Biography Today

Profiles
of People
of Interest
to Young
Readers

Volume 14 — 2005
Annual Cumulation

Cherie D. Abbey
Managing Editor

Kevin Hillstrom
Editor

Omnigraphics

615 Griswold Street
Detroit, Michigan 48226

Cherie D. Abbey, *Managing Editor*
Kevin Hillstrom, *Editor*

Peggy Daniels, Sheila Fitzgerald, Leif Gruenberg, Laurie Lanzen Harris,
Jeff Hill, Laurie Hillstrom, Sara Pendergast, Tom Pendergast, Diane Telgen,
Sue Ellen Thompson, Rebecca Valentine, and Rhoda Wilburn, *Sketch Writers*

Allison A. Beckett, Mary Butler, and Linda Strand, *Research Staff*

* * *

Peter E. Ruffner, *Publisher*
Frederick G. Ruffner, Jr., *Chairman*
Matthew P. Barbour, *Senior Vice President*
Kay Gill, *Vice President — Directories*

* * *

Elizabeth Barbour, *Research and Permissions Coordinator*
David P. Bianco, *Marketing Director*
Leif A. Gruenberg, *Development Manager*
Kevin Hayes, *Operations Manager*
Barry Puckett, *Librarian*
Cherry Stockdale, *Permissions Assistant*

Shirley Amore, Kevin Glover, Martha Johns,
Kirk Kauffman, and Angelesia Thorington, *Administrative Staff*

Copyright © 2005 Omnigraphics, Inc.
ISSN 1058-2347 • ISBN 0-7808-0692-1

The information in this publication was compiled from the sources cited and from
other sources considered reliable. While every possible effort has been made to ensure
reliability, the publisher will not assume liability for damages caused by inaccuracies in
the data, and makes no warranty, express or implied, on the accuracy of the information contained herein.

This book is printed on acid-free paper meeting the ANSI Z39.48 Standard. The infini-
ty symbol that appears above indicates that the paper in this book meets that standard.

Printed in the United States

INDEXED IN
Children's Magazine Guide

Contents

Preface

Biography Today is a magazine designed and written for the young reader—ages 9 and above—and covers individuals that librarians and teachers tell us that young people want to know about most: entertainers, athletes, writers, illustrators, cartoonists, and political leaders.

The Plan of the Work

The publication was especially created to appeal to young readers in a format they can enjoy reading and readily understand. Each issue contains approximately 10 sketches arranged alphabetically. Each entry provides at least one picture of the individual profiled, and bold-faced rubrics lead the reader to information on birth, youth, early memories, education, first jobs, marriage and family, career highlights, memorable experiences, hobbies, and honors and awards. Each of the entries ends with a list of easily accessible sources designed to lead the student to further reading on the individual and a current address. Retrospective entries are also included, written to provide a perspective on the individual's entire career.

Biographies are prepared by Omnigraphics editors after extensive research, utilizing the most current materials available. Those sources that are generally available to students appear in the list of further reading at the end of the sketch.

Indexes

Cumulative indexes are an important component of *Biography Today*. Each issue of the *Biography Today* General Series Annual Cumulation includes includes a **Cumulative General Index**, which comprises all individuals profiled in *Biography Today* since the series began in 1992. The names appear in bold faced type, followed by the issue in which they appeared. The Cumulative General Index also contains the occupations, nationalities, and ethnic and minority origins of individuals profiled. In addition, we compile three other indexes: Names Index, Places of Birth Index, and Birthday Index. These three indexes are featured on our web site, www.biographytoday.com. All

Biography Today indexes are cumulative, including all individuals profiled in both the General Series and the Subject Series.

Our Advisors

This series was reviewed by an Advisory Board comprised of librarians, children's literature specialists, and reading instructors to ensure that the concept of this publication — to provide a readable and accessible biographical magazine for young readers — was on target. They evaluated the title as it developed, and their suggestions have proved invaluable. Any errors, however, are ours alone. We'd like to list the Advisory Board members, and to thank them for their efforts.

Gail Beaver
Adjunct Lecturer
University of Michigan
Ann Arbor, MI

Cindy Cares
Youth Services Librarian
Southfield Public Library
Southfield, MI

Carol A. Doll
School of Information Science and Policy
University of Albany, SUNY
Albany, NY

Kathleen Hayes-Parvin
Language Arts Teacher
Birney Middle School
Southfield, MI

Karen Imarisio
Assistant Head of Adult Services
Bloomfield Twp. Public Library
Bloomfield Hills, MI

Rosemary Orlando
Director
St. Clair Shores Public Library
St. Clair Shores, MI

Our Advisory Board stressed to us that we should not shy away from controversial or unconventional people in our profiles, and we have tried to follow their advice. The Advisory Board also mentioned that the sketches might be useful in reluctant reader and adult literacy programs, and we would value any comments librarians might have about the suitability of our magazine for those purposes.

Your Comments Are Welcome

Our goal is to be accurate and up-to-date, to give young readers information they can learn from and enjoy. Now we want to know what you think. Take a look at this issue of *Biography Today*, on approval. Write or call me with your comments. We want to provide an excellent source of biographical information for young people. Let us know how you think we're doing.

Cherie Abbey
Managing Editor, *Biography Today*
Omnigraphics, Inc.
615 Griswold Street
Detroit, MI 48226

editor@biographytoday.com
www.biographytoday.com

Congratulations!

Congratulations to the following individuals and libraries, who are receiving a free copy of *Biography Today* for suggesting people who appeared in 2005:

Tina Anderson, Lake Orion, MI

Michelle Bosquez, San Saba, TX

Rachel Q. Davis, Thomas Memorial Library,
   Cape Elizabeth, MD

Philip Glanville, Sebastopol, CA

Anne Heidemann, Youth Services Coordinator Librarian,
   Chippewa River District Library System, Mt. Pleasant, MI

Mary Louise Helwig-Rodriguez, Little Falls Public Library,
   Little Falls, NJ

Kimberly Lentz, North Rowan High School Media Center,
   Spencer, NC

Miranda Louis, Cambridge, MA

Nicole Nava, Austin, TX

Joy Wald, Hobart Middle School, Hobart, OK

Joanna Wong, San Francisco, CA

Kristen Bell 1980-

American Actress
Star of the Critically Acclaimed TV Series
"Veronica Mars"

BIRTH

Kristen Anne Bell was born on July 18, 1980, in Huntington
Woods, Michigan, a quiet suburb of Detroit. She is the only
child of Tom Bell, a television news director, and Lori Bell, a
registered nurse. Her parents divorced before she turned two.
Kristen lived with her mother in Huntington Woods and
eventually gained a stepfather, radio account manager Ray

Avedian, and two stepsisters. Her father remarried and eventually moved to Phoenix, Arizona, but maintained a close relationship with Kristen.

YOUTH

Growing up, Kristen gained a reputation as an active, strong-willed girl. "She was a pill; she was a handful," her mother acknowledged. "She was always active, always knew her mind. She was the no-fear girl." At the age of four, Kristen announced that she no longer liked her first name. Instead, she declared that she wanted to be named after her favorite television characters, the Smurfs. "I cleverly swayed her away from the cartoon characters and towards her middle name, Anne, which is also her grandmother's name," her mother remembered. To this day, many of Kristen's old friends call her Annie.

> "She was a pill; she was a handful," her mother acknowledged. "She was always active, always knew her mind. She was the no-fear girl."

Bell began modeling for catalogs as a girl and signed with an agent by the time she entered her teens. Her first acting experience came at the age of 12 at the Stagecrafters community theater in Royal Oak, Michigan. She became so nervous before her first audition that she broke down in tears. Luckily, her mother was able to convince her to go through with the audition. "My mom said to me, 'Go in there and do what you said you were going to do and recite your Shel Silverstein poem or whatever in front of those 13 people,'" Bell remembered. "'You're so nervous; we never have to come here again. But you owe it to yourself.'"

Bell won a role in the Stagecrafters production of "Raggedy Ann and Andy." "It was a complex dual role actually," she joked. "I played a banana in the first act and I played a tree in the second act. I know you're thinking—how could I balance two characters like that? But somehow I did it." Despite her rough audition, Bell came to love appearing on stage. "The ability to pretend and the sense of family it provided became addicting," she related. "In youth theater, you get a whole bunch of kids together and allow them to think and create and receive recognition for their work. It gives them a voice and an outlet to explore their own creativity, which makes for a better adult, regardless of whether or not a child chooses acting as their profession."

When Bell was 17, her best friend was killed in a car accident. She has called the tragedy "both the best and worst thing that has ever happened to me. I think I'm a happier person because of it, as weird as that is to say, because once you learn not to take people for granted, you live a lot happier life." She also used this experience of early loss in creating her television character Veronica Mars.

EDUCATION

Bell attended the Burton International School, a multicultural school for gifted students in kindergarten through eighth grade. She went on to attend Shrine High School, a Catholic school in Royal Oak. Before graduating in 1998, she impressed audiences with her singing and acting ability as Dorothy in Shrine High's production of *The Wizard of Oz.*

Bell then moved to New York City to attend New York University's prestigious Tisch School of the Arts. She left the program in 2001, a few credits shy of earning her bachelor's degree, in order to accept a role in a Broadway play. Bell expressed some bitterness about the school's decision not to award her degree. "The weird thing is they gave me credit for bringing people coffee [as an intern], but they wouldn't give me credit for being on a Broadway stage every night," she explained.

CAREER HIGHLIGHTS

Appearing on Broadway

Bell became a fixture on the New York theater scene both during and after her time at NYU. Her first major role was as Becky Thatcher in the musical version of *Tom Sawyer* that played in New York in 2001. Bell also starred opposite the well-known film actors Liam Neeson and Laura Linney in the 2002 Broadway production of Arthur Miller's *The Crucible.*

Bell first gained widespread attention, however, for her portrayal of the squeaky-clean girl-next-door Mary Lane in the musical adaptation of *Reefer Madness* in New York. The play was based on a low-budget 1936 propaganda film about the dangers of marijuana. The original intent of the film was to scare people away from drugs. But it exaggerated the effects of marijuana use so dramatically (claiming that a few puffs could drive people insane and cause them to commit murder, for example) that it seemed campy, and it became a cult classic in the 1960s. "They were essentially B-movie actors who thought they were going to make a movie that would change the views of America; it was meant to be serious," Bell said of the original film. "It wasn't until they saw [the finished product] that they realized it was looking like a spoof."

Bell's character in the play, Mary Lane, falls in love with Jimmy, played by Christian Campbell. But Jimmy tries marijuana and is soon seduced into the world of drugs, which causes him to experience wild hallucinations and eventually go insane. Ultimately, though, the stage revival of *Reefer Madness* was intended to be a raucous musical comedy. In a review for *USA Today*, Elysa Gardner called it "a delirious romp, which at its best reaches highs of intoxicating goofiness."

In 2002 Bell moved to Hollywood. The creators of *Reefer Madness* planned to create a film version of the successful musical, and they wanted her to reprise her role as Mary Lane. In fact, they convinced her to move to California and offered her a place to stay for the first few months. The movie version of *Reefer Madness* appeared on Showtime in 2005. "Ultimately, the film's a bauble, unsubtle but full of such theatrical pep that one feels something real for these ridiculous characters in their exaggerated plight," Robert Lloyd wrote in a review for the *Los Angeles Times*. "Such are the intoxicating powers of musical theater—beware!"

Living in Hollywood

Living in Hollywood, Bell tried to make a career in television and film. She won a role on the 2002 season premiere of "The Shield," a gritty police drama broadcast on FX. She played a gang member's girlfriend who is raped and tattooed on the face. Although she auditioned for a number of TV series and movies over the next year, it took her a while to get another part. "It was very grounding to be that close to so many things and not get them," she recalled.

Finally, Bell received the starring role in the 2003 Lifetime original movie *Gracie's Choice*. As the teenaged daughter of a drug-addicted welfare mother, she had to decide whether to escape to a new life with her boyfriend or take responsibility for her younger siblings. *Detroit Free Press* reviewer Mike Duffy described the TV movie as "a powerful story of one working-class teen taking control of life despite the family-bruising trauma of her neglectful mother's drug abuse."

In 2004 Bell received her first major role in a theatrical release. In *Spartan*, a film by the respected independent director David Mamet, she played the wild daughter of the U.S. president. When she disappears with one of her college professors, she becomes the subject of an intensive search. Investigators eventually discover that she has been abducted into a white slavery ring. Some critics found *Spartan* difficult to follow, and the movie received mixed reviews.

The cast of "Veronica Mars."

Starring in "Veronica Mars"

In 2004 Bell heard about a new television series, "Veronica Mars," that would appear on the UPN network. The series was created by Rob Thomas, a former writer for "Dawson's Creek" and the author of the acclaimed young adult novels *Rats Saw God* and *Slave Day*. Bell soon auditioned for the lead role. She loved the script and the character, and she was thrilled to get the part over 100 other actresses who auditioned. "Kristen was actually the second actress who auditioned. And it was over for me. She was the person I wanted," said series creator Rob Thomas. "Veronica out-savvies people.

Kristen has to play really, really smarter than you. Hiring this NYU-trained Broadway actress is so much different from casting another pretty LA girl."

"Veronica Mars" is set in the wealthy oceanside community of Neptune, California. The main character, 17-year-old Veronica, is a student at Neptune High School. At one time she had been part of the popular crowd, along with her wealthy and beautiful best friend, Lilly Kane. But then Lilly was murdered, and Veronica's father, Sheriff Keith Mars (played by Enrico Colantoni), took charge of the investigation. Keith felt that the evidence pointed to Lilly's powerful and mysterious father, Jake Kane. When he was cleared of responsibility for the crime, Keith lost his job as sheriff. The scandal convinced Veronica's troubled mother to leave the family and turned Veronica into an outcast at school. Her father starts a private investigation business, and Veronica spends her evenings working as an apprentice detective to help him. She sneaks around Neptune with a camera, trying to uncover the town's dirty secrets and solve her friend's murder case.

—— " ——

"I think every character I've played, I've been able to draw on something in my life. I'm a fighter. I'm a little bit of a firecracker like Veronica is. And her strength appeals to me."

—— " ——

Bell drew upon her own experience of a friend's death to create the character of Veronica. "When you have a loss at such a young age, you become bitter and jaded and your whole perspective changes," she noted. "Veronica wouldn't be who she is without it." She identified with the character in other ways, as well. "I think every character I've played, I've been able to draw on something in my life," she stated. "I'm a fighter. I'm a little bit of a firecracker like Veronica is. And her strength appeals to me." Bell considers herself lucky to be part of a new and different kind of TV series — one that combines teen drama and murder mystery. "It's like nothing else out there," she said. "Rob Thomas has created so many twists, once you start watching you won't be able to stop. Yet he's been able to completely base it in a realistic setting. It's about a normal girl. She's not a super girl, she's just trying to live life."

"Veronica Mars" received acclaim from TV critics as soon as the pilot episode aired in fall 2004. "It's one of the freshest and most original new series of the year," Mike Duffy wrote in the *Detroit Free Press*. "Series creator Rob Thomas has written a really smart, witty pop noir with a twist of postmodern Nancy Drew in the form of 17-year-old detective Veronica

Veronica (Bell) and her friend Wallace Fennel, played by Percy Daggs III.

Mars. Kristen Bell's performance is funny, intelligent, and emotionally affecting, the sort of breakout performance that can make her a star." Critics reserved a great deal of praise for Bell's performance as the title character. A *Variety* reviewer, for example, called her "as charismatic as she is tough and intelligent, giving a multilayered performance that touches on simple 17-year-old insecurity and convincingly incorporates deeper issues concerning family, love, and disappointment."

Despite the critical acclaim, however, "Veronica Mars" failed to attract a large audience and consistently ranked near the bottom of the weekly TV ratings. The three million people who do watch "Veronica Mars" tend to be deeply dedicated to the show, discussing the plot twists in Internet chat rooms and sending e-mails to UPN begging for it to be renewed. Bell says that the show resonates with teenagers and their parents. "We've been doing these mall tours where we [the cast] go to a city and have thousands of people line up," she noted. "I have girls and guys alike come up to me and say that, You know, I started watching your show, and sort of the way Veronica handles things has given me strength to come out of my shell or out of my depression or whatever their problems were." Similarly, mothers approach Bell and tell her that watching "Veronica Mars" with their teens has helped open up a dialogue about important issues. Despite lackluster ratings, the UPN network decided to renew the show for a second season.

Enjoying Her Work

Bell is often told that she looks young for her age. "I'm carded for R-rated movies," she admitted. "And I get talked down to a lot. When I try to rent a car or buy an airplane ticket or other stuff adults do, I get, 'Okaaaay, honey.' I remember when I was 18, getting crayons in a restaurant." Although her youthful appearance helps in her role as a high school student, she looks forward to expanding her range of characters. "I like playing teenagers, but it'll be nice when I can start playing girls in their 20s—without their parents around," she said.

> "I'm proud of being able to do what I do. I'm really lucky to be able to have been involved in some amazing projects with some amazing people," she noted. "I'm in a very, very good place that hundreds of thousands of actresses wish they were in. Although my schedule is grueling, I have to realize how badly I wanted it."

Bell thoroughly enjoys her work as an actress, and she claims that would be the case even if she were not famous. "I'm not involved in the business of becoming famous," she stated. "And that's the advice I give to younger aspiring actors. Work on stage and do the little roles. In the end it's not important to be seen. It's important to do." Although she sometimes spends more than 15 hours per day on the set of "Veronica Mars," she still feels fortunate to be able to make a living doing what she loves. "I'm proud of being able to do what I do. I'm really lucky to be able to have been involved in some amazing projects with some amazing people," she noted. "I'm in a very, very good place that hundreds of thousands of actresses wish they were in. Although my schedule is grueling, I have to realize how badly I wanted it."

HOME AND FAMILY

Bell lives in Los Angeles with her boyfriend, Kevin Mann, who is a freelance writer, independent movie producer, and high school swim coach. They share their home with two dogs that they rescued from the pound.

HOBBIES AND OTHER INTERESTS

Bell is a big fan of the Detroit Red Wings and the Detroit Pistons. She celebrated when the Pistons won the 2004 NBA title by defeating the Los

Angeles Lakers. "I represented when the Pistons won," she related. "I wore my 'Bad Boys' T-shirts and got some dirty looks in LA."

SELECTED CREDITS

Television

Gracie's Choice, 2003 (TV movie)
"Veronica Mars," 2004- (TV series)
Reefer Madness, 2005 (TV movie)

Film

Spartan, 2004

Stage

Tom Sawyer, 2001
Reefer Madness, 2001
The Crucible, 2002
A Little Night Music, 2004

FURTHER READING

Periodicals

Bergen (NJ) County Record, Dec. 14, 2004, p.F9
Daily Variety, Aug. 30, 2004, p.A21
Detroit Free Press, Aug. 1, 2004; Dec. 23, 2004
Detroit News, Sep. 22, 2004, p.D1
Entertainment Weekly, Oct. 29, 2004, p.59; Dec. 10, 2004, p.36
Los Angeles Times, Mar. 20, 2005, p.E27; Apr. 16, 2005, p.E1
New York Times, Jan. 12, 2004, p.E8; Nov. 7, 2004, p.ST4
USA Today, Apr. 27, 2001, p.E13; Oct. 8, 2001, p.D5; Mar. 12, 2004, p.E6; Sep. 22, 2004, p.D4
Variety, Sep. 20-26, 2004, p.70; Feb. 7-13, 2005, p.74
WWD, Oct. 11, 2004, p.24

Online Articles

http://entertainment.iwon.com
(TV Guide Insider, "Is Veronica Mars a Pothead?" Apr. 15, 2005)

ADDRESS

Kristen Bell
UPN Television
11800 Wilshire Blvd.
Los Angeles, CA 90025

WORLD WIDE WEB SITES

http://www.tomsnet.net/kristenbell.html
http://www.upn.com/shows/veronica_mars_tmpl
http://www.upn.com/shows/veronica_mars/

Jack Black 1969-
American Actor and Musician
Star of *Shallow Hal* and *School of Rock,* Member of the
Spoof Rock Duo *Tenacious D*

BIRTH

Jack Black was born Thomas Black on April 7, 1969, in Santa
Monica, California, although his birthplace has also been listed as Edmonton, Alberta, Canada. He is the only child of Tom
and Judy Black, both of whom are satellite communications
engineers. Because his parents had both been married previously and divorced when he was still in grade school, he has
several half-siblings.

YOUTH

"Jack was my nickname and it just stuck," Black explains. He is reluctant to divulge much about his childhood, although he describes it as "hip and confusing." He was raised in Hermosa Beach, California, by parents who fought constantly and divorced when he was ten. His father left the country and started a new family, and Jack was raised by his Jewish mother. Although he describes both his parents as "loving," he felt like he never got enough attention from them and spent the rest of his life trying to compensate.

"I remember Hebrew school, which I had to go to three times a week," Black says. "We'd have recess when we weren't studying. We'd be playing around, and I remember getting some candy and putting it in the bathroom and then going outside and saying, 'There's a magic dragon in the bathroom.' And a couple of kids would run in there, and I'd turn off the lights and make dragon sounds and turn on the lights and say, 'Man, the dragon left some candy.' It was to try and make them believe in magic and stuff. I really liked being the source of entertainment."

> "I was really into [the rock band] Journey when I was a kid," Black recalls. "I went to the record store one day to get their new album, and this older kid was like, 'Oh man, you don't want to get that — get this.' He handed me Ozzy Osbourne's **Blizzard of Ozz**. It changed my world, and I became a heavy metal-er."

Black's interest in rock music also dates back to his childhood. "I was really into [the rock band] Journey when I was a kid," he recalls. "I went to the record store one day to get their new album, and this older kid was like, 'Oh man, you don't want to get that — get this.' He handed me Ozzy Osbourne's *Blizzard of Ozz*. It changed my world, and I became a heavy metal-er."

EDUCATION

Black was never a very good student and spent a lot of time pretending to be sick so he wouldn't have to go to school. He was kicked out of Culver City Junior High School for using drugs, after which he was sent to a Los Angeles school for troubled teens called the Poseidon School. It was here that Black first became interested in acting, appearing in his first commercial—for Atari, a pioneer in the computer and video games industry—at the age of 13. "I knew that if my friends saw me on TV, it would be the answer to all my prayers," he explains. "Because then they would have to worship me and everyone would know I was awesome. And I was awesome—for three days. Then it wore off. But it gave me the hunger."

After a year at Poseidon, Black went to Crossroads School, a private high school in Santa Monica with a strong performing arts program. At Crossroads he was the class clown, but he also got involved in school plays and started thinking about becoming a rock musician. "I performed in a band," he says. "We went and played at a high school party, and we were doing a real earnest serious version of [the Black Sabbath song] 'Iron Man.' No one paid attention, everyone was talking to each other, and we couldn't even hear ourselves play. . . . We stopped in the middle of the song, didn't even finish, and said, 'Let's just leave. This sucks.'" It wasn't until several years later that Black discovered he could make a career for himself in rock music by playing songs that were deliberately bad.

After graduating from Crossroads in 1987, Black attended the University of California at Los Angeles (UCLA), where he majored in theater. "I did some stuff in there that I was proud of. I had some good plays," he says of his UCLA days, but basically "I was an awful student. I slept through everything." He dropped out of college at the end of his second year.

CAREER HIGHLIGHTS

The Actors' Gang

Soon after leaving UCLA, Black joined the Actors' Gang, a Los Angeles-based theater company founded by actor and director Tim Robbins. He spent several years acting in the group's productions, which included classic dramas like *Peer Gynt* by Henrik Ibsen and a play called *Carnage,* written by Robbins and performed at the Edinburgh Theater Festival in Scotland. Black got his first movie role as a groupie in *Bob Roberts,* Robbins's 1992 satire about a right-wing politician. After that, Black had small parts in a string of not-very-successful films in the early to mid-1990s, including *Demolition Man, The Neverending Story III,* and *Waterworld.* He also appeared on a number of television shows during that time, including episodes of "Picket Fences," "Touched by an Angel," and "The X-Files."

While Black was performing with the Actors' Gang in 1994 he met Kyle Gass, who shared his interest in rock music. Together they formed a heavy metal acoustic rock duo called Tenacious D, which they named after a basketball term used by sportscaster Marv Albert to describe tough defensive action. Tenacious D played songs and performed skits that poked fun at the egotism, anger, and posturing of many rock stars. Soon, the duo began to attract attention with their appearances at Los Angeles clubs. Both men were overweight and Gass was balding, but this didn't stop them from strutting across the stage as if they were celebrity rockers. The *Los Angeles Times* called them "a mix of the Smothers Brothers, Cheech and Chong, Beavis and Butthead, and Spinal Tap."

In 1995 Black appeared in the Academy Award-nominated film *Dead Man Walking,* directed by Tim Robbins, which starred Sean Penn as a convicted criminal facing execution and Susan Sarandon as the nun who tries to help him. Black's performance as Penn's brother led to supporting roles in more films. In 1996 he appeared in *The Cable Guy,* which was directed by Ben Stiller and also starred Jim Carrey and Matthew Broderick. Black played Broderick's best friend, who suggests bribing the cable TV installer to get more channels. The movie didn't do very well at the box office, nor did any of the other movies in which Black appeared in the late 1990s, including the science fiction parody *Mars Attacks!,* a Bruce Willis thriller called *The Jackal,* and *Enemy of the State,* which starred Will Smith. In 1998 Black had a supporting role in *Johnny Skidmarks,* a thriller about a crime scene photographer starring Peter Gallagher and Frances McDormand, in which Black played Gallagher's former brother-in-law. While *Variety* found the movie "gloomy" and "not very convincing," it singled out Black's performance as noteworthy. The following year, Black played a would-be ventriloquist in another film directed by Tim Robbins, *Cradle Will Rock.*

> ——— **"** ———
>
> *Actor John Cusack commented that Jack Black "is great because . . . he's the king of somewhere. It might not be Earth, but it's definitely somewhere."*
>
> ——— **"** ———

The Rise of Tenacious D

While Black's acting career progressed slowly throughout the 1990s, he began to develop a cult following as part of Tenacious D. He and Gass started appearing in 10-minute spots following episodes of "Mr. Show with Bob and David," a comedy sketch series on HBO. They performed what *Entertainment Weekly* called "really terrific 'bad' songs," characterized by deliberately meaningless lyrics like, "It was a big day on Jesus Ranch/I fell in love with a baked potato." By 1999 they had their own series on HBO in which

they competed with each other for the attentions of a punk record store clerk named Flama. They also continued to parody the behavior of rock stars with songs that a critic from the Colorado Springs *Gazette* described as "the musical equivalent of gourmet marshmallows."

In 2001 Gass and Black released their first CD, called *Tenacious D*. It entered the *Billboard* chart at No. 33 and almost went platinum, selling far more copies than anyone had anticipated. The album had songs and skits with titles like "Kielbasa," "Karate Schnitzel," and "Sasquatch," and the pair's combination of heavy metal music and bathroom humor had an underground appeal that threatened to attract a mainstream audience. Actor John Cusack, another former Actors' Gang member and one of the duo's greatest fans, commented that Black "is great because . . . he's the king of somewhere. It might not be Earth, but it's definitely somewhere."

John Cusack, Jack Black, Todd Louiso, and Tim Robbins in the record store in a scene from High Fidelity.

High Fidelity

It was John Cusack who gave Black his first major movie role in *High Fidelity*, a film that Cusack himself starred in. In fact, Cusack also co-wrote the screenplay, which was based on the novel of the same name by Nick Hornby. Cusack's character, Rob Gordon, runs a record store, where he employs Barry (played by Black). A snobby music lover, Barry knows everything there is to know about vintage vinyl recordings and routinely insults customers who come in to buy mainstream music. As Owen Gleiberman wrote in *Entertainment Weekly*, "He plays Barry as an amusingly wired, passive-aggressive bully who holds the entire universe of popular music within his brain, all of it meticulously catalogued into the good, the bad, or the sublime. If you disagree with him, you're one of the unenlightened, and he can barely bring himself to speak to you."

Rob has recently been dumped by his girlfriend, and he spends most of his time hanging around the store making up "top five" lists of songs with Barry and another employee named Dick. The list-making leads to flashbacks about Rob's failed relationships with women. Barry, who dreams of being a musician himself some day, finally gets a chance to show off his talents as the movie draws to a close.

His performance as Barry was a breakout role for Black and led critics to compare him to John Belushi, the former "Saturday Night Live" comedian and star of the movie *Animal House*. Like Belushi, Black had a chubby physique, elastic face, and very expressive eyebrows. His "explosively bizarre" form of comedy reminded many people of Belushi as well. The *New York Daily News* commented that "When director Stephen Frears worked with this guy, he must have yelled, 'Let 'er rip!' instead of 'Action!'" *High Fidelity*, which was released in 2000, received favorable reviews, became a big audience favorite, and established Black as a comic actor.

Moving Up to Leading Roles

In 2001, Black appeared in a teen comedy called *Saving Silverman*. Black, Jason Biggs, and Steve Zahn play best friends who belong to a band that has modeled itself after Neil Diamond. They perform in long-haired wigs, wear tight black pants and flashy shirts, and call themselves Diamonds in the Rough. But when a beautiful psychologist (Amanda Peet) develops a romantic interest in Silverman (Biggs), she decides that he should stop seeing his friends. Desperate to save him—and their friendships—Black and Zahn take drastic steps. They kidnap Peet and try to reunite Silverman with his high school sweetheart, who is now training to become a nun. Teen audiences enjoyed the film, but it was a flop with movie critics—for example, the *Los Angeles Times* called it "a standard issue numbskull comedy" and "disposable as a paper towel." But Black and Zahn were singled out by the critics for their performances. "They're great together," a critic for the *Washington Post* said, "even in a bottom-of-the-barrel comedy like this."

> **"**
>
> *"He plays Barry as an amusingly wired, passive-aggressive bully who holds the entire universe of popular music within his brain, all of it meticulously catalogued into the good, the bad, or the sublime. If you disagree with him, you're one of the unenlightened, and he can barely bring himself to speak to you."*
> — *Owen Gleiberman,*
> **Entertainment Weekly**
>
> **"**

Black got a chance to play his first leading role in 2001. *Shallow Hal* is a romantic comedy about Hal Larson (Black), a less-than-perfect-looking man who has a very inflated view of his appeal to women. He only pursues gorgeous women, even though he is repeatedly rejected by them. He gets caught in an elevator one day with Tony Robbins, a self-help guru, who

Scenes from Saving Silverman *(top),* Shallow Hal *(center), and* Orange County *(bottom).*

hypnotizes him so that from now on, he only sees women's inner beauty. Larson immediately falls in love with Rosemary, a Peace Corps volunteer who he sees as slim and beautiful but who is really very overweight. Rosemary is played by Gwyneth Paltrow, who wears an inflated "fat suit" in many scenes. Directed by the Farrelly brothers, who also directed *Dumb and Dumber* and *There's Something about Mary,* the film provoked mixed reactions from critics. Much of the film's humor was based on "fat jokes" about Rosemary, which many critics and viewers found offensive. But almost all praised Black's performance as Hal. Roger Ebert, writing for the *Chicago Sun-Times,* found the movie "very funny, but . . . also surprisingly moving at times," especially in its portrayal of characters who are struggling to overcome the labels imposed on them by others. Ebert observed that Black "struts through with the blissful confidence of a man who knows he was born for stardom, even though he doesn't look like your typical Gwyneth Paltrow boyfriend."

In 2002 Black appeared in the suburban teen comedy *Orange County* as Lance, the deadbeat older brother of a high school over-achiever named Shaun (Colin Hanks). Shaun is desperate to get into Stanford University so that he can study with his literary hero, Marcus Skinner (Kevin Kline). But when Shaun is rejected because his school records have gotten mixed up, Lance tries to intervene and ends up burning down the admissions building. In addition to Kline, the impressive supporting cast included John Lithgow, Catherine O'Hara, Harold Ramis, Ben Stiller, and Lily Tomlin. Once again, Black's ability to portray inspired nuttiness triggered comparisons with the late John Belushi and won positive comments in the midst of otherwise lukewarm reviews. Still, the movie proved to be a big hit with teen viewers.

School of Rock

Black finally got a chance to play the kind of role he had dreamed of in the 2003 hit movie, *School of Rock.* He plays Dewey Finn, a failed rock musician who gets hired as a substitute teacher at a snobby prep school by impersonating his roommate. Dewey takes rock music — and himself — very seriously, sharing such bits of wisdom as "I serve society by rocking" and "For those about to rock, we salute you." In the classroom, he dispenses with his fifth graders' normal studies and concentrates instead on teaching them the only thing he really understands: rock music. They form their own rock band, and Dewey teaches them what songs to play, how to move, and what kind of faces to make as they prepare for a "battle of the bands" at the movie's end. Meanwhile, he must confront the school's uptight headmistress, played by Joan Cusack, who turns out to be a closet rock music fan herself.

The script was based on the true story of *The Langley Schools Music Project*, an album recorded in the late 1970s by a teacher in rural Canada who taught his students to perform rock and pop classics like "Good Vibrations," "Mandy," "Space Oddity," and "Desperado." The result was a cult hit album that, according to *School of Rock* script writer Mike White, "had both a comic aspect and a sweetness." White created the character of Dewey Finn expressly for Black, whom he knew from working on *Orange County*. "Dude, I was born to play this part," Black says. "Everything about it lines up perfectly with my strengths. Which include rocking. Which also include being superintense and passionate about stuff."

———— " ————

"Let's come right out and say it: School of Rock *made me laugh harder than any movie I've seen this year. . . . It's a bravura, all-stops-out, inexhaustibly inventive performance. I don't know how much was improvised, and how much comes from White's sharp screenplay, but Black may never again get a part that displays his mad-dog comic ferocity to such brilliant effect."*
— David Ansen, Newsweek

———— " ————

Praise for Black's performance was unanimous. Viewers loved it, as the film appealed to parents as well as their children; Black himself admitted that "kids respond to my high-energy kind of ridiculousness." And movie reviewers were equally enthusiastic. As the critic Owen Gleiberman wrote for *Entertainment Weekly*, "[In *School of Rock*, Black] reaches deep inside his riffing, strutting, head-banging self to give the most joyful performance I've seen all year. Black is still a happy geek in perpetual overdrive, only now he draws on his musical skill, and his hipster shamelessness, to deliver the acting equivalent of a perfect power chord crunched with a demon smile." Those accolades were echoed by David Ansen in *Newsweek*: "Let's come right out and say it: *School of Rock* made me laugh harder than any movie I've seen this year. The giggles start coming right at the get-go, when Jack Black, as the fiercely committed but less than inspired rock-and-roller Dewey Finn, howls his way through a song, then hurls himself shirtless and triumphant into the mosh pit . . . where the horrified crowd declines to catch him. . . . It's a bravura, all-stops-out, inexhaustibly inventive performance. I don't know how much

was improvised, and how much comes from White's sharp screenplay, but Black may never again get a part that displays his mad-dog comic ferocity to such brilliant effect."

Recent Projects and What Lies Ahead

Black's most recent movie project is the 2004 comedy *Envy*. Black plays Nick Vanderpart, a former factory worker who invented Vapoorize, a spray that makes dog poop evaporate. Now wealthy beyond belief, he is still de-

Black as Nick Vanderpart in the 2004 comedy Envy.

voted to his former co-worker and best friend, Tim Dingman, played by Ben Stiller. Tim had turned down the chance to invest just $2,000 in Vapoorize, thereby missing out on becoming rich himself. Now, he's sick with envy over his friend's success, which drives him to make some terrible choices. Despite the comic cast, the movie never really lived up to expectations, and it received generally lukewarm reviews.

Black claims that his first passion is still music. In late 2003 he released a DVD collection called *Tenacious D: The Complete Masterworks, Volume One*. It combines concert footage of Black and Gass with some of the short sketches they originally performed on HBO. Black hopes that the DVD will pave the way for a feature film that he has co-written with Liam Lynch about Tenacious D's "rise to power" from playing in obscure coffee houses to performing in front of huge concert audiences. "The weird thing is, nobody that's read it likes it so far," Black confesses. But he confidently predicts that the film will be "not just the best movie ever, but one of the great things ever. Like the pyramids."

Despite his recent successes and the over-inflated self-confidence of his on-screen persona, Black remains insecure about his talents. "I stress over career decisions and what people think of me," he says. "I'm always scared, thinking I'm going to be bad in everything." At the same time, the characters that he plays are usually "swaggering and cocksure, utterly convinced of their own studliness even when dressed in just a pair of sagging briefs," according to the *New York Times*. "To the rest of the world, these characters may look like losers and meatheads, but Black never mocks their delusions of grandeur, playing them instead with the sincere affection of a man who has himself spent hours playing air guitar in front of the mirror."

MARRIAGE AND FAMILY

Black has lived in the Hollywood Hills for several years with his girlfriend, Laura Kightlinger, whom he describes as "funnier than me." Kightlinger is an actress, a stand-up comedian, and a writer for the television series "Will and Grace." Black says that living with another comedian can be stressful. "When we're both working, we fight a lot. We both want the other one to be our personal assistant, and neither of us is willing to do it."

Will Black and Kightlinger get married and have a family some day? He doesn't see it happening. "I'm kind of a kid [myself]," he explains. "I'd have to do some growing up that I don't really want to do." Black also admits that his parents' failed marriage made a lasting impression on him.

MAJOR INFLUENCES

As a musician, Black has been influenced by what he calls "the school of heavy metal" — bands like Black Sabbath, Led Zeppelin, and AC/DC. He also likes Radiohead, the Foo Fighters, and Queens of the Stone Age. It was his mother who introduced him to heavy metal music, although she didn't do so deliberately. She went through a period where she was "trying different things and searching spiritually," Black recalls. "And there was this 'Jews for Jesus' phase where she gave me this tape that was some preacher saying rock is evil and here are some examples of music that would send you to hell." Although it wasn't what his mother intended,

> **"**
>
> *Black's characters are usually "swaggering and cocksure, utterly convinced of their own studliness even when dressed in just a pair of sagging briefs," according to the* **New York Times.** *"To the rest of the world, these characters may look like losers and meatheads, but Black never mocks their delusions of grandeur, playing them instead with the sincere affection of a man who has himself spent hours playing air guitar in front of the mirror."*
>
> **"**

Black says that the tape "exposed me to great heavy metal I hadn't heard before."

HOBBIES AND OTHER INTERESTS

Black describes himself as a "total shut-in" who rarely goes out to parties and would rather stay up all night and play Scrabble on the Internet. "When I'm relaxing," he says, "I just like to go to the movies, read a good book, or play video games."

SELECTED CREDITS

Films

Bob Roberts, 1992
Demolition Man, 1993
Airborne, 1993
Blind Justice, 1994
The Neverending Story III, 1994
Escape from Fantasia, 1994
Bye Bye, Love, 1995
Waterworld, 1995
Dead Man Walking, 1995
Bio-Dome, 1996
The Cable Guy, 1996
The Fan, 1996
Mars Attacks!, 1996
Crossworlds, 1996
The Jackal, 1997
Bongwater, 1998
Johnny Skidmarks, 1998
I Still Know What You Did Last Summer, 1998
Enemy of the State, 1998
Cradle Will Rock, 1999
Jesus' Son, 1999
High Fidelity, 2000
Saving Silverman, 2001
Shallow Hal, 2001
Orange County, 2002
Run Ronnie Run, 2002
School of Rock, 2003
Envy, 2004

Recordings

Tenacious D, 2001 (CD)
Tenacious D: The Complete Masterworks, Volume One, 2003 (DVD)

FURTHER READING

Books

Contemporary Theatre, Film, and Television, Vol. 32, 2000

Periodicals

Current Biography Yearbook, 2002
Entertainment Weekly, Nov. 16, 2001, p.102; Oct. 17, 2003, p.26
GQ, Oct. 2003, p.160
Los Angeles Daily News, Oct. 3, 2003, p.U6
Los Angeles Times, Apr. 1, 2000, p.F1
New York Times Magazine, Sep. 28, 2003, p.36
Newsweek, Sep. 29, 2003, p.52
Nickelodeon, Oct. 2004, p.78
People, Oct. 13, 2003, p.75
Premiere, Nov. 2001, p.28
Teen People, Nov. 1, 2003, p.62
Time, Oct. 6, 2003, p.73
Times (London), Jan. 24, 2004, magazine section, p.28
USA Today, Sep. 28, 2003, p.D1

Online Databases

Biography Resources Center Online, 2004, articles from *Contemporary Authors Online,* 2003; *Contemporary Theatre, Film, and Television,* 2000; and *Newsmakers,* 2002

ADDRESS

Jack Black
United Talent Agency
9560 Wilshire Blvd., 5th Floor
Los Angeles, CA 90212

WORLD WIDE WEB SITES

http://www.schoolofrockmovie.com
http://www.tenaciousd.com

Sergey Brin 1973-
Larry Page 1973-

Inventors of the Google Search Engine and Founders
of Google Inc.

BIRTH

Sergey Brin was born on August 21, 1973, in Moscow, the capital of the former Soviet Union (now Russia). His family
moved to the United States when he was six years old and
settled in College Park, Maryland. His father, Michael Brin, is a
professor of mathematics at the University of Maryland. His
mother, Eugenia Brin, works as a specialist for the National
Aeronautics and Space Administration (NASA).

Lawrence E. Page was born on March 26, 1973, in East Lansing, Michigan. His father, Carl Page, was a pioneer in the field

of computer science who served as a professor at Michigan State University. His mother, Gloria Page, was a database consultant who also taught computer programming at the university. Larry has one brother, Carl Jr., who is nine years his senior.

YOUTH

Sergey Brin and his family left Russia because they faced anti-Semitism. They often endured taunts about their Jewish religion when they walked through the streets of Moscow. "I was worried that my children would face the same discrimination if we stayed there," Michael Brin noted. "Sometimes the love for one's country is not mutual." They made a new life for themselves in the United States, where Sergey grew up loving math and science.

Meanwhile, Larry Page inherited an early interest in computers from his parents and older brother. "I never got pushed into it," he recalled. "I just really liked computers." The Page family had a computer at home as early as 1979. "I turned in the first word-processing assignment in elementary school," Larry remembered. "No one even knew what a dot-matrix printer was." By the time he was 18, he had constructed a working inkjet printer out of Lego building blocks.

EDUCATION

Teaming Up

Brin attended high school in College Park, where he was a star of the chess club and math team. In fact, the school yearbook compared him to the brilliant physicist Albert Einstein. After graduating from high school in 1990, Brin went on to earn a bachelor of science (BS) degree—with a double major in mathematics and computer science—from the University of Maryland in 1993. He pursued graduate studies at Stanford University in California, earning a master of science (MS) degree in 1995. He remained as a candidate for his doctorate (PhD) at Stanford, where he met Larry Page.

Page graduated from East Lansing High School in 1991 and then enrolled in the College of Engineering at the University of Michigan. During his undergraduate years, he served as president of Michigan's branch of the national engineering honor society, Eta Kappa Nu. After receiving his bachelor of science degree in engineering in 1995, he decided to pursue graduate studies at Stanford. Page initially felt intimidated by the intense academic environment he found in Stanford's computer science department. "At first, it was pretty scary," he acknowledged. "I kept complaining to my friends that I was going to get sent home on the bus."

Brin and Page met shortly after Page joined Stanford's PhD program in 1995. At first, each student found the other "obnoxious," and they argued about every topic they discussed. But then they discovered a common interest in finding new ways to locate information on the rapidly growing World Wide Web. "I was working on data mining, the idea of taking large amounts of data, analyzing it for patterns, and trying to extract relationships that are useful," Brin recalled. "When Larry joined, he started dabbling with the Web and started gathering large amounts of data. That data intrigued me, and I wanted to run various experiments on it."

> *"I was working on data mining, the idea of taking large amounts of data, analyzing it for patterns, and trying to extract relationships that are useful," Brin recalled. "When Larry joined, he started dabbling with the Web and started gathering large amounts of data. That data intrigued me, and I wanted to run various experiments on it."*

Inventing a New Kind of Search Engine

For two years—from the beginning of 1996 to the end of 1997—Brin and Page worked together on a research project they hoped would help people make sense of the vast amount of information available on the Web. They developed a new type of Internet search technology that they called PageRank. This program used a set of complex mathematical algorithms to rank Web sites in order of importance, based on the number of links they received from other sites. "There are millions of variables, but we manage to do a lot of math, very fast, and in the end we rank pages in a way that's very close to how you would do it intuitively," Brin explained.

The two PhD candidates then incorporated their PageRank system into a revolutionary new search engine. They called this program BackRub, for its ability to analyze the "back links" pointing to a given Web site. At that time, most search engines were compiled by "spiders," automated devices that crawled across the Web and created a database of terms appearing on Web sites. When users searched for a specific term, the search engines returned a list of sites on which the term appeared. The approach taken by Brin and Page expanded upon traditional search engines by indexing not only terms, but also the popularity of a given Web site, based on the number of links it received from other sites.

BackRub consistently returned more relevant results than the leading search engines, and it quickly grew in popularity among Stanford students and faculty. "We didn't even intend to build a search engine originally," Page noted. "We were just interested in the Web and interested in data mining. And then we ended up with search technology that we realized was really good. And we built the search engine. Then we told our friends about it and our professors. Pretty soon, about 10,000 people a day were using it."

In the early years of development, Brin and Page attempted to sell their search technology to several large Internet companies, but they received little interest. Although some of these companies found BackRub impressive, they were not interested in upgrading their search capabilities at that time. Instead, they were busy exploring new Web applications, like chat and instant messaging. Brin and Page, however, believed that searching was a vital—and neglected—usage of the Web. "Search is important," Brin stated. "It's important for people to be able to find information quickly, easily, accurately, and objectively." Thinking that they had discovered a great opportunity, the students decided to start their own search engine business. They both left Stanford in 1998, before completing their doctoral degrees.

CAREER HIGHLIGHTS

Founding Google Inc.

Brin and Page called their fledgling business Google. They based the name on the mathematical term "googol," which means 10 to the power of 100 (10^{100}). According to Brin, this enormous number represented the ambitious mission of their company: "to organize the world's information, making it universally accessible and useful." While they were still students at Stanford, the two men used credit cards (their own and their parents') to buy enough computer disks to store a terabyte (a million megabytes) of information. Then they built their own computer housings in Page's dorm room, which became Google's first data center.

In the spring of 1998, Brin and Page showed their business plan to Andreas ("Andy") Bechtolsheim, a co-founder of Sun Microsystems. "We met him very early one morning on the porch of a Stanford faculty member's home in Palo Alto," Brin remembered. "We gave him a quick demo. He had to run off somewhere, so he said, 'Instead of us discussing all the details, why

Brin and Page in the server room at Google.

don't I just write you a check?' It was made out to Google Inc. and was for $100,000." Unfortunately, "Google Inc." did not officially exist yet, so Brin and Page could not cash the check. Over the next few weeks, they rushed to complete the paperwork needed to incorporate their business. Finally, Google Inc. was born, with Page as its chief executive officer and Brin as its president.

Once Google gained the support of a high-profile computer-industry executive like Bechtolsheim, Brin and Page had little trouble finding other investors. By September 1998 they had raised nearly $1 million—enough to fund Google's first year of operations. They moved out of Page's dorm room, opened up an office in a friend's garage, and worked hard to perfect and expand their search engine. When they unveiled the final version of the program in 1999, it became a tremendous hit with Web users. In fact, even without advertising, Google's user base grew by a remarkable 20 percent each month. "Search is the number-one application on the Web," Page explained. "And it's easy for people to try out different search engines so they can compare. They notice differences and tell their friends. Friends tell friends. And that's how we grow."

Google's popularity attracted interest from several major venture capital firms, which are companies that invest in unproven business ventures, in hopes that the businesses will experience rapid growth and provide a good return on the investment. Brin and Page collected $25 million in venture capital from two computer-industry investment firms. This large investment brought a great deal of attention to the small, unproven company, and instantly raised the profiles of its young founders.

Around this time, the Google search engine started to attract a great deal of media attention. Both industry journals and mainstream periodicals commented on Google's unique approach to ranking Web sites based on their popularity, which consistently delivered search results of superior quality and relevance. "Just as you trust the links on a really good site to get you to other good pages, Google crawls the Web scooping up hyperlinks and uses them to figure out how important a page is by who is pointing at it," Margot Williams wrote in the *Washington Post.* "Google interprets connections between Web sites as votes," Chris Taylor added in *Time.* "The most linked-to sites win the Google usefulness ballot and rise to the top of search results. More weight is given to 'voters' with millions of links them-

___ *"* ___

"We didn't even intend to build a search engine originally," Page noted. "We were just interested in the Web and interested in data mining. And then we ended up with search technology that we realized was really good. And we built the search engine. Then we told our friends about it and our professors. Pretty soon, about 10,000 people a day were using it."

___ *"* ___

selves, such as Amazon or AOL." The *Wall Street Journal* praised Google for providing "a beacon in a sea of confusion" on the Web.

Growing with the Web

One of the challenges facing Brin and Page involved keeping up with the growth of the World Wide Web, which was expanding by more than 1.5 million pages every day. From the beginning, Google had to develop new software and increase its number of computers in order to keep pace. Some analysts compared Google's mission with finding a needle in an enormous haystack that grew larger every day. But Brin and Page refused to be intimidated by the exponential growth of the Web. In fact, Brin argued that the Google search engine would actually provide more accurate results over time because there would be more links for it to analyze. "That's our competitive advantage—we get smarter, not worse, as the Web gets bigger," he stated.

By mid-2000 Google had become the first search engine to index over a billion Web pages, making it the biggest in the world. Google also enjoyed an exceptional rate of customer satisfaction, with 97 percent of users reporting that they found the information they were looking for most or all of the time. These achievements helped Google earn a coveted Webby Award from the International Academy of Digital Arts and Sciences. In June 2000 Brin and Page announced the first in a series of lucrative partnerships with major Internet services: Google became the default search engine to complement Yahoo!'s directories.

Google's growth continued in 2001. By June of that year, the Google search engine handled over 100 million queries per day. Half of these searches were done using Google's Web site, and the other half were executed from the Web sites of various partners through licensing agreements. By the end of 2001, Google indexed 3 billion Web documents. Google Inc. also earned a profit that year—a feat that many Internet start-up companies never accomplish, and a particularly impressive achievement in the aftermath of the collapse of numerous Internet businesses in 2000. The success of Google attracted the attention of several large firms in the computer industry, but Brin and Page turned down all offers from prospective buyers. "We're growing at a good rate, we have been successful at attracting good [employees], and we are increasing our traffic tremendously," Brin said. "We believe we are going to dominate the market—and if you believe that, it's hard for anyone to pay you enough to justify selling."

In August 2001 Brin and Page decided to bring in an experienced manager to help them run their rapidly growing enterprise. They hired Eric E.

Schmidt, the former chief executive officer (CEO) of software maker Novell, to be Google Inc.'s new CEO. Page became president of products, while Brin became president of technology. "Larry focuses a little more on the operations side—computers and things like that," Brin explained. "I focus on research and marketing." One magazine described Page as "Google's clean-cut geek in chief, the brilliant engineer and mathematician who oversees the writing of the complex algorithms and computer programs behind the search engine," and called Brin "the company's earnest and impassioned visionary."

Going Public

A massive sign outside the NASDAQ stock exchange welcomes Google after the company went public.

Following the management reorganization, Google Inc. continued to grow. By the beginning of 2003, an amazing four out of every five searches conducted on the Web used Google, either directly from the Google home page or through another site that licensed its technology. The company stood far above virtually every other online business in terms of financial health, earning more than $100 million in profits on revenues of just under $1 billion.

In fact, Google had become so pervasive that the name of the search engine became a verb. For instance, people talked about "Googling" prospective dates and employers in order to obtain inside information. The search engine also helped people conduct academic research, locate long-lost relatives, recall old song lyrics, and simplify their lives in any number of ways. Google thus became "not only the place people go when looking for obscure factoids, but a pop-culture phenomenon," as Catharine P. Taylor wrote in *Brandweek*.

Google's remarkable success led many observers to speculate about when the company would "go public," or sell shares of ownership on the stock market for the first time. But Brin and Page resisted the idea of making

Charting Google's Growth

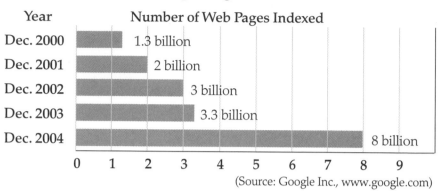

(Source: Google Inc., www.google.com)

Share of U.S. Search Engine Market

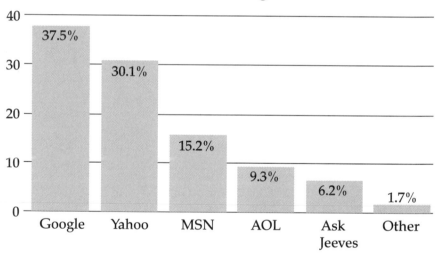

(Source: AP, July 7, 2005)

Google Inc. a publicly held company. They enjoyed having complete control over operations, rather than having to explain their decisions to stockholders. They also appreciated the fact that small, privately owned companies are not required to report their financial results to the outside world. Over time, however, the founders realized that Google had reached a point in its growth where it made sense to go public. The venture capitalists who had funded the company's early operations were eager to cash out their investments. In addition, since Google Inc. had accumulated more than 500 employees, it would soon be required to report financial results like a public company.

Brin and Page soon decided to prepare the company for an initial public offering (IPO). An IPO marks the first time that a corporation offers shares of stock for sale to investors on the public stock exchange. Many corporations stage an IPO, or "go public," as they grow in order to get money to pay for further expansion. Investors who purchase stock become part-owners of the company. They gain or lose money based on the company's financial performance.

When Brin and Page finally decided to take Google public, their company was so successful that they were able to dictate the terms of the IPO. They announced that the stock sale would be conducted on August 19, 2004, using the little-known Dutch auction process. Although this process was supposed to help stabilize the price of the stock, many investors found it confusing. Some analysts criticized Brin and Page during the IPO process, calling their demands for control "arrogant" and the stock price they suggested "exorbitant." But Brin and Page felt that their arrangements for the IPO were necessary in order to maintain Google's culture and long-term focus.

> *"Larry focuses a little more on the operations side — computers and things like that," Brin explained. "I focus on research and marketing."*

On the day that the highly anticipated stock sale took place, shares started selling at $85 each and ended above $100. These results gave Google Inc. a valuation of $27 billion, which was not only the highest among Internet companies, but also higher than many industrial giants, like General Motors. Experts estimated that Brin and Page's stock holdings gave them each a personal wealth of about $4 billion. The IPO also turned approximately 1,000 of Google's 2,300 employees into millionaires.

Facing the Future

In the months following the IPO, some analysts worried that shareholders might pressure the company to earn greater profits, which could affect Google's corporate culture. Google's dominance of the search business also led to increased competition, as other powerful Internet companies entered the market. Microsoft founder Bill Gates vowed to develop new search products to cut into Google's lead, for instance, while Yahoo! ended its partnership with Google and launched its own new search engine. Google also faced increasing threats from "optimizers" — computer

Employees at Google are encouraged to feel comfortable in the workplace, as the contents of this office show.

experts who used their understanding of the PageRank system to artificially raise the ranking of certain Web pages. Some users expressed concern that widespread optimization might reduce the quality of Google's search results.

Finally, Brin and Page had to make difficult decisions about what types of advertising to allow, what types of offensive material to censor, and what action to take against repressive governments that tried to block their citizens' access to Google. The founders tried to approach every decision with the best interests of Google users in mind. "We have a mantra: 'Don't be evil,' which is to do the best things we know how for our users, for our customers, for everyone," Page noted. "Obviously, everyone wants to be successful, but I want to be looked back on as being very innovative, very trusted and ethical, and ultimately making a big difference in the world," Brin added.

Over the years, Google Inc. has earned a reputation as a very innovative company in terms of the benefits it provides to employees. The company headquarters in Mountain View, California — called Googleplex — features a number of unusual workplace luxuries. The lobby holds a grand piano and a live projection of current search queries from around the world. Employees have unlimited access to workout facilities, yoga classes, a massage room, and pool and ping-pong tables. They can also eat three free meals per day in the company's cafeteria, which is headed by a gourmet chef. Finally, as a way to stimulate innovative thinking, Google encourages its employees to spend some of their time working on their own, original projects. "Engineers are supposed to spend 20 percent of their time doing whatever they want," Page explained. "That gets people working on things that they think are a good idea and that they're really excited about."

Partly due to the supportive atmosphere, Google has launched a series of innovative products over the years. Some of the notable innovations include the Google Toolbar, a downloadable browser plug-in that makes it possible to search with Google without visiting the home page; Google Zeitgeist, a periodic list of the top trending search terms; Local Search, a function that returns results within the user's community; and Gmail, a program that provides users with free email accounts and Web storage. "I think we've significantly raised the bar in Internet search, and I think we'll continue to do so," Page stated. "I don't see any limit to the significant innovations we can do to help people accomplish the tasks they're trying to do. We are quite optimistic that we can write interesting software that can make sense of information."

> *"We have a mantra: 'Don't be evil,' which is to do the best things we know how for our users, for our customers, for everyone," Page noted. "Obviously, everyone wants to be successful, but I want to be looked back on as being very innovative, very trusted and ethical, and ultimately making a big difference in the world," Brin added.*

Technology reporter Steven Levy summed up the impact of Brin and Page's invention in *Newsweek:* "Because of its seemingly uncanny ability to provide curious minds with the exact information they seek, a dot-com survivor has supercharged the entire category of search, transforming the masses into data-miners and becoming a cultural phenomenon in the process," he wrote. "Google has become a high-tech version of the Oracle of Delphi, positioning everyone a mouseclick away from answers to the most arcane questions—and delivering answers so efficiently that the process becomes addictive."

Advice to Young Inventors

Based on their own experiences as Internet entrepreneurs, Brin and Page offer the following advice to young inventors with a good idea: "You don't need to have a 100-person company to develop that idea," Page noted. "You can do it in your spare time, you can really work on ideas and see if they take off—rather than trying to raise tons of money, millions of dollars, for an idea that may or may not work. And once you have the product and people are using it, it's very easy to raise investment."

HOME AND FAMILY

Both Brin and Page are single. They both live in Palo Alto, California.

HOBBIES AND OTHER INTERESTS

In his spare time, Brin enjoys acrobatic sports. He has taken lessons in springboard diving and in flying trapeze. Page enjoys more earthbound pursuits like bicycling and in-line skating.

SELECTED HONORS AND AWARDS

Technical Excellence Award for Innovation in Web Application
    Development (*PC Magazine*): 1999
Top Ten Best in Cyberspace (*Time*): 1999
Best Search Engine (*Yahoo! Internet Life*): 2000
Best Search Engine (*The Net*): 2000
Webby Awards (International Academy of Digital Arts and Sciences):
    2000, People's Voice Award and Best Technical Achievement; 2001, Best
    Practices; 2002, Best Practices, People's Voice Best Practices, and People's
    Voice Technical Achievement; 2003, People's Voice Technical
    Achievement and News; 2004, Best Practices, Services, People's Voice
    Best Practices, and People's Voice Services; 2005, Best Practices, People's
    Voice Best Practices, and Best Navigation/Structure

Best Internet Innovation (*PC Magazine*): 2000

Search Engine Watch Awards: 2001, for Outstanding Search Service and Most Webmaster Friendly Search Service; 2002, for Outstanding Search Service, Most Webmaster Friendly Search Service, Best Image Search Engine, Best Design, and Best Search Feature; 2003, for Outstanding Search Service; 2004, for Outstanding Search Service, Most Webmaster Friendly Search Service, Best News Search Engine, Best Image Search Engine, and Best Design

Pandia Award for Best All-Around Search Site: 2001, 2002

Net Awards: 2001, for Best Site and Best Search Engine

World Class Award (*PC World*): 2001, 2002, 2004

Global Leaders for Tomorrow (World Economic Forum): 2002

Innovator of the Year (*Research and Development*): 2002 (Page)

Marketer of the Year (*Adweek Magazine's Technology Marketing*): 2002 (Brin)

World's 100 Most Influential People (*Time*): 2004

National Academy of Engineering: 2004 (Page)

America's 25 Most Fascinating Entrepreneurs (*Inc.*): 2004

Greatest Innovators of the Past 75 Years (*Business Week*): 2004

World Technology Award for Best Marketing Communications: 2004

FURTHER READING

Books

Hillstrom, Kevin. *Defining Moments: The Internet Revolution*, 2005
Who's Who in America, 2005

Periodicals

Brandweek, Oct. 14, 2002
Current Biography Yearbook, 2001
Fortune, Nov. 8, 1999, p.298; Aug. 23, 2004, p.19; Dec. 13, 2004, p.98
Internet World, June 1, 2001, p.54
Lansing (MI) State Journal, Apr. 29, 2001, p.E1
Maclean's, May 8, 2000, p.46
New York Times, Feb. 1, 2004, p.C1; Aug. 20, 2004, p.C1
Newsweek, Dec. 16, 2002, p.46; Mar. 29, 2004, p.48; May 10, 2004, p.40
Online, May-June 2000, p.41
People, Aug. 23, 2004, p.77
Technology Review, Nov.-Dec. 2000, p.108
Time, Aug. 21, 2000, p.66
Washington Post, Feb. 22, 1999, p.F20; Oct. 28, 1999, p.E1

Online Articles

http://www.linuxgazette.com
  (*Linux Gazette,* "Interview with Google's Sergey Brin," Nov. 2000)
http://www.businessweek.com
  (*Business Week,* "Google's Larry Page: Good Ideas Still Get Funded,"
  Mar. 13, 2001; "Larry Page And Sergey Brin: Information At Warp
  Speed," Dec. 27. 2004)
http://www.wired.com
  (*Wired,* "Google vs. Evil," Jan. 2003)

Online Databases

Biography Resource Center Online, 2005, separate articles on Sergey Brin and
  Larry Page
WilsonWeb, 2005, article from *Current Biography,* 2001

ADDRESS

Sergey Brin and Larry Page
Google Inc.
1600 Amphitheatre Parkway
Mountain View, CA 94043

WORLD WIDE WEB SITES

http://www.google.com/corporate
http://www-db.stanford.edu/~sergey
http://www-db.stanford.edu/~page

Adam Brody 1980-
American Actor
Star of the Hit TV Series "The O.C."

BIRTH

Adam Jared Brody was born on April 8, 1980, in San Diego, California. His father, Mark Brody, is an attorney, and his mother, Valerie Brody, is a graphic designer. He has fraternal twin brothers, Matt and Sean, who are five years younger.

YOUTH

Brody had a fairly typical Southern California childhood. He enjoyed going to the beach and spent a great deal of his time surfing. "I lived 20 minutes inland, which was a travesty because I surfed every day," he stated. As a teenager, Brody pictured himself becoming a professional surfer someday, or at least owning a surf shop.

Brody always showed signs of being a natural performer. For example, he loved to tell jokes as a kid. Yet he never did any acting during his school years. In fact, his only early involvement in film came at the age of 18, when he made a surfing video featuring his friends. "It was sort of a painstaking process—this was before digital film, so everything had to be done through an editing machine," he recalled. He ended up screening the completed film at the local YMCA for an appreciative audience of about 200 people. "Everyone was cheering and yelling for everyone's waves," he remembered. "It was great. It was the most energy I've ever felt in a room. Surfer movies are great, because unlike regular movies you're supposed to scream and shout. It was like a concert with blasting music and everything. My parents were blown away."

EDUCATION

Brody attended Scripps Ranch High School in San Diego. "I did fine in high school," he related. "I was popular enough. I had friends, I dated. I don't have any high school horror stories." After graduating in 1998, he took classes at Mira Costa College in Oceanside, California. But Brody soon abandoned college in order to pursue a career as an actor.

CAREER HIGHLIGHTS

Becoming an Actor

After graduating from high school, Brody struggled to figure out what he wanted to do with his life. He ended up working as a clerk at a video store, which helped turn his attention toward acting as a potential career. "I got a job at Blockbuster in La Jolla, and it was incredibly boring," he recalled. "I was not into school, there wasn't anything I wanted to do. The only thing in my career counseling class that looked at all interesting was acting. I was kind of drifting."

As he catalogued movies and thought about the people who starred in them—many of whom were his own age—Brody decided to try his hand at acting. "On a whim, I told my best friend we should move to Los Angeles," he remembered. "[I told him,] 'We have no girlfriends, we have no internships, and we're not even at four-year schools. We can do anything right now. Let's take this opportunity while we have no strings. Let's go up and try it for a year.'" Brody convinced his parents to let him enroll in a college near Los Angeles. Then he used some of the money that was supposed to pay his college expenses to take acting classes and attend auditions.

Brody and his friend shared a tiny studio apartment in Santa Monica. "The room was L-shaped, and we had bunk beds in one end," he related. "It was so small, only one person could be vertical at a time. We had to take turns eating because one person would have to be lying down on the bed. It wasn't much bigger than a cell at juvenile hall." Brody took a series of odd jobs as a waiter, valet, and department store clerk to help pay the bills. Although it was difficult, he viewed this period as a necessary part of starting his new career. "I made a deal with myself," he explained. "I would come here and give myself one year, try acting my absolute hardest."

Brody's first acting job was a seven-line part on the daytime drama "The Young and the Restless" in 1999. A short time later, he received two lines of dialogue on the Saturday morning kids' show "City Guys." Although small, these parts helped make him more determined to be an actor. "[Acting] turned out to be something I love, and that I really feel is my calling," he stated. "I really feel like I lucked out and found something I love to do."

"[Acting] turned out to be something I love, and that I really feel is my calling. I really feel like I lucked out and found something I love to do."

Shortly before his self-imposed one-year deadline, Brody received his first big break. He won the starring role in a made-for-TV movie called *Growing Up Brady,* which provided a behind-the-scenes look at the making of the hit 1970s series "The Brady Bunch." The movie was based on a tell-all memoir of the same name by Barry Williams, who played eldest son Greg Brady on the show. Brody played a dual role as the young actor Barry Williams and as Williams's TV character, Greg Brady. Although *Growing Up Brady* received generally poor reviews when it aired in 2000, it gave Brody some much-needed exposure. "Charmless acting, by-the-numbers directing, and a seemingly dashed-together script make for a thoroughly un-'Brady' experience," Phil Gallo wrote in *Variety.* The critic also acknowledged, however, that "Brody has some of the goofball charm of Greg's early years."

Growing Up Brady led to a series of acting jobs for Brody, which enabled him to quit his part-time jobs and focus all his attention on his new career. "I haven't had to have a job since then," he noted. In 2000 he appeared in the independent film *Never Land.* This modern retelling of the story of Peter Pan won several independent-film awards and was broadcast on PBS. Brody also had bit parts in *American Pie 2* (2001) and *The Ring* (2002). His biggest early film role came in *Grind* (2003), a comedy that follows four buddies from Chicago as they drive across the country to California in hopes of being discovered as professional skateboarders. Brody played Dustin, the uptight member of the group, who ends up financing the trip with his college fund. Unfortunately, *Grind* failed to connect with either audiences or critics.

Brody also earned several roles on television. He played Lucas on MTV's popular series "Undressed" and had a recurring role as Coop on the family drama "Once and Again." He attracted a following among teenaged girls in the recurring role of Dave Rygalski — boyfriend of Rory Gilmore's best friend, Lane — on the series "Gilmore Girls." Several critics claimed that Brody helped breathe new life and humor into the show.

"The O.C."

Brody received his ticket to stardom in 2003, when he was cast in a new TV series on the Fox network. The show was called "The O.C." in reference to Orange County, the area along the coast of California between Los Angeles and San Diego. The main story line concerns the Cohen family, led by idealistic attorney Sandy Cohen (played by Peter Gallagher). Working as a public defender, Sandy takes the case of Ryan Atwood (Benjamin McKenzie), a troubled teen from the rough neighborhood of Chino, California, who is accused of stealing a car. Sandy does not want to see Ryan put in prison or returned to his alcoholic mother, so he brings the boy home to his Newport Beach mansion. According to *Entertainment Weekly* writer Carina Chocano, however, Ryan "is just the kind of element the gates of the community were designed to keep out."

Sandy's desire to help Ryan creates a conflict with his heiress wife, Kirsten (Kelly Rowland), but she ultimately agrees to let the boy stay in their pool house. Their son Seth Cohen (played by Brody) immediately finds a kindred spirit in Ryan, and the teens become close friends. Despite his family's wealth, Seth too feels like an outsider among the shallow, image-conscious people who populate his high school and community — he is shy, naive, quirky, and somewhat nerdy, but also witty and endearing. Chocano described his character as "a nuanced portrait of a true-to-life dork, the odd product of the tension between his parents' ideology and their tax bracket." Writing in the *New Yorker,* Nancy Franklin added that "Brody is really too good-looking to be playing an unpopular kid, but he makes it

The cast of "The O.C.," from the first season.

work; he talks too much and too fast, he mumbles, and he projects zero physical confidence. In short, his character is adorable — except to people his own age."

Seth has a longstanding crush on Summer (Rachel Bilson), one of the most popular girls in his school. Unfortunately, Summer either treats Seth with contempt or pretends that he does not exist. Meanwhile, Ryan falls for the Cohens' troubled next-door neighbor, Marissa (Mischa Barton). The four teens' lives — as well as those of their parents — become intertwined in a web of dramatic story lines.

A Successful Series

"The O.C." made its debut during the summer of 2003 — several weeks before the official start of the fall TV season. The pilot episode attracted an impressive 7.5 million viewers, and the series continued to gain viewers over the course of its first season to become one of the Fox network's biggest hits. It proved to be particularly popular among young people.

Critics also liked the show. While acknowledging that "The O.C." was basically a teen soap opera, many reviewers insisted that it had more to offer than typical shows in its genre. Chocano, for example, pointed out that "somewhere in all the high-stakes soapiness and often deft and subtle drama, there is a pretty wicked satire of baby-boomer values." Writing in *Time*, James Poniewozik admitted that he found the basic story line "predictable," but nevertheless noted that "'The O.C.' looks to have enough heart, talent, and wit to generate a few seasons' worth of luxurious suds." Reviewer Chuck Barney described it as "a crowd-pleasing show that not only contained all the requisite gloss and gorgeous faces, but offered fleshed-out characters — both teens and adults — along with touches of subversive wit and self-mockery."

> "When we first started, I had no inkling of how popular [Seth would] be. I was like, whatever, so I'm not the hot guy. Just don't dress me in anything too lame and I don't really care. I'm just gonna have my fun and do my job and screw around and whatever. And now it's weird. . . . I'm surprised at how many people feel like this character is speaking for them."

Brody attributed the show's success to the fact that it "blends different-aged characters, comedy, drama, reality, and heightened reality." He also claimed that viewers of all ages could identify with the characters and their dilemmas. "Everyone's felt uncool or like an outsider," he noted. "Everyone's been pushed to do something they didn't want to do. Maybe the exact details aren't the same, but the overall themes of the show are going to resonate." At the same time, Brody admitted that "The O.C." is enjoyable as

From the left: Marissa (Mischa Barton), Ryan (Benjamin McKenzie), Summer (Rachel Bilson), and Seth (Brody).

"classic TV escapism. . . . You watch the drama of these people living extravagant lives and then you see them go down."

Of all the characters on "The O.C.," Brody's Seth Cohen seemed to make the deepest connection with fans. Many teenagers identified with the sincere, socially awkward, geeky aspects of the character, while also wishing that they could fire off witty one-liners like Seth. "When we first started, I had no inkling of how popular he'd be," Brody admitted. "I was like, whatever, so I'm not the hot guy. Just don't dress me in anything too lame and I don't really care. I'm just gonna have my fun and do my job and screw around and whatever. And now it's weird. I've got people coming up to me saying, 'Seth Cohen is our hero.' I'm surprised at how many people feel like this character is speaking for them." Still, Brody insisted that Seth's awkwardness is a bit overstated. "We call him a geek because he's into comics and might wear a button-up," he noted. "But truthfully, is he that nerdy? Is he that socially inept? No, not really. He's just a little goofy and has a great sense of humor."

For Brody, the most realistic aspect of "The O.C." is Seth's relationship with his father, Sandy. "The big similarity between my life and the show is

The cast of "The O.C.," from the second season.

Seth's relationship with his dad. In high school, my dad had this ungodly standard for me getting all A's and B's. I would be like, I'm going to the party because the girl I like is there, and then he and I would fight," he recalled. "Now I look back and I don't know why I was so mean. He was right every time. It's hard because I think, Why is Seth turning his back on his dad?"

By all accounts, Brody also resembles his character in another way: his tendency to toss off quips and one-liners. In fact, the creator of "The O.C.,"

Josh Schwartz, has adjusted Seth's personality in order to take advantage of Brody's natural wit. "[I've] started to write this character in ways that allow Adam to put some of what we call his 'sauce' into the dialogue," Schwartz stated.

By the time the first season of "The O.C." concluded, several critics noted that Brody had emerged as the breakout star of the show. "Thanks to Mr. Brody's appealing acting . . . Seth all but hijacked the series last year," Ari Posner wrote in the *New York Times*. "His blend of smarts, unapologetic weirdness, and self-consciously romantic yearning transformed a potentially secondary character into such an attractive figure that he all but eclipsed the show's more obvious, more glamorous stars."

Enjoying Stardom

Brody is under contract to appear on "The O.C." for six seasons. The 25-year-old actor looks forward to the time when Seth and his friends will graduate from high school and move on with their lives. In the meantime, the popularity of the show has created a number of new acting opportunities for Brody. In 2003, for example, he co-starred with Ed Asner in the straight-to-video movie *Missing Brendan*. He played Patrick, a young man who travels to Vietnam with his grandfather in hopes of finding the remains of an uncle who died in the Vietnam War. In 2005 Brody earned a

"I kind of missed out on a lot of what could've been an education. So now I'm always trying to educate myself. I won't put a TV in my trailer; I'm always reading books to fill in my gaps. I feel like I'm taking baby steps in this whole world of greater literacy, and I gotta say, I'm kind of proud of myself."

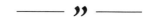

small but important role as Hector in *Mr. and Mrs. Smith,* a big-budget action-thriller starring Brad Pitt and Angelina Jolie. He is also scheduled to star opposite Meg Ryan in his first romantic comedy, *In the Land of Women*. His character is a screenwriter who travels from Los Angeles to suburban Michigan to care for his ailing grandmother, then becomes involved with the women who live across the street.

While Brody has enjoyed his rise to stardom, he claims that success has not spoiled him. "It's not so much that I can go buy that Ferrari I've always wanted or that white tiger," he explained. "It's more that I don't have to worry day to day. Now I'll get an appetizer or a glass of wine [at dinner]. I

Brad Pitt, Angelina Jolie, and Brody in a scene from Mr. and Mrs. Smith.

don't have to number crunch anymore." Brody hopes that he serves as inspiration to aspiring actors, helping them to believe that they can become successful through hard work. "If you really immerse yourself in Los Angeles and acting, if you go to acting class and start doing a good job, you're going to meet people who are agents, or who have agents," he noted. "It's almost unavoidable for anybody who wants to do it. Come up here, get in acting class, and get yourself out there. You make yourself known, and it will come to you, I think."

HOME AND FAMILY

Brody lives in an industrial-style loft apartment in West Hollywood with his dog, Penny, a pit-bull mix that he rescued from an animal shelter. He is single, although he has been linked romantically to his "O.C." co-star Rachel Bilson.

Brody remains close to his family, who have helped him remain grounded through his quick rise to stardom. "I will admit that I've caught myself about to act like a diva, totally," he noted. "But I try to check myself. When in doubt I look to my friends and family. They're so levelheaded, I figure if they're still hanging out with me I must be OK."

HOBBIES AND OTHER INTERESTS

In his spare time, Brody enjoys listening to music by indie bands like Interpol, Bright Eyes, and Death Cab for Cutie. He also plays drums in an alternative rock band called Big Japan. "Me and my friends are in a band, and it's fun," he said. "It's a great way to get out some aggression and it's just something that's really good and fun to put your energy into."

Brody also spends a lot of time reading—everything from comic books to nonfiction books about politics. "I kind of missed out on a lot of what could've been an education," he explained. "So now I'm always trying to educate myself. I won't put a TV in my trailer; I'm always reading books to fill in my gaps. I feel like I'm taking baby steps in this whole world of greater literacy, and I gotta say, I'm kind of proud of myself."

In addition, Brody watches a wide variety of movies on video, which helps him hone his craft as an actor. "I love movies. That's a big hobby," he stated. "I even love bad movies. Growing up, when I wasn't acting, I didn't want to watch bad movies. But now if it's bad, I notice other things [and think], 'OK, why did they put the camera there?' or 'What a horrible piece of dialogue.' Now, there are so many more things to look at."

SELECTED CREDITS

Television

Growing Up Brady, 2000
"Undressed," 2000
"Once and Again," 2000-01
"Gilmore Girls," 2002-03
"The O.C.," 2003-

Films

Never Land, 2000
American Pie 2, 2001
The Ring, 2002
Grind, 2003
Missing Brendan, 2003
Mr. and Mrs. Smith, 2005

HONORS AND AWARDS

Teen Choice Award: 2004, Favorite TV Actor in a Drama/Adventure

FURTHER READING

Books

Contemporary Theater, Film, and Television, Vol. 60, 2005
Krulik, Nancy. *Adam Brody: So Adorkable!,* 2004
Rizzo, Monica. *Meet the O.C. Superstars: The Official Biography!,* 2004
Zack, Elizabeth. *The Boys of Summer: The Unauthorized Biographies of Benjamin McKenzie and Adam Brody,* 2004

Periodicals

Boston Globe, Aug. 5, 2003, p.E6
Entertainment Weekly, Aug. 15, 2003, p.61; Sep. 5, 2003, p.43; Dec. 12, 2003, p.24; Nov. 5, 2004, p.34
New York Times, Oct. 31, 2004, Arts and Leisure, p.24
New Yorker, Aug. 18, 2003, p.144
Newsweek, Sep. 22, 2003, p.11
San Diego Union-Tribune, Aug. 5, 2003, p.E1
Teen People, Dec. 1, 2004, p.104; May 2005, p.110
Teen Vogue, Sep. 2004, p.165
Time, Aug. 11, 2003, p.63
Variety, May 15, 2000, p.39; Aug. 18, 2003, p.21
YM, Dec. 2003, p.74

Online Databases

Biography Resource Center Online, 2005, article from *Contemporary Theater, Film, and Television,* 2005

ADDRESS

Adam Brody
Fox Broadcasting Co.
P.O. Box 900
Beverly Hills, CA 90213

WORLD WIDE WEB SITES

http://www.fox.com/oc
http://www.kidzworld.com

Chris Carrabba 1975-

American Singer and Songwriter
Acclaimed Front Man for the Band Dashboard
Confessional

BIRTH

Christopher Ender Carrabba was born on April 10, 1975, in
Hartford, Connecticut. His mother, Anne Dichele, is the executive director of the National Ovarian Cancer Coalition of Boca
Raton, Florida. Not much is known about Carrabba's father,
Andrew, who was divorced from Dichele when Chris was only
three years old. Carrabba's family includes a stepbrother, Bill, a
brother, Nick, and a stepsister, Victoria.

YOUTH

Carrabba developed an interest in music at an early age. "I remember when we were kids, my little brother and I would collect the popcorn buckets, and we'd have popcorn bucket drum sets. Most kids were playing 'cops and robbers', but I was playing 'band'—so I was kind of a geek, I guess." He also said he's been singing as long as he can remember. When he was 15, his Uncle Angelo gave him his first acoustic guitar, but he didn't really focus on playing guitar until years later. His mother encouraged and supported this early interest in music, and he has credited her as his earliest musical influence. He told one reporter, "When MTV first came on the air, she sat me in front of the television and said, 'That's what you're going to do.'"

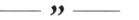

> "When MTV first came on the air, [my mother] sat me in front of the television and said, 'That's what you're going to do.'"

At that point, music took a backseat to skateboarding, though. Like many people his age, Carrabba was a big fan of skateboarding when he was young. This teenage passion earned him a few sponsorships and allowed the future musician to compete. "I had a small and nondescript career, but I'm proud of it," he declared. Skateboarding even had an effect on his musical tastes. With no car to get around in, Carrabba's early music education came not from record stores or concerts, and not from the conservative West Hartford radio stations, but from a skateboarding store in Avon, Connecticut. "I was huge into skateboarding, and the music that really shaped my life came when I was 13 or 14, watching skateboard videos and hearing Operation Ivy and trying to find a way to get their record," he remembered.

When he was 16, Carrabba and his family moved to Boca Raton, Florida, where he still lives today. As it turned out, that move would later provide material for his songwriting career. "I was incredibly in love with this girl, like you can only be when you're 16, and I just couldn't bear the idea of leaving."

EDUCATION

Carrabba attended Boca High School in Florida, where he suffered through a period of soul-searching. "I went through some rough times in high school. I skipped a lot, and went skateboarding. . . . For a while I wasn't doing that hot in school, then my family life started straightening out and I realized it was sort of silly to be doing so bad. . . . So I talked the guidance counselor into letting me take honors classes. I started going to class, and I did ok, I did well."

After graduating from Boca High School in 1994, Carrabba attended Florida Atlantic University, where he nearly completed a degree in education. But it was during his years as a college student that he began to get attention as a musician, and he decided he needed to make a choice. He chose to leave school and focus on turning his music hobby into a career.

EARLY JOBS

Aside from music, the singer had another interest worth pursuing. As a teen, Carrabba had spent summers as a camp counselor, a position that helped him realize how much he enjoyed working with children. During his time at Florida Atlantic University, he accepted a job as assistant director of after-school care at J.C. Mitchell Elementary School in Boca Raton. Known as "Mr. Chris," he was responsible for 150 kids, five days a week. He helped lead the kids' after-school activities, including homework, sports, games, and arts and crafts, and he even taught a weekly guitar class. Carrabba described children as his life's love, other than music. "I'll be working with kids before, during, and after my career as a musician. They just blow my mind."

While working at the elementary school, Carrabba made one concession to his students: he wore long-sleeved shirts every day to cover his heavily-tattooed arms. "All the kids seem to know, but I don't make an issue out of it either way," he said at the time. "Kids will sometimes do as they see, and I'm not trying to make all these kids out to be like me. I'm here to help them find out who they are."

He may have been Mr. Chris during school hours, but in his free time, he was busy writing songs and singing them with various bands. Shortly after graduating from Hall High School, Carrabba had joined a band called the Vacant Andys. The band played local hot spots and eventually earned a small but loyal fan base throughout south Florida. He eventually left the Vacant Andys to play with another local band, The Agency. After that, he joined the emo-rock band Further Seems Forever.

The definition of "emo" is controversial because it seems no two people agree completely on the meaning. Generally speaking, though, emo began in the 1980s hardcore punk scene in Washington, D.C. It's now a label given to bands and musicians who perform songs with confessional lyrics that are characterized by their emotional intimacy, intensity, and sincerity.

But the music accompanying those lyrics can take a variety of forms, including both softer acoustic sounds and pounding rock with loud guitars and vocals. As described by Kelefa Sanneh in the *New York Times*, "Emo songs tend to be passionate, skeptical, and grandly romantic, and the best of these bands seem intent on reinventing that most hackneyed of pop music forms: the love song."

Carrabba was singing with Further Seems Forever when it recorded its debut CD, *The Moon Is Down*, which was released to generally positive reviews in 2001. The CD features a Christian message on many of the tracks while also appealing to listeners from all walks of life. Carrabba decided to leave Further Seems Forever that same year, but he remained on good terms with former band mates and even joined them for a reunion at the 2005 Bamboozle Festival in Asbury Park, New Jersey.

> "I started [Dashboard] as a side project from the band I was in. I was going through something really tough at the time and since I don't write in a journal, this is what I did with it. . . . I played some for my friends and one of them who owned a little label talked me into recording."

CAREER HIGHLIGHTS

By the time Carrabba left Further Seems Forever, he had already gotten started on his next project, Dashboard Confessional. "I started [Dashboard] as a side project from the band I was in. I was going through something really tough at the time and since I don't write in a journal, this is what I did with it. . . . I played some for my friends and one of them who owned a little label talked me into recording." So for a while Carrabba was practicing, recording, and touring for two separate projects, Further Seems Forever and Dashboard Confessional.

When he decided to start doing solo work, he was reluctant to use just his own name. It seemed pretentious, since he knew he wanted to work with other musicians in the future. So he based the name on the lyrics of one of his songs, "The Sharp Hint of New Tears": "On the way home, this car hears my confessions."

The Swiss Army Romance

Carrabba began his career with Dashboard Confessional with the 2000 release of his debut solo album, *The Swiss Army Romance*. Like Further Seems

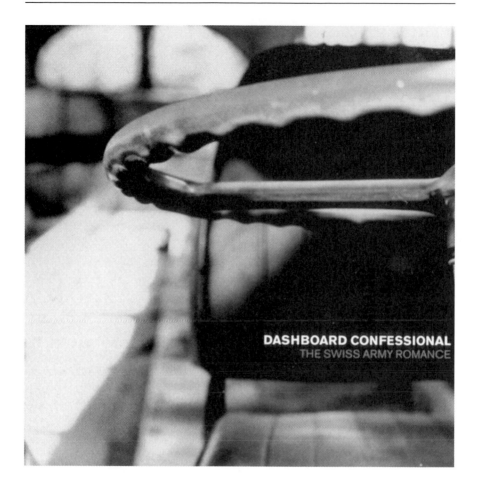

DASHBOARD CONFESSIONAL
THE SWISS ARMY ROMANCE

Forever, this band has also been given the emo label, something Carrabba isn't sure he likes. "I don't think that's what we are, but if that's what somebody wants to call me, that's fine," he explained. Carrabba's lyrics are intensely personal and reflect his life experiences. *Swiss Army Romance* is full of songs about broken hearts and lost love and pain, which he sings in a voice that alternates between a whisper and a scream.

Carrabba was actually still a member of Further Seems Forever when plans were being made for the *Swiss Army Romance* tour, and he looked at the scheduled gigs as "the equivalent of a fall break." He left FSF before the tour began, however, with plans to figure out what he'd do next when the tour ended and he returned to Florida. It took touring and playing night after night in front of live audiences for the singer/songwriter to realize how much he loved performing. "This is truly where my heart's at. I don't need to go home and find anything. It's right here in front of me," he explained. "So then it just sort of inadvertently became my main thing."

One of the reasons Carrabba and others believe his music is so successful is because of the way he began performing: seated on a stool, with an acoustic guitar, encouraging his audience to sing along with the lyrics. What shocked him was how many listeners knew the words. "Kids had already had the record because somebody had mailed them a mix tape with three of the songs from the record. . . . The kids from my hometown were really insistent on showing this thing to every person they knew out of town, so when I went on tour people would maybe be interested. . . . The first show out of town was in Florida but almost Alabama . . . where I had certainly never been with Dashboard. And I was overwhelmed that all these kids were singing." That sing-along quality continues to characterize his performance style to this day, in what the *Austin American-Statesman* once called "rock concert as irony-free campfire sing-along and therapy session."

> ———— " ————
>
> *"This is truly where my heart's at," Carrabba said about his love for performing. "I don't need to go home and find anything. It's right here in front of me. So then it just sort of inadvertently became my main thing."*
>
> ———— " ————

Carrabba's mother said that she isn't surprised at her son's success or at the way his audience interacts with him in concert. "Chris was a camp counselor for years. So when he's on-stage, it's like he's doing a really big sing-along." One fan explained his appeal like this: "His music tells me it's OK for punk kids to feel and not keep it all bottled up inside. In a way, Chris is the therapy for my generation, a way for us to vent without really hurting ourselves or each other."

Forming a Band

The popularity of Dashboard Confessional grew slowly. Carrabba was touring almost constantly at first, and the audience grew with each successive show. "The way that it's grown has been very word of mouth," he explained. "We kind of grew, as far as room size, with that word of mouth. So it never felt unusual. Now there's this influx of people, but it was very slow and steady—there'd be 50 people one time through the city, and then we'd be through the next time and there'd be 75 or 100, because everybody had told somebody to come. So it was a very slow and steady thing."

It was at that point of touring that Carrabba realized he needed a band to back him up. He had been accompanied on tour by his friend, Dan Bonebrake, a bassist who also acted as a sort of protective big brother. By the end of the tour, Bonebrake was playing various instruments on the songs to fill out the sound.

Upon returning home from the tour, Carrabba immediately set out to find more musicians he wanted to work with. He considered drummer Mike Marsh (of The Agency) the best in the business and asked him to join. Bonebrake eventually left to play with a different band, and Dashboard Confessional now consists of drummer Marsh, bass player Scott Schoenbeck, and guitarist-keyboardist John Lefler. "It's just the right combination of guys, the perfect circle of friends and musicians, for my taste," Carrabba said.

The Places You Have Come to Fear the Most

Swiss Army Romance sold better than expected, but with its success came an unexpected complication when several record companies approached Car-

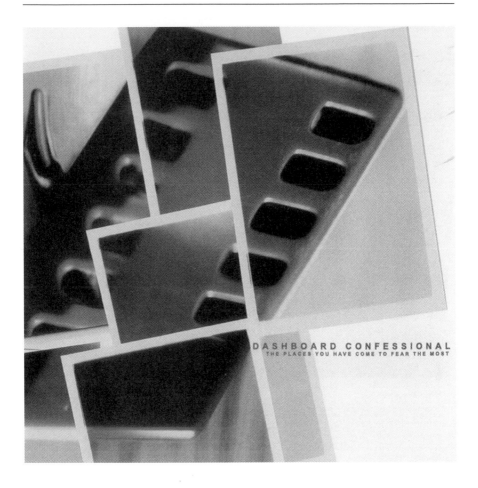

rabba with offers. Although the album was produced under the Fiddler label, a smaller company, he soon signed with Vagrant Records.

In 2001, Vagrant released *The Places You Have Come to Fear the Most*. The album was characterized by Carrabba's wrenching lyrics, many accompanied only by acoustic guitar. It included a new version of the tune "Screaming Infidelities" from *Swiss Army Romance*, which became the album's signature song. Record sales built steadily, and the album, an unexpected hit, reached the Billboard Top 200. It eventually sold over 400,000 copies, a phenomenal number for an independent release. That success was even more impressive since the album received little publicity from the record label and little radio play from record stations. "I'm a little confused by it all," Carrabba said about his success. "There's something universal about the songs, although I didn't know it when I wrote them. There's this honesty that helps people look inward."

Surprisingly, his mother's prediction that he would be on MTV one day came true. MTV chose to air "Screaming Infidelities" as Dashboard's first video, which shocked Carrabba. The band was signed with a lesser-known label, and they had spent just $5,000 to produce the video, compared to performers who spend millions of dollars per video. Said Carrabba, "I think it's been of incredible value to us. It's made us sort of look more legit [legitimate] in the professional sense, which is cool, because we want to be a real band and we are professionals." "Screaming Infidelities" went on to win a 2002 MTV Video Music Award.

That wasn't the end of Dashboard's relationship with MTV, either. In 2002 Carrabba and his band filmed an episode of "MTV Unplugged," a privilege usually reserved for bands that have already established themselves in the industry. Dashboard Confessional is the first band without a platinum record to ever record such a session. The 2002 album from that session, *Dashboard Confessional Unplugged*, went platinum.

——— " ———

Part of what makes Dashboard's success so phenomenal is the fact that Carrabba has always suffered from a serious case of stage fright. He explained his anxiety in a 2003 interview: "I have terrible stage fright," he confided. "I try to use it and draw energy from it, but it's difficult to go up onstage. Stage fright doesn't go away. I've done thousands of shows and I thought it would be gone by now, but I still have it."

"I have terrible stage fright," Carrabba confided. "I try to use it and draw energy from it, but it's difficult to go up onstage. Stage fright doesn't go away. I've done thousands of shows and I thought it would be gone by now, but I still have it."

A Mark, a Mission, a Brand, a Scar

——— " ———

The year 2003 turned out to be a good year for Dashboard. The band was signed by Interscope, one of the biggest labels in the business, and started receiving significant coverage in the national media. In August 2003, the group released *A Mark, a Mission, a Brand, a Scar.* "On this accomplished effort," according to a review in *People*, "Carrabba adds a crackerjack three-piece back-up band for a fuller rock sound that propels his acoustic earnestness to even greater heights." Indeed, this release represented a departure for Dashboard. Many of the songs were more upbeat than those on earlier releases. And instead of a single acoustic guitar, Carrabba's lyrics are accompanied by bass, drums, and electric guitar. Some fans challenged

DASHBOARD CONFESSIONAL
A MARK • A MISSION • A BRAND • A SCAR

Dashboard's integrity as an independent act. They questioned whether the addition of the band made the sound more mainstream, especially since Dashboard had just moved from an independent record label to a major label. But others welcomed the changes.

A Mark, a Mission, a Brand, a Scar debuted at No. 2 on Billboard's Top 200 chart and sold 122,000 copies in its first week. Until that time, the best week the band had ever had was selling 35,000 copies. Carrabba recalled a conversation from early in his career. "When I first signed at my label, the owner asked me what I thought I could do in the first week. The biggest number I could even conceive was 50,000. I told him if we sold that many, I'd flip out. . . . I'm going to frame that little Billboard number and show it off to my kids one day. They'll probably say, 'Yeah, Dad, we know you were quite the big shot back then. Enough already.' That's how it always ends up for everybody."

But if 2003 was a good year, 2004 was even better. Carrabba has been a life-long fan of Spider-Man, the comic superhero. So when movie producers approached him with the request that he write and perform a song for the soundtrack for *Spider-Man 2*, he couldn't believe his good fortune. "Do I get to see the movie early?" was all he wanted to know. Executives assured him he would, and that was all he needed to hear.

Carrabba submitted a song he'd already written, one he felt would fit in with the other songs from the soundtrack. After giving it more thought, though, the songwriter decided he wanted to write a song specifically for the movie, and he asked permission to resubmit. The next morning, he turned in the tune "Vindicated," and the movie executives loved it. They were so sure of its success, in fact, that they told Carrabba it would be one of two singles released from the soundtrack. To hear him tell it, the song seems to have written itself. "Some songs take a month, some songs take five minutes," he explained in an MTV interview. "This one took about an hour, and that was to write everything. The body of the song was written in about ten minutes. There must have been something else stepping in to help. It was almost like preordained rock."

"I'm not sure what the [next] record is going to be yet, it's too soon to tell. The next record is priority number one for me right now —just because it's the most fun thing for me to do—sit around and write songs."

Plans for the Future

With a new CD slated for release in 2005, Carrabba is enjoying his success. "I'm not sure what the record is going to be yet, it's too soon to tell. The next record is priority number one for me right now—just because it's the most fun thing for me to do—sit around and write songs," he told MTV.

Other than that, even Carrabba can't predict what lies ahead. "I think we'll just keep touring and working," he says. "We're one of those touring bands that just keeps going."

HOME AND FAMILY

Though he never comes right out and says it, Carrabba does hint about having a long-time girlfriend. His privacy is important to him, though, so he avoids giving out any details. Though he has no children, he hopes one day to have a family of his own.

Carrabba is close to his family; his mother even frequently edits his lyrics. "She is a musician herself, not professional, but she's very talented. She recognized whatever gifts I was given and encouraged them—not only just music, but especially when it came to music," he said.

HOBBIES AND OTHER INTERESTS

Carrabba enjoys reading, and his favorite author is John Irving, who wrote *A Prayer for Owen Meany* (which was made into the movie *Simon Birch*) and *The World According to Garp*, among other novels. Carrabba spends so much time on tour that he's always looking for ways to pass the time. "The days become a complete blur. Your forget what day of the week it is. Mike, our drummer, and I skateboard a lot around towns because we're both pretty avid skateboarders. We play basketball a lot. Eventually it becomes sleep-away camp almost, you're creating activities for yourself."

Carrabba recently listed some of his favorite music as Jawbox, Jawbreaker, Knapsack, Elvis Costello, the Beach Boys, The Refused, Stevie Wonder, Bruce Springsteen, Tom Petty, the Beatles, and They Might Be Giants. The songwriter makes it a point to say that he is influenced by the music he grew up listening to as well as the music he discovers now.

SELECTED RECORDINGS

(All recordings with Dashboard Confessional unless indicated.)

The Swiss Army Romance, 2000; reissued 2003
The Moon Is Down, 2001 (with Further Seems Forever)
The Places You Have Come to Fear the Most, 2001
Dashboard Confessional Unplugged, 2002
A Mark, a Mission, a Brand, a Scar, 2003

AWARDS

MTV Video Music Award: 2002, for "Screaming Infidelities"

FURTHER READING

Books

Contemporary Musicians, Vol. 44, 2004

Periodicals

Boston Globe, July 19, 2002, p.D1
Chicago Sun-Times, May 21, 2004, p.3

Hartford Courant, Mar. 28, 2002, p.8
Interview, Feb. 2002, p.68
New York Post, Sep. 5, 2003, p.58
Newsweek, Aug. 25, 2003, p.62
Palm Beach Post, June 11, 2000, p.1J
Rolling Stone, Aug. 30, 2001, p.108; July 25, 2002, p.38; May 4, 2004
Seventeen, Aug. 2002, p.178
South Florida Sun-Sentinel, Oct. 1, 2002, p.E1
Spin, Oct. 2003, p.66
Teen Vogue, Mar. 2004, p.114
Time, May 27, 2002, p.59

Online Databases

Biography Resource Center Online, 2005, article from *Contemporary Musicians,* 2004

ADDRESS

Chris Carrabba
Dashboard Confessional
P.O. Box 273645
Boca Raton, FL 33427

E-mail: chris@dashboardconfessional.com

WORLD WIDE WEB SITE

http://www.dashboardconfessional.com

Johnny Depp 1963-

American Actor
Star of the Hit Movie *Pirates of the Carribean*

BIRTH

John Christopher Depp III was born in Owensboro, Kentucky,
on June 9, 1963. His father, John Depp, Sr., was a city engineer.
His mother, Betty Sue (Palmer) Depp, worked occasionally as
a waitress. Johnny is the youngest of four children. He has two
older sisters, Debbi and Christi, and an older brother, Dan.

YOUTH AND EDUCATION

When Depp was about six, his family moved from Kentucky to Miramar, Florida, a working-class suburb of Miami. Depp disliked Florida. His parents didn't find jobs or a home right away, and the change was unsettling. Throughout his childhood, his mother and father had an unhappy relationship, and their home life was stormy. "They stuck it out for us all those years," Depp said of his mom and dad. "But we lived in a small house and nobody argued in a whisper. We were exposed to their violent outbursts against each other. That stuff sticks."

When he was a young boy, Depp's behavior could be a little unusual. "I made odd noises as a child. Just did weird things, like turn off light switches twice. I think my parents thought I had Tourette syndrome," he said, referring to the neurological syndrome that causes sufferers to make involuntary repetitive movements. Depp also idolized dare-devils. One of his favorites was stuntman Evel Knievel, who performed tricks like leaping the length of a bus on his motorcycle.

Depp became interested in the electric guitar when some relatives visited Florida to preach and perform gospel music. The religion didn't inspire him —but he was hooked on the guitar. "My mom bought [a guitar] from them for 25 bucks. I was about 12 years old," he said. "Then I locked myself in a room for a year and taught myself to play." At that stage of his life, all he wanted was to be a rock-and-roll star "for whatever reason—for girls, for money, for whatever. That's really the only plan I've ever had in my life."

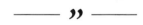

"My mom bought [a guitar] from them for 25 bucks. I was about 12 years old. Then I locked myself in a room for a year and taught myself to play."

Depp spent his early adolescence sitting in his room playing electric guitar and listening to music. "I was very lucky to have my brother, who is ten years older than me and a real smart guy," Depp said. "He turned me onto Van Morrison and Bob Dylan. I remember listening to the soundtracks to [the films] *A Clockwork Orange* and *Last Tango in Paris*. I loved Aerosmith, Kiss, and Alice Cooper, and when I was older, the Clash, the Sex Pistols, and the Ramones."

When Depp was a young teenager, he began to get into trouble. He experimented with alcohol, drugs, and sex. He stole from stores and "broke into a few classrooms, just to see what was on the other side of that locked door," he said. Looking back, he called it a mixture of curiosity and boredom that led him to misbehave. "I don't see what I was doing as a kid as 'bad boy,'" he said. "I wasn't a mean kid who did a lot of crime. It's not like I would run down the street and grab an old lady's purse. Anything I did was never malicious."

Depp was bright and inquisitive. But he felt that teachers were overbearing and unfair. He had trouble focusing his energy on books. "I wanted to be . . . one of the really smart kids. I always envied those guys," he admitted. But when he was 16, Depp dropped out of high school for good. At around the same time, his parents split up. "There was this kind of big scare," he said. "My mom got very ill and so the family really came together for a minute or two. By 'minute or two' I mean for a period of time. We bonded there, and then that sort of dwindled. So I guess anywhere from 12 to 17 I felt pretty weird."

> *Director Wes Craven recognized Depp's overwhelming charisma. "My teenage daughter and her friend were there at the reading and they absolutely flipped out over him," Craven said. "He's got real sex appeal for women."*

Depp spent part of that period living with a friend in the back of a car, a 1967 Chevrolet Impala. He held menial jobs like working as a gas-station attendant. His difficult youth has stayed with Depp. In the early 1990s, he said that despite his movie stardom, deep inside he still felt like "a 17-year-old gas-station geek." Several writers have observed that his sense of being an outsider has never left him. They suggest that his deep sympathy with oddball characters like Edward Scissorhands and Ed Wood is what enabled him to play these parts so well.

FIRST JOBS

As a teenager, Depp played guitar in several rock bands. He was too young to perform legally in bars, so he would sneak in the back door and leave after the first set of songs. His pay was about $25 a night. "That's how I made a living," he said. His most successful group was called the Flame, later renamed the Kids. They became popular enough to play as the opening act for the legendary rocker Iggy Pop and other nationally known acts. Two years later Depp took his band to Los Angeles to try and break into the big time. But the going was rough. "There were so many bands it was

A Nightmare on Elm Street.

impossible to make any money," he remembered. Depp and his band mates made ends meet with side jobs like selling ads over the phone. "We had to rip people off. . . . It was horrible," he said. His personal life hit a low note, too, as his early marriage to a Florida girlfriend ended in divorce.

CAREER HIGHLIGHTS

Depp fell into acting after his ex-wife introduced him to the actor Nicolas Cage, who was impressed by his dark good looks and moody manner. Cage recommended Depp to his agent (a professional who helps actors find work). The agent immediately sent Depp to film director Wes Craven, who was hiring actors for *A Nightmare on Elm Street* (1984). Depp had never acted but was eager to earn money. So he convinced an actor friend to stay up all night and coach him. Hours after his meeting with Craven, Depp was amazed to get a phone call saying he had landed the job.

Craven was struck by Depp's "very powerful and yet subtle personality." The director also recognized his overwhelming charisma. "My teenage daughter and her friend were there at the reading and they absolutely flipped out over him," Craven said. "He's got real sex appeal for women." Depp made his film debut as Glen, a teenager who gets viciously devoured by a bed. *A Nightmare on Elm Street* was a huge box-office success, becoming the first in a series of horror movies that have become cult favorites. Years later, as a thank-you to Craven for giving him his first break, Depp made an appearance in *Freddy's Dead: The Final Nightmare* in 1991.

After his first movie role, Depp began to study acting at the Loft studio in Los Angeles, a respected school. Still, he wasn't getting any work. To make matters worse, his band mates resented his focus on acting and kicked him out of the group. He was so broke that he stayed with friends, including Nicolas Cage, and searched their sofa cushions for spare change. When Depp was offered a part in a low-budget, sexy teen film called *Private Resort*, he hesitated — but then accepted it. The film got little attention, and Depp now omits it from his official list of credits.

In contrast, Depp's next role was in an Academy-Award winning war drama, *Platoon* (1986), made by the acclaimed director, Oliver Stone. The film is a hard-hitting view of the Vietnam War, a controversial conflict in Southeast Asia that the United States was involved in during the 1960s and early 1970s. Depp's part as Private Lerner, a language interpreter, was small but striking. After *Platoon* won four Oscars, including best picture, Depp hoped that similar, challenging work would come his way. In the meantime, he joined a new band, Rock City Angels.

"21 Jump Street" and TV Stardom

While Depp waited for more film work, his agent offered him a part as an undercover police officer in a new television series, "21 Jump Street," a cop show aimed at a young audience. It was to be a jewel in the line-up of the new Fox television network, which was just getting started at that time. "I said no, no, no, no, no," Depp recalled. "I didn't want to sign some big contract that would bind me for years." Fox hired another actor to play Tom Hanson, a narcotics officer who poses as a student at an urban high school. But soon the other actor left the series.

When his agent repeated the offer, Depp agreed. "21 Jump Street" quickly became a huge hit. Within months, soulful-eyed Johnny became a full-blown teen sensation. He attracted thousands of fan letters each week and inspired gushing features in teen magazines. A *Rolling Stone* reviewer wrote that he had "everything that makes little girls wriggle: a forest of eyelashes, sensitive eyes, spiked locks stiffened with several hair-care products of the 1980s, [and] dangly earrings." But Depp was not comfortable with his new status. "I would flip around the TV and there were all these commercials about me," he remembered. "I felt like a box of cereal."

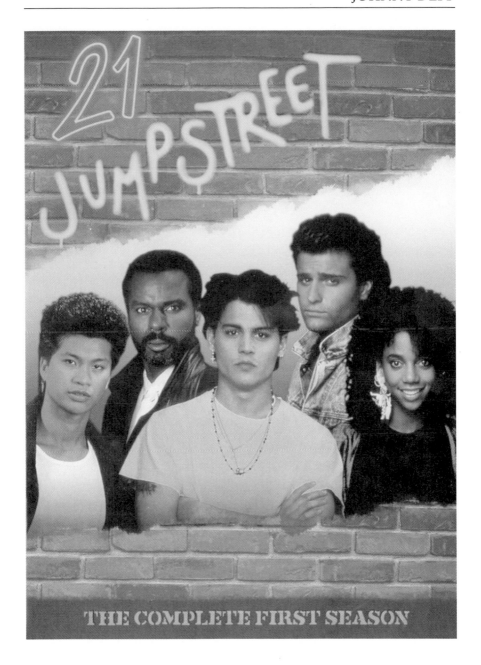

THE COMPLETE FIRST SEASON

Depp knew that fame could be a positive boost for his career, and he appreciated the on-camera experience. But he realized that few TV idols ever become serious actors. "It was a frustrating time," he recalled. "I didn't feel I was doing anybody any good on there. Not them. Not the people watching the show. Certainly not myself." Part way through his three-year run, Depp even tried to get fired from the job. He read his lines with rubber bands around his tongue. Once he turned up for work wearing a feathered turban and speaking in an Indian accent. But the show's producers knew they had a star on their hands. "They turned me into this great potential for a lunchbox and a thermos," Depp said. "Once I got out of that deal, out of that series, I swore to myself, you know, that I was only going to do the things that I wanted to do."

> Depp acknowledged his deep sympathy with misunderstood and damaged characters. "I do have an affinity for damaged people, in life, in roles," he said. "I don't know why. We're all damaged in our own way. Nobody's perfect. I think we are all somewhat screwy, every single one of us."

Oddballs and Outsiders: *Edward Scissorhands* **to** *Ed Wood*

Throughout his career, Depp has kept this vow. He has consistently selected films that are interesting to him, not those that would make him famous or rich. "I have a strange allergy to formula," he said, referring to plots that have been done many times. "Why do things that have been done a million times before?" Indeed, for the first part of his career, Depp was known for playing characters that were misfits and oddballs.

For his first role after "21 Jump Street," Depp was delighted to make a complete U-turn. He was hired by the offbeat cult filmmaker John Waters, who was then known best for shock-comic extravaganzas that starred a 300-pound transvestite named Divine. Waters was famous for turning expectations about gender, movies, and society upside down — with hilarious results. He wanted Depp to take the title role in *Cry-Baby* (1990), a spoof of 1950s films about bad-boy teenagers. "I thought, 'Who can I get to play this?'" Waters recalled. "I went and bought every teen magazine and [Depp] was on the cover of every one of them. I said, 'This guy looks perfect!'. . . Then I read these magazines, and they said that [he was] a juvenile delinquent! I thought, 'This is great!'" According to Depp, "It was important for me to do something as far away from 'Jump Street' as I could, to make fun of that image." His co-stars in *Cry-Baby* ranged from 1950s film idol Tab Hunter to rocker Iggy Pop to former political hostage Patti Hearst. The movie attracted mixed reviews from critics, but Depp sent a strong signal that he was eager to break out of the mold of television pretty-boy.

Edward Scissorhands.

One director who was intrigued by Depp's performance was Tim Burton. The creator of *Batman* and a filmmaker with a gothic, yet humorous, world view, Burton saw Depp's potential to play a misunderstood outsider. He chose him for the title role in *Edward Scissorhands* (1990), his portrait of a mysterious creature whose scientist-creator dies before completing him. The naive, bewildered Edward is left with deadly blades on his hands instead of fingers. He is sweet and vulnerable, but he could potentially kill anyone he touches. When a kindly Avon lady takes him home, he falls in love with her pretty teen-aged daughter (played by Winona Ryder, Depp's real-life fiancée at the time).

Edward Scissorhands became an unexpected box-office hit and a critical success. Depp's moving performance won him a wider fan base and boosted his reputation as a talented film actor. It also established a persona that he would revisit in a number of his films — the injured romantic on the edge of mainstream life. Depp acknowledged his deep sympathy with characters like Edward. "I do have an affinity for damaged people, in life, in roles," he said. "I don't know why. We're all damaged in our own way. Nobody's perfect. I think we are all somewhat screwy, every single one of us."

Burton chose Depp to play mysterious, misunderstood Edward partly because of the haunted quality in the actor's eyes. "They look like he's carried more years than he's lived," Burton said. Depp uses his face and body as expressively as the stars of silent films, according to the director: "He understands that a lot of the acting is not in the words."

In his next film, *Benny and Joon* (1993), Depp got the chance to actually impersonate his favorite silent-film stars. His character, Sam, likes to move, dress, and mug like Charlie Chaplin and Buster Keaton. To prepare for the part, Depp took up gymnastics, studied mime, and pored over old silent films. "I like Chaplin, but Keaton was something else, almost surrealistic in what he could say with his face," he said. Sam falls in love with an emotionally disturbed young girl, played by Mary Stuart Masterson. Depp received good reviews for his performance, but the quirky film didn't find mainstream success.

Depp's next film won even greater popularity and critical acclaim. In *What's Eating Gilbert Grape?* (1993), he played a small-town grocery-store employee who struggles to care for his needy family. The cast featured several gifted actors, including future superstar Leonardo DiCaprio as Depp's mentally disabled brother, Juliette Lewis and Mary Steenburgen as his love interests, and newcomer Darlene Cates as his obese, housebound mother. Critics praised his performance as an overburdened outsider. An *Entertainment Weekly* reviewer noted his subtle use of his face alone to create "a portrait of resigned claustrophobia."

Ed Wood (1994) reunited Depp with director Tim Burton in the story of a real-life eccentric who loved to dress in women's clothes—especially high heels and angora sweaters. Depp played Ed Wood, a film director known for making some of the worst movies of all time. But Wood so loves the act of creating that he never realizes that he is an object of scorn. Critics generally admired the film and singled out Depp for his strong, touching performance. They also credited him with contributing to the success of his co-star Martin Landau, who won an Academy Award for his role as the drug-addicted actor Bela Lagosi.

Surviving Some Low Points

By this point Depp had enjoyed a string of professional successes, but his personal life was in trouble. Since early in his career he had been known as a "Hollywood bad boy" who loved the party scene. Rumor had it that he turned up drunk at interviews with the press. Outrageous stories circulated about him—for example, that he and Nicolas Cage were found hanging from their fingertips from the top of a five-story parking garage.

In the early 1990s, Depp and some music friends opened a bar called the Viper Room in Los Angeles. They planned it as a place they could hang out and listen to 1930s-era jazz music. The club and Depp's reputation suf-

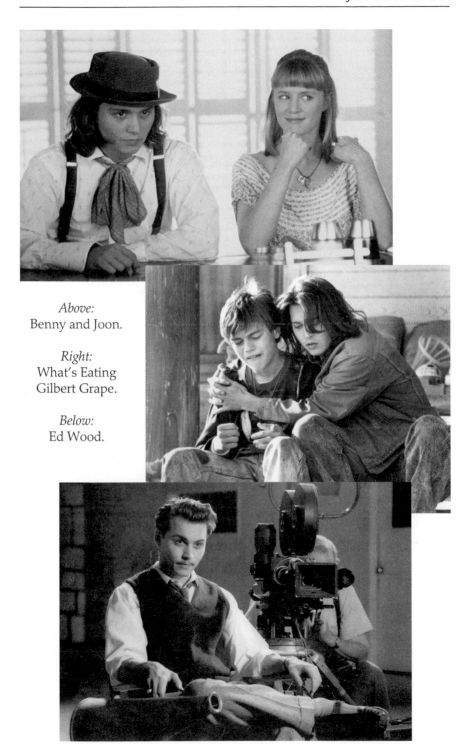

Above:
Benny and Joon.

Right:
What's Eating
Gilbert Grape.

Below:
Ed Wood.

fered in 1994, when the young actor River Phoenix died of a drug overdose just outside the club. That same year, Depp was arrested in New York City for trashing a hotel room he shared with his then-girlfriend, model Kate Moss. These low points led him to give up alcohol and drugs.

During this time, Depp acted in several movies that earned only a so-so response. In *Dead Man* (1995) he worked with the acclaimed, quirky director Jim Jarmusch for a film hardly anyone went to see. His work in *Fear and Loathing in Las Vegas* (1998), based on a famous, well-loved book by journalist Hunter S. Thompson, prompted some of Depp's most negative reviews ever. Some other films, *Nick of Time* (1995) and *The Ninth Gate* (1999), caused few ripples of attention.

―――― " ――――

Depp learned a lot from working with such distinguished co-stars as Marlon Brando and Al Pacino. "I watched them like a hawk. I sponged as much education as I could," he said. "Ultimately it solidified what I knew from being a musician: Do what's right for you. . . . [Don't] compromise unless you think it's right. Stick to your guns, no matter what."

―――― " ――――

In 1997, Depp took on a huge project: directing a film that he also starred in. Depp bought the rights to *The Brave* after the movie was abandoned by other filmmakers. It tells the story of a poor Native-American family who lives next to a junkyard. The father of the family fixes on a drastic and dangerous plan to pull the family out of their dire poverty. Depp is part Cherokee, thanks to a full-blooded great-grandmother who died at age 103. So he was interested in the Native-American issues raised in the story. And he always identified with the disadvantaged. Despite his heart-felt work—and his multi-million-dollar investment—critics torpedoed *The Brave* with horrible reviews. Depp was stung, but in the end was philosophical. "Whether the picture was good or bad, what they could never take away was that it was my movie," he said. He has not directed a film since then.

Career Highs in the 1990s

Depp survived some low points in the 1990s, but he also hit some high points. In 1995, he co-starred with legendary actor Marlon Brando in *Don Juan De Marco*. Depp played a deluded young man who enters psychotherapy with a therapist played by Brando. Two years later, Depp again co-starred with a famed older actor, this time Al Pacino, in *Donnie Brasco*. Depp played the title character, a conflicted undercover cop who tries to penetrate the Mafia underworld. Brasco befriends Pacino's character, a Mafia elder. Depp had a great time working with his distinguished co-stars. He also learned a lot. "I watched them like a hawk. I sponged as much education as I could," he said. "Ultimately it solidified what I knew from being a musician: Do what's right for you. . . . [Don't] compromise unless you think it's right. Stick to your guns, no matter what."

Both *Don Juan De Marco* and *Donnie Brasco* earned Depp generally a good response from critics and fans. "[He] was able to stand up to Pacino, who is really a power-

Sleepy Hollow.

ful actor. It was peer to peer," said Wes Craven, the director of *A Nightmare on Elm Street*. "At that point, I said, 'Wow. He can be on the screen with anybody, and he's going to give 'em a run for their money.'"

Depp finished off the 1990s with *Sleepy Hollow* (1999), his biggest money-maker up to that point. He rejoined director Tim Burton for this gory thriller, based on a classic tale by 19th-century American author Washington Irving. Depp startled interviewers when he revealed that the inspiration for his portrayal of the skittish Ichabod Crane was Angela Lansbury, an English actress who began her career in 1944 and is best known now for the TV series, "Murder, She Wrote." "I thought of Ichabod Crane as a very nervous, ultra-sensitive prepubescent girl. That's where Angela Lansbury came in," he explained. "Something happens to me when I'm reading a screenplay," he said about his strange inspirations. "I get these flashes, these quick images."

Captain Jack Sparrow and *Pirates of the Caribbean*

Depp's intriguing method of inspiration helped him to create an already-classic character for the Disney picture *Pirates of the Caribbean: The Curse of*

Pirates of the Caribbean:
The Curse of the Black Pearl.

the Black Pearl (2003). His pirate, Captain Jack Sparrow, is a swaggering, silly, unsinkable rogue, with an amazing look. He has feathers in his hair, thick black liner ringing his eyes, and significant gold in his ears and teeth. From the minute he appears on screen—sinking serenely into the Caribbean Sea—zany Sparrow steals the show.

Depp said that he based the character on his friend, the famous rock star Keith Richards of the British band the Rolling Stones. According to Depp, rock stars are the modern-day version of pirates. "They live dangerously," he confided. "They're wild and capable of anything, just like pirates." Depp's second inspiration for Sparrow was the classic cartoon character Pepe Le Pew. Pepe is a French skunk who lets nothing get him down. "As he's hopping along, people are falling over from the stink, but he never notices," Depp said. "I always thought, What an amazing way to go through life."

His portrayal of Capt. Jack Sparrow helped to make Depp an A-list movie star after nearly 20 years in Hollywood. Many critics initially disparaged the plan for the movie, saying that it was based on nothing more than a Disney theme-park ride. And Depp himself admitted he only took the part to be in a movie that his kids could watch. But many critics and fans felt that his performance alone lifts *Pirates* from humdrum to exhilarating. With the added attractions of Australian actor Geoffrey Rush and the young British heart-throbs Orlando Bloom and Keira Knightley, *Pirates of the Caribbean* became a massive hit. The film has earned more than $305 million to date.

Disney executives were uncomfortable at first with Depp's over-the-top interpretation of Sparrow. But producer Jerry Bruckheimer defended him, saying, "You don't hire Johnny Depp and not let him do what Johnny Depp does — create characters. He had something in his head he wanted to play, and I wanted him to do that. If I didn't want him to create a character I would have hired someone else." Reviewers marveled at the creativity that he put into Sparrow. One reviewer noted, "The effect of Depp's portrayal — commercially and culturally — is a victory for mysterious eccentricity (a very human trait) over computer-generated special effects."

Ultimately, Depp's performance won raves. He was named the year's best actor in a motion picture by the Screen Actors Guild; he was also nominated for an Academy Award as well as a Golden Globe award for best actor for the part of Sparrow. It's rare for a comic role to receive such honors. But to Depp, the best recognition comes from his fans. "Now I meet these little kids who go, 'Man — you're Captain Jack!' God, what a high that is, that somehow you've pierced that curtain and have made an effect to some degree," he said. "That little kid'll have that memory of watching that movie when he's a grown man or a grown woman. And to me, that means so much." Depp also enjoys the appreciation he gets from his fans at home. "My daughter is absolutely convinced that I'm a pirate," he said. "It doesn't register that Daddy's an actor. 'My dad's a pirate.'"

> **"**
>
> *For Depp, the best recognition comes from his fans. "Now I meet these little kids who go, 'Man — you're Captain Jack!' God, what a high that is, that somehow you've pierced that curtain and have made an effect to some degree," he said. "That little kid'll have that memory of watching that movie when he's a grown man or a grown woman. And to me, that means so much."*
>
> **"**

Above: Finding Neverland.

Right: Charlie and the Chocolate Factory.

Neverland and Charlie's Chocolate Factory

Depp appeared in another family-friendly film, *Finding Neverland,* in 2004. He played the real-life eccentric J.M. Barrie, the Scottish author of the classic children's story, *Peter Pan.* The movie is based on a real episode in Barrie's life. He befriends a widow (played by Kate Winslett), whose four sons help to inspire Barrie to create the Lost Boys of Neverland. Again, Depp's performance was hailed by moviegoers and critics alike. *Finding Neverland* received a Critics' Choice Award for Best Family Film, and Depp was nominated for the Screen Actors Guild Award for best actor.

In 2005, Tim Burton and Depp will collaborate for the fourth time, this time on another children's classic: *Charlie and the Chocolate Factory,* based on the novel by Raold Dahl. (For more information on Dahl, see *Biography Today*

Authors, Vol. 1.) The book was adapted into a very popular movie musical in 1971, starring Gene Wilder as Willy Wonka. Depp acknowledged that he has a hard act to follow as he creates the character of Wonka. "You'll never escape that memory that's seared into your consciousness of Gene Wilder as Willy Wonka. It was really amazing to watch that as a kid growing up, and I've watched it with my kids," he said. "So it's just, 'Okay, where do I go from there?' Gene Wilder did something very beautiful and it's time to take it somewhere else." Above all, he hopes the movie will escape being normal. "I hope it's going to be quite weird. Weird and wonderful," he said.

Other Recent Films and What's Next

Depp has not been devoting himself only to films for young people and families. He has also created critically acclaimed performances in such films as the romance *Chocolat* (2000), the thrillers *Blow* (2001) and *Once upon a Time in Mexico* (2003), and the suspenseful *Secret Window* (2004). In *The Libertine,* Depp played a real-life, 17th-century British poet destroyed by his wild lifestyle. The movie was completed in 2004, but had some delays in distribution. Up next for Depp is the much-awaited sequel, *Pirates of the Caribbean: Treasures of the Lost Abyss,* due to be released in 2006.

Depp never set out to attain commercial success. He has it now, along with widespread respect for his creative artistry. But more than these things, what matters to him is that acting gets more satisfying as his career goes on. "For a lot of years, I was really freaked out. Maybe I took it all too seriously, you know? I was freaked out about being turned into a product. That really used to bug me," he said. "Now, more and more, I enjoy the process. Creating a character, working that character into a scene, into the movie. I mean, the last couple of things have been just a ball."

MARRIAGE AND FAMILY

In 1983, when he was 20, Depp married Lori Anne Allison, a make-up artist. The couple divorced two years later. In the early 1990s, he was engaged to Winona Ryder, his co-star on *Edward Scissorhands.* When they split up after three years, he was said to be heartbroken. He later made and broke engagements with actresses Sherilyn Fenn and Jennifer Grey. Depp then had a stormy and much-publicized romance with English supermodel Kate Moss in the mid-1990s.

Life calmed down for Depp in 1998, when he became involved with Vanessa Paradis, a French actress, model, and former teen pop star. Their daughter, Lily-Rose Melody, was born in 1999 and their son, Jack, in 2002. Depp said that his kids "gave me everything. A reason to live. A reason not

to be a dumbass. A reason to learn. A reason to breathe. A reason to care."
Paradis has said that Depp is the perfect father—except that he gives his
daughter too many potato chips. Depp and his family divide their time between homes in Los Angeles, Paris, and the town of Plan-de-la-tour in the
south of France. They also own their own island in the Caribbean Sea.

HOBBIES AND OTHER INTERESTS

Depp loves vintage jazz music and rock, and he still plays the guitar. He is
a fan of the authors J.D. Salinger and Jack Kerouac. Above all, he enjoys
spending time with his family and playing with his children. They like to
watch movies and play games. One favorite computer game involves
dressing a princess. "You choose the dress and handbag and tiara," he said.
"I love it."

SELECTED ACTING CREDITS

Films

A Nightmare on Elm Street, 1984
Private Resort, 1985
Platoon, 1986
Cry-Baby, 1990
Edward Scissorhands, 1990
Freddy's Dead: The Final Nightmare, 1991
Arizona Dream, 1993
Benny & Joon, 1993
What's Eating Gilbert Grape, 1993
Ed Wood, 1994
Don Juan De Marco, 1995
Donnie Brasco, 1997
The Brave, 1997 (director and co-author)
Fear and Loathing in Las Vegas, 1998
Sleepy Hollow, 1999
Chocolat, 2000
Blow, 2001
Pirates of the Caribbean: The Curse of the Black Pearl, 2003
Once upon a Time in Mexico, 2003
Secret Window, 2004
Finding Neverland, 2004

Television

"21 Jump Street," 1987-1990

HONORS AND AWARDS

Lifetime Achievement Award (French Film Academy)
Best Lead Actor in a Motion Picture (Screen Actors Guild): 2004, for *Pirates of the Carribean: The Curse of the Black Pearl*

FURTHER READING

Books

Hawes, Esme. *Superstars of Film: Johnny Depp*, 1998
Robb, Brian J. *Johnny Depp: A Modern Rebel*, 2004

Periodicals

Biography, Fall 2004, p.38
Current Biography Yearbook, 1991
Entertainment Weekly, Sep. 19, 2003, p.28
Esquire, May 2004, p.94
Interview, Apr. 1990, p.84; Dec. 1995, p.86
Los Angeles Times, Dec. 12, 1993, p.3
New York Times, Jan. 10, 1991, p.C17
People, Oct. 3, 1994, p.100; Dec. 13, 1999, p.91; July 21, 2003, p.67
Time, March 15, 2004, p.76
TV Guide, Feb. 28-Mar. 5, 2004, p.29

Online Databases

Biography Resource Center Online, 2005, article from *Contemporary Authors Online*, 2004

ADDRESS

Johnny Depp
The Walt Disney Company
500 South Buena Vista Street
Burbank, CA 91521

WORLD WIDE WEB SITES

http://disney.go.com/disneyvideos/liveaction/pirates/main_site/main.html
http://www.miramax.com/findingneverland/

Eve 1979-
American Rap Artist and Actress
Star of the Hit TV Show "Eve"

BIRTH

Eve was born Eve Jihan Jeffers in Philadelphia, Pennsylvania, on November 10, 1979. Her mother, Julie Wilch, was a former model who worked for a medical publishing company. Her parents were never married, but Eve saw her father occasionally until she was 12. She and her mom lived in the Mill Creek housing projects in Philadelphia with extended family when Eve was young. They later moved to Germantown when her mother married fashion designer Ron Wilch and gave birth to Eve's younger brother, Farrod.

YOUTH

Growing up, Eve says she was a tomboy. "I do have girlfriends, but I've always hung around with a lot of guys ever since I was little. I always wrestled and climbed trees and did boy stuff. I was a tomboy, but I was very aware that I was a girl. I love being feminine." Although she liked to play outside, she also loved to shop and put together new outfits. She credits her mother with helping her develop her sense of style. When she was growing up, her mother and aunt would take her shopping on Saturdays at Strawbridge's in Center City. "I had my own style. I never wanted to look like the group, the pack of girls who just walk around. They all looked alike and that just annoyed me. I wanted to be fly, but I wanted my own identity." Eve says her family was never poor, just broke all the time. "I don't want to be broke again, ever," she emphasizes.

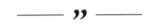

"I had my own style. I never wanted to look like the group, the pack of girls who just walk around. They all looked alike and that just annoyed me. I wanted to be fly, but I wanted my own identity."

While she was growing up, Eve wasn't star-struck. She only had one poster on her wall, and it was of Michael Jordan. She didn't go to many concerts, either. "I didn't like concerts, because I felt like I needed to be onstage. . . . When I was young, I was like, 'I'm not going to nobody's concert. If I'm not performing, I don't want to go.'" Eve liked to sing when she was young, but when she was 13 she switched from singing to rap. That brought her a lot of attention, because at that point most rappers were male. She took the name Eve of Destruction and went to talent shows around Philadelphia. She performed with a group of girlfriends named D.G.P., for Dope Girl Posse; she also performed with her friend, Jennifer Pardue, as the group EDJP (Egypt), which stood for Eve of Destruction Jenny-Poo. They patterned their music after their musical role models: Mary J. Blige, Lauryn Hill, Queen Latifah, and MC Lite.

EDUCATION

Eve attended Martin Luther King Jr. High School in Philadelphia. She wasn't very involved in her schoolwork. "I got punished a lot," she admits.

"I got in trouble for cutting school, staying out late, lying about detention, and lying about homework. I hated high school. I always knew there was something else." Instead of doing her schoolwork, she was putting a lot of energy into her music. "Once I got into high school I became really obsessed with it," she says. "When I graduated, I went full fledged." She also became obsessed with her image, even dying her hair blonde on a dare while she was in high school. "Me, I'm very comfortable being blonde. My hair was blonde for seven years before my first album came out. I love being blonde." She also got her well-known pawprint tattoos on a dare.

> ———— " ————
>
> *"I got punished a lot,"*
> *Eve admits. "I got in trouble*
> *for cutting school, staying*
> *out late, lying about*
> *detention, and lying about*
> *homework. I hated high*
> *school. I always knew there*
> *was something else."*
>
> ———— " ————

After high school, Eve thought about going to college like some of her friends, but she had always dreamed of a career in music. Her mother told her to go for it while she could. She had a period of confusion, where she worked as a stripper in the Bronx for a few weeks. "I did it because it was rebellious for me to do it. . . . I realized, 'You know what? This is not what I need to be doing with my life.'" After that, she decided to get serious about her music. She had started to go out on auditions, but she would have to keep working at it to get her big break.

CAREER HIGHLIGHTS

From Dr. Dre to Ruff Ryders

With the help of some friends, Eve had the good fortune to land an audition with Dr. Dre's label, Aftermath. The audition went well, and she was flown to Los Angeles to do a demo. She signed with the label and spent eight months in L.A. working on an album, but nothing ever came of it. Eve was sent back to Philadelphia with nothing to show for it. Devastated, she "walked around my mom's house in pajamas for a whole month," she now admits. Her mother told her it would all work out for the best, and she was right. Through friendships Eve had made while she was in L.A., she got an audition with the music label Ruff Ryders, located in New York. They put her in a studio with some other rappers and told her to show them what she had. It resulted in Eve being signed as their first female rapper.

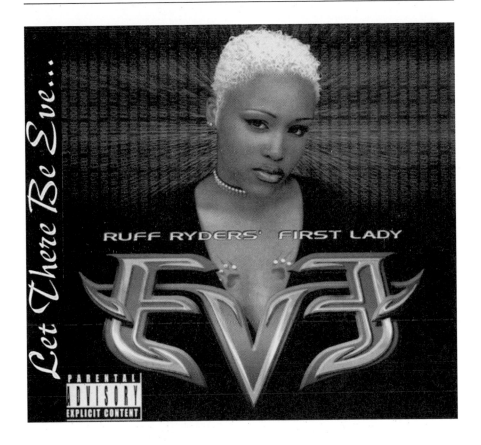

Let There Be Eve: Ruff Ryders' First Lady

Let There Be Eve: Ruff Ryders' First Lady, Eve's first album, was released in 1999. It debuted at No. 1 and eventually sold over two million copies, going multi-platinum. As a female rapper in a male-dominated field, Eve was getting a lot of attention. On one of the tracks, she described herself as a "pit bull in a skirt," and the name stuck. Fans seemed to love her defiant, in-your-face style. One reviewer said that unlike other female rappers, Eve "radiated power." Her good looks, signature blonde hair, paw-print tattoos, and fashion sense made her an instant star.

Eve's first tour was a difficult experience. When *Let There Be Eve* debuted at No. 1, the stress of almost instant fame was enormous. She fought with the friends who accompanied her on tour—they just didn't understand the pressure she was under. They wanted to party all the time, even when Eve had just finished a big performance late at night. Eve left the tour early and spent of couple of months seriously depressed. "I think everything was just so overwhelming for me. Everything happened so fast—friends, family, business associates, people, lawyers, contracts, budgets, everything. Just so much. I was 21. And there was nobody who I felt like I could really talk to, who really understood what I was going through. . . . I just crashed. I got out of it by talking to myself. I cried a lot. I prayed a lot. It was crazy. I don't ever want to go through that again, but I'm glad it happened. I learned from it."

——— " ———

"I think everything was just so overwhelming for me," Eve says about her first tour. "Everything happened so fast. . . . And there was nobody who I felt like I could really talk to, who really understood what I was going through. . . . I just crashed. I got out of it by talking to myself. I cried a lot. I prayed a lot. It was crazy. I don't ever want to go through that again, but I'm glad it happened. I learned from it."

——— " ———

Eve and her friends had always dreamed that rapping would make them rich. That dream was now a reality for her. When the first big checks arrived, she bought a mink and took some friends shopping, but she didn't do anything really crazy. Then she did some "responsible things" with her money—gave gifts to her family and bought a house and a car. She was the first woman in her family to own a house, which made her very proud. To this day, Eve continues to watch her spending. She has an accountant who manages her finances, monitors her expenses, and makes investments for the future. Eve is careful with her money, except for an occasional jewelry shopping spree, to ensure that she will be comfortable for life. She does admit, though, that she has a problem with shoes. "I am ridiculously into shoes. My accountant called me once and was like, 'What are you doing?' She put me on shoe punishment for a month."

Scorpion

Scorpion, Eve's second album, was released in 2001. The second album can be very important for a performer who has had a popular debut—it can show whether the artist has staying power. *Scorpion* had fairly good reviews and established Eve as a serious artist. "*Scorpion* is rooted in hardcore stomp, rhymes, boasts, and slams," David Browne wrote in *Entertainment Weekly*. "So much contemporary hip-hop feels sluggish and monochro-

matic, . . . [but] *Scorpion* pumps up the volume, the rhythms, everything." As Lorraine Ali wrote in *Newsweek*, "This record is more diverse than her debut—the formerly hard-nosed rapper now sings (and actually harmonizes) atop far-flung sounds: Latin horns here, reggae melodies there. The . . . swagger and party numbers that drove her debut still dominate, but a more complex musical backdrop and plausible, honest lyrics about everything from the hurtful deception felt at the hands of former friends to her disgust toward a weak boyfriend add needed substance."

In fact, *Scorpion* showed her taking some risks by moving away from the typical Ruff Ryders' hardcore lyrics. "I think it's a good balance of the hardcore from the first album and the artist I wanna become as I get older," Eve says. "Before, the lyrics were mine, but the vision was pretty much theirs [from Ruff Ryder]. Like there was a song about a heist that was totally the guys' idea. After that, I promised myself I would never make a song about shooting, robbing, anything like that, 'cause it's not me."

The album featured the hit song "Let Me Blow Ya Mind," which Eve performed with Gwen Stefani of No Doubt. (For more information on Stefani, see *Biography Today*, Sep. 2003.) The song was produced by Dr. Dre, who had dropped Eve from his Aftermath label a couple of years earlier. "I never had no animosity toward him. After a couple of months." She now thinks he is great, especially after the hit they made together, but she admits that things got a little ugly while they were working in the studio. "He's got his formula and I got mine. And we was clashin'."

Attending the Grammy Awards that year was exciting. Eve had received two Grammy nominations for *Scorpion*: she was nominated for Best Rap Album and for Best Rap/Sung Collaboration for "Let Me Blow Ya Mind." Eve attended the awards with her mother and was elated when she and Stefani won for "Let Me Blow Ya Mind." When asked about winning a Grammy, she said, "My mother was there, so she was able to share that with me. I cried, I screamed. I felt really blessed," she explains. "I never got awards in high school. So when they called my name, it was like, 'Mommy!' It was an incredible moment."

Eve-Olution

Eve's third album, called *Eve-Olution*, was released in 2002. It included several collaborations, with Snoop Dogg and Nate Dogg, Jadakiss and Styles, and Alicia Keys on the hit "Gangsta Lovin'." Eve said that the album title fit. "[I've] evolved as a person, mentally and spiritually. I think I've gotten closer to God. It's like a whole package. I've definitely grown. My ear for music has grown—you can hear it on the new album, both lyrically and musically. It's a little different from the first and second albums. I think it's more melodic."

By this point in her career, Eve was able to exert a lot more control over the album's artistic development. *Eve-Olution* was praised for its diversity of styles and influences, including reggae, rock, and gospel. Her songs on the album also reveal her interests, like relationships, men, love, or even the environment. She has been praised for speaking out against abuse toward women. "I don't listen to a lot of hip-hop anymore because I can't respect it," she admits. "Some people are gonna hate me for this, but it's like you're not busting guns anymore. We got in the business to get away from all of that. If you're gonna talk about it, at least have a moral to the story. You're not sellin' drugs anymore. It's like, 'C'mon! Talk about something else.'"

Eve-Olution gathered respect from many sources. Critic Marc Weingarten said that this album had "a fluid flow that glides effortlessly into double-time imprecations and snarling put-downs. Eve wields her new vocal weapon fearlessly, venturing into the stark noir-hop of 'What,' with its ominous staccato string section . . . before emerging into the bright daylight of 'Gangsta Lovin','" with its funky harpsichord fantasia." With three solid hit albums under her belt, Eve was ready to explore new challenges outside the music arena.

Barbershop and UPN's "Eve"

At the same time that Eve was working on *Eve-Olution*, she was already branching out into new areas. She started modeling and doing a few commercials and then made her break into film with a small part in *XXX* with Vin Diesel. It wasn't much, but it was enough to get noticed. She followed that with a role in the surprise 2002 hit *Barbershop*. This ensemble comedy is about a local barbershop that is more than a small business. Instead, it serves as the neighborhood social center—a center for gossip, for debate, for laughter, for community news, and for friendship. The shop is owned

Eve and the gang in a scene from Barbershop.

by Calvin (Ice Cube), who inherited it from his father. There are seven barbers — six males, one female, six blacks, one white — each with their own story. Eve plays Terri, a hard-edged woman who is trying but failing to leave her cheating boyfriend. When the story opens, Calvin is worried about the business and is on the verge of selling it, and the group rallies to save it.

> **"The character is very similar to me in real life,"** Eve said about the character Terri in **Barbershop.** *"I'm the only female involved with Ruff Ryders, so I'm used to being surrounded by testosterone all the time. I have to be tough with them the same way Terri is in the shop. She has a little bit of an attitude because she needs them to respect her."*

Eve's role in *Barbershop* delighted her fans and made her visible to people who hadn't noticed her before. She took her new acting career seriously, employing an acting coach and working very hard to improve her comedic skills. Eve has said that she loved playing Terri in *Barbershop*: "The character is very similar to me in real life," she says. "I'm the only female involved with Ruff Ryders, so I'm used to being surrounded by testosterone all the time. I have to be tough with them the same way Terri is in the shop. She has a little bit of an attitude because she needs them to respect her." Her performance was exactly what the director, Tim Story, had in mind for the character. "I was very adamant about getting the right person for Terri," he explains, "and when Eve came to read for us, I was interested as soon as she opened her mouth. I'd seen a lot of actresses, some of whom were phenomenal, but I was looking for somebody who was Terri, not somebody trying to be Terri. And although it's Eve's first movie role, she held her own. Her character is the only female in an all-male barbershop, so she has to show that character will stand up for herself, and she's been doing it. She gave me more than I expected every time."

The film was very successful with audiences, who enjoyed the fast-paced topical humor and the warm storyline. But *Barbershop* ultimately became controversial because some of its humor was considered offensive. The character Eddie, an elderly and outspoken barber played by Cedric the Entertainer, voices a lot of opinions that some viewers found objectionable. In particular, he disparages the civil rights icons Rosa Parks and Martin

Shelly and friends from the TV show "Eve."

Luther King, Jr., as well as other famous African Americans. That caused many civil rights leaders and others to criticize the film for its disrespectful comments—but it also led to widespread publicity and even more viewers.

In 2003, Eve made her move into the world of television with the premier of the UPN series "Eve," for which she serves as both star and co-executive producer. The show was originally titled "The Opposite Sex," but producers wanted fans to be able to identify Eve's show instantly among the dozens of other new shows that were also debuting at that time. She plays Shelly, a fashion designer living in Miami, having a good time but struggling with her relationships with men. Her two best friends—one of whom is single and gorgeous, while the other is married and out of the dating scene—try to help her navigate her way through the difficulties of balancing romance and career. While her girlfriends speak up for the female point of view, her guy friends speak up for the men. "Eve" presents a fresh and funny look at male and female relationships.

The show has been complimented for good chemistry between its characters, but it has also been called average and predictable. After a rough start that almost got it canceled, "Eve" quickly gained popularity. The show's connection with fashion was a bonus for Eve, who was already a fashion trendsetter preparing to debut her own clothing line that year. It gave her a chance to wear some of her new line in the show.

Fashion Line Fetish

It took work for Eve to expand beyond her fierce rap persona. The first images of her showed a scowling face and defiant pose. When she wanted to break into film and fashion, people were wary of her hard image. So Eve hired stylists to help her soften her look. They changed her hair and dressed her in more alluring styles, including the flowing peasant blouses that were popular at the time. The move worked; she began appearing in magazines, modeled for Tommy Hilfiger, and earned a reputation as a style trendsetter. She hoped that she could follow in the footsteps of Sean "P. Diddy" Combs, who had successfully moved from music into a number of other fields, including fashion design and restaurant ownership.

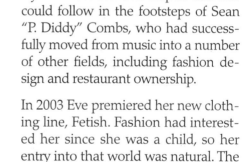

In 2003 Eve premiered her new clothing line, Fetish. "I am completely involved in this. Nothing gets done without my approval. I am so psychotic about it. Even down to the zipper pull. . . . This is my line. It carries my name. I have to be involved and I have to want to wear it."

In 2003 Eve premiered her new clothing line, Fetish. Fashion had interested her since she was a child, so her entry into that world was natural. The clothing line has had excellent initial sales; they hope to move into a full line that includes everything from fragrances to eyewear at some point in the future. Eve participates in all aspects of the project. "I am completely involved in this. Nothing gets done without my approval. I am so psychotic about it. Even down to the zipper pull. . . . This is my line. It carries my name. I have to be involved and I have to want to wear it."

Recent Films

The year 2004 proved to be a busy time for Eve, with three different movies scheduled for release. First up was *Barbershop 2: Back in Business,* a sequel to the hit 2002 film. The barbershop once again is threatened, and Calvin struggles to save it. Many of the actors reprised their original roles, and they

Eve and Storm P in The Cookout.

were joined by Queen Latifah, who plays a hair stylist in a nearby shop. Eve was excited to return to the role of Terri. "I just had to come back," she says. "I had such a great time doing the first *Barbershop*, and I just fell in love with Terri. Plus, it was fun because Terri has a love interest in *Barbershop 2*, and it's someone you'd never guess." While the sequel didn't achieve quite the same level of success as the original, fans of *Barbershop* enjoyed spending more time with the crew.

Eve followed that up with *The Cookout*, another feel-good ensemble comedy. It co-starred Queen Latifah, Danny Glover, Tim Meadows, Ja Rule, Farrah Fawcett, and Storm P, who plays a young basketball player who gets a $30 million deal to play for the New Jersey Nets. Pressured by his greedy girlfriend, he buys a house in an exclusive gated community, much to the chagrin of his conservative neighbors. When he gives a cookout for his friends, family, and new neighbors, everything seems to go awry. Eve plays his childhood friend and former girlfriend, one of many people who show up to enjoy the party. Audience response was strong, although the movie was largely overlooked by critics.

Perhaps Eve's most surprising project to date is her role in *The Woodsman*, which is scheduled for release in late 2004. The movie focuses on a convicted child molester named Walter, played by Kevin Bacon. Just released after 12 years in prison and trying to make a new life for himself, he gets a job at a lumberyard. That's where he meets a co-worker, played by Kyra Sedgwick, who gives him hope for the future, but that's also where he meets Mary Kay, played by Eve, a vindictive secretary.

This was Eve's first role in a serious drama, and she made the most of it. *The Woodsman* won widespread acclaim at film festivals throughout 2004, and critics singled out Eve for praise, as in these comments from Karen Durbin in the *New York Times*. "In an important secondary role, Eve . . . gives her character such complicated powers of attraction that you find yourself checking to see what she's up to even when she's just doing her job. Her Mary Kay is smart, a bit spicy, and frankly pleased with herself — the sort of person who makes a dull workplace feel special because she has to so she can feel special herself," Durbin wrote. "One of the best things about Eve's performance is the way she shows us indignation quietly simmering into malice, all the more toxic for being sincerely self-righteous. When she starts nosing around in Walter's background, the prospect of what she'll do with all that power gives you a little thrill of dread."

Future Plans

For the future, Eve has said that she wants to continue working in music, movies, and fashion. "I see myself definitely successful in whatever it is I'm doing," she remarks. "There are so many ideas in my head. But I definitely see myself being successful and well-off, and married with children." Recently, her spiritual life has become more important to her. "Prayer is very important. Keep God first. Believe in yourself at all times, stay positive, and stay original."

HOME AND FAMILY

Eve owns a home in New Jersey. She is single. She says that she hopes to get married one day and have several children.

HOBBIES AND OTHER INTERESTS

When she isn't acting, recording, or on tour, Eve likes to shop, sleep, and watch TV and movies in her pajamas. She says she is such a lazy person that she has to force herself to keep busy. Her "babies" are her two Yorkshire terriers: Spunky is a three pound teacup, and Bear is a seven pounder who loves to get in the trash, just like a real bear. They stay with her mom when Eve is on tour.

CREDITS

CDs

Let There Be Eve: Ruff Ryders' First Lady, 1999
Scorpion, 2001
Eve-Olution, 2002

Television

"Eve," 2003- (ongoing)

Films

XXX, 2002
Barbershop, 2002
Barbershop 2: Back in Business, 2004
The Cookout, 2004
The Woodsman, 2004

HONORS AND AWARDS

Grammy Awards: 2001, for Best Rap/Sung Collaboration, for "Let Me Blow Ya Mind" (with Gwen Stefani)

FURTHER READING

Books

Contemporary Black Biography, Vol. 29, 2001
Contemporary Musicians, Vol. 34, 2002
Who's Who among African Americans, 2004

Periodicals

Current Biography Yearbook, 2003
Detroit Free Press, Sep. 14, 2003, p.J1
Entertainment Weekly, Mar. 9, 2001, p.78; Sep. 20, 2002, Listen2This section, p.16
Essence, Mar. 2004, p.142
Interview, Nov. 2000, p.155; Sep. 2002, p.192
Jet, Apr. 9, 2001, p.58; Nov. 10, 2003, p.60; Feb. 9, 2004, p.58
Los Angeles Times, Aug. 29, 1999, p.3
Newsweek, Mar. 12, 2001, p.70; Sep. 2, 2002, p.60
Philadelphia Inquirer, Sep. 14, 1999, p.E1; Nov. 9, 2003, p.M1

Rolling Stone, Oct. 28, 1999, p.44; July 5, 2001, p.58; Oct. 31, 2002, p.42; Oct. 30, 2003, p.62
Teen People, Dec. 1, 2002, p.88
Time, Mar. 19, 2001, p.74
Variety, Sep. 1, 2003, p.S18

Online Databases

Biography Resource Center Online, 2004, articles from *Contemporary Black Biography,* 2001, and *Contemporary Musicians,* 2002

ADDRESS

Eve
Universal Music Group
2200 Colorado Avenue
Santa Monica, CA 90404

WORLD WIDE WEB SITES

http://www.upn.com/shows/eve
http://www.evefans.com
http://www.fetishbyeve.com/home.php

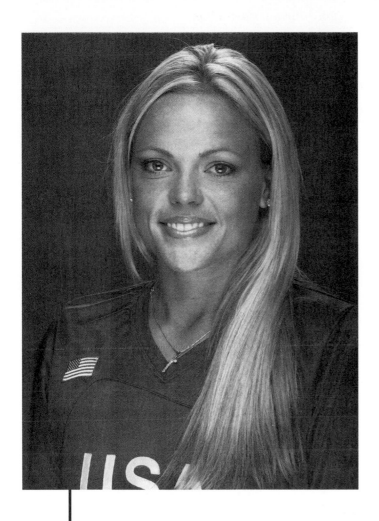

Jennie Finch 1980-

American Softball Player
Gold Medal-Winning Pitcher for Team USA at the
2004 Summer Olympics

BIRTH

Jennie Finch was born in the Los Angeles area on September 3, 1980. Her parents are Doug Finch, a cement-truck driver who later became a softball pitching and hitting instructor, and Beverly Finch, a secretary at an outpatient surgery clinic. She has two older brothers, Shane and Landon.

YOUTH

Finch grew up in a household that loved baseball. Her older brothers both played the game growing up, and Beverly Finch was a passionate fan of the Los Angeles Dodgers. In fact, she held season tickets to Dodgers games throughout Jennie's childhood. "She wasn't just like the normal person who would go to a Dodgers game," Jennie recalled. "It was like she had to be there with the radio [to listen to the broadcast of the game she was watching]."

Jennie's rise to softball stardom began when she started playing T-ball as a five-year-old. She quickly displayed an unusual talent for the game, and over the next couple of years she became one of the best players—boy or girl— in the area. By the time she was eight years old, she had switched to competitive junior softball. The following year, she began playing in distant softball tournaments as a member of various local all-star teams. "My family vacations were softball tournaments," she recalled. "Seeing the sacrifices [my parents] made growing up, understanding what they did for me and how hard it was and seeing the benefits I have from it, it's amazing."

> "My family vacations were softball tournaments," Finch recalled. "Seeing the sacrifices [my parents] made growing up, understanding what they did for me and how hard it was and seeing the benefits I have from it, it's amazing."

Around this same time, Doug Finch hurt his back. Ordered by his doctor to find a less physically demanding line of work, he combined his interest in softball and his talent for working with kids to launch a business as a softball instructor. He converted the Finch backyard into a virtual instructional facility and even patented a training machine for softball pitchers that remains popular with programs around the country. Before long he had dozens of young students clamoring for instruction. But his prized pupil was his own daughter. In one interview with "NBC Nightly News," for example, he recalled an amusing incident from one of Jennie's earliest tournaments. "She was 10 years old, and she started crying out on the mound and I said, 'Jennie, what's wrong?' And she goes, 'Did you hear what that coach called me?' And I said, 'No.' And she said, 'A pitching machine!' And I said, 'Jennie, that's a compliment.'"

As the years passed, Jennie continued to develop her talents as a pitcher, fielder, and hitter. She led her local 12-and-under softball team to a national title, and by the time she reached high school she was firing fastballs that were virtually unhittable. Jennie's love for softball deepened in 1996, when she watched Team USA claim the first Olympic gold medal ever awarded in women's softball at the Summer Games in Atlanta, Georgia. "When I watched that team with [pitcher] Lisa Fernandez and [shortstop] Dot Richardson, that's where I wanted to be," she said.

Despite spending much of her youth in dusty dugouts and seemingly endless car rides, Jennie's tomboy tendencies were balanced by a taste for more traditionally feminine pastimes. "Growing up, I loved to go to the dances, I loved getting dressed up, I loved getting my makeup done and my hair done," she remembered.

EDUCATION

Finch attended La Mirada High School in La Mirada, California. One of the finest athletes in the school's history, she left her mark not only in softball, but also in volleyball and basketball. She earned varsity letters as both a junior and senior (when she was team captain) in volleyball, and she made an even bigger impact on the basketball floor. Finch served as captain of the basketball team as a senior as well, and she earned team Most Valuable Player honors her last two years of school.

> "
>
> *Jennie's tomboy tendencies were balanced by a taste for more traditionally feminine pastimes. "Growing up, I loved to go to the dances, I loved getting dressed up, I loved getting my makeup done and my hair done," she remembered.*
>
> "

Still, softball remained Finch's best sport throughout high school. Named to the varsity team as a freshman, she rewrote the school's record books in the sport. By the time she had completed her high school career, she had compiled a 50-12 record as a pitcher, including 13 no-hitters, a 0.15 earned run average (ERA), and 784 strikeouts in 445 innings pitched. Displaying a rare combination of pitching talent and hitting power, she earned league Most Valuable Player honors in both her junior and senior years. Most impressively, she led La Mirada to four consecutive league championships—the last as captain of the team—while splitting time between the pitcher, shortstop, and first base positions.

By the time Finch graduated in 1998, she was acknowledged as one of the top softball prospects in the entire country. *Jump Magazine,* in fact, ranked her as the top softball recruit in the nation. Scholarship offers poured in

Finch's 2001 season was perhaps the greatest ever for a pitcher in NCAA softball history.

from a wide assortment of college programs, but in the end Finch decided to join the powerhouse softball program at the University of Arizona in Tucson. Four years later, in 2002, she graduated with a communications degree — and a fistful of NCAA records and honors.

CAREER HIGHLIGHTS

College — University of Arizona Wildcats

Finch made an immediate splash as a freshman at Arizona. "Jennie is just an awesome player," said one of her older teammates. "She can pitch, she can play infield, and she can hit for power." Most importantly, Finch showed resilience and determination when things didn't go her way. At the outset of the season, she was hit hard by a few opposing teams, but by season's end she was one of the team's top pitchers. "The biggest adjustment [from high school to college] has been not dealing with just batters one through four [in the nine-person batting line-up] being good, but the whole line-up being strong," she said. Finch's pitching and hitting helped lift the Wildcats all the way to the NCAA Softball World Series before they were defeated.

In the summer of 1999 Finch earned a silver medal with USA Softball at the Junior Women's World Championships. She then returned to Arizona for her sophomore campaign. As the season unfolded, it became clear to teammates and opponents alike that Finch had pushed her game to a new and more dominant level. By season's end she had posted a remarkable 29-2 pitching record, while also batting .327 and whacking 16 home runs, tied for best on the team. She continued her terrific performance in the postseason, earning NCAA Regional Most Outstanding Player honors on the strength of her 3-0 record and 0.35 ERA. Once again, her clutch pitching and hitting helped the Wildcats advance to the World Series before falling.

In 2001 Finch delivered perhaps the greatest season by a pitcher in NCAA softball history. At season's end she had a 32-0 record—an NCAA record for most victories in a season without a defeat. She also finished the season with a .309 batting average and 11 home runs, including 3 grand slams. Then, after helping Arizona reach the World Series for a third straight year, she lifted the team to the championship by throwing a four-hitter against the UCLA Lady Bruins for a 1-0 victory. In recognition of her stellar season, Finch easily won the 2001 Honda Award, presented each year to the best college softball player in the country.

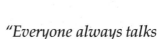

"Everyone always talks about how good-looking she is," admitted Arizona head coach Mike Candrea. "But Jennie Finch is a fierce competitor. . . . She also wants to be known for what she does on the field."

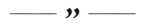

As Finch prepared for her senior season, she was surprised to find that the public spotlight was beginning to shine on her. Part of this attention was due to her amazing softball skills, but virtually everyone agreed that it also stemmed from her striking appearance. "Everyone always talks about how good-looking she is," admitted Arizona head coach Mike Candrea. "But Jennie Finch is a fierce competitor. . . . She also wants to be known for what she does on the field."

In 2002 Finch continued her dominant performance on the mound, extending her winning streak to an NCAA-record 60 games. Riding her blazing softballs to victory after victory, the Wildcats advanced once again to the season-ending College World Series, where their bid for a second consecutive championship fell short. This disappointment did not detract from Finch's incredible season, though. Once again, her exploits brought her the Honda Award.

Finch's incredible career at the Universita of Arizona will not soon be forgotten. In fact, her jersey number 27 was permanently retired by the team on May 9, 2003, in recognition of her years of excellence on the softball diamond.

Finch's pre-game jitters didn't show when she took the field at the 2004 Olympics.

After graduating from Arizona, Finch turned her attention to international competition. As a pitcher and first baseman for the U.S. national women's softball squad, she helped clinch a gold medal in the 2002 World Championships. One year later, she earned a gold medal as part of the victorious American team at the Pan American Games. It came as no surprise to anyone when she was named to the squad that would compete at the 2004 Summer Olympics in Athens, Greece.

Keeping Good Looks in Perspective

As the 2004 Olympics approached, American media outlets flocked to Finch's side like never before. Finch recognized that, as in college, the attention from television and magazine outlets was due at least as much to her appearance as her athletic skills.

Finch worked hard to keep this attention in perspective. She never sought to hide her looks or pretend that it was not a factor in her growing popularity. On the contrary, she recognized that the attention gave her an opportunity to improve her financial future through endorsements and personal appearances. For that reason, she willingly appeared on such shows as "Best Damn Sports Show, Period," and "The Late Show with David Letterman." She also agreed to appear in a regular segment on "This Week in

Baseball," in which she pitched against major league stars. Finally, she co-operated with various magazines that wanted to feature her in stories about the upcoming Olympic Games.

At the same time, however, Finch never embarrassed herself or her team-mates in the gathering pre-Olympic excitement. For example, she repeatedly turned down lucrative magazine offers to pose for photographs that were blatantly sexual in tone. She said that these offers never tempted her, partly because of her strong religious beliefs and partly because she felt that she would be letting teammates and fans down. "I had a lot more to lose than to gain," she stated. "I'm a role model for lots of young girls."

Finch also tried to make sure that the attention surrounding her advanced the sport of softball and helped her teammates gain greater recognition. "Whatever magazine I'm in, or we're in, we're excited because it does help softball," she stated. "I don't know how comfortable I am with the whole sex-symbol thing. I don't see myself that way. But it has helped the sport grow. I think it changes how people see women's athletics. For a long time, it wasn't cool or hip to be a woman and be a female athlete. Now, being athletic is the in thing to do. Athletic women are sexy now, whereas in the past they weren't."

— " —

"I don't know how comfortable I am with the whole sex-symbol thing. I don't see myself that way. But it has helped the sport grow. I think it changes how people see women's athletics. For a long time, it wasn't cool or hip to be a woman and be a female athlete. Now, being athletic is the in thing to do. Athletic women are sexy now, whereas in the past they weren't."

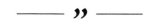

Finch's teammates seemed to appre-ciate the efforts she took to handle the attention with grace. "It's amazing how she takes all the attention in stride," said teammate Stacey Nuveman. "It's not something she thinks about or worries about. It doesn't affect her at all, and that's a special thing." "If she was bad, it would be completely different," added teammate Lori Harrigan. "You do have to take the publicity when you can get it, but at the same time it's too bad our society looks at Jennie as beautiful first, and a great pitcher second. . . . We have so many great players who don't get the recognition and if it's because of what they look like then that is too bad. But at the same time, if you have somebody who is good at what they do and is beautiful and people want to publicize it, then so be it."

Preparing for Athens

In the spring of 2004 the USA women's softball team went on a long pre-Olympics tour of the country, taking on a variety of top college teams and various all-star squads. The team went undefeated, usually romping by lopsided scores. Finch herself posted a 15-0 mark with a 0.27 ERA during the tour. The squad thus went to Athens brimming with confidence. "We want to experience that gold-medal experience," Finch said. "Anything less is unacceptable."

> "Walking out onto the field [at the Olympics], seeing thousands of young girls waving American flags" made her feel invincible, Finch later said. "I've dreamed of being an Olympian since I was little. And suddenly it was a reality."

Team USA was the heavy favorite in the softball competition. Experts agreed that the team's strong batting line-up—combined with an overpowering pitching staff led by Finch and Olympic veteran Lisa Fernandez—made them the team to beat. Still, Finch admitted that she was very nervous in the hours before the opening game. "This is a game I've been playing since I was five years old," she said. "I was telling myself you can't get too high or too low, but you can only do so much of that talking. It's the Olympics."

When Finch took the field to pitch, though, she felt a sudden surge of confidence. "Walking out onto the field, seeing thousands of young girls waving American flags" made her feel invincible, she later said. "I've dreamed of being an Olympian since I was little. And suddenly it was a reality."

Rolling to Gold

Team USA cruised through the opening rounds in Athens, with Finch and other pitchers posting four consecutive one-hit shutouts. In the meantime, the Americans' bats exploded for 31 runs during that span. Finch and her teammates continued to roll in the medal round, shutting out every opponent to reach the gold medal game against Australia. "This is absolutely the best Olympic team the U.S. has fielded and if you make one mistake you're done," declared Canadian coach Mike Renney.

In the gold medal game the Australians finally ended Team USA's string of shutouts, scratching out a single run. But it was not enough, as the Ameri-

Team USA was elated to win the gold medal at the 2004 Olympics. From left: Lisa Fernandez, Leah Amico, Lori Harrigan, and Jennie Finch.

cans knocked in five runs to claim Olympic gold. From that point forward, Finch savored every moment of the Olympics, from the medal ceremony to the closing ceremonies. "It was awesome," she told "Good Morning America." "It was the most incredible feeling standing up on that podium with my teammates, celebrating in this gold medal." Finch hopes to experience it all again in 2008, when she hopes to compete in the Olympics with the U.S. team.

HOME AND FAMILY

Finch is engaged to Casey Daigle, a pitcher with the Arizona Diamondbacks organization. She has said that she'd eventually like to have four or five children.

HOBBIES AND OTHER INTERESTS

Finch loves to relax by going shopping. In addition to her continued involvement with the Team USA softball program, she has signed promotional deals with a number of companies.

HONORS AND AWARDS

NCAA Regional Most Outstanding Player: 1999, 2000
First-Team All-American (NCCA): 2000, 2001, 2002
First-Team All Pacific-10 (PAC-10): 2000, 2001, 2002

Most Outstanding Player, NCAA Women's College World Series: 2001
Honda Award (as best collegiate softball player): 2001, 2002
PAC-10 Pitcher of the Year: 2001, 2002
International Softball Federation World Championships: gold medal, 2002
Pan American Games: gold medal, 2004
Olympic Women's Softball: gold medal, 2004

FURTHER READING

Periodicals

Arizona Daily Star, May 24, 2001, p.C1
Business Week, Aug. 2, 2004, p.61
Cincinnati Post, July 5, 2004, p.C1
Current Biography Yearbook, 2004
Glamour, July 2004, p.215
Grand Rapids (Mich.) Press, Aug. 17, 2004, p.F12
New York Post, May 14, 2004, p.88
New York Times, Aug. 8, 2004, p.L3; Aug. 15, 2004, p.SP4
Philadelphia Inquirer, June 29, 2004, p.F1
Rocky Mountain News, July 17, 2004, p.B1
Sports Illustrated, Aug. 23, 2004, p.32
Sports Illustrated Women, Mar./Apr. 2002, p.32
USA Today, Feb. 13, 2004, p.C15; Aug. 10, 2004, p.A1; Aug. 19, 2004, p.D4
Washington Post, June 22, 2003, p.E1

Online Articles

Additional information for this profile was obtained from the transcripts of "Good Morning America" (Aug. 24, 2004), "NBC Nightly News" (Aug. 23, 2004), and "Today" (May 24, 2004).

ADDRESS

Jennie Finch
USA Softball
2801 NE 50th Street
Oklahoma City, OK 73111-7203

WORLD WIDE WEB SITES

http://www.jenniefinch.net
http://www.usasoftball.com

James Forman 1928-2005

American Civil Rights Activist and Author
Former Executive Secretary of the Student Nonviolent
Coordinating Committee (SNCC)

BIRTH

James Rufus Forman was born on October 4, 1928, in Chicago,
Illinois. He was the older of two children born to Octavia (Allen) Rufus, a homemaker. His stepfather, John Rufus, worked
in the Chicago stockyards and also owned a gas station. James
grew up believing that his stepfather was his birth father, so

—————— **"** ——————

Forman had his first experiences with racism in Mississippi when he was eight years old and failed to say "yes, ma'am" to a white clerk in a store. Some men in the store thought that he was being rude to the clerk on purpose and warned his uncle that if James ever returned to town he would be lynched. This incident made an enormous impression on him. Forman recalled how pervasive racism was in his early life, saying simply, "Those are the kinds of things that I grew up with."

—————— **"** ——————

his name at that point was James Rufus. But when he was 14 years old, James learned that his real father was Jackson Forman, a cab driver in Chicago. He chose to add Forman to his name at that point.

YOUTH

When James was 11 months old, his mother took him to live with his grandparents near Holly Springs, Mississippi. He spent his first years living on his grandparents' farm in rural Marshall County. His grandparents were very poor, and worked their 180 acres of land with a mule-drawn plough. The family lived in a four-room house without electricity or running water. James was initially schooled at home by his Aunt Thelma, who taught him to read and spell, and encouraged his early interest in books. He returned to Chicago to live with his mother and stepfather when he was six years old, but continued to spend summers with his grandparents in Mississippi.

Experiencing Segregation and Racism

Forman grew up in a time of widespread legal discrimination against African Americans. Racial segregation was enforced throughout the southern United States by "Jim Crow" laws. This meant that African Americans and whites had "separate but equal" public facilities—housing, schools, bathrooms, drinking fountains, seating in movie theaters and on buses, and more. Although these separate facilities were called equal, in reality the facilities provided for whites were far superior to and cleaner than those provided for the African-American community.

Segregation was such a part of everyday life that African Americans were not allowed to sit in an ice cream shop or drink from a glass in a restaurant. They could go to a general store and purchase a coffee pot, but not a cup of coffee. African Americans were treated as inferior, and they were expected to act subservient to whites. In many places, African Americans were required to step aside to allow whites to pass by on the sidewalk. The "Jim Crow" laws made it very dangerous for African Americans to disobey the rules of segregation. Punishments ranged from harassment to being put in jail, and sometimes even lynching—a murder by a mob without a trial or legal protection.

Forman had his first experiences with racism at a very young age. One summer in Mississippi when James was eight years old, his uncle took him into town to go shopping. James failed to say "yes, ma'am" to a white clerk in a store. Some men in the store noticed this and thought that James was being rude to the clerk on purpose. The men warned his uncle that if James ever returned to town he would be lynched. This incident made an enormous impression on young James. His grandmother later assured him that she would protect him from harm, but the threat lingered. Forman recalled how pervasive racism was in his early life, saying simply, "Those are the kinds of things that I grew up with."

Later, when Forman was in graduate school, he wrote down every racist encounter he could recall ever happening to him. Many of these were recounted in his autobiography, *The Making of Black Revolutionaries*. Racial discrimination would become the central issue in Forman's life, and he would grow to devote himself to eliminating segregation in the United States. He would later write, "I realized that my purpose in life . . . came down to something very simple: If my life could make it possible for future black children not to have that experience, then it was worth living."

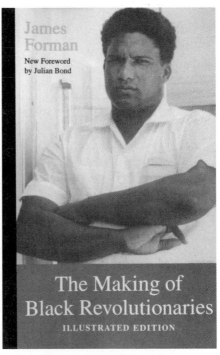

Forman's autobiography,
The Making of Black Revolutionaries,
*covered his life experiences as well
as his political philosophy.*

EDUCATION

In Chicago, Forman attended St. Anselm's Catholic elementary school. His parents were African Methodist Episcopal (AME) Church members, and the religious as-

121

pects of his early education caused problems for James. His teachers told him that he could not go to heaven because he was Protestant. This and other differences in the Catholic and Protestant faiths created conflicts that made James uncomfortable. He asked to switch to public school after sixth grade and was allowed to transfer to Betsy Ross School in Chicago. He performed very well in school and was always interested in learning, although his schoolwork was often not challenging enough for him. He pursued his own interests and studied subjects on his own.

————— " —————

"There was a constant thread running through my life. I had to get an education. I had to use this education. Whatever I did with this education, I had to put it to work for my people; somehow and somewhere, this had to be a reality."

————— " —————

Learning about Civil Rights

Forman's first exposure to the concept of civil rights also came at a young age. He worked as a paper boy in Chicago throughout his elementary school years. He sold copies of the *Chicago Defender*, a popular newspaper for African Americans. He liked to read newspaper articles about the experiences of African Americans and the problems they faced. This was Forman's introduction to the civil rights movement and the people who were working to change the racist attitudes that had threatened him in Mississippi.

These newspaper stories interested Forman so much that he began reading more about civil rights. As he progressed through school, he explored the writings of such prominent African-American thinkers as Booker T. Washington, W.E.B. Du Bois, and Richard Wright. He read Carl Sandburg's biography of Abraham Lincoln and studied the problems facing blacks throughout the United States. He also became interested in issues facing African people around the world.

The more he learned about civil rights issues, the more Forman wanted to help bring about changes. He began to attend protest meetings to learn about the ways he might contribute. His pastor, Joseph L. Roberts of Coppin Chapel AME church, encouraged his growing desire to serve in the civil rights movement. But it was not until much later that Forman would be able to act on his ambitions to become a leader in social change. He needed to experience more of life first.

Forman worked tirelessly for the cause of civil rights.

A Commitment to Education

Influenced by what he had read, Forman became committed to pursuing an advanced education. His plans were interrupted several times, but his strong desire to learn always brought him back to his studies. As he wrote in his autobiography, "There was a constant thread running through my life. I had to get an education. I had to use this education. Whatever I did with this education, I had to put it to work for my people; somehow and somewhere, this had to be a reality."

Before starting high school, Forman argued with his parents about the direction his education should take. He wanted to follow the example of intellectual leaders like Booker T. Washington and prepare for college. His parents wanted him to have vocational training so that he could find a job more easily. His parents won out, and Forman enrolled in shop classes at Englewood High School in 1943. He was very unhappy. For the first time, he began to fail his classes and get into trouble. He was suspended from school and began to spend all his time with a group of boys who were involved with gambling and drugs. Forman eventually rejected this way of life and returned to high school. He took general studies courses, and graduated with honors in 1947, receiving the *Chicago Tribune* newspaper's student honors award.

Forman went on to Wilson Junior College, where he studied English, French, and world history. His education was interrupted a second time when he decided to volunteer for the U.S. Army rather than wait to be drafted for service in the Korean War. He was rejected by the Army and told that their quota for African Americans had been met. He then joined the U.S. Air Force and spent four years in service. He was stationed at Lackland Air Force Base in San Antonio, Texas, Fairfield Air Force Base in California, and U.S. military bases in Okinawa, Japan. At first, Forman was assigned to a unit of all African-American soldiers. When he transferred to a mixed-race unit, he was infuriated to find that even the U.S. military practiced racial discrimination. Forman discovered that the Air Force provided better food and better living conditions for whites than for blacks. This bothered him and he continued to develop his interest in improving the status of African Americans. He was discharged from service in 1951.

> **Forman recalled that the Montgomery bus boycott "woke me up to the real — not the merely theoretical — possibility of building a nonviolent mass movement of southern black people to fight segregation."**

In 1952, Forman resumed his education at the University of Southern California at Los Angeles, where he studied public administration. Shortly into his time there, his education was interrupted once again when the Los Angeles police falsely accused him of robbery. Forman was jailed and beaten severely by police, held in jail for several days, and then released without charges. The episode stood in stark contrast to his studies of political science, law, and the basic human rights outlined in the United States Constitution. Forman wrote in detail about this experience in his autobiography. He was extremely disturbed by what happened, and the injuries he suffered from the beatings required a long period of mental and physical healing. It would prove to be a formative experience in his life.

After recovering from his experience in Los Angeles, Forman returned to Chicago in 1954 and entered Roosevelt University. There he studied anthropology, sociology, history, and philosophy. Forman excelled in his studies and was very involved in campus life. He became president of the

Minnijean Brown (center), age 15, along with six other African-American students, being blocked by the Arkansas National Guard. In 1957, Governor Orval Faubus ordered the Guard to prevent the students from entering all-white Central High School in Little Rock, hoping to stop school desegregation.

student body and was chief delegate to the 1956 National Student Association conference. It was at Roosevelt that he was finally able to devote time and energy to working in civil rights. He participated in a student group that met regularly to discuss civil rights issues and actions that might be helpful in bringing about change. Forman graduated from Roosevelt in 1957.

Changing Direction

In 1957, Forman registered at Boston University. He planned to enter the graduate program in African Research and Studies. But at that point, as he started graduate school, segregation was being challenged all over the South. African Americans had been organizing in groups to protest segregation. Desegregation efforts in the South, particularly in the areas of integrating transportation and schools, convinced him that the time was right for an immediate crusade for civil rights. The 1955-1956 bus boycott had just recently concluded in Montgomery, Alabama. Rosa Parks refused to give up her seat and sparked a city-wide boycott of the transportation system that eventually led to the integration of city buses. Forman recalled that the Montgomery bus boycott "woke me up to the real—not the merely theoretical—possibility of building a nonviolent mass movement of southern black people to fight segregation."

School desegregation was another major battle area throughout the South, particularly since the 1954 Supreme Court decision, Brown v. Board of Education. In that case, the Supreme Court ruled that segregation in public schools was unconstitutional and required the integration of all public schools. Southern states were forced to integrate their public schools—allowing African-American students to attend the same schools as whites. This action was fiercely opposed by many whites in the South. Some of the forced integrations required the United States military to be posted at schools, to protect the African-American students and also to control potential violence among the protestors.

In 1957, as Forman was starting at Boston University, Governor Orval Faubus of Arkansas used National Guard troops to prevent African-American students from integrating Central High School in Little Rock, an all-white school. President Dwight Eisenhower sent in federal troops to force compliance with the law. After getting press credentials from the *Chicago Defender* newspaper, where he had worked previously, Forman traveled to Little Rock to report on the issues. He felt that he could make an important contribution, and he soon decided to focus on civil rights activism.

CAREER HIGHLIGHTS

Becoming Involved in Civil Rights

In the late 1950s, Forman decided to set his formal education aside temporarily and become directly involved with those working for civil rights. He saw a need for a broadly based African-American civil rights organization. His ideal organization would promote social, political, and economic equality for everyone. He began to plan an outline for this organization, and wrote a novel about an interracial civil rights group that achieved sweeping social changes through the use of nonviolent tactics.

Forman took part in a number of civil rights projects and nonviolent protests during these years. He became involved with the Congress for Racial Equality (CORE). With CORE, he went to rural Tennessee to help sharecroppers who had been evicted from their farms after they tried to register to vote. The right to vote—along with the right to integrated transportation systems, education, and public places—was a key issue of the civil rights movement. Disenfranchisement, or preventing people from voting, was an important tactic by segregationists in maintaining the status

Forman was jailed several times while working for SNCC, including this arrest by Atlanta police, here shown forcing him into a car.

quo, and civil rights workers fought strenuously for voting rights laws. Segregationists used many different tactics to prevent blacks from voting, forcing them to take a test or pay a poll tax, or using outright intimidation and beatings.

Soon Forman was not only participating in protests, he was also arranging civil rights activism throughout the South. He officially joined the civil rights movement in 1961 in Monroe, North Carolina, working with a controversial leader of the National Association for the Advancement of Colored People (NAACP) who advocated the use of self-defense. That same year, he took part in a protest that challenged the segregated seating policy of the railroad transportation system in Georgia. Segregated seating on interstate transportation had been found illegal in the courts years earlier, but it was still the norm throughout the South. Then in 1961, the courts outlawed segregation in bus and train terminals. CORE organized Freedom Rides, in which black and white passengers rode together on buses across the South, from Washington, D.C., to New Orleans, Louisiana. On many stops the Freedom Riders were met with uncompromising racism, hatred, violence, arrests, and beatings. When Forman took part in a similar trip via train, he was arrested and put in jail with several Freedom

Riders from the Student Nonviolent Coordinating Committee (SNCC). This experience provided Forman with an opportunity to learn more about SNCC. He decided that their approach to civil rights activism was the closest to his own. After his sentence was suspended, he went to work full time with SNCC. Later in 1961, the Interstate Commerce Commission issued a tough new federal law banning segregation in interstate travel.

———— *"* ————

According to Julian Bond, "I thought he was the janitor. He immediately asked me what I could do — or thought I could do. Before I knew it, I had become the publicity director of the organization, editor of the newsletter, and the person who wrote the press releases. Because Forman made me do it. He had a compelling personality."

———— *"* ————

The Student Nonviolent Coordinating Committee

At that time there were several civil rights organizations working in the South. Some of the most prominent were CORE, the NAACP, the NAACP Legal Defense and Education Fund, the Southern Christian Leadership Council (SCLC) led by Martin Luther King, Jr., and SNCC. Based in Atlanta, Georgia, SNCC (pronounced "snick") was a loose coalition of student organizations that wanted to work together on civil rights issues. SNCC was considered more aggressive than some other civil rights groups.

After only one week of volunteering, Forman was named the group's Executive Secretary. This came about because many people in the organization trusted him and saw that his skills could lead SNCC effectively toward its goals. He recalled of this time, "I was in a quandary, for I didn't want to work as an administrator. I knew that I had some administrative qualities, more perhaps than any of those assembled, but I felt my best skills lay in other areas — agitating, field organizing, and writing. It was in these areas that I wanted to work. But this was a personal wish, and I had enough self-discipline to realize that when you are working with a revolutionary group, you don't do what you alone want to, but what the group desires of you." And so Forman agreed to become a leader of SNCC.

When he took over, Forman was at least ten years older than most of the SNCC members. He was a university graduate in his 30s and already a veteran of the Korean War. During the years he held the position, he transformed SNCC into one of the most influential and effective civil rights organizations of the time.

Organizing SNCC

One of the first things Forman did was convince the group to purchase its own office building and printing press. He also established a research department to provide volunteers with information and to document the civil rights movement. He even appointed an official photographer. This brought a professional approach to the somewhat disorganized group. Former SNCC volunteer Charles Cobb, Jr., described Forman as a trained historian who emphasized the importance of a written record.

Forman with Julian Bond, a fellow SNCC worker and later NAACP chairman.

"Of all the organizations involved in the southern movement during the early 1960s, SNCC left the clearest written trail," Cobb recalled. "SNCC's research department was the movement's best. It meant that we SNCC field secretaries entered rural counties with concrete information about who and what we were up against." Former SNCC volunteer and NAACP chairman Julian Bond also commented on Forman's administrative ability, saying that he molded "SNCC's near-anarchic personality into a functioning, if still chaotic, organizational structure."

Forman quickly gained a reputation for his willingness to do whatever was necessary to keep SNCC running effectively. Visitors and new volunteers sometimes found him in SNCC offices late at night, sweeping the floor or doing other maintenance jobs. According to Julian Bond, "I thought he was the janitor. He immediately asked me what I could do — or thought I could do. Before I knew it, I had become the publicity director of the organization, editor of the newsletter, and the person who wrote the press releases. Because Forman made me do it. He had a compelling personality."

Under Forman's leadership, SNCC was involved in nearly every major civil rights action that took place in the 1960s. He arranged voter registration drives and worked for new voting rights laws. He organized Freedom

Rides throughout the South and promoted the use of white civil rights workers in white communities. He led SNCC's participation in the 1963 March on Washington, which brought 200,000 demonstrators to the Lincoln Memorial in Washington, D.C., to bear witness to Martin Luther King, Jr., and his moving "I Have a Dream" speech. As a result of these actions, Forman was often arrested, jailed, and persecuted by police. "Accumulating experiences with the southern 'law and order' were turning me into a full-fledged revolutionary," he recalled.

> "
>
> *Three civil rights volunteers in Mississippi — Andrew Goodman, James Chaney, and Michael Schwerner — were arrested, jailed, and then disappeared. The FBI concluded that they were killed by about 20 members of the Ku Klux Klan. According to the U.S. State Department, "It was later determined that the civil rights workers had been murdered as a result of a conspiracy between elements of Neshoba County law enforcement and the Ku Klux Klan."*
>
> "

Within the arena of nonviolent action, Forman's style was more confrontational than that of other major civil rights groups of the time. SNCC took a more aggressive position that encouraged activists to push boundaries in order to bring about more changes, more quickly. Forman publicly criticized other civil rights leaders, including Dr. Martin Luther King, Jr. He thought that King's approach was too passive. Forman also wanted to prevent too much dependence on one person as the civil rights savior. "A strong people's movement was in progress. And the people were feeling their own strength grow. I knew how much harm could be done by injecting the Messiah complex — people would feel that only a particular individual could save them and would not move on their own to fight racism and exploitation." Instead of waiting for King to provide direction to the civil rights movement as a whole, Forman worked to develop leadership among the students of SNCC.

He put in place a network structure for volunteers, which helped to recruit and support young activists throughout the South. Taylor Branch, a former SNCC volunteer and an award-winning historian and biographer of the civil rights era, recalled that Forman made it possible for young SNCC members to go out into the field and do very difficult work. "He'd say, 'Go organize South Louisville—here is the contact.' He made people believe they could do that." Others who knew him at this time describe Forman as a fearless civil rights pioneer who was a fiercely revolutionary and visionary leader. His intellect and passion for equality and justice allowed him to be forceful without shouting. He is remembered as a leader who believed that massive change was possible, but only through vigilance, dedication, and persistence.

An FBI poster seeking information as to the whereabouts of the civil rights workers Andrew Goodman, James Earl Chaney, and Michael Henry Schwerner.

Mississippi Freedom Summer

In 1964, Forman was involved in organizing efforts for the Mississippi Freedom Summer Project. The idea for this project came from the Council of Federated Organizations, of which SNCC and CORE were member groups. The volunteer work was coordinated and managed by SNCC leadership, especially Forman. This effort brought about 1,000 volunteers to Mississippi, many of them white, to work on a number of projects, including registering citizens to vote; establishing freedom schools and community centers; and creating a grass-roots freedom movement among residents to fight against repression. Mississippi had a reputation as perhaps the most segregated and repressive state in the nation, and it had the lowest percentage of registered black voters in the country, just 6.7 per cent. Violence against the volunteers was brutal, including the burning or bombing of 60 black churches, businesses, and homes. Many volunteers were beaten by white mobs and police, and many more were arrested. The volunteers persisted despite this intimidation, and their efforts helped pass the Voting Rights Act of 1965.

A tragedy occurred during the Mississippi Freedom Summer. Three volunteers—Andrew Goodman, James Chaney, and Michael Schwerner—were sent to investigate the fire-bombing of a black church. They were pulled over afterward, arrested, and jailed; then they disappeared. Their bodies were found buried six weeks later, and the FBI eventually concluded that they were killed by about 20 members of the Ku Klux Klan. According to the U.S. State Department, "It was later determined that the civil rights workers had been murdered as a result of a conspiracy between elements of Neshoba County law enforcement and the Ku Klux Klan." Forman felt responsible for their deaths because he had always worked so hard to protect SNCC field volunteers.

In 1967, 19 people faced charges in the crime, but the charges were dismissed on a technicality. Over the next few years there were several trials and several men were convicted on conspiracy charges. But none were ever charged with or convicted of murder, and Forman never received the resolution of knowing what really happened. Three days after Forman died in 2005, Edgar Ray Killen was charged with three counts of murder in the 1964 deaths of the three volunteers.

Leaving SNCC

Forman left his position as Executive Secretary in the midst of turmoil in 1966, although he continued to work with SNCC in an administrative capacity until 1969. Newer members of the organization thought that SNCC leadership should be more radical, even more than it already was. Forman was under a lot of pressure to lead SNCC in more direct and militant actions. He was forced out of his leadership position during an organizational shake-up in which younger, much more radical members took over. His leadership had been the backbone of SNCC, and when he left the group it became significantly less effective. Without Forman's clearly defined agenda and ability to lead people to achieve productive goals, SNCC fell apart.

In the late 1960s, Forman worked with another organization called the Black Panther Party for Self-Defense. Known as the Black Panthers, this group was very militant and believed that change would only come through a complete social revolution. Forman was attracted to the Black Panthers because of his deep beliefs about how a revolutionary struggle should be carried out. He saw the Black Panthers as a continuation of the work SNCC had begun. He served briefly as the Black Panthers' Minister of Education. The position was short-lived, and Forman left the Black Panthers soon after arriving.

Leaving behind his SNCC leadership duties and no longer working directly with any one civil rights organization, Forman was able to speak out on his own. He began to concentrate on writing, publishing several books on topics central to the civil rights movement. One of the first was *Sammy Younge,*

A protest march featuring Ralph Abernathy, James Forman (in overalls and jacket), Martin Luther King, Jr., S.L. Douglas, and John Lewis.

Jr.: The First Black College Student to Die in the Black Liberation Movement (1968). It tells the story of Sammy Younge, a SNCC volunteer who was murdered by a white man in Tuskegee, Alabama. Some of Forman's other writings focused on his thoughts on various political schools of thought, including socialism and democracy. One book was written in French and published in Europe, reflecting Forman's growing international view of racism and worldwide issues for people of African descent.

Reparations for Slavery

While he continued to study civil rights issues and work for changes in American society, Forman began to form a new understanding of the lasting effects of the slave trade in the United States. As his understanding grew, the idea of monetary reparations for slavery took shape. Forman based the idea of reparations on a promise made by the United States government at the end of the Civil War: every freed male slave would be given 40 acres of land and a mule, to establish a new life as a free man. This promise was later revoked and never delivered upon, but it was also never forgotten by many African-American activists. The idea of reparations for slavery was radical and revolutionary, and Forman began to develop it further.

In 1969, Forman helped to organize the first meeting of the National Black Economic Development Conference, held on April 26 in Detroit, Michigan. It was here that he developed his "Black Manifesto." This speech demanded monetary payment to African Americans, to partially compensate for slavery and the many years of continued discrimination and suffering that followed the freeing of slaves in America. He felt that the most effective way for the United States to advance the cause of human rights and civil rights for African Americans would be to redistribute money and resources so that all people would be truly equal. Only then could real opportunities for African Americans be developed. Forman planned to publicly deliver these demands in May 1969. The National Black Economic Development Conference had chosen a date for protestors to interrupt church services around the United States, in order to draw attention to civil rights issues that were still not being addressed.

> *Charles Cobb, Jr., a former SNCC volunteer, recalled that Forman always kept the bigger picture in mind. Forman reminded the volunteers that "you have to constantly think about what it is you are really fighting for . . . to think about more than a cup of coffee at a lunch counter or even voting rights."*

On the designated day, Forman chose to attend Riverside Church in New York City. He interrupted the communion service to deliver his "Black Manifesto." With this speech, Forman called for white churches and synagogues to pay $500 million to African-American organizations as reparations for slavery. Specific demands included the creation of the Southern Land Bank, four major publishing companies and four television networks for African Americans, a Black Labor Strike and Defense Fund Training Center for African Americans, and a new African-American university. Late in his life, Forman recalled this day and the delivery of his *Black Manifesto* as his greatest moment in civil rights.

Forman's speech received a range of responses. Some called his demands ridiculous, while others publicly denounced his tactics as blackmail and intimidation. His demands did not produce the requested amount of money, but did result in enough funding to establish Black Star Publications and to support the League of Revolutionary Black Workers in Detroit, Michigan. Perhaps most importantly, Forman's speech raised awareness and re-opened public discussion of the continuing unequal conditions for

African Americans. Historians point to Forman's speech as the start of the modern reparations movement. The topic of reparations is still discussed today by prominent African-American thinkers and theorists.

In the early 1970s, Forman focused on writing *The Making of Black Revolutionaries*, published in 1972. This autobiography is also a first-hand account of the civil rights movement from its beginnings in southern African-American churches through the violence of the 1960s struggle against segregation. The book includes eyewitness accounts of all the major civil rights demonstrations that made news headlines around the country in the 1960s. Forman also included stories and memories of lesser-known people and events, making this book

Forman speaking at Riverside Church in New York City, where he delivered his "Black Manifesto" articulating his demand for $500 million in reparations for slavery, May 1969.

unique in its point of view. His memoir has been called a civil rights document of unequaled importance. It has also been used as a textbook in university civil rights history courses.

In 1974, Forman founded the Unemployment and Poverty Action Committee (UPAC). This was a civil and human rights organization that promoted political education and created economic development opportunities for African-American communities. The group also supported voter registration and voting right, issues that he continued to champion throughout his life.

Later Years

In the late 1970s and early 1980s, Forman returned to his pursuit of advanced education. He received a Masters of Professional Studies in African and Afro-American History from Cornell University in 1980. He went on to earn a doctorate degree from the Institute of Policy Studies at the Union of Experimental Colleges and Universities in Cincinnati, Ohio, receiving his PhD in about 1982.

In 1981, Forman moved to Washington, D.C., and started the Black American News Service. He continued writing and produced numerous pamphlets on civil rights and voting issues. He served a one-year term as legislative assistant to the president of the Metropolitan Washington Central Labor Council (AFL-CIO) in 1983. He continued to be active in civil rights, working for various social justice causes and participating in protests and demonstrations in Washington. During this time Forman also became involved with the Democratic Party, working to influence party policies and political platforms. Because of his lifelong work to ensure voting rights for everyone, he was invited to witness President Clinton's signing of the 1993 National Voter Registration Act. This Act removed any remaining restrictions on voting in the United States, making it easier for people to exercise their right to vote.

> "
>
> *Taylor Branch, a former SNCC volunteer and an award-winning historian and biographer of the civil rights era, recalled that Forman made it possible for young SNCC members to go out into the field and do very difficult work. "He'd say, 'Go organize South Louisville—here is the contact.' He made people believe they could do that."*
>
> "

Forman was diagnosed with colon cancer in the early 1990s. This illness limited his activities, but he remained a vital contributor to human rights campaigns and a vocal supporter of the right to vote. He participated in his final political protest in July 2004. While severely ill, Forman traveled from Washington, D.C., to Boston, Massachusetts, for the Democratic National Convention. He took part in a demonstration styled after the Boston Tea Party. This time, demonstrators tossed tea bags into the Boston Harbor to protest the lack of voting rights for residents of Washington, D.C. Forman spent his last days in a hospice in Washington, D.C., listening to music that he loved and surrounded by his family and old friends. After a long battle with cancer, James Forman died on January 10, 2005.

LEGACY

Today James Forman is recognized as one of the driving forces behind the advancement of civil rights in the United States. Best remembered for his work with SNCC, he has been called a pillar of the modern civil rights movement. Those who knew him then describe Forman as an angry young

Teaching the next wave of civil rights activists.

man who was a brilliant organizer, serious and unbending in his dedication to the cause of civil rights. He was characterized as robust, very energetic, outspoken, and feisty. Because he was older than most of the students he organized, Forman was also sometimes a father figure for the young people working in civil rights.

According to Eleanor Holmes Norton, a former SNCC volunteer and delegate to the U.S. Congress for Washington, D.C., "James Forman, at the zenith of his powers, was a one-man virtuoso who brought to bear each and every skill that made it possible for men like him to change America. We were often transient students . . . but Jim was the stable rock, just as militant, but older, with a level head and a strong, strategic intellect. Jim performed an organizational miracle in holding together a loose band of nonviolent revolutionaries who simply wanted to act together to eliminate racial discrimination and terror. As a result, SNCC had an equal place at the table with all of the major civil rights organizations of the 1960s. Americans might not know Jim's name . . . but if they look around them at the racial changes in our country, they will know Jim by his work."

Charles Cobb, Jr., another former SNCC volunteer, recalled that Forman always kept the bigger picture in mind. Forman reminded the volunteers that "you have to constantly think about what it is you are really fighting for . . . to think about more than a cup of coffee at a lunch counter or even voting rights." In this way, Forman tried to bring a global consciousness to the American civil rights struggle. He had the perspective to offer insightful analysis of the movement, and could accurately predict which actions would succeed and which would be less effective.

> ——— " ———
>
> *"My warmest and most tender feelings are for the masses of black people in the United States and poor people the world around. My life has been dedicated to the struggle of all exploited people against their oppressors. It is this objective that sustains me every day."*
>
> ——— " ———

Cobb also had this to say: "Forman was a radical intellectual but oriented toward action more than words and political babble, not that he was ever shy about his political thoughts. But in the south of those days, more often than not, Forman kind of commandeered you and sent you into action. And without discussing it, he somehow made it clear that he believed you had the ability to do the job. This is a rare quality, a gift. . . . In the end, this is the great debt to Forman owed by those of us who worked with him. Whatever we did in SNCC, we would have been lost were it not for Forman's strong steady hand helping to guide our efforts."

Perhaps the clearest example of Forman's legacy is in the very real way the world changed around him. In 1961 in Albany, Georgia, Forman was jailed for his role in a demonstration to protest segregation of public transportation. In 1998, in the very same place, Forman was presented with a key to the city of Albany as part of the opening ceremonies for the Albany Civil Rights Museum.

In describing his life's work in civil rights, Forman wrote, "My warmest and most tender feelings are for the masses of black people in the United States and poor people the world around. My life has been dedicated to the struggle of all exploited people against their oppressors. It is this objective that sustains me every day."

MARRIAGE AND FAMILY

Forman was married three times, to Mary Forman, Mildred Thompson, and Constancia Romily. All of his marriages ended in divorce. Forman had two sons with Constancia. James Robert Lumumba Forman, Jr. is a professor at Georgetown University Law Center and a founder of the Maya Angelou charter school in Washington, D.C. Chaka Esmond Fanon Forman is an actor. Forman had one granddaughter.

WRITINGS

1967: High Tide of the Black Resistance, 1967
Sammy Younge, Jr.: The First Black College Student to Die in the Black Liberation Movement, 1968
Liberation: Viendra d'une Chose Noir, 1968
"The Black Manifesto," 1969
The Political Thought of James Forman, 1970
The Makings of Black Revolutionaries: A Personal Account, 1972
Self-Determination: An Examination of the Question and its Applications to the African-American People, 1980

HONORS AND AWARDS

Eleanor Roosevelt Key Award (Roosevelt University Alumni): 1963
Hall of Fame Member (Ward I Democrats of the District of Columbia): 1966
Fannie Lou Hamer Freedom Award (National Conference of Black Mayors): 1990

FURTHER READING

Books

Allen, Robert L. *Black Awakening in Capitalist America: An Analytical History*, 1969
The African-American Desk Reference, 1999
Carson, Claybourne. *In Struggle: SNCC and the Black Awakening of the 1960s*, 1981
Contemporary Black Biography, Vol. 7, 1994
Encyclopedia of World Biography, 1998
Forman, James. *The Makings of Black Revolutionaries: A Personal Account*, 1972
Lader, Lawrence. *Power on the Left: American Radical Movements since 1946*, 1979
Notable Black American Men, 1998
Sellers, Cleveland, and Robert Terrell. *The River of No Return: The Autobiography of a Black Militant and the Life and Death of SNCC*, 1973

Periodicals

Atlanta Journal-Constitution, Jan. 12, 2005, p.B6
Guardian (London), Jan. 14, 2005, p.29
Los Angeles Times, Jan. 15, 2005, p.B8
New York Times, Jan. 12, 2005, p.A18
Times (London), Jan. 17, 2005, p.50
Washington Post, Jan. 12, 2005, pp.B6 and C1; Feb. 6, 2005, p.C3; Feb. 10, 2005, p.T2

Online Databases

Biography Resource Center Online, 2005, articles from *Contemporary Black Biography,* 1994; *Encyclopedia of World Biography,* 1998; and *Notable Black American Men,* 1998

Online Articles

http://www.courier-journal.com/apps/pbcs.dll/article?AID=/20050217
/COLUMNISTS09/502170363/-1/SCENEarts
(*Louisville Courier Journal,* "Civil Rights Hero Forman Never Stopped Engaging in the Struggle," Feb. 17, 2005)
http://www.stanford.edu/group/King/about_king/encyclopedia/enc_SNCC
.htm
(Stanford University, Martin Luther King Papers Project, "Student Nonviolent Coordinating Committee," no date)
http://www.stanford.edu/~ccarson/articles/left_2.htm
(Stanford University, Clayborne Carson, "James Forman," no date)
http://www.washingtonpost.com/wp-dyn/articles/A1621-2005Jan11.html
(*Washington Post,* "Civil Rights Leader James Forman Dies," Jan. 11, 2005)

WORLD WIDE WEB SITES

http://www.thehistorymakers.com
http://www.cr.nps.gov/nr/travel/civilrights
http://memory.loc.gov/ammem/aaohtml/exhibit/aopart9.html
http://www.voicesofcivilrights.org/index.html
http://www.time.com/time/newsfiles/civilrights
http://afroamhistory.about.com
http://www.civilrightsmuseum.org
http://www.usm.edu/crdp/index.html

Wally Funk 1939-

American Aviation Pioneer
Member of the Historic "Mercury 13" Group of
Female Astronaut Candidates

BIRTH

Mary Wallace Funk—who insists on being called "Wally"—
was born on January 31, 1939, in Taos, New Mexico. Her parents, Lozier and Virginia Funk, owned a five-and-dime store
in Taos. She had one older brother, Clark, who was born in
1936.

———— " ————

"I grew up in an area where you had free spirit," Funk said. *"[Indian friends] taught me how to fish and hunt and camp at a very early age, and survive the wilderness. So I had all that going for myself. . . . That's why I thank the good Lord for putting me where he put me."*

———— " ————

YOUTH

Funk first explored the wonders of flight as a five-year-old. It was then that she took to jumping from the roof of the family barn into waiting haystacks, a Superman cape clasped around her neck. These jumping stunts reflected the fun and carefree nature of Funk's childhood. When she wasn't selling rabbits, squash, strawberries, corn, and arrowheads to tourists outside her father's store, she could usually be found exploring the wild country outside Taos with friends from a local Tiwa Indian tribe. "I grew up in an area where you had free spirit," she said. "[Indian friends] taught me how to fish and hunt and camp at a very early age, and survive the wilderness. So I had all that going for myself, where a youngster today is in a city, in an apartment, and that's all they know. They don't know ocean and skiing and snow and air as I was able to know it, and that's why I thank the good Lord for putting me where he put me."

As Wally grew older, she developed a strong fascination with machines — and especially airplanes. "Mother wanted a froufrou girl with frills, and all I wanted was an Erector set," she recalled. When it became clear that Wally's interest in planes was not a passing fancy, though, both of her parents were very supportive. Her father brought home model airplanes for her to build, and her mother drove her out to the tiny local airport to watch the planes come and go. By the time she was a teenager, Wally's hero was Amelia Earhart, a famous American aviator who disappeared over the Pacific Ocean during a 1937 flight.

Wally later learned that her mother's encouragement stemmed from her own experiences as a young woman. After taking a ride with a "barnstormer" — a stunt flyer who performs at county fairs and carnivals — Virginia Funk burst into her home talking excitedly about learning to fly. But her hopes were immediately shot down by her father. "He told her that she would become a fine young woman, a good wife, and an excellent mother," reported Wally. "And she was all of those things. But she also passed along those flying genes to me, and she supported me all the way."

Wally's love for adventure and the outdoors took other forms, too. She became an expert rifle marksman, receiving the Distinguished Rifleman's Award at age 14. She also competed in various slalom and downhill skiing competitions throughout the West until a serious back injury forced her to hang up her skis.

EDUCATION

Funk attended schools in the Taos area until age 16, when she enrolled at Stephens College in Columbia, Missouri. This two-year college, one of the oldest women's colleges in the country, offered several aviation courses. Not surprisingly, Funk wasted little time in signing up.

Funk made her first flight in a single-engine, four-seat airplane with her teacher and one other student. "What impressed me the most was that the airplane just kind of took itself off, and the ground was so beautifully packaged as north, south, east, west — it was all field we flew over, near the Missouri River," she remembered. "The earth was so pristine, and I was up there looking down at the perfect pattern on the ground, at the cows and the cars and the houses and the river and the town. The bug bit and that was it."

Afterward, Funk's parents agreed to pay for flight lessons for their excited daughter. Years later, she discovered that paying for her lessons constituted a major financial burden for her parents. But despite the expense, they remained steadfast in encouraging her to pursue her flying dreams.

Funk made her first solo flight at age 16 and earned her pilot's license at age 17. She then joined the Flying Susies, the intercollegiate flying squad at Stephens College. She loved the hours she spent in training flights and flying competitions, but sometimes even all this flying action was not enough to satisfy her. On one occasion, she remembered, "I snuck out the window

"What impressed me the most was that the airplane just kind of took itself off, and the ground was so beautifully packaged as north, south, east, west — it was all field we flew over, near the Missouri River," Funk remembered. "The earth was so pristine, and I was up there looking down at the perfect pattern on the ground, at the cows and the cars and the houses and the river and the town. The bug bit and that was it."

Funk was the top female pilot with the Flying Aggies for two years.

from a formal [dance] one time to go night flying and snuck back in by midnight so I wasn't caught."

In 1958 Funk graduated from Stephens College with an associate of arts degree. That same year, she received the Outstanding Female Pilot Trophy at the National Intercollegiate Flying Meet in Minneapolis, Minnesota. Most of the other awards handed out at the meet, however, went to members of the Oklahoma State University Flying Aggies.

Funk was so impressed by the Flying Aggies that she decided she had to fly with them. She subsequently enrolled at Oklahoma State, and by the close of 1959 she was one of the school's top female flyers. Meanwhile, she continued her studies in both aviation and education. By the time she graduated with a bachelor of science degree in secondary education in 1960, she had also qualified to pilot a wide variety of aircraft, from single-engine seaplanes to commercial planes.

FIRST JOBS

After graduation, Funk worked to get a job as a commercial pilot. But she was turned down flat by all the airlines, none of which had ever had a female pilot on their payroll (the first female commercial pilot in the United States was not hired until 1973). "I was told by United and Continental Airlines I couldn't be hired as a commercial pilot because there were no ladies' bathrooms in the training facilities," she recalled with a mixture of amusement and sadness.

With that avenue blocked, Funk went to Fort Sill, Oklahoma, where at age 20 she became the first civilian flight instructor of noncommissioned and commissioned officers in the history of the U.S. military. She was limited to teaching flying on propeller-driven aircraft, though, since the U.S. military did not allow women to operate jets in that era.

CAREER HIGHLIGHTS

As Funk carried out her work at Fort Sill, she—like millions of other Americans—followed with great interest the accelerating "space race" between the United States and the Communist-led Union of Soviet Socialist Republics (USSR), also known as the Soviet Union. Both nations desperately wanted to be the first to achieve certain landmarks, like putting a man on the moon. This race for supremacy was also waged in the development of nuclear weapons and economic and political power, and it dominated news coverage of the era.

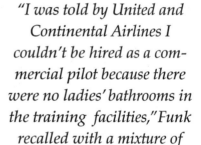

"I was told by United and Continental Airlines I couldn't be hired as a commercial pilot because there were no ladies' bathrooms in the training facilities," Funk recalled with a mixture of amusement and sadness.

The modern age of space exploration began in 1957 when the Soviet Union launched Sputnik I, the first satellite sent into space. The United States became determined to beat the Russians in developing its space program. In 1958, the United States founded the National Aeronautics and Space Administration (NASA), which screened over 580 military pilots who had expressed interest in becoming astronauts. During the screening process, 159 pilots were selected to undergo a series of challenging physical and psychological tests. The seven men with the highest scores became the "Mercury 7" —seven astronauts who led America's first expeditions into space.

Training to Be an Astronaut

In 1960 Funk was leafing through an issue of *Life* magazine when she came across an article describing a budding NASA plan to train female astronauts. This news stunned and excited Funk, who promptly wrote a letter to the director of the fledgling program, Dr. W. Randolph Lovelace II. She boldly asked for a spot in the program, then backed up her request with a listing of her credentials, including her various collegiate flight team awards, flight instructor training, and 3,000 flying hours — over three times the number of hours Lovelace was seeking from candidates.

Impressed by Funk's ambition and aviation experience, Lovelace agreed to place her in the "Women in Space" program, which had the support — but not the official sponsorship — of NASA. Funk and 24 other women began the program in February 1961. Of all the candidates in the program, Funk was the youngest.

> "The [sensory deprivation] tank was a piece of cake," Funk later said. "The only thing that really hurt was when they injected freezing water into my ear [to trigger disorientation]. Now that was really painful. But I wanted to go into space so badly, I would have endured anything."

The testing program, which was identical to the one used on the male astronaut candidates, was divided into three phases. Phase one consisted of 87 different tests to check physical health. Some of these tests were very unpleasant. For example, Funk and the others were forced to swallow three feet of rubber hose for a stomach test, and on another occasion 18 needles were stuck in each of their heads to record brain waves. They even were forced to consume glasses of radioactive water. "I just gulped it down," Funk recalled. "I can't say it really bothered me."

The second phase involved a combination of psychological and psychiatric testing. For many prospective astronauts — both male and female — the most disorienting and frightening of these tests was the isolation tank. In this test, candidates were placed in a pitch-black tank of warm water that was constructed to completely eliminate input for all five senses. Even the water in which the subjects floated could not be felt, since the water temperature was perfectly matched to the body temperature of each participant.

This sensory deprivation test was designed to create a feeling of weightlessness such as one might feel in space, but it also commonly caused prospective astronauts to lapse into uncontrollable hallucinations. Funk, however, never succumbed to hallucinations. Instead, she spent 10 hours and 35 minutes in the tank without hallucinating, a longer period of time than any

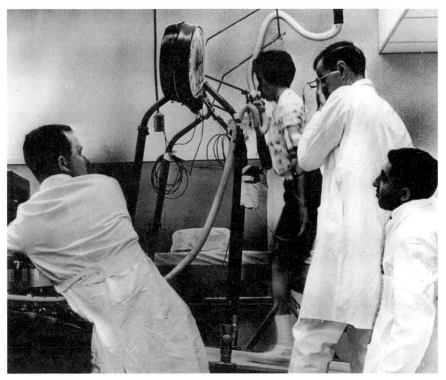

For the Mercury 13 astronaut training program, Funk underwent a series of physical, psychological, and psychiatric tests.

other man or woman who participated. "The tank was a piece of cake," she later said. "The only thing that really hurt was when they injected freezing water into my ear [to trigger disorientation]. Now that was really painful. But I wanted to go into space so badly, I would have endured anything."

Phase three of the training program was conducted at different test sites. During this process, Funk and the other astronaut candidates were tested for their reactions to high altitudes, fierce gravitational forces, and other potential elements of the space environment. "I did whatever they asked without asking questions," she said. "We hadn't been to space yet, so there was no idea what the human body would have to endure in terms of stress. That's why they tested us to the limit."

A Dream Deferred

Funk and 12 other women — dubbed the "Mercury 13" — passed the battery of tests. In fact, one doctor who helped test the women told *National*

Geographic Online that "their results were so astonishing that, at the time, I didn't see how NASA could turn them down. All of the Mercury women were extraordinary."

Nonetheless, the so-called Mercury 13 program was abruptly terminated by NASA, just when Funk and the other women had come to believe that their dream of space flight might actually come true. Director Lovelace and other Mercury 13 supporters strenuously objected to the decision, but they were told that the U.S. government had decided that America was not ready for female astronauts. "It was the era when women were in the kitchen," explained Funk. "[It was] terrible. I mean, they never gave us a chance to prove ourselves."

> ————— **"** —————
>
> *The so-called Mercury 13 program was abruptly terminated by NASA when the U.S. government decided that America was not ready for female astronauts. "It was the era when women were in the kitchen," explained Funk. "[It was] terrible. I mean, they never gave us a chance to prove ourselves."*
>
> ————— **"** —————

Funk and the other Mercury 13 members held out hope that NASA might eventually reconsider its decision. "I thought, 'Wally, you're still going into space, just not right now,'" she recalled. But in 1963, Congressional hearings conducted to study the feasibility of sending women into space determined that all astronauts should be military jet pilots. Since the U.S. military did not let women fly military jets at that time, the decision effectively killed all hopes.

Breaking New Ground in Aviation Circles

After the Mercury 13 program was suspended, Funk accepted a position in the fall of 1961 as a flight instructor and pilot with an aviation company in Hawthorne, California. She also continued her education, rising to new heights of her profession with each passing year. In 1971, for example, Funk became the first woman to successfully complete the Federal Aviation Administration's General Aviation Operations Inspector Academy course. This accomplishment qualified her to test pilots for flight certification and investigate flight violations, accidents, and other aspects of plane operation.

In 1973 Funk became the first woman in the United States to hold the position of specialist in the FAA's Systems Worthiness Analysis Program. In

*In about 1961 or 1962, Funk flew this Cessna 310 as a flight instructor
and pilot with an aviation company.*

the ensuing months she became an inspector of both flight schools and
air taxi operations. In December 1974 Funk relocated to Washington,
D.C., where she became one of the first female air accident investigators
in the history of the National Transportation Safety Board (NTSB). Over
the next decade, she investigated more than 450 airplane accidents across
the country.

The task of investigating accidents—especially fatal airplane crashes—
could be a very depressing one. But it never eroded Funk's love for aviation. In fact, she participated in several air races across the American West
in the 1970s and 1980s. Her biggest triumph in this sport came on October
4, 1975. On that day, Funk flew a red and white Citabria plane to victory
over a field of 80 competitors in the Pacific Air Race, a contest that took
competitors from San Diego to Santa Rosa, California.

In 1985 Funk left the NTSB. She spent the next several years working as a
flight instructor and promoting flight safety at conferences and other

events around the world. Funk has estimated that her work as a sort of "goodwill ambassador" for flying took her to more than 50 countries in Europe, the Middle East, and Africa. These activities put her in the public spotlight, and she has since been profiled on numerous television and radio programs and in several national publications.

"Wally should have been the first woman in space, she could have been the first woman in space," said Randa Milliron, Chief Executive Officer of IOS. "Wally is the most qualified person in the world for this as well. You want somebody who can think on her feet for an activity like this. So when I fly, I want to fly with Wally."

Watching Female Astronauts Make History

As Funk grew older, she continued to follow the U.S. space program with great interest. In 1983 she celebrated when Sally Ride became the first American female astronaut to go into space (the first female astronaut in the world was Valentina Tereshkova, who was part of a 1963 Soviet space flight). Twelve years later, Funk became just as excited when American Eileen Collins became the first female astronaut to serve as pilot on a space shuttle mission.

In a gesture of appreciation for their trailblazing efforts three decades earlier, Collins invited all surviving members of the Mercury 13 group to be her guests at the launch. It was an emotional day for Funk, who still harbored dreams of going into space. As the rocket left the launchpad, Funk felt tears streaming down her cheeks as she yelled, "Go Eileen! Go for all of us!" Collins's historic flight signaled an end to the days when women astronauts were kept to the sidelines of space flight.

Today, female astronauts are part of virtually every space shuttle crew, serving as commanders, pilots, and scientists. But Funk knew that her age made it highly unlikely that she would ever fulfill her dream of space flight on a NASA mission. In fact, NASA has rejected Funk's application to join its astronaut program four times over the years.

Certified to fly more than 30 types of airplanes, Funk continued to work as a flight instructor. She also continued to give motivational speeches to women's organizations, college groups, aviation conferences, and other

*Funk and other Mercury 13 astronaut candidates watched the
1995 launch when Eileen Collins became the first female astronaut
to pilot a space shuttle mission.*

gatherings. Her public pronouncements have drawn fire from some critics, who accuse her of exaggerations and excessive boastfulness in her recollections of her Mercury 13 days. Funk, though, says that she pays no attention to these complaints.

Moreover, Funk continued to explore alternative ways of getting into space. In 2000, for example, she paid a hefty fee to train at the Yuri Gagarin Cosmonaut Training Center in Russia's Space City complex. She had hoped that these sessions might lead to an opportunity to visit the Russian Space Station Mir orbiting above the earth. In March 2001, however, the aging satellite — which had housed dozens of astronauts over the previous decade — was brought back to Earth in a controlled crash.

Since that time, Funk has become involved with a privately funded aerospace corporation called Interorbital Systems (IOS), based in Mojave, California. Founded in 1996, IOS is developing commercial rocket systems for spaceflight in hopes of launching a profitable "space tourism" business. For the past several years, the company has been working to develop Solaris X, a rocket capable of carrying people into orbit. In fact, the Solaris X vehicle was entered in the Ansari X Prize, a privately financed international commercial spaceflight competition. This contest, organized by aerospace entrepreneur Peter Diamandis, offered a $10 million prize to the first team that could send a rocket carrying three people to the threshold of space — about 60 miles from Earth — and return them safely, then duplicate the feat in the same spacecraft within two weeks.

In 2002 Interorbital Systems announced that it had reached an agreement with Funk for her to pilot the Solaris X went it goes into space. "Wally should have been the first woman in space, she could have been the first woman in space," said Randa Milliron, Chief Executive Officer of IOS. "Wally is the most qualified person in the world for this as well. You want somebody who can think on her feet for an activity like this. So when I fly, I want to fly with Wally."

> "I want to be in space in the worst way," Funk said. "I've tried in every way to kick a lot of doors in. I still have the heart of that 20-year-old. . . . What I am already dreaming about is the roar of the take-off, followed by the absolute silence as we go into orbit, and then seeing Earth outside my window."

For her part, Funk expressed great excitement about the flight, which is scheduled to take place in late 2004 or 2005. "I want to be in space in the worst way," she said. "I've tried in every way to kick a lot of doors in. I still have the heart of that 20-year-old. . . . What I am already dreaming about is the roar of the take-off, followed by the absolute silence as we go into orbit, and then seeing Earth outside my window."

Unfortunately, the Interorbital Systems flight will not win the Ansari X Prize. That honor went to the American Mojave Aerospace Team, which was led by research aircraft developer Burt Rutan and financier Paul Allen. The team completed two successful suborbital space flights — on September 29 and October 4, 2004 — and was awarded the $10 million prize. But Interorbital Systems later announced that it is continuing its plans to open the space frontier to tourists. Interorbital is currently constructing two new rockets: the Nano, which will send tiny satellites into orbit, and the Neptune, a rocket capable of ferrying up to eight people into orbit. The team plans to compete for the America's Space Prize that is being offered by entrepreneur Bob Bigelow for a private vehicle that can carry passengers to orbit Earth.

HOME AND FAMILY

Funk, who has never been married, lives in Roanoke, Texas, in a home that is heavily decorated with model airplanes, flight-related ribbons and awards, and photographs documenting her decades as an aviator.

HOBBIES AND OTHER INTERESTS

Funk enjoys restoring antique automobiles and participating in firearm shooting competitions. She has also engaged in a wide variety of "extreme" sports over the years, including parachuting, bungee jumping, ballooning, and hang gliding.

HONORS AND AWARDS

Outstanding Female Pilot (National Intercollegiate Flying Meet): 1958
Pacific Air Race: 1975, First Place
International Hall of Fame for Pioneer Women in Aviation: 1995

FURTHER READING

Books

Ackmann, Martha. *The Mercury 13*, 2003
Nolen, Stephanie. *Promised the Moon: The Untold Story of the First Women in the Space Race*, 2002

Periodicals

Chicago Tribune, Feb. 1, 1995, p.C2
Dallas Morning News, Mar. 27, 1995, p.A1
Fort Worth (Tex.) Star-Telegram, Nov. 20, 1996, Metro, p.1; Sep. 25, 1999, Metro, p.1
Life, Aug. 29, 1963, p.72; June 28, 1963, p.31
Los Angeles Times Magazine, Jan. 18, 2004, p.16
People, July 7, 2003, p.114
Weekly Reader (senior edition), Apr. 2, 2004, p.2

Online Articles

http://www.houstonchron.com
(*HoustonChronicle.com*, "Wally Funk Is Still Determined to Get Her Shot at Space," Feb. 11, 2000)

http://www.guardian.co.uk
  (*Guardian Unlimited,* "Space Cowgirl," Apr. 2, 2002)
http://www.scottsdalejournal.com
  (*Scottsdale Journal Online,* "Wally Funk — From Cowgirl to Space Girl,"
  Feb. 2003)
http://www.nationalgeographic.com
  (*National Geographic.com,* "Mercury 13's Wally Funk Fights for Her Place
  in Space," July 9, 2003)

Additional information for this biographical profile was gathered from
transcripts of NASA's Oral History project.

ADDRESS

Wally Funk
Interorbital Systems
P.O. Box 662
Mojave, CA 93502-0662

WORLD WIDE WEB SITES

http://www.ninety-nines.org
http://www.interorbital.com

Cornelia Funke 1958-

German Writer of Books for Children and
Young Adults
Author of *The Thief Lord, Inkheart,* and *Dragon Rider*

BIRTH

Cornelia Caroline Funke (pronounced FOON-keh) was born
in 1958 in Dorsten, Westphalia—a small, industrial town in
central Germany that she has described as "not very pretty"
and "a place you're a little bit bored by all the time." Her father was a lawyer, and her mother was a homemaker. She was
the oldest child in her family, with younger brothers and a
younger sister.

YOUTH

Funke was an imaginative child who loved to draw and paint. She often made up stories for her younger siblings, and she also loved to read fantasy and adventure tales — especially *The Chronicles of Narnia* by C.S. Lewis. "Most authors I read were British or American," she noted. Her father was also a great reader, and he often took her to the library. Despite her love of books and stories, however, Funke never really considered becoming an author. Instead, her early career plans included becoming an astronaut or a pilot. "Then I thought I wanted to marry a chief of a large American Indian nation and live with him and his people in the wide prairies," she recalled.

EDUCATION

Funke attended schools in Dorsten where, like most German students, she studied English for nine years. She has described herself as a good student but "not ambitious (which means quite lazy)." English was one of her favorite subjects, and she also "loved to write essays, though always too long and not always strictly on the topic."

At the age of 18 Funke moved to Hamburg, Germany. She earned a degree in education theory at the University of Hamburg, then completed coursework in book illustration at the Hamburg State College of Design. "I studied education (the most stupid idea of my life) because I wanted to work in some way with children, not as a teacher, but as a social worker," she related. "I think I wanted to make the world a better place, but I found out that you can't live against your gifts. And my gifts are writing and drawing."

CAREER HIGHLIGHTS

After completing her education, Funke began working with troubled children as a social worker. "I did work with children on an activity playground for a while, building huts and generally teaching them not to hit others as soon as they didn't get what they want," she remembered. Although Funke soon realized that the job would never make her completely happy, she did learn a great deal about the spirit and determination of children. "I still have the greatest respect for the little ones I met in those years — they all had bad, bad things to deal with, and did it so bravely," she noted. "I have often been impressed by children who come from very different social backgrounds: how much they care for siblings or friends, help each other, try to be strong."

Funke soon left social work and began applying her artistic talents as a designer of board games and illustrator of children's books. Dissatisfied with the quality of the stories she was asked to illustrate, she decided to start writing her own books. "I found that I am better at writing than illustrating, and more passionate about it," she stated. She sent her first effort, *The Great Dragon Quest,* to a German publisher in the mid-1980s. It was accepted immediately, and Funke launched a new career as an author of children's books. Over the next 15 years, Funke became one of Germany's most popular writers. She published more than 40 works, including picture books, early readers, chapter books, and young adult novels.

Herr der Diebe (The Thief Lord)

Although Funke speaks fluent English, she has written all of her books in German, her native language. To date, only a few have been translated into English. The first was *Herr der Diebe,* which was later published in English as *The Thief Lord.*

Funke first got the idea for *Herr der Diebe* during a visit with her family to Venice, Italy. She had always loved Venice—with its historic buildings, romantic atmosphere, and endless system of canals—and longed to share it with readers. "Venice is an enchanted place, but it is also very real—you can touch it, smell it, and taste it," she explained. "I wanted to tell children that there is a place in this world that is real and full of history, but also contains magic and mystery—not an imagined world, but right here, in a place they can visit."

"Venice is an enchanted place, but it is also very real—you can touch it, smell it, and taste it. I wanted to tell children that there is a place in this world that is real and full of history, but also contains magic and mystery—not an imagined world, but right here, in a place they can visit."

The trip to Venice also brought back feelings from Funke's childhood, when she often wished that she could magically become an adult. "As far as I know, there is not one story about all those children who want to be an adult, so they can buy a dog at once, get a horse, or something else, watch movies all night or whatever, just have this freedom," she related. "So one day I had the idea of writing a story about a boy who has the same dream and who even pretends to be an adult."

Herr der Diebe tells the story of 12-year-old Prosper and his five-year-old brother, Boniface ("Bo"). When their mother dies, the boys are sent to live with their wealthy, cold-hearted aunt and uncle in Hamburg, Germany.

While the aunt is interested in raising cuddly Bo, she wants no part of the intense Prosper and plans to send him away to boarding school. Faced with the prospect of being separated, the boys run away to Venice, which their mother had once described to them as a magical city of moonlit canals. The orphans end up taking refuge in an abandoned movie theater with other street children. The leader of the street children is 12-year-old Scipio, who calls himself the Thief Lord. Dressed in boots and a mask like Robin Hood, Scipio steals jewels from rich people to support his young friends.

Publication in English

———— " ————

"It thrills me that English and American children will come to love the story as much as German children do, which proves that we are not that different," Funke stated.

———— " ————

At first, *Herr der Diebe* and Funke's other works were popular primarily in Germany. That changed in 2002, when the book was first published in English. The translation was inspired by a bilingual girl named Clara, who spoke both German and English and had recently moved from Germany to England. She wrote a letter to Barry Cunningham, an editor at the British publisher Chicken House. He had become famous several years earlier as the editor who discovered J.K. Rowling's talent and published her "Harry Potter" series in England. In the letter, Clara asked Cunningham why her favorite book, *Herr der Diebe*, was not available in English translation. Cunningham contacted Funke's German publisher, read a translation that had been prepared by Funke's cousin, and immediately arranged to publish the book in English as *The Thief Lord*.

The Thief Lord became an instant success, selling out its first printing in ten days in England, and reaching the number two spot on the *New York Times* children's bestseller list in the United States. It also won several awards in Europe, as well as the American Library Association's Mildred L. Batchelder Award as the best foreign-language children's book published in the United States in 2002. "It thrills me that English and American children will come to love the story as much as German children do, which proves that we are not that different," Funke stated.

In a review for *School Library Journal,* John Peters called *The Thief Lord* "a compelling tale, rich in ingenious twists, with a setting and cast that will linger in readers' memories." Writing for the *New York Times,* Rebecca Pepper Sinkler added that "There is magic here, but what lifts this radiant novel beyond run-of-the-mill fantasy is its palpable respect for both the struggle to grow up and the mixed blessings of growing old."

Exploring the World of Books with *Inkheart*

Following the success of *The Thief Lord,* Funke's young adult novel *Inkheart* was published in English in 2003. She drew upon her lifelong love of books in writing this story. "I have dreamed for a long time of writing a story in which characters from a book come into our world," she explained on her Web site. "Which book addict doesn't know the feeling that the characters in a book can seem more real than the people around us?"

> ———— **"** ————
>
> *"I have dreamed for a long time of writing a story in which characters from a book come into our world. Which book addict doesn't know the feeling that the characters in a book can seem more real than the people around us?"*
>
> ———— **"** ————

Inkheart tells the story of Meggie, a 12-year-old girl who lives with her father, Mo. Mo is a bookbinder who shares his love of books with his daughter. Unbeknownst to Meggie, however, Mo's connection with books goes much deeper than his job. He is a Silvertongue, meaning that he possesses an ancient gift that enables him to bring the characters of a book to life by reading their stories aloud. Unfortunately, when the book's characters come to populate the real world, real people also disappear into the pages of the book.

Nine years earlier, when Mo read the exciting novel *Inkheart* aloud to his wife, he had accidentally released the evil character Capricorn into the real world, while Meggie's mother had disappeared into the pages of the novel. Meggie learns about her father's secret when the mysterious Dustfinger, another character from *Inkheart,* shows up to ask Mo to read him back into the book. Her father is unable to reverse the process, however, and Meggie is soon drawn into an adventure rivaling any that she had read about.

Upon completing the novel, Funke sent a copy of the manuscript to Clara, the young fan whose letter had led to the English-language publication of *The Thief Lord*. Funke wanted Clara's input to make sure that her villains were not too frightening for young adults. "When I decided to do something with villains, I thought I'd like to do them really real and not fool children with evil, because they have to meet it at some time—it is not something abstract, like some stories depict," she explained. "I experience evil in the world as something very real and threatening." Clara responded that the villains were not too scary for her age group.

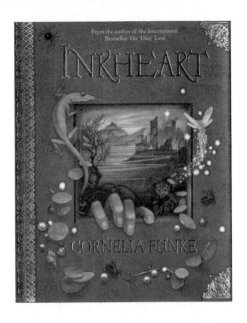

Inkheart quickly earned outstanding reviews. A writer for *Kirkus Reviews* called the novel "a true feast for anyone who has ever been lost in a book." A *Publishers Weekly* reviewer added that "Funke once again proves the power of her imagination; readers will be captivated by the chilling and thrilling world she has created here." Reviewer Jean Boreen noted in the *Journal of Adolescent and Adult Literacy* that "Funke does a wonderful job illuminating the difficulties faced by various characters as they choose between their own safety and that of a loved one, or debate the choices they might have to make to prove their loyalty to a friend. *Inkheart* will definitely catch the attention and admiration of most readers as it is, overall, a delightful read."

Funke has said that she found *Inkheart* the easiest to write among all of her books. In fact, once she had prepared an outline, the characters seemed to come to life and demand to tell their own stories. "I opened a door and all these characters ran out," she said. The vivid characters in her imagination eventually convinced Funke to expand *Inkheart* into a trilogy. "I love my characters to take me for a surprising ride," she explained. "You have to be confident enough to follow them. It is like walking to a cliff edge.... If you want to develop as a writer, you have to jump off—and fly." She planned to set the sequels mostly within the world that Dustfinger came from. "Dustfinger will go back home and some of the others will follow, either because they want to or because they are made to," Funke stated.

Writing Popular Children's Series

By the summer of 2004, Funke's books had sold five million copies in 28 countries around the world. Yet only a handful of her books had been translated into English by this time. In fact, one of her most popular series among German readers, *The Wild Chicks*, was not available in the United

States. This realistic fiction series features five books about a group of schoolgirls who call themselves "The Wild Chicks."

Another one of Funke's most popular books, *Dragon Rider,* made its American debut in 2004. This fantasy-adventure novel for young readers had helped establish Funke's reputation among German readers several years earlier. *Dragon Rider* tells the story of Firedrake, an unusual dragon who sets out to find the Rim of Heaven — the mythical home where dragons can live in peace forever. He is accompanied on his quest by a human boy named Ben, who turns out to be his dragon rider, and a feisty Scottish brownie girl named Sorrel. Along the way, they meet new friends but must also battle with the evil Nettlebrand, who is determined to exterminate all the world's dragons. "Exciting adventures abound, albeit counterbalanced with some implausible motivations, a few plot holes, and a dollup of syrupy sentiment," wrote Anita L. Burkam in *Horn Book.* "But for younger readers who want fantastical events straight up, . . . this book delivers." *Dragon Rider* reached the top position on the *New York Times* children's bestseller list shortly after its release.

Some of Funke's books for younger readers have recently been published in the United States. *The Princess Knight,* released in 2004, is a picture book about Violetta, a little princess whose father trains her to ride horses and engage in sword fights alongside her brothers. When she turns 16, however, the king insists that she behave like a traditional princess and marry the winner of a jousting contest. Determined to control her own destiny, Violet sneaks into the woods every night and trains herself to be the most clever, nimble knight in the kingdom. She competes in the jousting contest in disguise and wins her own independence. "Funke handles the picture book form just as deftly as her novels, with sure-footed pacing and a well-placed thrust through the cardboard princess stereotype," wrote a reviewer for *Publishers Weekly.* "Despite the fairy-tale surroundings, the heroine earns her triumph with believable determination, and readers young and old will root for her from start to finish."

> "
>
> *"There are people who know already at the age of six that they want to become a doctor or a teacher. Just don't worry if you're not one of these people. Take your time finding out what kind of work gives you so much joy that you could imagine doing it for the rest of your life. And then you can still change your mind completely halfway through your life and do something completely different. Why not?"*
>
> "

The popularity of Funke's books in English has led to several movie-production deals. *The Thief Lord, Inkheart,* and *The Wild Chicks* are all scheduled to be filmed in 2005. While Funke was thrilled at the prospect of see-

Funke and the actor Brendan Fraser surrounded by fifth-grade students at a book-signing for Inkheart.

ing her work on the big screen, she also expressed concern about the filmmakers' ability to capture her artistic vision. "I get more and more the feeling that I should be very careful of the Hollywood influence," she stated. "Some people have given casting ideas that are just ridiculous. I don't want to make *Inkheart* with Jim Carrey or with Tom Hanks or with Brad Pitt [as Mo]. . . . If they do a movie that crushes the imagination, I'll never forgive myself. You write a book that you're passionate about and they spoil it!" Funke envisioned actor Brendan Fraser—star of *Gods and Monsters, The Mummy,* and *George of the Jungle*—in the role of Mo. In fact, she sent him a copy of *Inkheart,* and they ended up establishing a friendship. Fraser has since read some of Funke's books when they were recorded on audiotape.

Enjoying Her Work

Funke claims that she has more ideas for stories than she could ever write. "I have the feeling more and more that the story is just there and you have to find it," she stated. She spends about a year on a typical book, including six months of research and planning, followed by six months of writing and revising. Sometimes her books seem to write themselves. While she continues to illustrate some of her own books with line drawings, she no longer illustrates picture books by other authors.

Funke often reassures young people by telling them that it took her a while to discover her life's work. "I love my work. I love writing books and telling stories so much that I could not imagine doing anything else. But it took me a very long time to figure out that this was what I wanted to do, let alone that I could actually do it well enough to make a living from it," she explained. "Of course there are people who know already at the age of six that they want to become a doctor or a teacher. Just don't worry if you're not one of these people. Take your time finding out what kind of work gives you so much joy that you could imagine doing it for the rest of your life. And then you can still change your mind completely halfway through your life and do something completely different. Why not?"

Funke attributes her success as a writer partly to her ability to understand children and their interests. "I am an adult now, at least I look like one. But I still am amazed by the rituals and everything in the adult world and I still don't get it," she admitted. "Sometimes I feel like a spy for children, offering them a glimpse into the strange world of adults. The worst thing that can happen as an adult is to forget how the world felt when it was new."

—— **"** ——

"I am an adult now, at least I look like one. But I still am amazed by the rituals and everything in the adult world and I still don't get it. Sometimes I feel like a spy for children, offering them a glimpse into the strange world of adults. The worst thing that can happen as an adult is to forget how the world felt when it was new."

—— **"** ——

Funke enjoys connecting with her young readers, especially those who share her deep love of books. "I like when a child comes to me at a reading and they have a book that looks like it's been read a dozen times," she stated. "A collector who brings me a book that is perfectly clean—that is kind of a creepy feeling. I feel like that book is dead. Nobody will ever touch it again. If I was a book, I would like to be a library book, so I would be taken home by all different sorts of kids. A library book, I imagine, is a happy book."

MARRIAGE AND FAMILY

Funke has been married to her husband, Rolf, for 25 years. Rolf worked as a book printer until his wife's writing career took off, then he quit his job to care for their children, Anna and Ben. Funke and her family live in the

165

countryside north of Hamburg, Germany, in an older brick house "with a huge, wild garden, two horses, a guinea pig, and a hairy dog called Loony —because she is."

HOBBIES AND OTHER INTERESTS

One of Funke's hobbies is collecting dragons. "Ever since I wrote *Dragon Rider*, I have been a mad collector of dragons—stuffed dragons, paper dragons, china dragons, small ones, big ones, green ones, red ones—but there is still not a single one in my collection that can fly like Firedrake," she noted. In her spare time, she enjoys watching movies with her family and has an extensive collection of DVDs. Funke also lends her support to several German charities that serve underprivileged, ill, or refugee children.

SELECTED WRITINGS

The Thief Lord, 2002
Inkheart, 2003
The Princess Knight, 2004
Dragon Rider, 2004

HONORS AND AWARDS

Zurich Children's Book Award: 2000, for *The Thief Lord*
Venice House of Literature Award: 2001, for *The Thief Lord*
Notable Book Award (*New York Times*): 2002, for *The Thief Lord*
Mildred L. Batchelder Award (American Library Association): 2003, for *The Thief Lord*
Torchlight Prize (Askew Library Services): 2003, for *The Thief Lord*
Corinne 2003 International Book Award: 2003, for *The Thief Lord*
Children's BookSense Book of the Year: 2003, for *Inkheart*
Amelia Bloomer Project Award (American Library Association): 2005, for *The Princess Knight*

FURTHER READING

Periodicals

Bookseller, June 20, 2003, p.32
Buffalo (NY) News, Apr. 7, 2004, p.N6
Detroit Free Press, Dec. 5, 2002, Yak, p.2
Duluth (MN) News-Tribune, Jan. 7, 2004

Guardian (London), June 22, 2002, p.32; Oct. 29, 2003, p.17
Horn Book, Sep. 1, 2004, p.583
Journal of Adolescent and Adult Literacy, Sep. 2003, p.91; Feb. 2004, p.433
Kirkus Reviews, Sep. 15, 2003, p.1174
New York Post, Dec. 6, 2003, p.26
New York Times, Nov. 17, 2002, p.31
Observer (London), July 11, 2004, p.17
Publishers Weekly, July 21, 2003, p.196; Jan. 26, 2004, p.253
School Library Journal, Oct. 2002, p.163
Time, Apr. 18, 2005, p.120
USA Today, Sep. 5, 2002, p.D5
Variety, Oct. 20-26, 2003, p.12

Online Articles

http://www.bordersstores.com/features
  (Borders.com, "Hey American Kids, Meet Cornelia Funke," 2003)

Online Databases

Biography Resource Center Online, 2005, article from *Contemporary Authors Online,* 2005

Further information for this profile was taken from a National Public Radio interview with Funke, conducted Oct. 13, 2002.

ADDRESS

Cornelia Funke
Scholastic Inc.
557 Broadway
New York, NY 10012

WORLD WIDE WEB SITES

http://vbreitrein.layer2.de/projekt01 (click on the British flag for English translation)
http://www.doublecluck.com
http://www2.scholastic.com/teachers/authorsandbooks
http://www.bookbrowse.com

Bethany Hamilton 1990-
American Amateur Surfer and Shark-Attack Survivor

BIRTH

Bethany Hamilton was born on February 8, 1990, on the island of Kauai in Hawaii. Her father is Tom Hamilton, who works as a waiter. Her mother is Cheri (Lynch) Hamilton, who works in food service. She has two older brothers, Noah (who is about eight years older than Bethany) and Timmy (who is four years older).

YOUTH

Given her heritage, it's not surprising that Hamilton has spent much of her life on a surfboard. Both her father and mother have been avid surfers for decades. In fact, it was a love of waves that led both of them to the Hawaiian island of Kauai, where they met and were married. Their children were raised on the island, and the Hamiltons introduced Bethany to the ocean at a young age. She rode her first surfboard when she was just eight months old, though these outings were more like floating than surfing. "She was just tiny when my wife and I took her out," her father remembered. "I would push her on a longboard [a type of surfboard] and my wife would catch her. . . . She was always in the water."

The island of Kauai has a lot of water—and not all of it is in the ocean. It gets a large amount of rain, so beautiful waterfalls cascade down the steep mountainsides. The rain and warm temperatures make everything green and tropical. It is more remote and less commercial than some of the other Hawaiian islands, so the pace of life is slow. In her memoir, *Soul Surfer*, Hamilton noted that "having a home on a tiny island in the middle of the Pacific Ocean isn't for everybody. There are no big shopping malls, only a couple of movie theaters, no ice-skating rinks, no miniature golf or go-cart places." Still, she loves Hawaii and "wouldn't live anywhere else on the planet." Her favorite things about Kauai are its warm temperatures, its delicious tropical fruits, and, of course, the ocean.

Hamilton rode her first surfboard when she was just eight months old, though these outings were more like floating than surfing. "She was just tiny when my wife and I took her out," her father remembered. "I would push her on a longboard [a type of surfboard] and my wife would catch her. . . . She was always in the water."

Hamilton began real stand-up surfing when she was five years old. In the beginning, her parents would help her by pushing her into the waves, but by age seven she was able to get started by herself. She was always aware that there was a dangerous side to the ocean. While she believes that "surfing is a pretty safe sport," she has also been "bounced" off the sharp coral of the sea bottom after wiping out (falling off the board). In some cases, the force of a big wave has held her down under the water for a long period of time. "For a few minutes you become a little panicky," she said of such incidents, "and the thought 'I might drown' enters your mind. Then the wave lets you up again and you can breathe and you forget you were scared." Hamilton also knew that there were sharks lurking in the sea, but she and her friends didn't worry about them too much. "We were afraid of them," she said, "but we didn't really think anything would happen to us."

EDUCATION

During her elementary-school years, Hamilton attended regular public schools, one of which was Hanalei School, which is in the town of Hanalei. Beginning in the sixth grade, she entered a home-schooling program through the Myron B. Thompson Academy in Honolulu. One reason she switched to home schooling was that she needed to keep her schedule flexible. By that time she was becoming serious about competitive surfing, and the flexible schedule allowed her to train and attend surf meets. "There is no way I could go to a regular school and participate in professional surfing," she wrote. She knows that some people think that home-school students don't work hard at their education, but Hamilton says that isn't the case. "Let me tell you, homeschooling is no way easier than your traditional classroom. I have tests, and a mom who's pretty tough when it comes to making sure I hit those books and pull straight A's."

> "Let me tell you, home-schooling is no way easier than your traditional classroom. I have tests, and a mom who's pretty tough when it comes to making sure I hit those books and pull straight A's."

MAJOR INFLUENCES

The Hamilton family attends the North Shore Community Church on Kauai, and her Christian faith has long been one of the touchstones that Bethany relies upon. "All my life is based on God and Jesus," she has said. "If I didn't have them I'd be lost in the world." In addition to regular worship services, she attends weekly church-sponsored activities that involve games and barbecues mixed with Bible study. She also takes part in annual church camps that include such offbeat games as turkey football (using an uncooked turkey), concerts, speakers, and devotional activities.

Bethany and her best friend, Alana Blanchard, have been a duo since they were eight years old.

CAREER HIGHLIGHTS

Hamilton's first surfing contests were "push-and-ride" competitions, where parents assist the children. At age eight she was ready for the more advanced meets where she would be on her own for the entire ride. The first of these was the Rell Sun competition, which is held on the Hawaiian island of Oahu. Hamilton took first place in both divisions she entered (short board and long board) and went home with two trophies and two new surfboards. Soon, Hamilton became a regular on the amateur surfing circuit, and she continued to rack up wins. Her family encouraged her to work toward a career as a professional surfer—one of the select group of athletes who earn their living by competing in meets. It was a long-term goal—most people don't become professionals until they're adults—but Hamilton began a serious training program to make it happen.

As an amateur, Hamilton couldn't hope to win big cash prizes, but there was one financial incentive she could shoot for: a sponsorship. The most promising young surfers sign deals with companies that make surfing clothing and equipment. This provides them with free surfboards and accessories and also helps to cover the expenses of attending surf meets. Hamilton's brother Noah played a big role in seeking out a sponsorship for his sister. He created promotional packages and sent them off to companies in the surfing industry. His efforts and Hamilton's talent eventually won her a deal with Rip Curl.

Though she's known as a fierce competitor, Hamilton believes that "a surf contest is really about having fun." At most meets, she wrote, "winning is secondary to enjoying the surf, the beach, and all the companionship." In fact, Alana Blanchard, one of Hamilton's closest competitors, is also her best friend. Blanchard, who is also sponsored by Rip Curl, lives on Kauai, so she and Hamilton often train together and spend a lot of time together out of the water, too. "We are more like sisters than friends," Hamilton explained. "I can almost read her mind and she can read mine, so we don't have to spend a lot of time with words."

By the time she was 13, Hamilton was considered a very promising surfer. She was ranked No. 8 in the world in her age group. In October 2003, she scored one of her most impressive performances at the National Scholastic Surfing Association National Championships in San Clemente, California. She came in second in that meet, despite the fact that many of the competitors were older than she was. After the meet, she returned to Kauai and went right back to work. Even on Halloween, Hamilton planned to head for the ocean and another day of surfing.

> "*It's funny," Hamilton wrote in* Soul Surfer, *"you would think having your arm bitten off would really hurt. But there was no pain at the time. I felt pressure and kind of a jiggle-jiggle tug, which I know now was the teeth. They have serrated edges like a steak knife and they sawed through the board and my bones as if they were tissue paper."*

Shark Attack

That morning, she awoke at 5 a.m., and her mom drove her to "Tunnels," one of the surf spots along the north shore of the island. She paddled out with Alana Blanchard and Alana's brother and father. After a half-hour of surfing, the group was floating on their boards, waiting for a good-sized wave to roll in. Hamilton was dangling her left hand in the water, just as she had done countless times before. But this day was different—she was attacked by a shark.

"It's funny," Hamilton wrote in *Soul Surfer*, "you would think having your arm bitten off would really hurt. But there was no pain at the time. I felt pressure and kind of a jiggle-jiggle tug, which I know now was the teeth. They have serrated edges like a steak knife and they sawed through the board and my bones as if they were tissue paper." Hamilton had been attacked by a tiger shark, one of the most deadly predators in the ocean. "It was over in a few seconds," she wrote. "I remember seeing the water around me turn bright red with my blood. Then I saw that my arm had been bitten off almost to the shoulder. There was just a three- or four-inch stub where my limb had once been."

"It was over in a few seconds," Hamilton said about the attack. "I remember seeing the water around me turn bright red with my blood. Then I saw that my arm had been bitten off almost to the shoulder. There was just a three- or four-inch stub where my limb had once been."

Hamilton was in grave danger. Because blood was pouring from the severed arm, she could easily have bled to death. Fortunately, her companions did exactly the right things to keep her alive. After helping her get into calmer water closer to shore, Holt Blanchard (Alana's father) tied his rash guard (a protective shirt made of swimsuit material) around the arm to help slow the blood loss. He then towed Hamilton to shore. On the beach, he created a more effective tourniquet from a surf leash—a piece of rubber tubing that prevents surfers from losing their boards when they fall off. These tourniquets probably saved Hamilton's life. Even with them in place, she lost 60 percent of her blood, which could have been fatal in itself. The doctor who later treated her said that her conditioning had been a help. "This is a woman who is a highly trained athlete, and because of that she's able to handle a huge blood loss really well."

As for Hamilton, she attributed her survival to another source. "I might not be here if I hadn't asked for God's help," she said. "I was talking. I was praying. I don't know the exact words. I just asked for help." She also considered some less spiritual topics in the moments after the attack: "One thought that went through my head was 'I wonder if I'm going to lose my sponsors?'" After a long ambulance ride to Kauai's Wilcox Memorial Hospital, Hamilton underwent surgery to cleanly amputate her arm, then a second operation several days later. Strangely, when she was first brought to the hospital, her father was in the surgery unit, about to under-

go a non-emergency knee operation. In fact, his surgery was postponed when the surgeon learned that a shark-attack victim was on the way. Tom Hamilton was horrified to learn that the victim was his own daughter.

Bethany remained in the hospital for six days. Flowers and presents from well-wishers—many she had never met—filled her room. Even before she was released, she was showing that she was ready to get back on her feet. She played practical jokes on her nurses and visited with other patients. After being released, she admitted that the shark attack was "pretty much all I think about," but even then she was determined to come to terms with her misfortune. "There's no time machine," she said. "I can't change it. That was God's plan for my life and I'm going to go with it. . . . If you don't get over it, . . . then you'll just be sad and cry."

A Media Celebrity

Hamilton's story quickly became a sensation. Three days after the attack, such major TV shows as "The Today Show" and "Good Morning America" ran stories that included interviews with Hamilton's doctor and members of her family. The next day, a story on the attack made the front page of the *New York Times*. Kauai filled with members of the international media, who were eager for stories about Hamilton's ordeal. Her brothers created a web site about their sister, and thousands of e-mails arrived each day offering encouragement. By the time Hamilton was released from the hospital, journalists and TV crews were staking out the family home. Rather than face the cameras right away, the Hamiltons retreated to a borrowed beach house on Kauai so they could have some privacy.

> ———— " ————
>
> *"I might not be here if I hadn't asked for God's help,"Hamilton said. "I was talking. I was praying. I don't know the exact words. I just asked for help."*
>
> ———— " ————

The quiet didn't last for long. On November 21, Hamilton herself appeared on four major television shows in one day, including "Good Morning America" and "20/20." By this point, however, the family was taking a more careful approach to the publicity surrounding Bethany. They had hired Roy Hofstetter, an entertainment entrepreneur acquainted with the family, to serve as Hamilton's agent. It was Hofstetter's job to see that Hamilton got paid in addition to getting famous. "What I'm trying to do is make this 15 minutes of fame into Brand Bethany Hamilton," Hofstetter said in *USA Today*.

Within a few months of the accident, Hofstetter had arranged publicity tours for Hamilton. Soon, a book deal was signed, which led to the October 2004 publication of *Soul Surfer*. Rather than losing her sponsorship from Rip Curl, as Hamilton had feared after the accident, she was able to negotiate a more lucrative deal than she had before. The company was pleased to be associated with such a high-profile figure. "She's the most recognized surfer on the planet," said Adam Sharp, vice president of sales and marketing for the company.

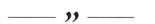

"It's hard for me to describe the joy I felt after I stood up and rode a wave in for the first time after the attack," Hamilton wrote in her book. *"I was incredibly thankful and happy inside. The tiny bit of doubt that would sometimes tell me 'You'll never surf again' was gone in one wave!"*

In addition to news/entertainment shows and talk shows, including "The Oprah Winfrey Show," Hamilton took part in an episode of the reality show "Switched," where she traded places with actress/songwriter Chantilly. She also starred in a promotional video for Volvo automobiles with horseracing jockey Greta Kuntzweiler. Contracts have been signed for a movie version of her life story. Hamilton is expected to do some of the surfing scenes for the film.

Being a celebrity has allowed Hamilton to earn some money, but she has found fame to be bittersweet. "Some parts are fun and some aren't so fun," she said. The fun included being able to meet other celebrities, receiving first-class treatment, and getting to tell a lot of people about her belief in Christianity. On the down side, she had to answer the same questions over and over about the shark attack. "I wish we had recorded my answers so we could just play them back," she said. She also dislikes the fact that strangers will sometimes interrupt her when she is out with her friends.

The Comeback

The main question asked by interviewers in the first weeks after the accident was whether Hamilton would return to surfing. She vowed that she would. "I'm definitely going to get back in the water," she said. "If I was like a person that just quit surfing after this, I wouldn't be a real surfer." Before hitting the surf, however, she had to get used to everyday life with just one arm. She learned how to tie her shoes with just one hand and

Hamilton's courageous return to her sport earned her the ESPY Award for Best Comeback Athlete in 2004.

how to peel an orange by holding it between her feet. She also had to deal with pain, which affected her for several weeks after she was released from the hospital.

Despite the difficulties, Hamilton wouldn't stay out of the ocean for long. Around Thanksgiving, just four weeks after the accident, she and her family headed for a secluded beach, and she once again stepped into the water. When she was later asked if she had any fear of the ocean, Hamilton said "I don't feel differently about the water, but I think of sharks more often." These thoughts didn't keep her off the waves. Just a few moments after wading into the sea, she reached for her surfboard. "This is the deal I made with myself," she later recalled: "I have to stand up and catch the first wave on my own." In other words, she didn't want any special assistance. Apparently she didn't need it. On just her third attempt she was up and surfing. "It's hard for me to describe the joy I felt after I stood up and rode a wave in for the first time after the attack," she wrote in her book. "I was incredibly thankful and happy inside. The tiny bit of doubt that would sometimes tell me 'You'll never surf again' was gone in one wave!"

Soon she was back to her daily workouts and planning to return to competition. There are only two differences in the equipment she uses now versus the gear she used before the accident: her board is slightly longer, and she uses a special strap that allows her to more easily guide the board out through the waves to her takeoff spot.

In January 2004, less than three months after the attack, Hamilton returned to surfing competition at Kailoa-Kona in Hawaii. In her first outing, she placed fifth. "It was definitely fun," she said of the contest. "But I've got a lot more work to do." In June, she won the junior girls' short-board competition at a meet in Hawaii. Then it was on to the National Scholastic Surfing Association (NSSA) Nationals, one of the most prestigious meets of the year. Hamilton showed she was again a serious competitor, finishing fifth. When the NSSA season resumed in August, she turned in one of her strongest performances since the attack. She won the women's open division in a meet held on her home island, Kauai.

> "I am not saying that God made the shark bite me. I think He knew it would happen, and He made a way for my life to be happy and meaningful in spite of it happening." In this way, Hamilton sees the horror of the accident working toward something positive. As she put it, "I think I may be able to do more good having one arm than when I had two."

Coping with Physical Disability

Some people who lose an arm are fitted with an artificial limb—a prosthesis. Thanks to technology, some of these devices can do many of the things that a real arm and hand can do—grasping objects, for instance. The problem in Hamilton's case is that her arm had been severed above the elbow and very close to the shoulder, which makes it more difficult to employ a technologically advanced prosthesis. Thus far, the only artificial arm that doctors have been able to provide for her is more for looks than anything else—it can't move by itself, and the hand can't hold objects. She hasn't worn the arm very often. "Maybe I look a little different without it," she wrote, "but that's okay. I'm cool being me."

Though her own life has plenty of challenges, Hamilton is using her fame to assist others. She has teamed up with the Christian humanitarian agency World Vision to raise money for disabled children all around the world. Hamilton also hopes that her story will serve as an inspiration. "I am sticking with surfing and following my dream," she said. "I hope people can learn to follow what they want to do and not give up."

But more than anything else, Hamilton hopes that she can use her notoriety to focus more attention on the teachings of Jesus. In doing this, she believes that she is fulfilling God's plan for her life. "I am not saying that God *made* the shark bite me," she wrote. "I think He knew it would happen, and He made a way for my life to be happy and meaningful *in spite* of it happening." In this way, Hamilton sees the horror of the accident working toward something positive. As she put it, "I think I may be able to do more good having one arm than when I had two."

HOME AND FAMILY

Hamilton lives with her family in the town of Princeville on Kauai. "They're my number one fans," she says of her parents and brothers. "Win or lose, they think I'm awesome, and I know I have their love and support no matter how I place in a contest." The family has a shar-pei dog named Ginger.

HOBBIES AND OTHER INTERESTS

Hamilton played on a soccer team for six years beginning when she was in the first grade. She also enjoys playing outdoor games with her friends such as "kick the can." When they're feeling more mischievous, they opt for "ding-dong ditch," where they ring someone's doorbell, then run away. Romance hasn't yet played a big part in her life. "Boys are fine," she wrote, "but to be honest, I am *so* busy right now that I don't have any time to think about them."

FAVORITE MUSIC AND TV PROGRAMS

Hamilton is a big fan of Christian-oriented rock bands, which she listens to on her way to and from the beach or while traveling by plane. When she finds time to watch television, she likes old programs like "Leave It to Beaver" and "Mr. Ed," though she also enjoys more recent shows, including "The Simpsons" and "SpongeBob SquarePants."

HONORS AND AWARDS

Chutzpah Award (*O* magazine): 2004
ESPY Award for Best Comeback (ESPN): 2004
Teen Choice Award for Courage: 2004
Wahine O Ke Kai Award (Surf Industry Manufacturers Association): 2004

FURTHER READING

Books

Hamilton, Bethany, with Sheryl Berk and Rick Bundschuh. *Soul Surfer: A True Story of Faith, Family, and Fighting to Get Back on the Board*, 2004

Periodicals

Honolulu Advertiser, Nov. 2, 2003, p.A1; Nov. 14, 2003, p.A1; Nov. 21, 2003, p.A1
Los Angeles Times, June 1, 2004, p.F4
New York Times, Nov. 4, 2003, p. A1
People, Dec. 1, 2003, p.62
Teen People, Nov. 2004, p.122
USA Today, Mar. 19, 2004, p.C15
YM, Feb. 2004, p.90

Online Articles

http://www.timeforkids.com/TFK/surfer
(*Time for Kids Online*, "Meet Bethany Hamilton, 13-Year-Old Surfer," Jan. 27, 2004)

ADDRESS

Bethany Hamilton
P.O. Box 863
Hanalei, HI 96714

WORLD WIDE WEB SITE

http://www.bethanyhamilton.com

Anne Hathaway 1982-

American Actress
Star of *The Princess Diaries* and *Ella Enchanted*

BIRTH

Anne Hathaway was born on November 12, 1982, in Brooklyn, New York. (She has the same name as the playwright William Shakespeare's wife—an early sign that she was bound for the world of drama.) Hathaway's mother is Kate McCauley, a retired actress, and her father is Gerald Hathaway, who works as a lawyer. She has two brothers, one older and one younger.

YOUTH

Hathaway spent her first years in Brooklyn, but her family moved to Milburn, New Jersey, when she was young, and she spent most of her childhood there. Acting grabbed her attention early on. Her mother, Kate McCauley, was a professional actress whose credits included the role of Fantine in a touring production of *Les Miserables*. McCauley gave up her acting career when Anne was about eight years old. But by that time Anne had already gotten a good look at the world of the theater, and she decided that that was where she belonged. "I just never imagined myself doing anything else," Hathaway said. "Even before I knew that acting was a profession that you could actually make money at."

Hathaway's parents weren't eager to have their daughter get into show business at a young age, however. They allowed her to study acting but kept her from pursuing professional roles until she was in her teens. "They so wanted me to have a normal life as a kid," Hathaway said. Though Anne ("Annie" to her family and friends) wasn't happy with her parents' decision, she later agreed that they were right to make her wait. "You can have a career at any age. You can't relive your childhood," she once said. "I hate to say I had a 'normal' childhood because I don't think anyone does, but you know, I had tea parties. I played soccer." In fact, Hathaway played a lot of other sports, too — softball, basketball, track, swimming, and tennis. She confesses to being a tomboy who didn't give much thought to maintaining a neat appearance. "I was a rough-and-tumble kid," she said, "and I broke a lot of bones."

> "
>
> *Hathaway wasn't happy with her parents' decision that she had to wait until her teens to act professionally, but she later agreed that they were right. "You can have a career at any age. You can't relive your childhood," she once said. "I hate to say I had a 'normal' childhood because I don't think anyone does, but you know, I had tea parties. I played soccer."*
>
> "

The Awkward Phase

As she approached her teen years, Hathaway had some trouble adjusting to the changes she was going through. "I had an awkward phase that lasted for years," she recalled. "I was a 15-year-old who was 5-foot-8 and looked like I was 12." She grew more clumsy as she got taller. Even years later she called herself "a dork." Love also shook up her life. In an article she wrote for *Seventeen*, Hathaway described how she adapted her appearance and attitudes to try to impress a guy she liked. When the relationship later ended, she had trouble rediscovering her own opinions.

One of her convictions never wavered, however: She wanted to be an actress. As she got older, her mother and father began to allow her more freedom to pursue her passion, and she had her first professional audition at age 15. "They were supportive," Hathaway said of her parents' attitude toward her acting. "But they never shied away from telling me how tough it was. They let me know exactly how tough it was. And I didn't care."

EDUCATION

Hathaway got her first taste of serious acting at the Paper Mill Playhouse in her hometown of Milburn. It's a well-respected professional theater that also offers theater education programs. Hathaway attended the Paper Mill Conservatory and appeared in several productions at the theater while she was in middle school. As Robert Johanson, artistic director of the Paper Mill, told the *New York Times*, "Annie always had this beautiful luminous quality about her. There are certain indescribable things that indicate star quality, and Annie has got it."

Hathaway also studied with the Barrow Group, a famous theater group in New York City. The fact that she was able to gain admittance to the Barrow Group showed that her acting talents were beginning to impress people. In fact, she was the first teenager that Barrow ever accepted.

Hathaway did well in her other studies, too. She was an honor student at Milburn High School, where she received top grades in all of her classes — except for math. "I was not in the most-popular clique," she said of her high-school days, but she had a group of good friends, some of whom have stayed close to her since graduation. High school also gave her the chance to develop her singing talents. She was part of the All-Eastern U.S. High School Honors Choir, which performed at the famed Carnegie Hall in New York City when Hathaway was 16.

Part-Time College Student

After graduating from high school, Hathaway enrolled at Vassar College in Poughkeepsie, New York, where she is majoring in English. Because her film career took off at about the same time that she entered college, she has taken several extended breaks from Vassar in order to work on movies.

(She usually has to withdraw for an entire semester because film productions can extend over several months.) Hathaway remains committed to getting her education, however. "In school, I can be in a place where reading 500 pages by Wednesday is more important than losing 5 pounds before the audition Wednesday," she said. "It's good for me to be around that. And there are other times when I can't concentrate [on school work] and I need to go and burn off some career energy."

During her first college semester in 2001, *The Princess Diaries* had just been released, so Hathaway didn't receive any special attention on campus. "I'm not Annie the movie star," she said then, "I'm just Annie." But as she became better known, she found herself being noticed more often. Sometimes other students approach her and ask if she's "that movie star." Hathaway usually responds, "I don't think I am." Otherwise, her college experience has been pretty typical. "You've never lived until you've shared a dorm bathroom with 10 guys," she said. "And then walked down the hallway with zit cream all over your face."

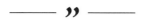

> *Hathaway's college experience has been pretty typical. "You've never lived until you've shared a dorm bathroom with 10 guys," she said. "And then walked down the hallway with zit cream all over your face."*

CAREER HIGHLIGHTS

Hathaway's first big break came when she was 16. She landed a role in "Get Real," a drama series on the Fox Network that premiered in the fall of 1999. She played Meghan, a smart but rebellious teenager who is a central figure in the Green family, which also includes two anxious parents and two brothers. Though she was the same age as the character she was playing, Hathaway found that she didn't always identify with her onscreen persona. "I like Meghan very much," she said, "but there are times when I just go, 'Oh, you're such a shallow wench!'" The show ran just one season before being canceled, despite the fact that it had earned decent reviews and some enthusiastic fans.

While the series wasn't a huge success, it did bring Hathaway to the attention of more casting directors. She soon landed a supporting role in the movie *The Other Side of Heaven* (2001), in which she played the wife of a Mormon missionary in the 1950s. It was a modest role in a modest film, but like the television series, it led to something larger. *The Other Side of Heaven* was filmed in New Zealand, which forced Hathaway to make a

The cast of "Get Real."

very long flight halfway around the world. She decided to stop off in Los Angeles on the way. While there she got the chance to audition for another film. It was some sort of modern fairy tale — a story about a girl who suddenly becomes something much different than what she was before.

Becoming a Princess

Hathaway had the good fortune to land an audition for a part in the movie *The Princess Diaries*, based on the novel by Meg Cabot. (For more information on Cabot, see *Biography Today Authors*, Vol. 12.) "I was shaking during the entire audition, but apparently nobody noticed," Hathaway later re-

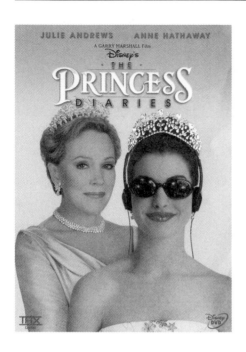

called. She had good reason to be nervous: she was meeting with Garry Marshall, the Hollywood producer and director who had helped create such motion pictures as *Pretty Woman* and *Runaway Bride*, as well as oodles of TV series, including "Happy Days," "Laverne & Shirley," and "Mork & Mindy."

This time, Marshall was getting ready to direct *The Princess Diaries*, and he needed a princess. Hathaway did her best to impress him, but then she goofed up and acted like a klutz. "It was just one of those things where you get up and your foot kind of hits the leg of the chair as you're doing it," she said. "And you sort of trip a little, and sit back down and get up very gracefully. Then you pretend like nothing ever happened while you're trying to ignore other people laughing at you. . . . I'm such a dork. I can't believe I fell off my chair."

Fortunately, a klutz was just who the director was looking for. "That's what we wanted," Marshall said. "Pretty and vulnerable and ungainly." Hathaway got the part, and once production began on the movie, she found herself tripping all over the place — on purpose. In *The Princess Diaries* she played Mia Thermopolis, a teenager from San Francisco who is quite clumsy and far from glamorous. Little does she suspect that she's actually a member of a royal family. Her father, who Mia never met and has recently died, was the prince of Genovia, a tiny European kingdom. Her mother kept this fact from Mia, but when her grandmother — Queen Clarisse of Genovia — arrives for a visit, the truth comes out. Mia is heir to the throne, and Queen Clarisse, played by Julie Andrews, sets out to transform Mia into a fitting princess.

The Princess Diaries was released in 2001 and became a big hit, especially with girls and their mothers. Movie critics were less impressed with the film as a whole, but many of them liked Hathaway's performance. *Newsweek* reviewer Devin Gordon praised her "gawky, witty performance." Elvis Mitchell, writing in the *New York Times*, stated that "Ms. Hathaway is royalty in the making, a young comic talent with a scramble of features: a

Anne Hathaway, Heather Matarazzo, and Robert Schwartzman
in a scene from The Princess Diaries.

loveably broad Grecian nose, a cloud of curly hair and charisma that recalls Julia Roberts. The camera is mad about her."

Flattering Comparisons

Mitchell wasn't the only one to compare Hathaway to Julia Roberts. The two actresses did have a few things in common. Both had become known for their wide smiles and both made their breakthroughs in films directed by Garry Marshall. Roberts had become a star after appearing in Marshall's *Pretty Woman*, and more than a few reviewers stated that *The Princess Diaries* had a very similar story. Hathaway was flattered by the comparison. "I suppose if you're going to be compared to someone, who better to be compared to," she said of Roberts. "I only hope one day I can be as good as her." Marshall himself said that Hathaway reminded him of Roberts, as well as screen legends Audrey Hepburn and Judy Garland.

Julie Andrews, Hathaway's co-star in *The Princess Diaries*, was also a big influence on the young actress. Hathaway had admired Andrews long before the two worked together. "I was so nervous," Hathaway said of meeting Andrews. "But she pulled me into an enormous bear hug and made me feel at ease. She is just so lovely." Andrews, a legendary star of stage and film musicals (including *The Sound of Music* and *Mary Poppins*), even complimented Hathaway on her singing voice. "To hear that from Julie Andrews, who has been one of my heroes since I was three years old, was one of the defining moments of my life," Hathaway said.

On Stage

Once she had a hit movie under her belt, Hathaway found lots of offers coming her way. Many movie actors go immediately from one film project to the next, but Hathaway didn't commit to her next motion picture right away. This was partly because she wanted to devote some time to her college studies but also because the scripts she read didn't thrill her. "Nothing has spoken to me the way *The Princess Diaries* did," she said. "I'm holding out."

> ―――― " ――――
>
> *When Hathaway first met actor Hugh Dancy during the auditions for* Ella Enchanted, *she found herself looking forward to the production more than usual. "I thought, 'Oh my God, I get to work with this guy for three months? Woo-hoo!'"*
>
> ―――― " ――――

When she did return to acting, it wasn't in the movies. She joined a production of the musical play *Carnival* that was part of the *Encores!* series presented in New York City in early 2002. Taking the part of Lili, Hathaway got a chance to show off her singing talents. Because it was part of a larger presentation, just five performances of the play were staged. But that was enough for Hathaway to make a big impression. She won one of the Clarence Derwent Awards, which honor the most promising newcomers to the New York drama scene. Though she enjoyed performing in the play, Hathaway said that, for her, singing was "just for fun." She has entertained the idea of recording an album but claims that she doesn't want a Britney-Spears-style music career. "I have no aspirations of world domination through the pop charts," she clarified. "That's not me."

Ella Enchanted

Hathaway's next film role was as a supporting character in *Nicholas Nickleby* (2002). After that, she turned her attention to a starring role in *Ella Enchanted* (2004), based on the best-selling book for young readers by Gail

Ella Enchanted.

Carson Levine. (For more information on Levine, see *Biography Today Authors*, Vol. 17.) The movie relates the adventures of Ella of Frell, in a reworked version of the fairy-tale character Cinderella. Thanks to a misguided fairy, Ella receives the curse of obedience; any time she is told to do something, she immediately obeys. Desperately unhappy with this condition, Ella tries to escape the spell. In the process, she meets the dashing Prince Charmont, played by British actor Hugh Dancy.

Hathaway found the real-life Dancy just as dashing as his character. When she first met him during the movie auditions, she found herself looking forward to the production more than usual. "I thought, 'Oh my God, I get to work with this guy for three months? Woo-hoo!'" A few press stories tried to link the two romantically, but Hathaway said that she and Dancy were only friends. "He's too busy enjoying the bachelor lifestyle right now," she declared.

In the style of *Shrek*, *Ella Enchanted* mixed hip, semi-modern elements (such as medieval-style shopping malls) into the fairy-tale setting of Levine's book. It also included jokey gags and plot devices borrowed from other movies. A lot of movie critics found this combination too uneven, and they gave the movie mixed reviews. Hathaway's performance generally got high marks, however. A review in *Variety*, for instance, stated that "the glue that holds the sweet teen-fantasy together is star Anne Hathaway, who continues to evolve into a luminous young lead."

More Royal Treatment

Shortly after she completed work on *Ella Enchanted*, Hathaway began work on *The Princess Diaries 2: The Royal Engagement*, the sequel to her breakout film. "I was very wary of doing a sequel," she said, but she ended up enjoying the experience. "We had so much more fun on the second one," she explained, because she was less nervous about her performance. One part of the process wasn't very fun, though — the auditioning of Mia's love interest. Director Garry Marshall made her go through a kissing scene with all of the actors he was considering for the part. "Don't get me wrong, I love kissing," Hathaway said, "but the idea of having to kiss 12 different people that I've just met in one 10-hour period of time is a little much for me."

> "It's going to sound so cheesy, but I just love acting," Hathaway said. "I love learning about new parts of myself through characters, and getting lost in people and learning how to breathe differently because all of a sudden you're this different person."

The sequel proved popular with young moviegoers, cementing Hathaway's reputation as a big star in the 'tween and teen market. She has often been asked if she feels any responsibility to set a good example for her young fans. She said that her characters might serve as role models, but that she herself doesn't want to be one. "Ultimately I can't live my life based on the hopes that people are inspired by my actions," she said. "I'd feel very phony."

Putting Away the Tiara

The Princess Diaries 2 was the third film in which Hathaway played a princess-type figure. She has joked that she's the "go-to tiara girl," but also feels that it may be time to leave those roles behind. "In terms of the princess role, there is only so long that you can play those as a young lady before you start feeling really ridiculous," she admitted. "I think I've done a lot in this genre, and I'm ready to tackle new ones." Hathaway has already shot two movies that allow her to try new roles. Both are expected to be re-

A scene from The Princess Diaries 2: The Royal Engagement.

leased in 2005. One is *Brokeback Mountain*, which is set in the 1960s and focuses on the relationship between two cowboys, played by Jake Gyllenhaal and Heath Ledger. Hathaway plays a former rodeo rider who is married to Gyllenhaal's character, while Michelle Williams plays the wife of Ledger's character.

An even bigger departure from Hathaway's wholesome image is her role in *Havoc*. Her character is part of a group of affluent teenagers who become obsessed with gang culture and get into drugs, violence and sex. Hathaway has even admitted that she appears topless in the movie. She felt that the nudity "was necessary for the film," but some of her fans have been shocked at the news. "It's not sexy," she explained. "I have seen the scenes and they are so uncomfortable. You look at this girl and think: 'What are you doing?' You want to smack her across the face." Hathaway has also made it clear that *Havoc* is not intended for the young viewers who loved her other films. There has been some media concern about the motion picture and whether Hathaway was wise to have starred in it. At times, she has seemed unsure of the movie herself. "Let's just say my process for choosing films is different because of *Havoc*," she said, suggesting that she isn't completely happy with the choice she made.

Hathaway may not be thrilled with all of her movies, but she remains committed to a life on stage and screen. "It's going to sound so cheesy, but I just love acting," she said. "I love learning about new parts of myself through characters, and getting lost in people and learning how to breathe differently because all of a sudden you're this different person." Though she's had a lot of success, she claims that fame and fortune aren't what motivate her. "Honestly, I love acting so much, I just find the success part of it hysterical. I would be acting in church basements if I had to."

> *Hathaway claims that fame and fortune aren't what motivate her. "Honestly, I love acting so much, I just find the success part of it hysterical. I would be acting in church basements if I had to."*

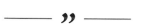

HOME AND FAMILY

Hathaway divides her time among several different places. When she's not working on location or attending college in Poughkeepsie, New York, she usually lives in New York City. On occasion, she also spends extended periods in Los Angeles. She remains close with her family and even employs her cousin Meredith, who she considers her best friend, as her personal assistant. Hathaway has had several boyfriends over the years but doesn't seem to have settled on the love of her life. "I still do believe that in my future I will end up with one person," she said, "but I have no assurances of that so I'm just having fun in the interim." She also claims that men pay little attention to her. "I never ever, ever, ever get hit on, wherever I go. . . . Guys really don't come up to me, or they come up and get autographs for their little sisters and then they go away. So I usually do most of the approaching. . . . I mean, how else am I going to get a date?"

HOBBIES AND OTHER INTERESTS

Hathaway enjoys writing, yoga, and cooking. "For the most part I lead a very healthy lifestyle," she said. "I just feel better that way, especially when I'm working." On the other had, she confesses to occasionally cutting loose. "I am your average, red-blooded 21-year-old girl, and every so often I brush up on my partying skills." Hathaway listens to a lot of different kinds of music. She has declared that "Bob Marley is God," and her other favorites include the Dandy Warhols, the Strokes, and Bjork.

SELECTED CREDITS

Television Series

"Get Real," 1999-2000

Movies

The Other Side of Heaven, 2001
The Princess Diaries, 2001
Nicholas Nickleby, 2002
Ella Enchanted, 2004
The Princess Diaries 2: The Royal Engagement, 2004
The Cat Returns, 2005 (voice of the animated character Haru)

Plays

"Carnival" at Encores!, 2002

HONORS AND AWARDS

Clarence Derwent Award (Actors' Equity Association): 2002, for *"Carnival"
at Encores!*

FURTHER READING

Periodicals

Bergen County (NJ) Record, Apr. 21, 2002, p.E4; Apr. 6, 2004, p.F7
Los Angeles Daily News, Apr. 8, 2004, p.U4
Los Angeles Times, Apr. 18, 2004, p.E29
Milwaukee Journal Sentinel, July 30, 2001, p.01E
New York Times, Aug. 5, 2001, p.3; Feb. 18, 2002, p.E1
Newark (NJ) Star-Ledger, Apr. 11, 2004, p.1
Seventeen, Sep. 2001; Feb. 2003, p.102
Teen People, June 1, 2004, p.69
USA Today, Aug. 3, 2001, p.E2

Online Database

Biography Resource Center Online, 2002

Online Articles

http://actionadventure.about.com/cs/weeklystories/a/aa040704.htm
(About.com, "Anne Hathaway's Enchanting Interview," undated)

http://elle.com
(*Elle* magazine, "Later, Princess," Nov. 2004)
http://www.kidzworld.com
(*Kidzworld*, "Biography: Anne Hathaway," undated)
http://www.seventeen.com
(*Seventeen.com*, Anne Hathaway, "I Was Lousy at Being Myself," Sep. 2001)
http://www.teenhollywood.com/d.asp?r=64953
(*Teen Hollywood*, "The 'Enchanting' Anne Hathaway," Apr. 7, 2004)
http://www.usaweekend.com
(*USA Weekend*, Kevin Maynard, "Up-and-Comers: Beyond the Fairy Tale," Apr. 11, 2004)

ADDRESS

Anne Hathaway
The Walt Disney Company
500 South Buena Vista Street
Burbank, CA 91521

WORLD WIDE WEB SITES

http://disney.go.com/disneyvideos/liveaction/princessdiaries/main.html
http://disney.go.com/disneyvideos/liveaction/princessdiaries2
http://www.miramax.com/ellaenchanted

Priest Holmes 1973-

American Professional Football Player for the
Kansas City Chiefs

BIRTH

Priest Anthony Holmes was born on October 7, 1973, in Fort
Smith, Arkansas. Holmes never knew his biological father,
and he has never revealed the man's name. In fact, he never
laid eyes on his dad until he attended his funeral in 1989. "I
just stared at the casket," Holmes said, recalling the event,
"and I didn't know who the man was." Fortunately, his mother, Norma, has always been a very big part of her son's life.
When Priest was four years old, Norma married Herman

Morris, who became the father figure that helped guide Holmes as he grew up. "He is my dad," Holmes said of Morris. "He was always there for me. He always encouraged me in everything I did." The family, which included Holmes's older sister, settled in San Antonio, Texas, where Morris worked as a civilian aircraft technician at Kelly Air Force Base.

It was Norma who chose the unusual name of Priest, which he hasn't always embraced. He was known as Anthony Holmes during high school and his first two years of college, but he eventually came to accept his given name.

YOUTH

Early on, Holmes discovered the sport that would one day make him famous. "He just loved football," his mother recalled. "It seemed like every time you wanted to find him, he'd be outside playing football. He was just a natural at it." While plenty of kids fall in love with a sport, not many of them give it the same dedication that Holmes did. "All my energy went toward making me a better football player," he said. "I wasn't gonna go ride my bike just to ride it. I was gonna go ride it for endurance."

> "All my energy went toward making me a better football player," Holmes said. "I wasn't gonna go ride my bike just to ride it. I was gonna go ride it for endurance."

While football was important, it wasn't the only force that shaped Holmes's personality as he grew up. "Religion is a very big part of my life," he said. "I was brought up with the Lord." His family attended Greater Lincoln Park Temple, a non-denominational church in San Antonio. One day, when Holmes was still in middle school, Pastor Ronald Smith called him to the front of the church. After bowing his head in prayer, the pastor announced that he was bound for greatness. "He said God had revealed to him that Priest was going to do well in football," recalled his stepfather, Herman Morris. "He said that God had his hands on Priest, that he was going to mold him and shape him." Holmes has held onto this idea ever since — that his success on the playing field is a matter of divine fate. Even as a pro, his locker contains a framed copy of the Prayer of Jabez, which thanks God that "Your hand would be with me." Holmes's faith has helped him overcome many obstacles in his career. "I think God already has determined everything for me," he said, "and I'm just going to do my best to follow along."

Though Holmes possessed athletic ability, desire, and a sense of mission, there was one thing he didn't have: size. By the time he was a teenager, it was becoming clear that he was going to reach a rather average height and weight. Even today, he's smaller than most running backs in the NFL, standing just five feet, nine inches tall and weighing just 213 pounds. But Holmes knew that other average-sized players had made it to the pros, and one of them became his idol—Dallas Cowboys running back Tony Dorsett. "He wasn't the biggest guy," Holmes said of Dorsett, "and seeing him kind of made me think that I could do what he did."

To help make up for his small size, Holmes worked hard to get himself in the best shape he could. He used what was available—which turned out to be his sister's car. To build his muscles, Holmes would pick up the back end of her car and move it around the driveway. He also developed his leaping ability by hurdling over the hoods of parked cars in his neighborhood.

EDUCATION

Holmes attended John Marshall High School in San Antonio. He joined the varsity team as a sophomore and became the centerpiece of the offense in his junior and senior years. In his final year at Marshall, Holmes emerged as one of the best players in Texas. He rushed for 2,000 yards, scored 26 touchdowns, and was named Offensive Player of the Year. He led his team to the 5A, Division II state championship game. Though Holmes scored an important touchdown in the game, Marshall was defeated 27-14.

Though his athletic ability made him the center of attention on the field, Holmes was shy and quiet elsewhere. "He never said anything in high school," said his friend and Marshall teammate Mike Gann. This side of his character hasn't changed much over the years, even after he became a pro. "To this day, you can count the words he has said around the locker room," said his Kansas City teammate Will Shields. "We all knew he could run, but we kind of wondered if he could talk." In high school, the only memorable thing about Holmes's off-the-field personality was his wardrobe. He was voted the school's best dresser.

Holmes has made few comments about his classroom studies in high school, but he did well enough to earn his diploma in 1992. He was recruited by many colleges, but he chose to attend the University of Texas (U-T) in Austin, which is about 90 miles northeast of San Antonio. Holmes began his studies there in the fall of 1992. Not much is known about his college academic interests. He never earned a degree from the university.

CAREER HIGHLIGHTS

College — The University of Texas Longhorns

U-T has produced many legendary running backs over the years, and Holmes hoped to become one of that select group. One of the best runners ever to wear the Longhorn uniform was Earl Campbell, who won the Heisman Trophy, which honors the best college player in the nation. He later went on to a Hall-of-Fame professional career with the Houston Oilers and New Orleans Saints. While Campbell was an example of what a talented running back could accomplish, he also served as a warning about the dangers of football. After six strong seasons in the pros, the physical punishment began to take its toll on Campbell, who now has difficulty walking. This served as a lesson to Holmes, who got to meet him at U-T. "We had Earl Campbell come around during practice," Holmes remembered. "We would see him and the condition he was in. It made you think as a running back if you would end up the same way."

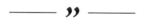

> "We had Earl Campbell come around during practice," Holmes said about the Hall-of-Fame running back, who now has trouble walking as a result of his punishing professional career. "We would see him and the condition he was in. It made you think as a running back if you would end up the same way."

Like many other college players, Holmes saw only limited playing time in his first two seasons. In his junior year in 1994, however, he became the Longhorns' top back. He rushed for more than 100 yards in each of the first three games and helped power Texas to a successful season. The team earned a post-season invitation to play in the Sun Bowl, where they met the University of North Carolina. Holmes had the break-out game of his college career in the bowl game. He rushed for 161 yards and scored four touchdowns. His final score came when he made a soaring leap into the end zone, vaulting over the Carolina defenders in the same way that he used to clear the hoods of parked cars. The score gave Texas a hard-fought 35-31 win.

Holmes was expected to be the key to the Longhorn offense the following season — his senior year — but it was not to be. During a spring practice just a few months after the Sun Bowl, another player rolled into Holmes's

Holmes scored three touchdowns in this 1996 Big 12 Championship game against the Univeristy of Nebraska.

left leg, and he felt pain shoot through his knee. He had torn his anterior cruciate ligament, or ACL. Just like that, he was through with football for 1995. Holmes decided to delay his senior season for one year so that he could concentrate on getting his knee back to its old condition. He did that by spending a lot of time in the weight room. "He went in trying to fix his knee," said Texas running-back coach Bucky Godbolt of his weight-room workouts, "and came out a hulk." Holmes packed on muscle, going from 185 to 210 pounds while retaining his slender build.

Pumping iron wasn't enough to get Holmes back into the starting lineup for 1996, however. In the year that he had been sidelined, two new running backs had taken over the Texas backfield. One of them was Ricky Williams, a superstar in the making, who went on to win the Heisman Trophy before playing in the NFL. With the other backs doing so well, Holmes's playing time was limited. Many players would have become frustrated by this situation, but not Holmes. "He never complained," said Texas head coach John Mackovic. "He only worked." He became a short-yardage specialist and racked up 13 touchdowns for the year. He also proved himself a big-game player, scoring three touchdowns in the

Longhorns' victory in the Big 12 championship game. Though his college career had had its ups and downs, Holmes remained positive about the experience—even about his knee injury. "It's the best thing that ever happened to me," he said. "I matured so much in the year I was hurt." He also became better acquainted with the divine force that he felt was directing his life. "I just had faith that God has a plan," he said.

———— **"** ————

When Holmes became a pro, he didn't adopt a lavish lifestyle that he couldn't afford. He didn't buy an expensive car, and he didn't move into a mansion, either. Instead, he rented an apartment and didn't even bother to buy much furniture. "He had blankets and pillows, linens, but no bed," his stepfather said. "He used boxes and stuff as tables. He had a small TV and a VCR to watch game films. It was very humbling."

———— **"** ————

The Pros, Part 1—The Baltimore Ravens

If God did have a plan, it wasn't a simple one. When the NFL draft took place in April 1997, Holmes wasn't chosen by any of the professional teams. He was then forced to offer his services as a free agent, which meant that he couldn't hope for a big contract. He signed with the Baltimore Ravens, and his initial payday was indeed humble: while top professional prospects receive millions of dollars in signing bonuses when they accept their contracts, Holmes received just $2,500.

Fortunately, he didn't adopt a lavish lifestyle that he couldn't afford. Unlike many new pros, he didn't buy an expensive car—he kept the nine-year-old Mustang he had driven in college. He didn't move into a mansion, either—he rented an apartment in Baltimore, and he didn't even bother to buy much furniture. "He had blankets and pillows, linens, but no bed," his stepfather said. "He used boxes and stuff as tables. He had a small TV and a VCR to watch game films. It was very humbling."

His first season as a pro was also humble. He played in just seven games as a rookie, all on kicking teams. Still, Holmes worked hard in practice and in the weight room and waited for his chance. It came during the second season. In his first game as a starter, he ran for 173 yards and scored two touchdowns. He was named AFC Offensive Player of the Week for that performance, and there were more to come. Several weeks later he rolled up a whopping 227 yards against the Cincinnati Bengals. By the close of the season, Holmes had run for 1,008 yards and scored seven touchdowns. The unknown free agent suddenly found himself being compared with the better running backs in the league.

Second Fiddle

For Priest Holmes, history has a way of repeating itself. At Texas, his promising junior year had been followed by a serious injury. He had learned that the legs he depended on could come up lame. In Baltimore in 1999, he learned that lesson again. On a different field, a different ligament gave way—this one in his

Holmes in action with the Baltimore Ravens.

right knee. He played in only nine games that season, stalling his run toward greatness. The second injury didn't sideline him as long as the first, but the effect was the same. Just as at Texas, another running back took over his starting position. Fearing that Holmes might not recover from his injury, the Ravens made running back Jamal Lewis their number one pick in the 2000 draft. When the following season began, Lewis was the starter, and Holmes was once again the backup.

But Holmes's response to adversity has a way of repeating itself, too. "To me, it was just another setback, but I wasn't going to let that stop me," he said. Just as he had at Texas, he kept a positive attitude and did what he could for the team. He even helped teach Jamal Lewis how to handle NFL defenses. "Even though Priest knew Jamal was going to get his job, he supported Jamal through the whole process," said Ernest Byner, the director of player development for the Ravens. "Not a lot of guys would do that."

Lewis had a big year, and so did the rest of the Ravens. Though Holmes never regained his starting spot, he came off the bench when needed, rolling up 588 yards in rushing. Powered by an excellent defense, the Ravens marched through the playoffs and earned a spot in Super Bowl XXXV. There, the Ravens became world champions in a 34-7 win. Holmes had earned a Super Bowl ring, but he had also played his final game as a

Baltimore Raven. His four-year contract expired at the end of the season. This meant that he was free to sign with another NFL team, and Holmes was determined to find a new home where he could be the starting running back.

The Pros, Part 2 — The Kansas City Chiefs

"It had to be the right place," Holmes said. "I wanted to go someplace where everything fit, so I sat down and made a list." When he matched his list against prospective teams, he came up with an answer: the Kansas City Chiefs. In April 2001 Holmes signed a five-year, $8 million contract with the Chiefs. He collected a $2 million signing bonus — 800 times more than the bonus he had gotten from the Ravens in 1997.

> *Holmes's running is explosive — he can accelerate quickly, which allows him to burst through small openings created by his blockers. "My strength is breaking people down,"* he said. *"I may not outrun or outsize you, but I will make you miss."*

And then Homes set out to fulfill his destiny as a great NFL player. In his first two games as a Chief, he had some difficulty getting adjusted to the new system. But in game three, he hit his stride. As the season progressed, he put together a string of seven straight 100-yard games and ended with 1,551 rushing yards for the season — the most in the NFL. He also chalked up an additional 600 yards on passing plays and scored 10 touchdowns. In short, he became one of the top running backs in football in the course of one season. "This guy — the more you give him the ball, the better he gets," said Chiefs head coach Dick Vermeil. "No one has ever given him the ball as many times as we have. Maybe nobody's ever found out how good he is."

This stellar performance wasn't enough to turn the Chiefs into winners: the team finished with six wins and 10 losses for 2001. Still, it was a sweet year for Holmes. He capped the season by being named to the AFC Pro Bowl team. On hearing the news, he was so excited that he invited his entire team to join him in Hawaii for the game — at his expense. "I think he put his foot in his mouth when he said he'd take the whole team to Hawaii," said Tony Gonzalez, one of Holmes's teammates. "That's gotta hit him in the pocket." In the end, about 12 players made the trip to Hawaii, and the Chiefs' other Pro-Bowler, Will Shields, helped pay their way.

Holmes's explosive speed allows him to accelerate quickly past his opponents.

Work and Will

Pinning down the secret to Holmes's success isn't simple. He's not a large back, and in terms of all-out speed, he's not that fast, either. His running is explosive, however—he can accelerate quickly, which allows him to burst through small openings created by his blockers. "My strength is breaking people down," he said. "I may not outrun or outsize you, but I will make you miss." Perhaps more important than his physical abilities is the all-out effort he brings to each play. "Priest is a beast," said Marcellus Wiley of the San Diego Chargers. "A lot of guys have talent, but he gets a lot of yards because of his will." Coach Dick Vermeil makes a similar point. "There are a number of guys in the NFL who are darned good running backs, but they don't give the third and fourth little extra effort at the end of certain runs. They are thinking about protecting their careers. But not Priest Holmes. This guy runs with violence, and with continual violence all through the run, until there is no more run."

Holmes also works very hard before the game even begins. He studies films relentlessly—footage of his opponents and of himself—searching for ways to improve his performance. For example, following the 2001 season, he spent days reviewing the 411 plays he had been involved in during the year, analyzing each play over and over to see what he had done right and wrong. "His mental preparation is second to nobody I've ever been around," said Vermeil.

> ———— " ————
>
> *The day before each game, Holmes walks through each play in the Chiefs' game plan, rehearsing the moves he will need to make the following day. "I have to go through it, I have to visualize it, I have to see it happen," he explained. "It's a matter of muscle memory. I've already practiced it, so I shouldn't even be thinking of any of this stuff on Sunday. It should be very natural."*
>
> ———— " ————

During the season, Holmes follows an unusual routine the day before each game. After the Chiefs' regular practice concludes, he remains on the field by himself. Beginning on one end of the field, he walks through each play in the Chiefs' game plan, rehearsing the moves he will need to make the following day. "I have to go through it, I have to visualize it, I have to see it happen," he explained. "It's a matter of muscle memory. I've already practiced it, so I shouldn't even be thinking of any of this stuff on Sunday. It should be very natural."

As the 2002 season opened, many experts felt that Holmes wouldn't be able to equal his performance from the previous year. Some questioned his endurance. Others felt that opponents would be keying on the Chiefs' star player and would have more success in shutting him down. As the season unfolded, Holmes did not match his 2001 numbers—he exceeded them. He rushed for 1,615 yards and added more than 600 yards as a pass receiver. He scored more touchdowns than anyone in the league with 24. He was named NFL Offensive Player of the Year. All of this was made even more impressive by the fact that he missed the final two games of the season. Had he played those games, he would have had a very good chance to have set the NFL single-season records for yards rushed and touchdowns scored.

Feeling the Pain, Counting the Dollars

But Holmes did not play in those final 2002 games. On a mid-December day in Denver, he was hauled down after a long run, and when his hip hit the ground, something felt wrong. As quickly as that, he was out of the game and out for the season. He had surgery on his injured hip in March 2003, then began the rehabilitation process once again. In some ways he was as determined as ever. He told his old high-school coach "I will outwork this injury." Yet there was also a note of caution in his voice shortly after he was sidelined. "I think this is my body telling me, 'Hey, you're not Superman. . . . You can't ignore this.'"

After injuring his hip in this December 2002 game against the Denver Broncos, Holmes missed the rest of the season.

Holmes had something else on his mind during the off-season: money. The contract he had signed with the Chiefs in 2001 was still in effect, but in the two years since, he had proven himself one of the best running backs in pro football. He felt that he deserved a new, higher-paying contract. The Chiefs didn't disagree, but his most recent injury made them nervous about handing over more money. Relations between Holmes and the Chiefs' front office became somewhat strained. Usually quiet and unassuming, he made public comments about how he wanted to "get paid," which angered the Chiefs' management. Eventually, however, Holmes convinced team president Carl Peterson that he was fully recovered from his hip injury, and the two sides came to an agreement that extended his contract by four years and has the potential to pay him $35 million. Holmes was pleased with the deal. "I have three kids," he said, "and this money allows me to take care of them and my extended family."

Then it was back to work for the 2003 season. It was a typical outing for Holmes — which is to say, it was exceptional. He ran for 1,420 yards. He caught passes for 690 yards. He scored touchdowns. In fact, he scored 27 of them — more than any player has ever scored in a single season in the history of the NFL. The Chiefs as a team had a great year, too. They won the first nine games and finished the regular season with 13 wins and three losses, winning their division. When he had first joined the Chiefs, Holmes had said "I believe we can put it together and push this team over the hump." That finally seemed to be happening in 2003. As the Chiefs entered the playoffs, they had hopes of reaching the Super Bowl.

The team lined up against the Indianapolis Colts in their first playoff contest. It was a high-scoring game where the offenses of both teams put on a show. Holmes scored two touchdowns in the game and rolled up 176 yards in rushing. One of his longest gains took place early in the second half, when he busted free for a 48-yard run. Unfortunately, he fumbled the ball at the end of the play—something he very rarely does—and the Colts recovered. Holmes performed well for the rest of the game, at one point racking up 44 yards in rushing in the course of a single drive. But in the end, the Colts offense ended up winning the duel, posting a 38-31 victory and bringing the Chiefs' excellent season to a disappointing finish.

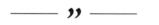

> "There are so many different reasons why I did not retire," Holmes said after the 2003 season. "There were my teammates. There was the coaching staff that brought me here. . . . And it's just the desire that I have inside me. I definitely don't believe I'm done. I have so much more to do on the field."

End of the Line?

Holmes went into the off season wrestling with a very large question: Was it time to hang up his helmet? He had gotten through 2003 without a major injury, but his hip still bothered him, not to mention the general aches and pains that went with playing professional football. "In terms of getting your body beat up, it only takes one NFL season and you feel like you've been in a car wreck," he said. He also knew that running backs can't keep running forever. NFL history is full of people like Earl Campbell who probably played longer than they should have and paid the price later on. "It's a thought that I have every year," he said of retirement. "It's a matter of going to the table every year and deciding what you want to do." His doubts seemed to be stronger in early 2004, because for the first time in his career Holmes approached his coaches and fellow players and told them he was considering retirement. Coach Vermeil told him to take some time to make up his mind, and Holmes returned to San Antonio to think things over.

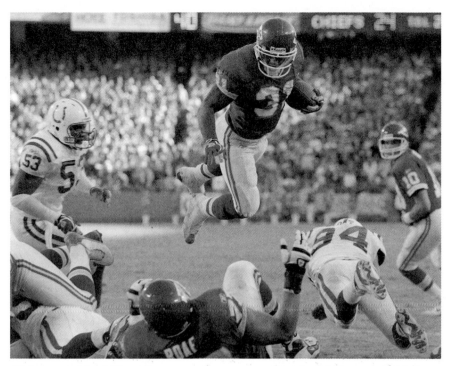

Holmes put his ability to leap over players to good use in this January 2004 play-off game against the Indianapolis Colts.

In the end, he decided to keep on playing. "There are so many different reasons why I did not retire," he explained. "There were my teammates. There was the coaching staff that brought me here. . . . And it's just the desire that I have inside me. I definitely don't believe I'm done. I have so much more to do on the field." He didn't waste any time in trying to prove that point. In the first eight games of 2004, Holmes picked up where he had left off the previous season. He led the league in rushing and touchdowns and was named the AFC Player of the Month for October. While the Chiefs were once again struggling as a team (they won only three of the first eight games), it looked as if Holmes was on his way to another fantastic year.

But on November 7 in a game against Tampa Bay, Holmes's right knee came back to haunt him. After scampering for a 13-yard gain, he went out with a strained medial collateral ligament (MCL). Initially, doctors thought that the injury wasn't serious and that he would only miss a few games. But Holmes didn't recover as quickly as expected. In early December, it was decided that he wouldn't play again in 2004.

Given his recurring injuries and his previous thoughts of retirement, some have speculated that Holmes's playing days may be over. He claims that they're not. "I'm definitely 100 percent preparing to play," he said of the 2005 season. "The injury just gave me an opportunity to rest up and get the body 100 percent." If the past is any indication, he may come back better than ever, since he has a long history of turning in strong seasons following major injuries. "It's a God-given talent," he said. "I'm able to weather the storm despite whatever is in front of me." Holmes still believes that his football skills were granted by God, and he doesn't intend to waste them. "I just believe I was given a gift. And I believe I can touch people's lives with my gift."

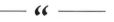

Holmes believes that his football skills were granted by God, and he doesn't intend to waste them. "I just believe I was given a gift. And I believe I can touch people's lives with my gift."

HOME AND FAMILY

Holmes has three children with his former girlfriend, Stephanie Hale: a son named De'Andre, who was born around 1993; a son named Jekovan, who was born around 1997; and a daughter named Corion, who was born around 2002. Speaking of the period when De'Andre was born, Holmes once commented that "Stephanie and I didn't know each other well enough to make babies. . . . We made a mistake." On the other hand, he has also made it clear that he feels "really fortunate" to have had children and has faced up to his responsibilities as a father. Because the kids live with their mother in San Antonio, Holmes has to do a lot of traveling to be part of his children's lives. During the football season, he makes weekly visits to Texas so that he can spend time with them, and he usually spends the off-season in San Antonio. In addition, Holmes took primary custody of De'Andre for two years while he was playing with Baltimore, though De'Andre later returned to San Antonio to live with Hale.

Holmes remains close to his mother and stepfather. In 2003 Herman Morris was called to serve in Iraq as a member of the United States Army Reserve. When Holmes was weighing retirement in early 2004, one of the reasons he decided to keep playing was that he knew that his stepfather would enjoy watching him play on television while stationed overseas. Morris's service to his country also made Holmes reflect on the meaning of courage. "I don't like it when people call football players 'heroes,'" he said.

"Those people who fight for our country, those are the real heroes. They are the ones that put their lives on the line for freedom."

HOBBIES AND OTHER INTERESTS

Holmes has been an avid chess player ever since he was young. "Nobody can tell you who you are when you're playing chess," he commented, and he proved that point while in the seventh grade. His victory in a school chess tournament surprised the other entrants, who had dismissed him as a football-playing jock who wouldn't be able to master strategy. Holmes feels that the board game has a direct relationship to his actions on the football field. "Chess is a game of patience, and that pretty much defines how I run the ball," he said. "I'm patient, always looking for the opportunity and trying to capitalize off the other person's mistake."

Holmes uses chess as a means to help kids. He regularly visits a center operated by the Kansas City Police Athletic League, where he helps youngsters learn the game. "It gives kids the opportunity to try something outside of the usual football, lifting weights, and playing basketball," he explained. "It allows them to think a little differently, and at the same time, it allows them to be very aggressive."

His stepfather's service to his country, as a member of the United States Army Reserve stationed in Iraq, made Holmes reflect on the meaning of courage. "I don't like it when people call football players 'heroes,'" he said. "Those people who fight for our country, those are the real heroes. They are the ones that put their lives on the line for freedom."

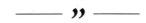

Holmes is also involved in a number of charity efforts. His foundation Team Priest provides assistance to underprivileged kids and minority-owned businesses. In addition, Holmes has aided a wide variety of organizations, including the Maryland Department of Education, McDonald House Charities, and the Children's Miracle Network. He's a member of the Fellowship of Christian Athletes.

HONORS AND AWARDS

Member of the American Conference Pro-Bowl Team: 2001-2003
Offensive Player of the Year (National Football League): 2002
NFL All-Pro Team selection (Associated Press): 2001-2003

FURTHER READING

Books

Althaus, Bill. *Priest Holmes: From Sidelines to Center Stage*, 2003
Who's Who in America, 2003

Periodicals

Football Digest, Apr. 2002, p.26
Houston Chronicle, Dec. 26, 1996, sports section, p.6
Kansas City (Mo.) Star, Dec. 23, 2001, p.C1; Oct. 6, 2002, sports section, p.1;
    Dec. 19, 2002, p.D1
Los Angeles Times, Sep. 29, 2002, sports section, p.4
Montreal Gazette, Dec. 2, 2003, p.C1
San Antonio Express-News, Dec. 29, 1996, p.C10
Sporting News, July 22, 2002, p.42; Dec. 31, 2002, p.21
Sports Illustrated, May 20, 2002, p.56; Sep. 2, 2002, p.182; Sep. 29, 2003, p.68
Sports Illustrated for Kids, Dec. 1, 2003, p.31
St. Louis Post-Dispatch, Dec. 8, 2002, p.E1

Online Databases

Biography Resource Center Online, 2005, articles from *Biography Resource
Center*, 2004, and *Who's Who among African Americans*, 2004

ADDRESS

Priest Holmes
Kansas City Chiefs
One Arrowhead Drive
Kansas City, MO 64129

WORLD WIDE WEB SITES

http://www.nfl.com/players
http://www.kcchiefs.com
http://www.nflplayers.com

T.D. Jakes 1957-

American Minister, Author, Broadcaster, and
Community Advocate
Pastor of The Potter's House and CEO of The Potter's
House Ministries

BIRTH

Thomas Dexter Jakes was born in South Charleston, West Virginia, on June 9, 1957. His father, Ernest Sr., was the owner of a
custodial service. His mother, Odith, was a schoolteacher. He
was the youngest of three children.

YOUTH

Jakes's religious faith has been an important part of his life for as long as he can remember. He loved going to the local Baptist church as a boy, and when he got home he spent hours preaching to imaginary congregations. "We were all brought up in the church," his older brother Ernest told the *Dallas Morning News*. "But it stuck with him. With me, I would go outside and play. He would want to read the Bible and go to choir practice." Jakes's enthusiasm for worship and religious study eventually became so widely known around the community that folks started calling him "Bible Boy."

In addition to exploring his religious faith, Jakes spent a lot of time helping out around the house. He learned to cook and sew, and he earned extra money for the family by delivering newspapers and selling Avon products. These extra dollars became vital in the late 1960s, when Ernest Jakes Sr. developed a serious kidney ailment that eventually took his life. Jakes was 10 years old when his father first became ill, and he has described the five years of suffering that his father endured before his death as a nightmare for the whole family. It also left him with an enduring respect for the pain and suffering that afflict countless people every day. "That's how I grew up, sleeping in waiting rooms and hospitals, suspended between life and death," he recalled. "And riding an emotional roller coaster at a time that I desperately needed the solidarity of my father's hand and the attention of my mother. My mother was distracted with my father, and my father was distracted with death."

> *"That's how I grew up, sleeping in waiting rooms and hospitals, suspended between life and death," Jakes recalled about his father's long battle with illness. "And riding an emotional roller coaster at a time that I desperately needed the solidarity of my father's hand and the attention of my mother. My mother was distracted with my father, and my father was distracted with death."*

EDUCATION

Jakes dropped out of high school two months before graduation to help care for his family. He eventually passed a high school equivalency exam, then enrolled as a part-time student at West Virginia State College in

Charleston. He took several psychology courses at West Virginia State. By this point he had started a part-time ministry, however, and his academic studies gradually fell by the wayside.

Jakes later resumed his education at Friends International Christian University, a correspondence school located in Merced, California. He eventually earned a bachelor's degree, a master's degree, and a doctoral degree from the school. "It's for guys like me who have already gone on [with their careers] and are halfway up the hill," he explained. "They take credits you have accrued from school and experience and round out with courses until you are eligible for a diploma."

CAREER HIGHLIGHTS

Jakes's career as a minister began in 1979, when he founded a small store-front church in Montgomery, West Virginia. This church, called the Greater Emmanuel Temple of Faith, had only ten members when it first opened its doors. But Jakes's energetic leadership seemed to bring in a trickle of new members with each passing month.

The part-time post fulfilled Jakes's need to share his faith, but it did not provide him with the money he needed to support a family. In 1981 he married Serita A. Jameson and took a factory job with Union Carbide, but the plant closed down a year later. Unable to find another stable job, Jakes dug ditches and took odd jobs for several months.

After a while, however, the Greater Emmanuel Temple of Faith expanded to the point that it was able to pay Jakes a full-time salary for his pastoral activities. This development freed him to focus all his attention on his ministry. He started a local radio program called "The Master's Plan," and in 1987 he was ordained as a bishop by Dr. Quander L. Wilson, presiding Bishop of Greater Emmanuel Apostolic Churches. Although Jakes resigned from that denomination two years later, he maintained a relationship with a small fellowship of churches collectively known as the Higher Ground Always Abounding Assemblies.

Emerging as a Gifted Counselor to Women

In 1990 Jakes moved his growing church to South Charleston, West Virginia. At the time of the move, the congregation numbered only 100 or so, but within three years the church membership tripled in size. It was during this period that Jakes developed a Sunday school lesson plan specifically tailored to address the pain and sadness he saw in many of the church's women. "I was counseling married couples and started to see that behind

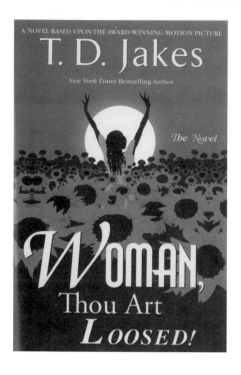

the perfect exterior were a lot of women dealing with the same problems of oppression," he recalled. "I called them all together. Part of healing is knowing that others have been through it."

Jakes was profoundly moved by the number of women in his congregation who seemed to take comfort from his program. Determined to help women deal with their emotional pain, he wrote and self-published a book called *Woman, Thou Art Loosed!* In this 1993 work, Jakes emphasized the universality of the experiences of women and urged them to take pride in their worth and responsibility for their happiness. The book proved enormously popular, and over time it became the foundation of an entire "Woman, Thou Art Loosed!" program devised by Jakes. This program—which includes audiotapes, books, and symposiums—also was instrumental in building his reputation as a skilled minister to poor, depressed, and unhappy women of all ages, races, and economic backgrounds.

Jakes's ministry continued to grow in other ways as well. In 1993 his weekly services began appearing on the Trinity Broadcasting Network. The same year, he moved his church to Cross Lanes, West Virginia. Before long, his congregation grew to about 1,100 members. About 40 percent of the congregation was white, an unusually high percentage for a church led by a black pastor.

In 1994 Jakes expanded his television ministry to Black Entertainment Television (BET). Two years later, he made the biggest move of his career, relocating his ministry to Dallas, Texas. Jakes later admitted that moving to the Dallas area was scary in some respects. "We literally felt like the Beverly Hillbillies coming out of West Virginia to a place where I couldn't get out of [Dallas/Fort Worth] Airport effectively," he said. "It was an adventure." But the move gave Jakes the resources he needed to bring his ministry to a whole new level. Accompanied by 50 staff members and their families from West Virginia, Jakes settled into a huge, modern church located on a compound of about 30 acres. This ideal property had become available after the previous occupant, a televangelist, had been imprisoned for tax evasion.

Founding the Potter's House

Jakes decided to name his nondenominational church The Potter's House — a tribute to Jeremiah's description of God as a potter who puts broken vessels back together. The name reflected his decision to focus his ministry on helping people who are broken in spirit. "My assignment is to open the door of the Church for hurting people and refocus what the Church was meant to be in our society," he said. "The Church has become stereotyped as a 'spiritual club' for elitists and yuppies who portray themselves as persons who 'have arrived.' I believe the Church was meant to be a hospital for hurting people."

The first church service Jakes held at The Potter's House drew over 2,000 people and was televised on BET stations around the country. With each passing week, the number of worshipers swelled. They were drawn partly by the service's energetic mix of music and dancing, but also by Jakes's sermons, which used Biblical lessons to discuss the challenge of leading a spiritually rewarding life in the modern world. "When T.D. Jakes opens his mouth, what comes out is liquid fire," declared a fellow evangelist. "It impacts your life with a message that doesn't stop when you walk out of there."

> "My assignment is to open the door of the Church for hurting people and refocus what the Church was meant to be in our society," Jakes said. "The Church has become stereotyped as a 'spiritual club' for elitists and yuppies who portray themselves as persons who 'have arrived.' I believe the Church was meant to be a hospital for hurting people."

By the end of his first year in Dallas, Jakes had added another 7,000 members to The Potter's House. The next year, another 10,000 people joined the church. The surging popularity of his ministry enabled Jakes to branch out into a number of different areas. In addition to book writing, he established a theatrical company to produce Christian-themed plays and began recording gospel music. The Potter's House also launched a number of community outreach programs, including ambitious efforts to reach inmates in prisons around the country.

In 1999, Jakes's sermons attracted a record crowd of 87,500 at the Georgia Dome in Atlanta.

By 1999 it was clear that in the space of a few short years, Jakes had become one of the best-known evangelists in the country. That year, he preached to a record crowd of 87,500 people at the Georgia Dome in Atlanta. He was also the keynote speaker for a National Day of Prayer in Washington, D.C. In 2000 he gave the keynote addresses at annual conferences of the National Council of Black Mayors, the National Black Police Association, and the Congressional Black Caucus.

In 2001 Jakes's fame reached a new plateau when *Time* featured him in a long cover story, calling him "America's best preacher." "He is a virtuoso, a prodigy," declared David Van Biemathe in *Time*. "The only thing more exhilarating than the style of T.D. Jakes's sermons is their rigor and compassion. . . . As a preacher, Jakes takes on still-taboo topics like physical and sexual abuse and the shame of incarceration with a cathartic and psychologically acute explicitness." Around this same time, other major media outlets turned their spotlight on him as well. The *Washington Post,* for example, described him as "perhaps the greatest preaching phenomenon in black America and by some people's reckoning, all of America."

Establishing Himself as a Powerful, Prolific Writer

During Jakes's rise to stardom, he used a variety of creative avenues to express his religious faith. For example, he unveiled a theatrical version of

Woman, Thou Art Loosed!, in which a physically and emotionally abused woman struggles to build a new life for herself. That later led to a film version of the play, starring Jakes himself, which was released in 2004 to acclaim from church groups around the country. His gospel albums have been similarly successful. A 2001 gospel album called *The Storm Is Over*, featuring Jakes and the Potter House Choir, became the No. 1 gospel album in the country, and other recordings have earned Grammy and Dove Award nominations.

But book writing remained perhaps Jakes's favorite artistic means of declaring his faith and reaching out to people struggling to find happiness in the world. Since the 1993 publication of *Woman, Thou Art Loosed!* — which has sold more than 1.5 million copies —he was written more than two dozen other books. In virtually all of these works, Jakes uses his interpretations of Jesus's teaching to help guide readers to more satisfying and rewarding lives.

"When T.D. Jakes opens his mouth, what comes out is liquid fire," declared a fellow evangelist. "It impacts your life with a message that doesn't stop when you walk out of there."

In 1998, for example, Jakes published *The Lady, Her Lover, and Her Lord*, which provides instruction to women seeking positive relationships with both God and their life partners. "Here, he demonstrates an unusual ability to inspire, uplift, teach, and comfort," commented a reviewer in *Publishers Weekly*. "An eloquent wordsmith, this African-American minister writes with an abundance of memorable metaphors and yet speaks to women's hearts in practical, often humorous terms." In *The Great Investment: Faith, Family, and Finance* (2000), meanwhile, Jakes turns his attention to economic empowerment for Christians. *Publishers Weekly* praised this work as well, stating that it "quite effectively addresses nontraditional [family] configurations such as blended, one-parent, and grandmother-headed families in a supportive and non-judgmental tone."

In 2002 Jakes released another book that vaulted onto the religious bestseller list. *God's Leading Lady* combined the examples of highly successful women with personal experiences from his own life to provide readers with guidance on navigating a wide assortment of challenges. "This is a book for women of all ages and of all economic and social statuses, and it speaks to a range of issues from single motherhood to ill health to financial crises to troubled marriages," observed *Booklist*. "Jakes's fans will love this latest message of encouragement and spiritual empowerment."

Other recent books penned by Jakes include *Cover Girls* (2003), a novel of spiritual hope and inspiration, and *He-Motions: Even Strong Men Struggle* (2004), which features what *Publishers Weekly* called a "distinctly unmacho vision of fatherhood, friendship, and lifelong marital romance." In addition, Jakes contributes regular columns to national magazines like *Gospel Today*, *Christianity Today*, and *Ministries Today*, and he has joined with Hallmark Cards to produce a popular line of "Loose Your Spirit" inspirational greeting cards.

Promoting a Philosophy of Self-Worth

"The greatest gift you can give to a person is a resolution, so they can move on," Jakes has said. "Getting over the past has nothing to do with the person who hurt you way back when coming back to ask forgiveness. I try to help people take the past in hand and say, 'It's over, I'm moving on.'"

Both in his sermons and in his books, Jakes emphasizes his belief that unhappy people can change their lives for the better. "Too often, I'm afraid, [people] think they've identified their life story's genre and feel compelled to live it out without questioning the areas they could change," he wrote in *God's Leading Lady*. "Have you already decided you know how the story ends? What kinds of things do you allow yourself to hope for? Do you keep your hopes safe and predictable, like a familiar sitcom's ending, or do you dare believe that the impossible can happen? I believe [everyone] must harbor at least one impossible dream, an area [he or] she feels led to pursue despite the odds. It may be with [a] job, or with your broken marriage, with estranged children or with health, but I believe God wants us to expect the unexpected from Him. Too often, many people write off the end of the story before the show has ended. Leave room for Him to work in your life. . . . Hold on to your dreams, and with calm perseverance you, too, will see your promise fulfilled."

Jakes is convinced that if people can learn to put pain and suffering behind them, they can begin walking a new path of renewal and self-regard. "The greatest gift you can give to a person is a resolution, so they can move on," Jakes has said. "Getting over the past has nothing to do with the person

Jakes's ministry has been especially valuable to women.

who hurt you way back when coming back to ask forgiveness. I try to help people take the past in hand and say, 'It's over, I'm moving on.'"

Jakes believes that his ministry can be especially valuable to women. "I bring a fresh perspective to women's problems," he said. "Women have women friends to talk to, they go to women's seminars, read women's books. But their problems are with men. I tell them what men are all about." In addition, he insists that women not judge whether their lives are successful simply by the presence or absence of a romantic partner in their lives. "Your self-esteem is not tied to having a man in your life, for that's too much power to give to one person," he declared. "But when you are valuable in and of yourself and think highly of yourself, you are much more likely to draw someone who thinks highly of you as well."

Despite his immensely popular ministry, however, Jakes claims that his success is due to God. "It has more to do with God's timing and His purpose for my life than my gifts or abilities," he said. "My responsibility to the Body of Christ is almost like a spiritual physician who has discovered some medicine in the Word of God. I believe this medicine will help heal some of the hurts that are in this world. As the physician, I am careful always to acknowledge that I am not the cure, but that I have been able to facilitate the cure because Jesus Christ lives within me."

Addressing Controversy

Not surprisingly, Jakes's interpersonal skills, his oratorical abilities, and his seemingly limitless energy have drawn praise not only from his congregation, but from community activists, fellow ministers, and other observers. "He's pretty darn impressive," said Joel Fontinos, director of religious publishing at Putnam. "He draws huge crowds, sells hundreds of thousands of books, he has record deals and inner-city ministries. There's so much to him. He's so complex and multifaceted. He cuts across a lot of boundaries."

Jakes's emergence as a national figure has not been completely trouble-free, however. Some critics have complained that his ministry places too much emphasis on financial and material gain and not enough on spiritual matters. Minister Eugene Rivers, for example, charges that "[Jakes] is not offering black Christians a developed sense of biblical justice, like we got from [Martin Luther] King. The prophetic dimension of biblical faith is absent from Jakes's teaching. . . . I want to know what the end game is beyond wealth accumulation and marketing." This criticism has been sharpened by Jakes's friendships with various celebrities and sports stars, as well as by the minister's lifestyle. He lives with his family in a huge mansion, selects luxurious accommodations wherever he travels, and displays very expensive taste in suits and jewelry.

Jakes rejects claims that he dwells too much on economic matters, though. "[I have to] talk about economic empowerment because it is a reality for my people," he stated. "The only solution to our generation, particularly in the inner cities where there are racial issues and academic issues and people are on their second and third chances, is [to teach economic empowerment]. . . . If we don't teach economic empowerment, we will subtly create atmospheres that promote crime and drugs and pestilence in our community. I'm not evaluating the integrity of your faith by the depth of your wallet."

In addition, Jakes makes no apologies for his lifestyle. "I see no need to hide the fact that God has blessed me as a business person, investor, and author," he wrote on his web site. "Any time Christians become very, very successful, others attempt to discredit us. . . . In a time when we're saying to African-American men — and men in general — to take care of their children, we ought to celebrate any man who has found financial security and is also a minister. I don't see that as a minus." In fact, Jakes told the *Washington Post* that he sees his success as an inspiration to others. "Once [young African Americans] see a black man who is successful, who has written several books and been celebrated [across] the country and overseas, and he's not selling drugs but he's driving the same kind of car the pimp or drug dealer is, and he's not illegal and he's not immoral, it encourages young men. . . . They say, 'Hey, if God can do it for him, he can do it for me, too.'"

Some Pentecostal religious leaders have also questioned aspects of Jakes's theological beliefs—specifically his continued affiliation with the Higher Ground Always Abounding Assemblies. Churches in this organization follow a doctrine commonly called "Oneness Pentecostalism," a belief that Jesus Christ alone is God. Other Pentecostal denominations, however, embrace the traditional Christian concept of a Holy Trinity consisting of the Father, Son, and Holy Spirit.

When criticism of Jakes in this area was publicized in *Christianity Today* in 2000, the leader of The Potter's House responded quickly. "My association with Oneness people does not constitute assimilation into their ranks any more than my association with the homeless in our city makes me one of them," he wrote in a response published in the same magazine.

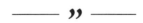

"I see no need to hide the fact that God has blessed me as a business person, investor, and author," he wrote on his web site. *"Any time Christians become very, very successful, others attempt to discredit us. . . . In a time when we're saying to African-American men—and men in general—to take care of their children, we ought to celebrate any man who has found financial security and is also a minister. I don't see that as a minus."*

"While I mix with Christians from a broad range of theological perspectives, I speak only for my personal faith and convictions. . . . I believe in one God who is the Father, the Son, and the Holy Spirit. I believe these three have distinct and separate functions—so separate that each has individual attributes, yet are one. I do not believe in three Gods. . . . When I think of the Trinity, I consider how Jesus prayed under the unction of the Holy Spirit that we would be one even as He and the Father are one. To that end, I preach, write, and work."

The Potter's House has grown into a multiracial, nondenominational church with more than 28,000 members.

Building an Empire

Today, Jakes leads a religious empire of truly amazing size and scope. The Potter's House has grown into a multiracial, nondenominational church with 59 active internal and outreach ministries and more than 28,000 members. The church facility is also one of the largest and most technologically modern in the country. In addition to seating capacity for 8,200 (Sunday attendance is spread over three services), the church features a concert-quality sound system and laptop terminals that enable worshipers to download sermon notes and other information directly from their pews. The weekly services from The Potter's House appear on the Trinity Broadcasting Network (TBN), Black Entertainment Television (BET), the Daystar Network, and an assortment of foreign networks. In addition, Jakes has developed "The Potter's Touch," a daily 30-minute talk show focusing on religious and self-help issues that appears on both TBN and BET.

Jakes is particularly proud of the church's outreach programs, which target virtually every needy demographic group in America. Programs include the Guardians, which reaches out to homeless people; Rahab International, which helps prostitutes and women in abusive domestic situations; a Transformation Treatment Program for drug and alcohol abusers; an AIDS outreach initiative; a Fire House youth ministry; and the Prison Satellite Network, which provides gospel programming to more than 350,000 inmates in 375 prisons in 40 states. "Most of our Bible was written in prison, by inmates," Jakes explained on his official web site. "Some of the greatest men that God ever used were incarcerated. In fact Jesus himself was incarcerated, locked up and executed. Jeremiah, Joseph, Peter, and the Apostle Paul were incarcerated. Many of the great people of faith, received their faith in prison—and were able to make a significant contribution to the world."

Other notable institutions established by Jakes and The Potter's House include Clay Academy, a private Christian preparatory school for children from kindergarten through eighth grade, and the Metroplex Economic Development Corporation (MEDC), a nonprofit organization. The MEDC was founded to "transform urban America by creating a platform for social and economic awareness," according to The Potter's House web site. The corporation's activities include employment services, business development, political outreach, and strategic partnerships with corporate and civic organizations. Jakes also serves as Chief Executive Officer (CEO) of The Potter's House Ministries, a nonprofit organization that each year produces several major national conferences for Christian men, women, and youth.

——— " ———

"I'm certainly a Type-A, high-energy person," Jakes observed. "There's never enough time in the day to do everything that I want to do. I finally realized I'm the kind of person who enjoys being busy. When I'm overwhelmed, I back away. Get some rest and then go back and do it again. . . . I feel as though my area of expertise is to work with people who are emotionally hurt or wounded and to watch them recover. And to see them restored."

——— " ———

In addition to all his evangelical and community oriented work, Jakes directs the for-profit company T.D. Jakes Enterprises. Many of Jakes's books, videotapes, and audiotapes of various sermons and speeches are made available through this company. Other resources managed by T.D. Jakes Enterprises include Touchdown Concepts, his theatrical production company; and Dexterity Sounds, his gospel music label.

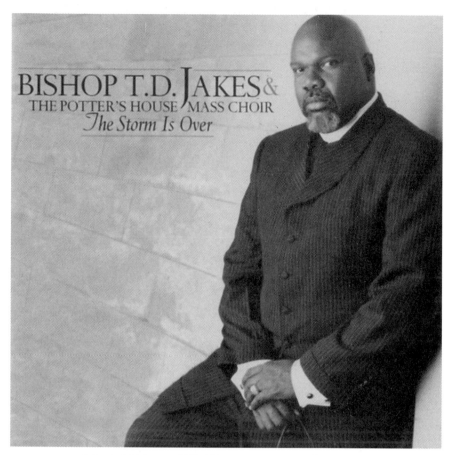

BISHOP T.D. JAKES&
THE POTTER'S HOUSE MASS CHOIR
The Storm Is Over

Jakes's 2001 gospel CD The Storm Is Over *became the
No. 1 gospel album in the country.*

Jakes admits that it is a challenge to stay on top of his many responsibilities. "My struggle is the scheduling, stress, busyness, weariness—the loss of normalcy and privacy," he said. "Sometimes the crowds are overwhelming. Those kinds of things are perplexing for a country boy from West Virginia." But he notes that he only needs about four hours of sleep a night. "I'm certainly a Type-A, high-energy person," he observed. "There's never enough time in the day to do everything that I want to do. I finally realized I'm the kind of person who enjoys being busy. When I'm overwhelmed, I back away. Get some rest and then go back and do it again. . . . I feel as though my area of expertise is to work with people who are emotionally hurt or wounded and to watch them recover. And to see them restored."

MARRIAGE AND FAMILY

Jakes married Serita A. Jamison in 1981. They have three sons, Jamar, Jermaine, and T. Dexter, Jr.; and two daughters, Cora and Sarah. Jakes commonly tells people that he could never have built his successful ministry without the support of his wife, a fellow author who helps direct various Potter's House programs. "She's the butter in my biscuit, she's the gravy on my grits," declared Jakes. "She's essential to the running of this place."

HOBBIES AND OTHER INTERESTS

Jakes's many evangelical, community, and entrepreneurial activities leave him little time for hobbies. He has said, however, that "my idea of having a good time is sitting around with the kids acting crazy. You know, stuff you could do if you was broke."

SELECTED WORKS

Writings

Woman Thou Art Loosed!, 1993
Can You Stand to Be Blessed?, 1995
Help Me, I've Fallen, 1995
The Harvest, 1995
Naked and Not Ashamed, 1995
Loose That Man and Let Him Go!, 1996
Daddy Loves His Girls, 1996
Water in the Wilderness, 1996
Why? Because You Are Anointed, 1996
T.D. Jakes Speaks to Women!, 1996
Help! I'm Raising My Child Alone, 1996
A Fresh Glimpse of the Dove, 1997
When Shepherds Bleed, 1997
T.D. Jakes Speaks to Men!, 1997
I Choose to Forgive, 1997
So You Call Yourself a Man?, 1997
Lay Aside the Weight, 1997
The Lady, Her Lover, and Her Lord, 1998
His Lady, 1999
Maximize the Moment, 2000
The Great Investment, 2001
God's Leading Lady, 2002
He-Motions, 2004

Recordings

Live at The Potter's House, 1999
The Storm Is Over, 2002
Follow the Star, 2003
A Wing and a Prayer, 2004

HONORS AND AWARDS

Gospel Heritage Award for Ministry (*Gospel Today* magazine): 1999
Living Legend Award (National Professional Network): 2000
Chairman's Award (National Religious Broadcasters): 2002
NAACP Image Award: 2002, for *The Storm Is Over*

FURTHER READING

Books

Contemporary Black Biography, Vol. 17, 1998; Vol. 43, 2004
Hinds, Patricia M., ed. *50 of the Most Inspiring African Americans,* 2002
Religious Leaders of America, 1999

Wellman, Sam. *T.D. Jakes,* 2000
Who's Who among African Americans, 2003

Periodicals

Baltimore Sun, Aug. 24, 1998, p.E5
Boston Globe, Oct. 21, 2004, p.D1
Christianity Today, Feb. 7, 2000, p.52; Feb. 21, 2000
Cleveland Plain Dealer, Sep. 22, 2000, p.E1
Current Biography Yearbook, 2001
Dallas Morning News, Jan. 24, 1999, p.E1
Detroit News, Oct. 16, 2004, p.D1
Ebony, Oct. 1998, p.92; Jan. 2001, p.108; Oct. 2002, p.24
Essence, Dec. 2001, p.126; Feb. 2003, p.210; Aug. 2003, p.116
Houston Chronicle, July 12, 2003, p.1
Jet, Dec. 22, 2003, p.57
Los Angeles Times, Aug. 20, 1998, p.E1
New York Times, Jan. 1, 1999, p.A1
People, Nov. 9, 1998, p.121
Time, Sep. 17, 2001, p.52
USA Today, Dec. 27, 2000, p.D8

Wall Street Journal, Aug. 21, 1998, p.A1
Washington Post, Sep. 11, 1999, p.B1; Mar. 25, 2001, p.S1

Online Databases

Biography Resource Center Online, 2004, articles from *Contemporary Authors Online,* 2004; *Contemporary Black Biography,* 2004; *Religious Leaders of America,* 1999; and *Who's Who among African Americans,* 2004

ADDRESS

T.D. Jakes
The Potter's House
6777 West Kiest Blvd.
Dallas, TX 75236

WORLD WIDE WEB SITES

http://www.tdjakes.org
http://www.thepottershouse.org
http://www.thepotterstouch.org

Pope John Paul II 1920-2005
Polish Religious Leader
Head of the Roman Catholic Church

[Editor's Note: John Paul II, the charismatic "people's pope" who helped topple Communism while championing Catholic values and the culture of peace, died on April 2, 2005. He died after a long struggle with illness that was characterized by his humble and graceful acceptance of suffering. His papacy was marked by his great personal popularity and the great esteem in which he was held by millions around the world. John Paul II was first profiled in Biography Today *in October 1992; this retrospective marks the occasion of his death.]*

BIRTH

Karol Jozef Wojtyla (pronounced voy-TIH-wuh), who adopted the name John Paul II when he became pope in 1978, was born May 18, 1920, in the market town of Wadowice in southern Poland. He was the second of two sons born to Karol Wojtyla, an administrative officer in the Polish Army, and Emilia (Kaczorowska) Wojtyla, a schoolteacher of Lithuanian descent. His brother, Edmund, was 15 years his senior.

YOUTH

Like most of the population of Poland, where people are known for their fierce devotion to the Catholic Church, the Wojtylas were a deeply religious family who prayed together and went to mass every day. In fact, the building that housed their modest apartment was located in the shadow of the 600-year-old Cathedral of St. Mary in Wadowice, where young Karol was baptized a month after his birth. Karol was not particularly pious as a boy, however, and his early years provided little indication that he would eventually enter the priesthood.

The Wojtylas lived a simple life, as did most of the people in their town, and Karol divided his time among school, church, and outdoor play. He was an athletic child who loved every imaginable sport, from the street game *palant* (played with two sticks), to soccer, to swimming and canoeing. His favorite sport, though, was skiing, and he practiced on the hills around his home until he was old enough to go to the steep slopes of the nearby Tatra mountains.

Karol's boyhood was marred by sadness. His beloved mother died when he was barely nine years old. Then tragedy struck again a few years later when his brother Edmund, by then a physician, died after contracting scarlet fever from a patient. From this time on, father and youngest son were left to fend for themselves. The senior Karol's military background made him a strict parent who expected obedience, but he was a warm father as well. Friends from those days remember the special bond forged between the elder Wojtyla and his son. The two attended mass every morning and often strolled the streets together after their evening meal. During these years, they lived frugally on a small army pension, with the retired father doing all of the washing, mending, and cooking. He also guided his son in his studies and checked the boy's schoolwork each day.

EDUCATION

Young Karol Wojtyla was a good student from the time he entered primary school at the age of seven, but it was in the upper grades that he excelled.

A young Karol Wojtyla, age two, with his father in a formal portrait taken in Krakow, Poland.

His father chose to send him to the state high school for boys rather than to either of the private schools in Wadowice. During high school, Karol's interests broadened to include literature and drama, Latin, poetry, and music. He loved acting, too, and his friends and teachers felt that he would one day choose the theater as his profession. The church remained a major part of his life, though, and he continued to serve as an altar boy, as he had done in his very young years, and also headed a student religious society. After high school, Karol enrolled at Krakow's ancient Jagiellonian University. His studies revolved around language and literature, but he also was a prominent member of a drama group.

World War II

Wojtyla's life as a student was interrupted a year later by the beginning of World War II. Germany invaded Poland on September 1, 1939, and soon closed all universities. In *The People's Pope*, James Oram discussed the goal of the Third Reich, as the Nazi government was known. "The Germans were determined," Oram explained, "to wipe out all Polish intellectual thought because they saw the Poles only as slaves and there was no room in the plans of the Reich for those who studied, debated, and questioned."

Young Karol was issued a work card by the Germans after their invasion of his country and forced to labor in a limestone quarry outside Krakow. He spent three years at the backbreaking job, and his meager pay was the only income to support him and his father, whose military pension had been cut off when war broke out. During this time, Karol attended informal classes at night wherever young students could hide from the Nazis, and he began to write memorable and touching poetry. He also helped an old friend form an underground drama group, the Rhapsodic Theater, which would play to small audiences in secret in an effort to keep Polish pride alive.

Studying for the Priesthood

Several biographers claim that Karol Wojtyla's calling to the priesthood began with the unexpected death of his cherished father in 1941. At that time, the horrors of war were everywhere: innocent people were snatched away in the night, never to be seen again, and rumors had begun to circulate about the Nazi gas chambers at Auschwitz, not far from Krakow, where millions of Jews were murdered. Although these tragedies undoubtedly influenced his decision, Wojtyla rarely spoke openly about this period of time, when "the most important questions of my life were born and crystallized," he revealed, "and the road of my calling was decided." Upon deciding to become a Roman Catholic priest, Wojtyla continued his studies at a secret and illegal "seminary" at Cardinal Adam Sapieha's palace in Krakow.

After the war ended, Wojtyla finally was able to return to his studies. He was ordained as a priest on November 1, 1946, and sent to study at the Angelicum, or Papal University, in Rome. He received a doctorate of divinity from this institution in 1948. After returning from Rome, he was assigned to a small village church. But within a year he was back in Krakow at the Jagiellonian University, which had reopened after the war. He eventually earned two PhD degrees from the Jagiellonian, in ethics and phenomenology—the study of human consciousness and self-awareness. When he received his second doctorate, he was appointed to the faculty at the university.

CAREER HIGHLIGHTS

Serving the Catholic Church

Wojtyla began his priestly duties around the time that the Soviet Union evicted the Nazis from Poland and installed a Communist government there. The ruling Communists took a hostile view toward religion and shut down many Catholic institutions in Poland. In 1954, Wojtyla began to teach at the Catholic University of Lublin, the only Catholic institution of higher learning in Poland that had not been shut down by the Communists. He soon became head of its ethics department. Around this time, several religious leaders were arrested under trumped-up charges of "disloyalty" to the Polish nation. The popular Cardinal Stefan Wyszynski was among them. After his release in 1956, however, Wyszynski was able to effect a degree of church autonomy unrivaled in any other Communist country by agreeing that the church would not become involved in politics.

Religion in Poland thrived afterward, and it was during these years that Wojtyla began his rise through the ranks of Polish church leaders. He be-

Pope John Paul II making his first official appearance as pope, October 1978.

came auxiliary bishop of Krakow in 1958. Two years later he went to Rome for the Second Vatican Council, the first general assembly of Catholic Church leaders in nearly a century. Under the guidance of the beloved Pope John XXIII, Vatican II announced a modernization and liberalization of church practices. It was here that Bishop Wojtyla "first established the international regard and contacts that were to make him pope," according to *Time* magazine.

More church honors followed. In 1964 Wojtyla was named archbishop of Krakow, and in May 1967, at the age of 47, he became the second-youngest cardinal in Vatican history. As cardinal, he moved easily in the elite circles of the Vatican, the independent state within the borders of Rome that houses the headquarters of the Catholic Church. When Pope Paul VI, successor to John XXIII, died in August 1978, Cardinal Wojtyla was among those who voted for a new pontiff. The cardinals chose from among themselves the gentle and fragile Albino Luciani of Italy, who became Pope John Paul I.

Only one month into his papacy, however, Pope John Paul I died. The College of Cardinals convened again and, this time, did the unexpected. After several attempts to decide between the two leading Italian candidates resulted in a deadlock, they elected the first non-Italian pope since 1522, Karol Wojtyla of Poland. *Time* called him "the first international pope to lead the global church" and "a man of extraordinary qualities and experience." Out of respect for the recently deceased pope—and also because of his reverence for Paul VI, whom he called "my inspiration and strength"—Wojtyla chose the name John Paul II.

Spreading His Message around the World

Almost immediately upon being elected pope, John Paul demonstrated his determination to spread the message of Catholicism around the world. As Robert D. McFadden wrote in the *New York Times*, "Almost from the start, it was evident to many of the world's Roman Catholics, and to multitudes of non-Catholics, that this was to be an extraordinary papacy, one that would captivate much of humanity by sheer force of personality and reshape the church with a heroic vision of a combative, disciplined Catholicism." He launched an ambitious series of overseas trips that, over the course of his 26-year papacy, made him the most-traveled pope in history. He eventually made more than 100 trips abroad and visited 129 different countries. His journeys, which covered nearly 690,000

—— *"* ——

As Robert D. McFadden wrote in the New York Times, *"Almost from the start, it was evident to many of the world's Roman Catholics, and to multitudes of non-Catholics, that this was to be an extraordinary papacy, one that would captivate much of humanity by sheer force of personality and reshape the church with a heroic vision of a combative, disciplined Catholicism."*

—— *"* ——

miles, ensured that he was seen and heard in person by more people than any other public figure in history. "He was determined from the start to make the world his parish and go out and minister to its troubles and see to its spiritual needs, "McFadden explained. "He saw himself primarily as a spiritual figure who transcended geographical and ideological boundaries, and he saw it as his mission to deliver a clear set of Catholic ideas and to foster peace and human dignity through the power of faith."

Some of John Paul's travels had far-reaching political effects. His first official visit to his homeland in 1979, for example, is widely credited with helping to topple Communism in Eastern Europe. Although the Communist government that ruled Poland tried to mute the impact of the pope's visit—by refusing to allow him to speak in large cities or to give workers time off to hear him—he was nonetheless met by huge, enthusiastic crowds. The large turnout—estimated at 13 million people during his 10-day visit—demonstrated that Poles were largely united in their discontent with the Communist government. This revelation gave some Polish leaders the courage to launch a democratic revolution.

One year after John Paul's visit, Polish dockworkers ignored Communist rules and started a trade union movement called Solidarity. The pope repeatedly expressed his support for Solidarity over the next few years, and the popular movement grew steadily in strength and influence. In 1989 Poland held free elections and the Solidarity party won an overwhelming victory, ending 40 years of Communist rule. The fall of Communism in Poland soon encouraged similarly successful movements in Germany and the Soviet Union. Although many historians credit the pope with aiding the fall of Communism, John Paul was reluctant to accept responsibility for the wave of democracy that swept across Eastern Europe. "The tree was already rotten," he once said. "I just gave it a good shake and the rotten apples fell."

> ――― " ―――
>
> *Although many historians credit the pope with aiding the fall of Communism, John Paul was reluctant to accept responsibility for the wave of democracy that swept across Eastern Europe. "The tree was already rotten," he once said. "I just gave it a good shake and the rotten apples fell."*
>
> ――― " ―――

In all of his public appearances, the pope charmed crowds with his personal warmth and enthusiasm. He would charge into the crowds to talk to people, reaching out to touch them. In return, they offered their affection and trust. John Paul was fluent in seven languages (Polish, Latin, Italian, French, German, Spanish, and English) and conversant in several others, which allowed him to connect with people around the world in their native tongues. His charismatic presence on the world stage helped broaden the geographic and ethnic diversity of the Catholic Church and increase membership from 750 million to more than 1 billion. His travels also focused world attention on the problems of poverty and repression affecting the people of many countries. He gained a worldwide reputation as a champion of human rights and human dignity, providing a voice for people throughout the world who are poor, oppressed, victimized, and powerless.

The pope was greeted warmly wherever he went, especially among children.

John Paul's penchant for traveling and meeting with followers once nearly cost him his life. On May 13, 1981, the pope became the target of an assassination attempt. As he circled St. Peter's Square in the white vehicle that the press had dubbed "the popemobile," a man fired several shots at him. The bullets hit John Paul in the abdomen, right arm, and left hand. He underwent five hours of surgery to repair the damage. His assailant was Mehmet Ali Acga, a Turk already wanted for murder in his own country. Agca was believed to have been an agent of the Bulgarian government, a Communist regime that resented the pope's unbending stance against repression. The pope eventually forgave Acga and visited him in prison. Security around the pope was tightened in the ensuing years, but John Paul often defied attempts to keep him from potentially dangerous situations.

Just as he had reached out to Catholics around the world, the pope used his position to improve relations between the Church and other major religions. As a witness to the horrors of the Holocaust, John Paul made it a priority of his papacy to forge stronger ties with the Jewish people. He emphasized the ancient connections between Christianity and Judaism, for example, and he issued an apology for the failure of some Catholics to aid Jews during the Holocaust. In 1986 John Paul II made a historic visit to

The pope prays at the Western Wall, Judaism's holiest site, during his historic visit to Jerusalem.

Israel, where he became the first pope to pray in a synagogue and placed a note in Jerusalem's Western Wall. In 1993, the Vatican formally recognized the state of Israel, which was formed after World War II and the Holocaust to serve as a homeland for the world's Jews. John Paul made similar efforts to improve relations with Muslims. In a historic visit to the Middle East in 2001, for instance, he became the first pope ever to set foot inside a mosque.

Defending Conservative Traditions

Traveling and spreading his message of peace and hope around the world was just one part of John Paul's legacy. From the beginning of his tenure, the pope also embarked on a mission to "solidify the foundations of Catholicism, which he believed were beginning to crumble under the weight of the modern age," according to biographer Timothy Walch. Schooled in the staunchly conservative Catholic Church of Poland, John Paul steadfastly defended the traditional moral authority of Church doctrine throughout his papacy. He repeatedly called "for a return to traditional Catholic ethical values: he condemned homosexuality as morally wrong; he called on priests to honor their vows of obedience and celibacy; he told the laity that premarital sex, contraception, and abortion were repugnant, . . . and he put severe limits on Catholic academic freedom and theological inquiry," Walch noted. "Pope John Paul II was a man who used the tools of modernity to struggle against the modern world," an editorial stated in the *New York Times*. "He traveled more than a half-million miles through 129 countries, waving to crowds from his popemobile. He wrote best sellers and took advantage of every means of communication to spread his message: a cry against what he saw as the contemporary world's moral decadence, moral degradation, and abandonment of values."

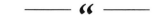

"Pope John Paul II was a man who used the tools of modernity to struggle against the modern world," an editorial stated in the **New York Times.** *"He traveled more than a half-million miles through 129 countries, waving to crowds from his popemobile. He wrote best sellers and took advantage of every means of communication to spread his message: a cry against what he saw as the contemporary world's moral decadence, moral degradation, and abandonment of values."*

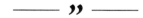

Some supporters appreciated the pope's conservative stance on social issues, viewing him as a rock of moral values in a confused world. But more liberal Catholics, especially in the United States, questioned some of John Paul's teachings—especially his rejection of birth control, his refusal to address a chronic shortage of priests by allowing priests to marry, and his refusal to allow the ordination of female priests to give women an equal voice in the church. These dissenters felt that the pope was out of touch with the modern world and argued that his conservative stances held back social progress. In fact, some American Catholics adopted a "cafeteria" approach to religion, observing the parts that suited their lifestyles and ignoring others.

Over the years, many observers commented on John Paul's demand for loyalty and intolerance for dissent within the Church. He took a number of steps to centralize authority in the Vatican, rather than allowing individual parishes to choose their own approaches. In fact, he drew criticism by dismissing a number of bishops and cardinals who did not agree with his conservative philosophy. "He was a pope who thought you could deal with the confusion after the Second Vatican Council—the inevitable, necessary confusion of growth and change—by putting a lid on it, by clamping down, by tightening things up," Father Andrew Greeley asserted. "This didn't work. It was the wrong strategy applied by a great man."

Criticism of John Paul's handling of internal affairs peaked in 2002, when he finally took steps to address a sex abuse scandal that had been brewing for many years. Since the 1950s, there had been thousands of allegations in the United States of young children being sexually abused by Catholic priests. In Boston alone, for example, approximately 1,000 children were sexually abused by pedophile priests. In some cases, bishops had tried to cover up suspected incidents of abuse by transferring the accused priests to other parishes—where they would be free to continue the pattern of abuse on a new group of unsuspecting children. In 2002 the pope ordered the release of Church documents detailing abuse allegations and adopted a zero-tolerance policy toward sexual abuse. He authorized the payment of reparations to confirmed victims, and he also condemned offenders, calling sexual abuse an "appalling sin" and saying that there was "no place in the priesthood or religious life for those who would harm the young." Still, some critics claimed that John Paul had not acted swiftly enough to protect young Catholics from abuse, while others claimed that his focus on the global stage had caused him to neglect internal problems. Overall, the crisis challenged the moral authority of the church in the eyes of many Americans.

Declining Health and Death

Over the course of John Paul's 26-year pontificate, the world watched as the pope's health underwent a gradual decline. He started his tenure as a robust 58-year-old skier and mountain-climber who insisted on building a lap pool inside the Vatican for his daily exercise. In his later years, however,

Millions of mourners poured into Rome and Vatican City to mark the passing of the pope.

he became increasingly frail until he was barely able to carry out his duties. "His physical decay unfolded before the eyes of a world both dazzled by his will and sometimes aghast at the cruelty of a vocation that would impose such burdens," John L. Allen, Jr., wrote in the *National Catholic Reporter.* "The pope struggled to walk, he slurred his speech and drooled badly, his hearing failed, and his facial expression became increasingly frozen. Yet he soldiered on, bearing his thorns in the flesh with grit and good humor."

The pope's decline began in 1992, when doctors removed a cancerous tumor from his abdomen. Over the next few years, he suffered a series of falls that resulted in broken bones. By 1999 he had grown so frail that he needed a cane, and the Vatican acknowledged that he was suffering from both arthritis and Parkinson's disease, a progressive neurological disorder that causes tremors and paralysis. By 2002 his symptoms were so severe that he could no longer walk, and aides either carried him or pushed him in a wheelchair. Still, the pope continued writing, traveling, and making public appearances almost until the end of his life. Throughout his courageous struggle with failing health, John Paul became an international symbol of aging with dignity.

In early 2005 the pope began to experience problems with his kidneys and lungs, and he was hospitalized several times with fevers and infections. He spent his final days in his papal apartment in the Vatican, attended by friends and colleagues. Thousands of followers maintained a prayerful vigil in the courtyard outside. Pope John Paul II died on April 2, 2005, at the age of 84. An estimated 4 million pilgrims came to Rome to mourn his death, some of whom stood in line for up to 24 hours just to get a glimpse of the pope's body. In addition, mourners filled churches around the world, testifying to the pope's deep personal popularity on the international stage. At his funeral, an impressive array of current and former world leaders gathered to pay their respects, as millions more thronged the streets of Rome.

> "He was a magnificent pope who presided over a controversial pontificate, at turns daring and defensive, inspiring and insular," wrote John L. Allen, Jr. "[John Paul II] leaves behind the irony of a world more united because of his life and legacy, and a church more divided."

The passing of a pope sets in motion a series of events that are dictated by centuries of tradition. For instance, within a short time the 117 members of the College of Cardinals travel to the Vatican and lock themselves in the Sistine Chapel to elect a new pope. They chose Cardinal Joseph Ratzinger of Germany, who had served as one of John Paul II's closest aides. Cardinal Ratzinger chose to be known as Pope Benedict XVI. One of his first acts was to set aside the usual five-year waiting period in order to put his predecessor on a "fast track" to sainthood.

The obituaries that appeared following the death of the pope provided a mixed assessment of John Paul's legacy. Many observers noted the charismatic appeal that made him popular among people of faith around the world. "Bells tolled solemnly across the continents, prayers and hymns filled great cathedrals and modest churches, and around the world mourning multitudes remembered Pope John Paul II . . . as the torchbearer of peace and human dignity, a tireless traveler whose journey finally ended," wrote Robert T. McFadden. But other observers were more critical of his resistance to change and modernization within the Church. "He was a magnificent pope who presided over a controversial pontificate, at turns daring and defensive, inspiring and insular," wrote John L. Allen, Jr. "[John Paul II] leaves behind the irony of a world more united because of his life and legacy, and a church more divided."

One expert on the Vatican, Giancarlo Zizola, summarized his legacy like this: "This pope will have a place in history. Not just for what he is glorified for now, for attracting the great masses, as a sporty pope — this won't last. Not even the fall of the Berlin Wall, the defeat of Communism, because he himself said it would destroy itself. But he will be remembered for the seeds he laid. He will be remembered for his great favoring of dialogue between different religions, for the culture of peace, and the courage to speak against wars. For having saved the values of the West from the West itself. And the human form he gave to the papacy. It is not negative or positive: it is a complete pontificate."

SELECTED WRITINGS

Pope John Paul II published more than one million words in his lifetime. He authored hundreds of books, essays, articles, and poems, as well as encyclicals (papal documents) defining the religious, moral, and political policy of the Catholic Church. The following selections are among his best-known works or those intended for a juvenile audience.

Crossing the Threshold of Hope, 1994
Pope John Paul II: In My Own Words, 1998
My Dear Young Friends: Pope John Paul II Speaks to Teens on Life, Love and Courage, 2000
For the Children: Words of Love and Inspiration from His Holiness John Paul II, 2000
Every Child a Light: The Pope's Message to Young People, 2002
The Poetry of Pope John Paul II, 2003
Lessons for Living, 2004

HONORS AND AWARDS

Smithson Medal (Smithsonian Institution): 1979
Olympic Order (International Olympic Committee): 1981
Man of the Year (*Time*): 1994

FURTHER READING

Books

Bernstein, Carl, and Marco Politi. *His Holiness: John Paul II and the Hidden History of Our Time,* 1996
Fischer, Heinz-Joachim, and others. *Pope John Paul II: A Pope for the People,* 2004

Kwitny, Jonathan. *Man of the Century: The Life and Times of Pope John Paul II,* 1997

Oram, James. *The People's Pope: The Story of Karol Wojtyla of Poland,* 1979

Sullivan, George. *Pope John Paul II: The People's Pope,* 1984

Walch, Timothy. *Pope John Paul II,* 1989

Weigel, George. *Witness to Hope: The Biography of Pope John Paul II,* 1999

Who's Who in America, 2005

Wilson, Jay. *Pope John Paul II,* 1992 (juvenile)

Wilson, M. Leonora. *Karol from Poland: The Life of Pope John Paul II for Children,* 1999 (juvenile)

Wolfe, Rinna. *The Singing Pope: The Story of John Paul II,* 1980 (juvenile)

Periodicals

Catholic New Times, Apr. 24, 2005, p.4

Christian Century, Oct. 14, 1987, p.876; Oct. 12, 1988, p.887; Apr. 19, 2005, pp.8, 12

Christian Science Monitor, Apr. 4, 2005, p.1

Commonweal, Oct. 7, 1988, p.516

Los Angeles Times, Apr. 3, 2005, p.A1

National Catholic Reporter, Apr. 15, 2005, p.3

New York, Oct. 30. 1978, p.93

New York Times, Apr. 3, 2005, pp.A1, A39, A46 (multiple articles); Apr. 9, 2005, p.A1

New York Times Biographical Service, May 1979, p. 614; Oct. 1982, p.1331; May 1985, p.549

New Yorker, Oct. 17, 1994, p.50

Newsweek, Oct. 30, 1978, p.78; May 25, 1981, p.24; Apr. 11, 2005 (multiple articles); Apr. 18, 2005 (multiple articles)

Time, Oct. 30, 1978, p.84; May 25, 1981, p.10; Jan. 9, 1984, p.27; Apr. 11, 2005 (multiple articles); Apr. 18, 2005 (multiple articles)

Times (London), Apr. 4, 2005, Features, p.50

USA Today, Apr. 8, 2005, p.A14

Washington Post, Apr. 3, 2005, pp.A1, A31, B6 (multiple articles)

WORLD WIDE WEB SITE

http://www.vatican.va

Toby Keith 1961-

American Country Music Singer, Songwriter,
and Guitarist
Two-Time Winner of the Entertainer of the Year
Award from the Academy of Country Music

BIRTH

Toby Keith was born Toby Keith Covel on July 8, 1961, in Clinton, Oklahoma. His mother, Joan Covel, was a homemaker
who loved to sing. His father, Hubert K. Covel, was an oil com-

pany executive. Keith is the oldest of three children in his family. He has a younger brother, Tracy, and a younger sister, Tonni.

YOUTH

Toby Keith spent most of his childhood on the family farm in Moore, a town on the outskirts of Oklahoma City. He believes that he got his singing talent from his mother and his songwriting abilities from his father. Hubert Covel, a Korean War veteran, also taught his children to be patriotic. "He was like John Wayne," Keith recalled. "He lost his eye in a jeep accident. Went through the windshield. I was 16 or 17 before I knew that discolored eye was blind." Keith grew up sharing his father's strong loyalty to the United States, a characteristic that surfaces repeatedly in his songs.

With the support of his family, Keith started playing guitar when he was eight years old. His first instrument was a Christmas present from his maternal grandmother. His paternal grandfather, who played music in church, taught Keith his first guitar chords. Keith soon began attending jam sessions with some older boys who lived nearby. He became inspired to write his own songs, and sometimes he composed up to nine in a day. Although he admitted that these songs were not very good, he was proud that he finished every one he started.

Keith's first significant musical influences were the country musicians who performed at a supper club his grandmother owned. Keith worked in the kitchen of the restaurant as a teenager, and the band would let him join them on stage when he finished working. This early exposure to country music helped hone his songwriting style.

Another early influence was his father's record collection. Keith listened to the legendary country singer-songwriter Merle Haggard, whom he would later cite as his main influence. He also discovered country star Willie Nelson, with whom he would later record a hit song. Other artists, including rock musicians like the Eagles and Bob Seger, inspired him as well.

EDUCATION AND FIRST JOBS

Keith received his education in the public schools in Moore. While attending Moore High School, Keith worked summers as a rodeo hand, test-riding bulls and broncos. In addition, he organized a number of his fellow music-loving rodeo hands into a country-rock band called Easy Money, which performed at local bars on weekends.

Because of his imposing physical size, Keith was sometimes called upon to break up barroom fights during his early musical career. "The places I first played in, if a fight broke out, it could clear the bar," he remembered. "They couldn't afford bouncers [security people], so I'd have to do something to keep from losing my audience. If I saw a big fight fixing to happen, I'd put down my guitar and jump off the stage. I'm 6-foot-4, 235 pounds, plus I'd be sober and the other guys were drunk. That's a great advantage."

After graduating from high school in the late 1970s, Keith worked with his father in the local oil fields. He started out as a low-level laborer and worked his way up to operational manager over the next few years. Eventually he traded the oil fields for the football field and played defensive end for the Oklahoma City Drillers, a semi-professional football team. In 1984 Keith tried out for the Oklahoma Outlaws—a professional franchise in the now-defunct United States Football League (USFL)—but failed to make the team.

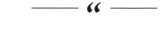

Easy Money was "up against the best bands in the world," Keith acknowledged. "The competition's fierce, and if you can make it there, you can make it anywhere. I'm not bragging when I say that the Easy Money Band and I can hold our own against any of them."

CAREER HIGHLIGHTS

Throughout his years working in the oil industry and playing football, Keith continued playing with his band, Easy Money. After his unsuccessful tryout with the Outlaws football team, he decided to focus on music. His band went on tour, playing at clubs in Oklahoma, Texas, and Louisiana. Meanwhile, Keith sent demo tapes of his own music to record companies in Nashville, Tennessee—the country music capital of the United States. None of the record companies expressed any interest at first, but Keith refused to abandon his dream of a big music career.

This grit and determination eventually paid off. Toby Keith and Easy Money gained momentum throughout the mid-1980s. By 1988 they had moved beyond the Texas and Oklahoma club circuits and were playing at bigger, more profitable venues throughout the western United States. Hopeful that they were on the verge of national success, Keith even purchased a tour bus for the band. Easy Money was "up against the best bands in the world," he acknowledged. "The competition's fierce, and if you can make it

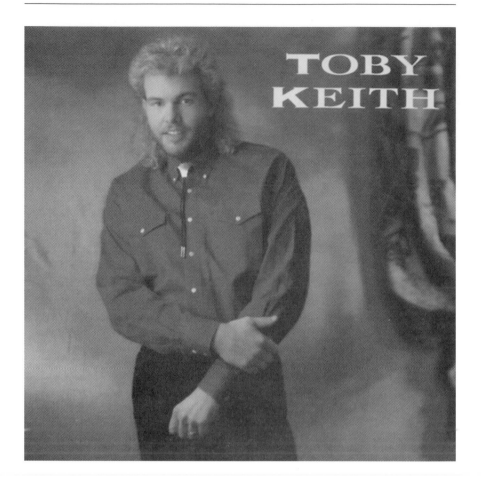

there, you can make it anywhere. I'm not bragging when I say that the Easy Money Band and I can hold our own against any of them."

Signing His First Recording Contract

Easy Money had been together almost 10 years when its leader finally got his big break. While in Nashville, Keith gave a demo tape to Harold Shedd, the president of Mercury Records. He was shocked when Shedd called him a few days later and offered to fly out to one of his Oklahoma City shows. Shedd signed Keith to a record deal over breakfast on the day after the concert.

Keith released his first album, entitled *Toby Keith,* in 1993. It was a remarkably successful debut effort, producing three No. 1 hits. The first single, "Should've Been a Cowboy," topped the *Billboard* magazine country singles chart, followed by "Wish I Didn't Know Now" and "A Little Less Talk and a Lot More Action." Another song, "He Ain't Worth Missing," reached the No. 5 spot. *Toby Keith* eventually sold more than two million copies, earning "double platinum" status.

Shedd soon left Mercury and joined Polydor Records. Eager to continue their working relationship, Keith followed him and signed a new deal with Polydor. He released his second album, *Boomtown*, in 1994. Although it was not quite as successful as his debut effort, it sold more than 500,000 copies. It also produced a No. 1 hit single, "Who's That Man," and a Top 5 hit, "You Ain't Much Fun."

The songs on Keith's first two albums cemented his reputation as a working-man's poet. The title track on *Boomtown*, for example, tells the story of an oil town that experiences a fleeting boom and then goes bankrupt. "I lived that song, watched it happen in Elk Town, Oklahoma," Keith explained. "Elk Town went from being Small Town USA to Boomtown overnight, as they brought in 1,500 oil rigs and started pumping. For six years, you had corporate people coming in from Houston and Saudi Arabia. . . . Everybody had money, even people who were living under overpasses, because there wasn't enough housing for everybody." Then the oil industry went into a slump, with disastrous results for the town. "The wells ran dry," Keith recalled. "The rich people got rich by saving their money. The fools who got it and spent it were broke."

> *"I lived that song, watched it happen in Elk Town, Oklahoma," Keith said about "Boomtown." "Elk Town went from being Small Town USA to Boomtown overnight, as they brought in 1,500 oil rigs and started pumping. . . . Everybody had money, even people who were living under overpasses, because there wasn't enough housing for everybody. . . . [Then] the wells ran dry. The rich people got rich by saving their money. The fools who got it and spent it were broke."*

Keith released his next record, a collection of 12 holiday songs called *Christmas to Christmas,* in 1995. "It doesn't have any traditional Christmas songs on it," he noted. "Instead of this just being a Christmas album, I wanted this to be an album like I usually do, but with a Christmas theme. This sounds like anything else of mine that you would hear on the radio. It just happens to be about Christmas." Keith's fourth record, *Blue Moon,* was

*Keith and Sting performed their hit song "I'm So Happy I Can't Stop Crying"
at the 1997 Country Music Association Awards.*

released in 1996 and went platinum, meaning that it sold over a million copies.

Around this time Polydor ceased operations in Nashville. Keith then returned to Mercury, which maintained offices in the country music capital. He released his next record, *Dream Walkin'*, on the Mercury label in 1997. It featured two songs that reached the No. 2 spot on the *Billboard* country charts: the ballad "When We Were in Love," and a duet with the rock musician Sting called "I'm So Happy I Can't Stop Crying." This song, which Sting composed, was nominated for a Grammy Award—one of the most coveted awards in the music industry. Sting joined Keith on television later that year to perform the song on the Country Music Association's awards show.

Breaking Through to a Wider Audience

In 1998 Keith released his *Greatest Hits, Volume I*. By this time, he was regarded as one of the rising stars of country music, but he had not yet broken through to attract a mainstream audience. He placed part of the blame on Mercury, which he felt had not done a satisfactory job of promoting his records. After the release of his *Greatest Hits* album, Keith left Mercury and signed with a new label, DreamWorks Nashville.

His next album proved to be a breakthrough effort. *How Do You Like Me Now?!*, released in 1999, marked Keith's first collaboration with Dream-Works and producer James Stroud. It featured two No. 1 hits. The song "How Do You Like Me Now?" sat at the top of the country charts for five weeks and became Keith's first Top 40 hit on the pop charts. The next hit single, "You Shouldn't Kiss Me Like This," remained at No. 1 on the country charts for three weeks.

How Do You Like Me Now?! eventually sold more than one million copies and brought Keith several long-awaited award nominations. He claimed two prestigious honors at the 2000 Academy of Country Music Awards: Male Vocalist of the Year and Album of the Year.

That success was repeated on Keith's 2001 album, *Pull My Chain,* which produced three No. 1 singles and a slew of award nominations. Two songs from the album, "My List" and "I Wanna Talk About Me," each spent five weeks at the top of the charts. The Country Music Association honored Keith as the year's best male vocalist.

> **"**
>
> *"I'm stalking him," stated Warren Littlefield, former president of the NBC network, about his efforts to sign up Keith for a TV sitcom. "He's a personality, he's a performer, and he's funny. Last time I checked, that's what makes for great television."*
>
> **"**

As Keith's music began to achieve crossover success, the singer received several opportunities to try his hand at acting. He made brief television appearances in the series "Touched by an Angel" and in the "Dukes of Hazzard" reunion movie. He also starred in television commercials for Ford Trucks, Mr. Coffee, and other products.

Television executives noticed Keith's screen presence and approached him to star in a situation comedy series. "I'm stalking him," stated Warren Littlefield, former president of the NBC network. "He's a personality, he's a performer, and he's funny. Last time I checked, that's what makes for great television." Keith admitted that he was tempted by the offer to star in his own TV show, but he decided that it would take too much time away from his music. "I just can't do that," he said.

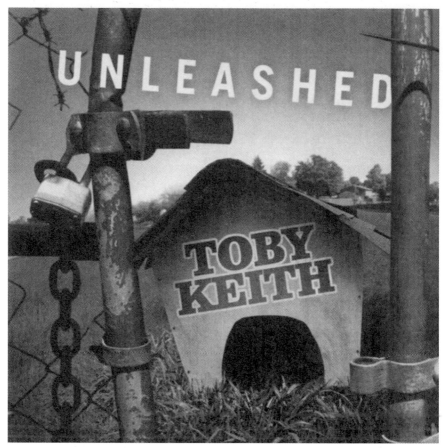

*The emotionally volatile song "Courtesy of the Red, White, and Blue
(The Angry American)" appeared on Keith's CD* Unleashed.

Responding to the September 11 Tragedy

Despite his growing personal success, the year 2001 was tragic for Keith, as
it was for all Americans. On March 24 his father died of a heart attack
while driving. Six months later, the entire nation reeled from the September 11 terrorist attacks on the World Trade Center in New York City and the
Pentagon in Washington, D.C., along with the plane crash in Pennsylvania.

The loss of his father, coupled with the events of 9/11, inspired Keith to
write what is probably his best-known song: "Courtesy of the Red, White,
and Blue (The Angry American)." Its emotionally charged lyrics denounce
terrorist groups: The song condemns Al Qaeda, the terrorist organization
that orchestrated the attacks, and the Taliban, the radical Islamic government of Afghanistan that sheltered terrorist leader Osama bin Laden. The

song also pays tribute to Hubert Covel and the patriotism he instilled in his children. "I really wanted it as an honor and a tribute to my dad," Keith explained. "I wanted to go out and sing it to military people."

"Courtesy of the Red, White, and Blue" appeared on Keith's 2002 album, *Unleashed*. Keith originally had not planned to record the song. But after he performed it at a military event in Washington, D.C., a general in attendance told him that it was his "responsibility" to record it. It later proved extremely popular with the U.S. troops that took part in the 2003 invasion of the Middle Eastern nation of Iraq. "Courtesy of the Red, White, and Blue" became a sort of anthem for the American forces during the Iraq War. Many soldiers painted the song's title on bombs and tanks. One soldier, Private First Class Patrick Miller, told reporters that after he was taken prisoner by Iraqi forces in an ambush, he sang it to his captors "just to make 'em mad."

After September 11, "Courtesy of the Red, White, and Blue" generated strong responses from listeners, both positive and negative. "The response was so tremendous," Keith stated. "I know how angry I was when those towers came down, and this is my way of serving my country."

Creating Controversy

From the beginning, the song generated strong responses from listeners, both positive and negative. Many people, furious over the 9/11 attacks, applauded its angry call for revenge and unabashed patriotism. "The response was so tremendous," Keith stated. "I know how angry I was when those towers came down, and this is my way of serving my country." Other listeners, though, condemned the song as overly aggressive.

An ABC television special stirred up additional controversy about the song. The network invited Keith to sing it on "In Search of America: A July Fourth Musical Celebration." A short time later, Peter Jennings, the show's host, convinced ABC to rescind its invitation. Jennings felt that the song's lyrics were inappropriate for the show. Keith's fans were outraged by the network's decision. They swamped ABC with calls, letters, and e-mails in protest, but Keith remained off of the guest list.

Keith soon found himself at the center of another flap. Natalie Maines, lead singer of the all-female country group the Dixie Chicks, gave an interview in which she harshly criticized "Courtesy of the Red, White, and Blue." "I hate it," Maines stated. "It's ignorant, and it makes country music sound ignorant." Keith reacted to this criticism by saying, "You've got to be in my league as a songwriter before I'll even respond to you." The ABC incident, Maines's comments, and Keith's response made him the center of a great deal of media attention. The publicity actually worked in his favor, however, because it shined a spotlight on the song and album. Partly as a result, *Unleashed* debuted as the best-selling album on both the pop and country charts in July 2002. It eventually sold three million copies and was certified triple platinum.

Although "Courtesy of the Red, White, and Blue" generated the strongest response, others songs on the record proved immensely popular as well. "Who's Your Daddy?" and "Beer for My Horses" both became hits. "Beer for My Horses" is a duet that Keith recorded with his longtime idol Willie Nelson. The two men performed the song at the Farm Aid benefit concert in Pittsburgh in 2002. The lyrics talk about justice and the way it was served in the Old West. Although the song was written before September 11, its harsh sentiments struck a chord with many people outraged by the terrorist attacks.

Keith and Nelson reunited to perform the song at the Academy of Country Music's 2002 awards show. The Dixie Chicks were unable to attend and arranged instead to be broadcast live on a television screen at the ceremony. Maines appeared wearing a T-shirt with an insulting slogan and Keith's initials on it. When Keith failed to show up a short time later to accept the "Entertainer of the Year" award, some believed that he had left the theater in anger. But he later said that he had retired to his tour bus to write a song with Nelson.

Speaking for Soldiers and Hard-Working Americans

Keith followed up on the success of *Unleashed* with *Shock'N Y'all*, which debuted at number one upon its release in 2003. Like most of his records, the album was tinged with patriotic sentiments. It also demonstrated Keith's sense of humor. "We were looking for album titles while the war was going on," he explained. "Then the 'Shock and Awe' [military] campaign started, and it became such a funny phrase; I thought it would be funny to take that, add a 'y'all' on the end and throw a little hillbilly at 'em."

Keith recorded *Shock'N Y'all* at the Shrimp Boat Sound Studio in Key West, Florida, the recording facility owned by singer-songwriter Jimmy Buffett. While he was making the album, Keith was called away by the president of the United States. President George W. Bush invited Keith to attend a

*Along with President George W. Bush, Keith visited soldiers at
MacDill Air Force Base in Florida.*

speech he was giving to General Tommy Franks and his troops at MacDill
Air Force Base in Tampa. The singer proudly accepted, and he treated soldiers and their families to a brief performance, using only an acoustic guitar.

Shock'N Y'all added to Keith's reputation as a songwriter who speaks to
the concerns of American soldiers and other hard-working people. The
song "American Soldier," for example, tries to see the world through the
eyes of a U.S. enlisted man stationed in Iraq. Keith continued to express
his patriotism and his support for American troops. "I'm not for every war,
and I'm not against every war," he noted, "and I don't consider myself
smart enough to say whether or not we should be [in Iraq]. This is just my

way of letting everybody know exactly what a soldier is: just another American that gets up and goes to work."

In 2004 Keith released his *Greatest Hits, Volume 2* album, featuring favorite songs recorded before *Shock'N Y'all.* He continues to tour constantly and perform at awards shows and other high-profile venues. He headlined a nationally televised pre-kickoff concert at the 2004 Super Bowl, for example, and he took the stage again at halftime to perform "Walk This Way" and "Sweet Emotion" with the rock group Aerosmith.

> ——— **"** ———
>
> *"I'm not for every war, and I'm not against every war," Keith noted, "and I don't consider myself smart enough to say whether or not we should be [in Iraq]. This is just my way of letting everybody know exactly what a soldier is: just another American that gets up and goes to work."*
>
> ——— **"** ———

Over the course of his 20-year career, Toby Keith has gone from breaking up fights in small clubs to headlining concerts in sold-out stadiums. Despite his success, however, he has never lost track of his roots. In fact, he claims that being in big cities like New York only makes him yearn for the country. "After three days, I've got to find some grass," he stated. "You can go to Central Park, but that's just a quick fix. I've got to be able to see grass way off in the distance. I'm always going to be a country boy."

MARRIAGE AND FAMILY

When he is not traveling with his band, Keith loves to spend time with his family. He met his wife, Tricia Lucus Covel, at a club where he was playing with Easy Money. "I was 19, and he was 20," she recalled. "He was just one of those larger-than-life guys, full of confidence." They dated for three years before marrying in 1984. Keith has two daughters, Shelley and Krystal, and one son, Stelen. The family makes their home on a 160-acre ranch near Norman, Oklahoma, called Dream Walkin' Farms, where Keith raises and trains about 50 racehorses.

HOBBIES AND OTHER INTERESTS

Keith has always loved sports. He works out at the gym, runs, and is an avid golfer. He is a devoted fan of the University of Oklahoma Sooners basketball and football teams. Both of his daughters attend Oklahoma, and he frequently makes financial donations to the university.

The singer also does charity work. In 2003 he organized the "Toby Keith and Friends Golf Classic," which raised an estimated $250,000 for "Ally's House," a nonprofit organization that assists the families of pediatric cancer patients. The foundation takes its name from Ally Webb, the daughter of Keith's former band mate, Scott Webb. Ally died of liver cancer at the age of two.

In 1999 an elementary school in Keith's hometown of Moore was flattened by a tornado. The country music star responded by holding a benefit concert to raise money to rebuild the school. In December 2000 the students planted a tree in Keith's honor.

Keith is also becoming involved in various business interests. He purchased the Belmar Golf Club in Norman in 2004. He also purchased a 12,000-square-foot piece of property that will one day be home to "Toby Keith's Road House," a $4.5 million restaurant and music hall.

RECORDINGS

Toby Keith, 1993
Boomtown, 1994
Christmas to Christmas, 1995
Blue Moon, 1996
Dream Walkin', 1997
Greatest Hits, Volume I, 1998
How Do You Like Me Now?!, 1999
Pull My Chain, 2001
Unleashed, 2002
Shock'N Y'all, 2003
Greatest Hits, Volume 2, 2004

HONORS AND AWARDS

Male Video Artist of the Year (Country Music Television): 2000
Video of the Year (Country Music Television): 2000, for "How Do You Like Me Now?!"
Male Vocalist of the Year (Academy of Country Music): 2001, 2004
Entertainer of the Year (Academy of Country Music): 2003, 2004
Favorite Country Album (American Music Awards): 2003, for *Unleashed*
Flameworthy Male Video of the Year and Cocky Video of the Year (Country Music Television): 2003, for "Courtesy of the Red, White, and Blue"
People's Choice Award: 2004, for *Unleashed*, for Favorite Album
Album of the Year (Academy of Country Music): 2004, for *Shock'N Y'all*
Video of the Year (Academy of Country Music): 2004, for "Beer for My Horses"
Flameworthy Video of the Year (Country Music Television): 2004, for "American Soldier"
Flameworthy Video Collaboration of the Year (Country Music Television): 2004, for "Beer for My Horses" with Willie Nelson

FURTHER READING

Books

Contemporary Musicians, Vol. 40, 2003

Periodicals

Airplay Monitor, Oct. 24, 2003, p.31
Arizona Daily Star, Sep. 27, 2002, p.F4
Baltimore Sun, Nov. 19, 2002, p.E1
Boston Globe, July 23, 2004, p.C1

Daily Oklahoman, May 25, 2004, p.A1
Entertainment Weekly, Oct. 31, 2003, p.38
GQ, Jan. 2004, p.46
Minneapolis Star Tribune, Feb. 28, 2003, p.E1
National Catholic Reporter, Sep. 6, 2002, p.12
People, June 25, 2001, p.71
Phoenix New Times, Sep. 26, 2002
Rolling Stone, Jan. 22, 2004, p.43
Sunday Oklahoman, Aug. 22, 2004, p.C1
Time, Mar. 1, 2004, p.75
USA Weekend, Aug. 20, 2000; Nov. 2, 2003, p.6

Online Articles

http://launch.yahoo.com
   (Launch Music, "Toby Keith: The Sting of Success," Aug. 28, 1997)
http://www.usaweekend.com
   (*USA Weekend,* "An Outsider and Proud of It," Aug. 20, 2000; "Red,
   White, and Cowboy Blues," Nov. 2, 2004)
http://www.usatoday.com
   (*USA Today,* "Singer Toby Keith Speaks Out on ABC Censorship," June
   13, 2002)

Online Databases

Biography Resource Center Online, 2004, article from *Contemporary
Musicians,* 2003

ADDRESS

Toby Keith
TKO Artist Management
1107 17th Avenue
South Nashville, TN 37212

WORLD WIDE WEB SITES

http://www.tobykeith.com
http://www.tobykeith.dreamworksnashville.com
http://www.allmusic.com
http://www.cmt.com/artists

Alison Krauss 1971-

American Bluegrass Singer and Fiddler
Creator of the Hit Album *Now That I've Found You: A Collection*

BIRTH

Alison Maria Krauss was born on July 23, 1971, in Decatur, Illinois. Her father, Manfred "Fred" Krauss, is a German immigrant and a psychologist who manages apartment buildings for students at the University of Illinois. Her mother, Louise Krauss, is a freelance illustrator for magazines and textbooks.

258

Alison has one brother, Viktor, who is two years older and plays the bass in country music star Lyle Lovett's band.

YOUTH

Alison and her brother grew up in Champaign, Illinois, the university town where her parents first met. "We were pig kids," she says, "rolling around and getting dirty. We had a ball." Their parents encouraged them to learn something new every day and took them to factories and doctors' offices so they could see what went on there. They enrolled Alison and her brother in gymnastics, art, and swimming lessons. "They just wanted to make sure that if we had a talent, we got the chance to develop it," Alison says.

> *Krauss's parents enrolled her and her brother in gymnastics, art, and swimming lessons. "They just wanted to make sure that if we had a talent, we got the chance to develop it," she says.*

Both Fred and Louise Krauss were musical—Fred used to sing opera, and Louise played the guitar and banjo—and they took their children to classical and jazz concerts as well as to the local roller rink, where they skated to rock 'n roll. Viktor took piano lessons and Alison would sit under the piano while he practiced, thinking that she might like to be a pianist some day. But her mother encouraged her to be different and learn to play the violin instead. Fred and Louise Krauss had both taken instrumental lessons as kids but had not stuck with it, and they told their children repeatedly how much they regretted it. "It made a big impression: To be a quitter was the worst thing," Alison says.

Alison began studying classical violin at the age of five, and it was immediately clear that she had a gift. Having been exposed to all different kinds of music as a child, she had no preconceived ideas about any one style of playing and was willing to try anything. A banjo and guitar player herself, Louise Krauss suggested that her daughter try fiddling—a "fiddle" is basically a violin used to play folk music. She entered her first fiddling contest at the age of eight, having taught herself how to play traditional fiddlers' music from a book called *Old Time Fiddling*. She came in fourth in the competition for kids 12 and under, and soon she was entering contests all over the Midwest. "My parents and I drove all the time, sometimes even hit two or three a weekend," she recalls. "Yeah, I was a real contest queen." By the age of 12, she had won the Illinois state fiddling championship.

BECOMING A BLUEGRASS MUSICIAN

It was around this same time that Krauss discovered bluegrass music (see box). John Pennell, a musician and songwriter who was studying for his PhD in music composition at the University of Illinois, heard about her winning the state fiddling championship and invited her to audition for his bluegrass band, Silver Rail. "He changed my whole focus," she said many years later. "He got me into the timeless quality of bluegrass. I wouldn't be playing now if not for John." She joined Silver Rail—which would later become known as Union Station—and began playing in local clubs.

What Is Bluegrass Music?

The origins of bluegrass music can be traced back to the Scotts-Irish settlers of western North Carolina, who brought with them ballads that had been passed down from generation to generation in the British Isles. It was the pioneer women who taught their daughters to sing these songs, because it wasn't considered proper for women to play instruments like the fiddle or the banjo. Most of the songs were about death, and they tended to have a sad or somber tone that has been described as a "high lonesome sound." They were sung in a shrill, high-pitched voice that only women could produce, and sometimes they were accompanied by the fiddle—one of the few valuable possessions that many of the immigrants from the British Isles brought to America with them.

Bill Monroe (1911-1996) is known as "the father of bluegrass music," named for the bluish-green grass grown for fodder in his home state of Kentucky. He had learned the high-voiced style of singing from his Scotts-Irish ancestors and also played the mandolin. In 1946 he formed what is considered to be the first classic bluegrass band, whose members included Lester Flatt (guitar), Earl Scruggs (banjo), and Chubby Wise (fiddle). They had a number of hit songs on the radio in the 1950s and 60s, and Monroe was inducted into the Country Music Hall of Fame in 1970.

Today, bluegrass music is known for its virtuoso fiddle, banjo, and guitar playing and for its vocals, consisting of high-pitched voices singing in close harmony.

Pennell discovered that she was not only a champion fiddler, but that she also had "the most beautiful voice I had ever heard."

At age 13 Krauss won the National Flatpicking Championship in Winfield, Kansas, and was voted the Most Promising Fiddler by the Society for the Preservation of Bluegrass Music in America. The following year she purchased the fiddle she still plays, which was part of a collection belonging to a World War II veteran in western Kentucky. He was unwilling to part with the instrument she wanted, but after he died, Krauss bought it from his widow. By the time she was a sophomore in high school, she was appearing regularly at bluegrass competitions and had even played at the prestigious Newport Folk Festival in Rhode Island, her first introduction to New England bluegrass fans.

EDUCATION AND FIRST JOBS

Krauss attended Central High School in Champaign, where she sang in the swing choir. "We had pink sweaters with gray skirts and did the Pointer Sisters' [song] 'I'm So Excited,'" she recalls. After only two years in high school, she was admitted to the University of Illinois as a music education major. "I wasn't into [musical] theory at all, but I kicked at ear training," she says.

> *After only two years in high school, Krauss was admitted to the University of Illinois as a music education major. "I wasn't into [musical] theory at all, but I kicked at ear training," she says.*

Krauss worked briefly in a guitar store during her year-and-a-half at the university, spending most of her time dusting and tuning guitars. But she wasn't really committed to either schoolwork or her job. She claims that "All I could think about all day while I was sitting in class was Ralph Stanley, Larry Sparks, and Del McCoury" — all well-known bluegrass musicians. She did, however, spend time studying with Willliam Warfield, a well-known vocal coach at the university, before dropping out to pursue a career as a professional musician.

CAREER HIGHLIGHTS

Early Recordings

In 1985, when she was about 14, Krauss had signed a contract with Rounder Records, a small independent recording label. Two years later her first album, *Too Late to Cry*, was released. But because it was a bluegrass

album, it didn't draw much attention. The following year, the National Council for the Traditional Arts chose her as one of six fiddlers to participate in a concert tour that would introduce American audiences to different fiddling styles. Krauss represented "western fiddling," which uses a long bow and enables the fiddler to play a long series of notes very rapidly. It is also known for requiring a great deal of improvisation, which is music that is created spontaneously rather than learned and rehearsed in advance. The concert tour exposed more audiences to Krauss's talents and added to her reputation as one of America's best young fiddlers.

In 1989 Krauss made a second album with Rounder, this time performing with Union Station, which consisted of guitarist Dan Tyminski, banjoist Ron Block, bass player Barry Bales, and mandolin player Adam Steffey. *Two Highways* triggered an ongoing argument among fans and reviewers as to whether it was a country or a bluegrass album. It actually stayed on the

Billboard country album chart for 10 weeks, and the video for the title track was played repeatedly on the Country Music Television (CMT) station. Even more significantly, it was nominated for a Grammy.

Devoted to Bluegrass

Even before her next album, *I've Got That Old Feeling,* was released in 1990, country music producers were pressuring Krauss to make more "commercial" music. She had the looks to become a major country music star, and her voice—described as "a pure, melting soprano" by the *New York Times*—had been compared to that of Dolly Parton and Emmylou Harris, two of the biggest stars in country music. "They wanted me to do records that were more geared toward country radio," she explains. "That just wasn't something I was interested in doing. . . . I finally decided I hadn't had my fill of playing bluegrass. I don't think I ever will."

I've Got That Old Feeling attracted listeners who had never before shown much interest in bluegrass music. While *Rolling Stone* said that "Krauss makes traditional bluegrass seem utterly contemporary," the reviewer for *Bluegrass Unlimited* was more critical, as Krauss recalls here: "He didn't like the songs and the singing, and he didn't like the way [the album] was put together and the drums and piano that I had on there." But she included these non-traditional instruments because "I thought the songs demanded it." And there was no denying the album's success: It stayed on the *Billboard* country album chart for 10 weeks and sold more than 100,000 copies. The video she made for the title track was so popular that it went to No. 1 on CMT and brought Rounder Records hundreds of calls from country music programmers. Best of all, it won a Grammy for Best Bluegrass Recording and was named Album of the Year by the International Bluegrass Music Association.

> **"**
>
> *"I just want people to get a chance to hear bluegrass music,"Krauss told* **Rolling Stone.** *"I think the only reason it isn't more popular is just that people haven't been lucky enough to hear it."*
>
> **"**

By this time, Krauss had made it clear that she was not interested in making money by playing more mainstream country music. Rather than expanding her reputation as a "hot" fiddler capable of dazzling audiences, she would play with more restraint and stay true to the bluegrass tradition. "I just want people to get a chance to hear bluegrass music," she told

Rolling Stone. "I think the only reason it isn't more popular is just that people haven't been lucky enough to hear it."

The Road to The Grand Ole Opry

Krauss released two more albums in the early 1990s. *Every Time You Say Goodbye* (1992) showed the influence of country music even though it won her a second Grammy for Best Bluegrass Album. The *New York Times* praised Krauss's "high, pure vocals and impressive fiddling," describing her voice as "angelic." Union Station "shines alongside her," the *Los Angeles Times* commented, "with a completely revamped lineup contributing strong lead vocals, good original songs and standout playing."

I Know Who Holds Tomorrow (1992) was an album Krauss made with The Cox Family, an acoustic country band that she'd first met at a bluegrass festival when she was 16. It was Sidney Cox who had written "I've Got That

Old Feeling," the title track for her third album, and she had been doing everything she could to promote the band. Although this new album displayed what a critic for *All Music Guide* called a combination of "jaw-dropping fiddling and breathtaking singing," it did not get the rave reviews that Krauss had received for *Every Time You Say Goodbye*. It did, however, bring her a third Grammy, this time for Best Southern Gospel, Country Gospel, or Bluegrass Gospel Album.

In 1993 Krauss was invited to become a member of the Grand Ole Opry, the country's best known venue for country music performers in Nashville, Tennessee. As the first bluegrass singer to receive this honor in almost 30 years and as the Opry's youngest musician ever, Krauss was well aware of the significance of this event. On the evening of her induction, she was introduced by country music star Garth Brooks—a sure sign that Krauss's talents had been embraced by the country music establishment.

"Their harmonies were so different,"Krauss said after listening to the music of the British rock band Def Leppard."They layered so many things. So I got all wigged out and wanted to try that stuff on [my next] record."

Bluegrass Goes Double Platinum

By the mid-1990s Krauss had begun singing harmony on albums by other mainstream country music stars, including Patty Loveless and Dolly Parton. She had co-hosted the International Bluegrass Music Awards show and was opening for Garth Brooks on a regular basis. But no one was prepared for what happened when she released her fifth album, *Now That I've Found You: A Collection.* Consisting of the most popular songs from her first four albums, collaborations with other musicians including The Cox Family, and four new songs written especially for her, the CD was the first bluegrass album to experience significant "crossover" success. The centerpiece of the album was Krauss's rendition of Keith Whitley's "When You Say Nothing at All," the song that had helped her get into the Grand Old Opry. The album also included cover versions of several classic pop and rock songs: "Baby, Now That I've Found You," originally recorded by the Foundations, "Oh, Atlanta," by Bad Company, and "I Will," by the Beatles—all played with Krauss's unique bluegrass style.

Now That I've Found You made the pop chart's Top 15 and remained on the country chart's Top 10 for more than 30 weeks. It was the first record produced by Rounder to go platinum, eventually selling more than two mil-

lion copies. It was nominated for four Country Music Association Awards, all of which Krauss won, and earned two more Grammys. One critic called it "a greatest hits album from a bluegrass band that never had a hit." Despite her intention to ignore fame and fortune and remain true to bluegrass traditions, Alison Krauss was well on her way to becoming a star.

So Long So Wrong

Krauss took a few months off to recover from the unanticipated success of *Now That I've Found You*. She spent time settling into the house she had just bought in Nashville and listening to the music of Def Leppard, the British rock band. "Their harmonies were so different," she explains. "They layered so many things. So I got all wigged out and wanted to try that stuff on [my next] record."

The result was *So Long So Wrong,* her first album of new material in five years. It marked a return to traditional bluegrass but with subtle differences, including layered instruments and a fuller sound. It featured a song written by Krauss's brother Viktor and what *Entertainment Weekly* called "the deft and impeccably layered ensemble playing" of Union Station. *Time* magazine called it "48 minutes of beautiful music. . . . Krauss has the voice of a lost angel, beckoning you into the beyond."

Going Solo

Krauss's next release, *Forget About It* (1999), was a solo album made without Union Station. The theme was regret and sadness, although Krauss preferred to think of it as "the positive kind, still looking for the way up to the good, wherever people can find it." It gave her a chance to display two distinct styles at which she excelled — traditional bluegrass and what *Billboard* called "soft, lush ballads" — and featured the work of dobro player Jerry Douglas. Dolly Parton and Lyle Lovett provided guest vocals, and Krauss's new husband, Pat Bergeson, played electric guitar on a few of the tracks.

While *The Tennessean* called the album as a whole "understated and flawlessly executed," *People Weekly* said, "Still, one can't help but thirst for some of the pure, mountain stream sparkle that graced many of Krauss's previous recordings." The album was nominated for three Grammys but didn't win any.

Bluegrass Goes Mainstream

In 2000 Krauss contributed three songs to the successful soundtrack for the movie *O Brother, Where Art Thou?* starring George Clooney and Holly Hunter. Emmylou Harris and other country music and bluegrass stars appeared on the album, a huge mainstream success that went double platinum and brought bluegrass music to millions of American listeners. Krauss sang a cappella (unaccompanied by instruments) with Emmylou Harris and Gillian Welch on "Don't Leave Nobody But the Baby"; she also performed "Down to the River to Pray" and "I'll Fly Away." The soundtrack won Album of the Year from the International Bluegrass Music Association as well as a Grammy for best album.

Krauss released two more CDs of her own within the next year. *New Favorite* (2001) was her second album featuring dobro player Jerry Douglas, who had replaced former Union Station member Adam Steffey. *New Favorite* broke some of the strict stylistic rules governing bluegrass music

Emmylou Harris, Gillian Welch, and Krauss perform a piece from
O Brother, Where Art Thou?

and gave what *All Music Guide* called a "progressive slant to Union Station's traditional bluegrass feel." The two-disc *Live* (2002), which was recorded at the Palace Theater in Louisville, Kentucky, combined "blazing old-fashioned fiddle and banjo drivers [with] patiently arranged acoustic singer-songwriter music," according to *The Tennessean*. It was the first of Krauss's albums to go platinum since the 1995 release of *Now That I Found You: A Collection*.

Recent and Upcoming Projects

Recently, Krauss has been busy playing in concert and performing songs for various movies. In addition to *O Brother, Where Art Thou*, she recorded two songs for the soundtrack of *Cold Mountain*; she has also been featured on the soundtracks of a number of other movies, including *Divine Secrets of the Ya-Ya Sisterhood, Twister,* and *Buffy, the Vampire Slayer.* She has worked with a wide range of artists that includes cellist Yo-Yo Ma, Linda Ronstadt, Reba McEntire, Vince Gill, Dolly Parton, Ricky Skaggs, and the rock group Phish. Most recently, she participated in the 2004 Great High Mountain Tour, which featured songs and performances by artists from the soundtracks of *O Brother, Where Art Thou?* and *Cold Mountain.*

The most recent recording by Krauss and Union Station, *Lonely Runs Both Ways*, came out in late 2004. On this first new studio recording in three years, they stayed true to their bluegrass roots. Like their previous works, this album was characterized by Krauss's hypnotic singing and the superb instrumental skills of Krauss and the other musicians, all put to use on songs by a range of the top songwriters in the business. "What ultimately holds the album together is its embrace of sweet melancholy," Greg Crawford wrote in the *Detroit Free Press*. "Nobody does sadness quite as well as Krauss and company, and whether they're performing Woody Guthrie's Depression-era 'Pastures of Plenty' or Gillian Welch and David Rawlings's contemporary 'Wouldn't Be So Bad,' they tackle familiar themes of loneliness, despair, and restlessness with deep feeling." Writing in *Entertainment Weekly*, Alanna Nash summed up the response of many listeners: "While it can be unbearably sad, *Lonely Runs Both Ways* is ultimately a beautiful meditation on heartbreak."

In addition to performing and recording, Krauss remains committed to promoting the careers of lesser known musicians in whom she believes. She has produced three albums for The Cox Family and two albums for Nickel Creek; she even won a Grammy for her production work on the Nickel Creek recording *This Side*. She is also thinking about producing a debut album for Sierra Hull, a teenager who plays the mandolin.

Writing in **Entertainment Weekly,** *Alanna Nash summed up the response of many listeners:* "While it can be unbearably sad, **Lonely Runs Both Ways** *is ultimately a beautiful meditation on heartbreak."*

Loyal to Her Roots

Despite her unprecedented success as an artist — Krauss has won a record 17 Grammy Awards, more than any other female musician in the history of the awards — she has remained fiercely loyal to bluegrass and to Rounder Records. She is afraid that if she signs a contract with a more commercial record label, they will want her to "tone down" the traditional bluegrass sound of her music and make it sound more like pop or country, with electric guitars and drums. She has also remained loyal to Union Station — "It's a band, for gosh sakes, it isn't something I'm going to grow out of" — and she prefers sharing the lead vocals with them rather than doing all the singing herself.

One of Krauss's most important contributions to bluegrass music is her willingness to record new songs. Most bluegrass musicians stick to traditional tunes or rearrange pop or country songs, but Krauss has assembled a small group of talented songwriters to come up with new songs for her albums. The result, according to *Country Music* magazine, is a combination of "country music subject matter, modern-folk lyrics, and bluegrass music." Krauss herself describes her songs as "not traditionally bluegrass, and . . . not commercial country. They're in this weird folkie/string-band category where we want to be." Others have referred to her music as "newgrass."

In a field of entertainment that is largely ego-driven, Krauss is uncomfortable with the fame that her best-selling albums have brought her. "All she has ever wanted to do is play good music," explains Denise Stiff, her manager. "She hasn't changed the music to try to get into the public eye; she hasn't tried to get into the public eye at all. This has never been about what works on the radio. It has always been about what songs we really love and do well." Krauss herself admits that she can't imagine recording a song she doesn't love. "To me, a song has to have a timeless feel. . . . Maybe it's something I learned from [bluegrass legend] Bill Monroe. You listen to one of his songs and they could have been written yesterday or tomorrow because they just tell a human story. That's all I try to do in my music."

MARRIAGE AND FAMILY

In 1997, Krauss married guitarist Pat Bergeson, a friend of her brother's whom she had first met when she was only 12. They have a son, Sam, who was born in 1999; they were divorced in 2001. She has managed to keep her personal life very private, and few of her fans even knew she was going to have a baby. Krauss and her son live in Nashville, where she can be close to the studios where she records.

MAJOR INFLUENCES

Krauss cites a range of musical influences, including the Electric Light Orchestra (ELO) and Foreigner. Some of the bluegrass musicians who have most influenced her include Ralph Stanley, Tony Rice, and Ricky Skaggs. The country performer who has had the greatest influence on her is Dolly Parton, with whom she has recorded. "She's special, so terrific . . . she is one of the most talented songwriters," Krauss says.

"To me, a song has to have a timeless feel," Krauss says. "Maybe it's something I learned from [bluegrass legend] Bill Monroe. You listen to one of his songs and they could have been written yesterday or tomorrow because they just tell a human story. That's all I try to do in my music."

MEMORABLE EXPERIENCES

Some of Krauss's most memorable moments have come to her through her fans. "There's one little girl who's autistic and can't hardly walk; the parents encourage her to walk over to the tape player to turn it on because she likes our music and it gets her to do her physical therapy. The parents of another child who can't talk wrote a letter to me saying our version of 'When You Say Nothing at All' let them know how their kid feels about them, even though the child can't tell them." This same song appeared to

have a calming effect on a severely handicapped child who cried "and was out of control" all the time.

FAVORITE MOVIES

Krauss loves to watch "girly movies" like *Steel Magnolias*. Her favorite movie of all time, however, is *The Color Purple*.

RECORDINGS

Too Late to Cry, 1987
Two Highways, 1989
I've Got That Old Feeling, 1990
Every Time You Say Goodbye, 1992
Now That I've Found You: A Collection, 1995
So Long So Wrong, 1997
Forget About It, 1999

O Brother, Where Art Thou?, 2000 (with various artists)
New Favorite, 2001
Live, 2002
Lonely Runs Both Ways, 2004

HONORS AND AWARDS

Country Music Association Awards: 1995 (four awards), Female Vocalist of the Year, Horizon Award, Single of the Year, for "When You Say Nothing At All" (with Union Station), and Vocal Event of the Year, for "Somewhere in the Vicinity of the Heart" (with Shenandoah); 2001, Album of the Year, for *O Brother, Where Art Thou?*; 2004 (two awards), Music Video of the Year, for "Whiskey Lullaby"; Musical Event of the Year, for "Whiskey Lullaby" (with Brad Paisley)

Grammy Awards: 1990, Best Bluegrass Recording, for *I've Got That Old Feeling*; 1992, Best Bluegrass Album, for *Every Time You Say Goodbye* (with Union Station); 1994, Best Southern Gospel, Country Gospel, or Bluegrass Gospel Album, for *I Know Who Holds Tomorrow* (with The Cox Family); 1995 (two awards), Best Female Country Vocal Performance, for "Baby, Now That I've Found You," and Best Country Collaboration with Vocals, for "Somewhere in the Vicinity of the Heart" (with Shenandoah); 1996, Best Country Collaboration with Vocals, for "High Lonesome Sound" (with Union Station and Vince Gill); 1997 (three awards), Best Bluegrass Album, for *So Long So Wrong* (with Union Station), Best Country Instrumental Performance, for "Little Liza Jane"(with Union Station), and Best Country Performance By a Duo or Group with Vocal, for "Looking In the Eyes of Love"(with Union Station); 1998, Best Country Collaboration with Vocals, for "Same Old Train" (with various artists); 2001 (three awards), Best Bluegrass Album, for *New Favorite* (with Union Station), Best Country Performance by a Duo or Group with Vocal, for "The Lucky One"(with Union Station), and Album of the Year, for *O Brother Where Art Thou?* (with various artists); 2002, for Best Contemporary Folk Album, for *This Side* (as producer for Nickel Creek); 2003 (three awards), Best Country Collaboration with Vocals, for "How's the World Treating You" (with James Taylor), Best Bluegrass Album, for *Live* (with Union Station), Best Country Instrumental Performance, for "Cluck Old Hen" (with Union Station)

International Bluegrass Music Association Awards: 1990, Female Vocalist of the Year; 1991 (three awards), Female Vocalist of the Year, Entertainer of the Year, Album of the Year, for *I've Got That Old Feeling*; 1993 (two awards), Female Vocalist of the Year, Album of the Year, for *Every Time You Say Goodbye*; 1995 (two awards), Female Vocalist of the Year,

Entertainer of the Year; 2001 (two awards), Gospel Recorded Event of the Year, for "I'll Fly Away," Album of the Year, for *O Brother Where Art Thou?*

Dove Award (Gospel Music Association): 1998, Bluegrass Recorded Song of the Year, for "Children of the Living God"

FURTHER READING

Books

Contemporary Musicians, Vol. 10, 1994; Vol. 41, 2003

Periodicals

Billboard, June 5, 1999, p.3
Chicago Tribune, Jan. 19, 1992, Arts section, p.12; Mar. 30, 1997, Arts section, p.3; Mar. 17, 2000, p.33
Country Music, May-June 1994, p.49
Current Biography Yearbook, 1997
Entertainment Weekly, Sep. 29, 1995, p.32
Los Angeles Times, Apr. 6, 1997, Calendar section, p.4
New York Times, Apr. 24, 1994, Section 2, p.28; Apr. 30, 2000, p.15; Jan. 24, 2002, p.F1
New Yorker, Dec. 6, 1999, p.54
Rolling Stone, Jan. 25, 1996, p.48

Online Databases

Biography Resource Center Online, 2005, articles from *Contemporary Musicians,* 2003

ADDRESS

Alison Krauss
Union Station Land, Inc.
P. O. Box 121711
Nashville, TN 37212

WORLD WIDE WEB SITE

http://www.alisonkrauss.com

Wangari Maathai 1940-
Kenyan Environmentalist, Feminist, Human Rights
Activist, and Educator
Winner of the 2004 Nobel Peace Prize

[Editor's Note: Wangari Maathai first appeared in Biography
Today *in 1997. Since then, she has continued to distinguish herself
as an internationally known environmental and political activist
and was named the winner of the 2004 Nobel Peace Prize. This
entry covers her life to date, with a special focus on her accomplishments since the late 1990s.]*

BIRTH

Wangari Muta Maathai (pronounced wan-GAH-ree mah-DHEYE) was born Wangari Muta on April 1, 1940, in Nyeri, a town in south-central Kenya, about 60 miles north of Nairobi, the country's capital. She later lived near the towns of Solai and Kanungu. Her family was part of the Kikuyu people, one of the many cultural groups that live in east-central Africa. She has described her parents as "very simple farmers" and said that her father was "a squatter on a white settler's farm." This means that her family worked and lived on land that they did not own, though she also said her father was on good terms with the landowner. Her family practiced subsistence farming. In other words, the food they raised was primarily used to feed their family, rather than being sold as a cash crop. Her father also served as farm mechanic. Of the family's six children, Maathai was the oldest daughter.

BACKGROUND ON KENYA

At the time Maathai was born, Kenya did not exist as an independent country. Instead, the area, known as British East Africa, was a colony ruled by the United Kingdom. The British had entered the region in the mid-1800s and established large agricultural plantations and other businesses. This region, and indeed all of Africa, was fundamentally transformed by colonialism. The colonial rulers regarded most aspects of African life as inferior to those of Europe. They tried to change the Africans' way of life, imposing their own social customs, languages, and religious beliefs. The Europeans also erected governments and legal systems that ensured that they would maintain political and economic power over the Africans. They took Africa's land and natural resources for themselves, accumulating great wealth in the process, but they shared little of this wealth with Africans. Instead, Africans were herded into the colonies' most difficult and lowest-paying jobs.

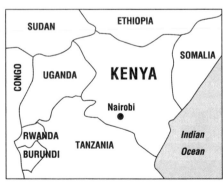

ABOVE: Closeup of Kenya and surrounding countries.

RIGHT: Kenya in relationship to the continent of Africa.

Under British rule, the African residents of British East Africa were forced into a social and economic position below that of the colonists. Some worked as laborers on the plantations, while others maintained their own small farms. Beginning in the late 1940s, colonized people all around the world began to demand their independence in the aftermath of World War II. In British East Africa, Jomo Kenyatta (1891?-1978) led the battle to end British rule. After several years of fighting, the independence forces triumphed, and in 1963, the country of Kenya was created. Kenyatta became the country's first prime minister and later its president. His political party, the Kenya African National Union (KANU), dominated the country's government for the next 40 years. (For more information on Kenyatta, see *Biography Today World Leaders Series,* Vol. 2: *Modern African Leaders.)*

———— **"** ————

At the time Maathai grew up, it wasn't common for a Kenyan girl to receive an education. But her family had an eye toward the future. "My parents were progressive people," she said, "and they decided that I should have a chance to go to school."

———— **"** ————

MAATHAI'S EDUCATION

At the time Maathai grew up, it wasn't common for a Kenyan girl to receive an education. But her family was looking toward the future. "My parents were progressive people," she said, "and they decided that I should have a chance to go to school." Maathai began attending classes when she was eight years old, enrolling at Ihithe Primary School near her home in Kanungu. She later studied at Mathari Girls Intermediate School, and in 1955 she entered Loreto Convent Limuru Girls High School. She did very well in her studies, and her teachers singled her out as a promising student.

As Maathai was finishing her high school studies in the late 1950s, her homeland was moving toward independence. Maathai's education suddenly became joined with her country's political future. Surprisingly, it all began in another part of the world. A group of United States politicians, which included John F. Kennedy, started a program to bring gifted Africans to America to receive a college education. They hoped this program would develop future leaders who would help guide the newly independent African countries. Maathai was chosen to be part of the program, and in 1960, she moved to the United States. The trip to the U.S. included her first airplane trip and her first ride on an escalator, where she lost her shoe.

Then she took a Greyhound bus from New York City to Atchison, Kansas, and enrolled at Mount St. Scholastica College.

"I'd never seen so much flat land or so much corn," Maathai said of her new home on the plains. The school was operated by members of the Benedictine religious order, and she was inspired by the nuns that taught her. "On a daily basis, I saw women working hard for higher goals and inner peace," she later recalled. "This must have impacted my own conscience and values as I matured." She graduated with a Bachelor of Science (BS) degree in biology in 1964. She then entered a post-graduate program at the University of Pittsburgh, where she earned a Master of Science (MS) degree in biological science in 1966. Next, she attended the University of Munich in Germany for a short time, but she began to feel the pull of her homeland once again. Believing that she "had to go back home . . . and make a contribution," she returned to Kenya in 1966. She took a job shortly after she arrived, but she wasn't finished with college. She enrolled in a doctoral program at the University of Nairobi, and in 1971 she received a doctoral degree (PhD) in anatomy. She was the first woman in all of eastern and central Africa to earn a doctorate.

——— **"** ———

At the University of Nairobi, many of her colleagues weren't happy to have a female in their ranks. "The typical African woman is supposed to be dependent, submissive," Maathai explained. Some men questioned the education she had received in the United States. "They wondered if it was really a master's degree or if it was just a joke," she said.

——— **"** ———

CAREER HIGHLIGHTS

Maathai chose to work in the field of veterinary medicine, which allowed her to assist the many people in Kenya who raise livestock. When she first returned to Kenya, she took a position as a research assistant in the department of veterinary medicine at the University of Nairobi in 1966; she remained with the school for the next 16 years. Many of her colleagues weren't happy to have a female in their ranks. "The typical African woman is supposed to be dependent, submissive," Maathai explained. Some men questioned the education she had received in the United States. "They wondered if it was really a master's degree or if it was just a joke," she said.

Maathai didn't let sexism stand in her way. After earning her PhD, she became chair of the university's Department of Veterinary Anatomy in 1976 and was appointed associate professor in 1977. She was the first woman to hold these positions at the university. "Others told me that I shouldn't have a career, that I shouldn't raise my voice, that women are supposed to have a master," she explained. "Finally I was able to see that if I had a contribution I wanted to make, I must do it, despite what others said."

A Changing Environment

Maathai's book tells the story of the Green Belt Movement: its history, organization, objectives, and philosophy. The book also explains how to start a similar organization devoted to environmental and social justice issues.

One of Maathai's projects at the university was to conduct research about ticks that infested livestock. In the process, she found a more basic issue. "When I spoke to farmers, their real problems were not the tick but the availability of water, the productivity of the soils, and the shortage of fuelwood," she said. These conversations made her reflect on a change she had noticed in Kenya. Upon her return to the country after six years studying abroad, she found that there were far fewer trees. This condition is known as deforestation—the removal of forests. Also, there was less ground water than in previous decades. "I noticed springs that I knew as a child drying up, and I saw water levels going down," she said, "and I could see there was no longer firewood."

All of these were symptoms of desertification, which means that more and more land in Kenya was being taken over by desert. The northern part of the country had long been arid and inhospitable to growing crops, but now the infertile, desert-like conditions seemed to be expanding. Though the causes and processes of desertification are complex, one of the key factors is trees. Tree roots help bind the soil together and hold it in place. As trees are cut down for lumber and to create pastures and fields, the rich

279

topsoil can erode away. Also, the loss of shade dries out the soil and may even cause the climate to change, reducing the amount of rainfall.

There was a human side to this environmental issue. Like many former colonies in Africa, Kenya was a poor country where many people struggled to get by. The loss of trees and the expansion of the desert made the situation worse. The farmers' fields weren't as productive, so food became more scarce and more expensive. With fewer trees, firewood became harder to find. This had a big effect on people in rural areas, most of whom used wood fires to cook their meals. They began to eat more foods that didn't require cooking, and many of these items proved less nutritious than traditional cooked dishes. This contributed to the country's malnutrition problem.

> "The Green Belt Movement is about hope. It tells people that they are responsible for their own lives. It suggests that at the very least, you can plant a tree and improve your habitat. It raises an awareness that people can take control of their environment, which is the first step toward greater participation in society."

Maathai's personal life had an effect on her growing concern about the environment and poverty. In the late 1960s she married Mwangi Maathai, a business leader who had political aspirations. In 1974 her husband ran for a seat in Kenya's Parliament (similar to Congress in the United States), and Maathai accompanied him on the campaign trail. This gave her an even better look at the difficult lives of the country's underprivileged residents. "I had grown up in a poor rural area, but it was nothing like what I encountered in the slums of Nairobi," Maathai recalled. "These people were desperate. All they wanted was a promise from my husband that we would find them jobs. Of course he said he would, because that is what you say on a campaign. However, I took the promise very seriously."

Green Belt: Beginning a Movement

Faced by two large problems—a lack of trees and a lack of jobs—Maathai hit upon a solution that addressed both: pay people to plant trees. Her program was launched in 1977 under the direction of the National Council of Women of Kenya, a group that she had recently joined. The program was originally called Save the Land Harambee, using the Swahili term that

Wangari ready to plant a seedling for the Green Belt Movement.

means "let us all pull together." But the program later took on a new title: The Green Belt Movement, which also became the title of her book on the subject, *The Green Belt Movement: Sharing the Approach and the Experience*, first published in 1985 and reprinted in 2003. The program she developed provides free tree seedlings to the members of a community, who in most cases are women. The women plant the seedlings and care for them. For each tree that survives more than three months outside the nursery, the planter receives 50 Kenya cents (about 2.5 U.S. cents). This sounds like a very small amount of money, but one person can plant a lot of seedlings. Also, the income of poor Kenyans is so low that even a few dollars can make a huge difference in their lives.

A key to the success of the Green Belt Movement is that it is practical. As Maathai has noted, those struggling to make ends meet can't afford to volunteer their time for a cause that doesn't directly touch their lives. "Conservation cannot be presented to them as a luxury issue," she explained. "The trees have been planted to meet immediate community needs—to provide fuelwood and material for fencing and building, and to give shade." Early on, the organization received help from government nurseries that provided tree seedlings for free. The program grew quickly, however, and the demand became so great that the government had to start charging for the trees. Eventually, the organization established its own nursery in Nairobi, then encouraged women's groups around the country to do the same. By the late 1990s, 6,000 of these nurseries were in operation in Kenya.

Much of the group's funding comes from international organizations, but Green Belt relies on the knowledge and abilities of local people. The women use common-sense agricultural practices rather than complex scientific knowledge. These "foresters without diplomas," as Maathai calls them, were largely successful: about half of the trees planted in dry areas grew into adulthood, while about 8 of every 10 planted in wetter areas survived. By 1999, the movement had planted more than 20 million trees throughout Kenya and had employed about 50,000 people. The Green Belt program proved so successful, it spread to many other countries in Africa. In addition to planting trees, Green Belt also offers educational programs addressing civic affairs, the environment, health, nutrition, and other subjects. "The Green Belt Movement is about hope," Maathai said. "It tells people that they are responsible for their own lives. It suggests that at the very least, you can plant a tree and improve your habitat. It raises an awareness that people can take control of their environment, which is the first step toward greater participation in society."

―――― " ――――

"When you start working with the environment seriously," Maathai said, "the whole arena comes: human rights, women's rights, environmental rights, children's rights, you know, everybody's rights."

―――― " ――――

"Too Educated, Too Strong, Too Successful"

In addition to growing trees and putting people to work, Maathai began to focus on a variety of political issues. "When you start working with the environment seriously," she said, "the whole arena comes: human rights, women's rights, environmental rights, children's rights, you know, everybody's rights." Eventually, her concerns would make her an outspoken critic of her country's government, but first she had a personal matter to deal with.

In the early 1980s Maathai's husband filed for divorce, claiming that his wife had committed adultery with another member of Parliament. His case also asserted that she was "too educated, too strong, too successful, too stubborn, and too hard to control." She denied the adultery charge, and the case was settled in a well-publicized trial. When the court found in favor of her husband, Maathai charged that judges were either "incompetent or corrupt," which earned her a brief jail sentence for being in contempt of court. In the end, she believed that her marriage came to an end because her husband considered her a threat. "I think from his point of view I was a woman who was a little too, er . . . conspicuous for him," she said. "He was a politician and he wanted to be successful and I think I was a bit overshadowing to him, and I didn't realize."

Maathai didn't become any less conspicuous after the divorce. In 1982, her political activities forced her to give up her position at the University of Nairobi. According to one account of the incident, she decided to become a candidate for a Parliament seat and quit her job to concentrate on the campaign. She was later prevented from running because of a technicality, and the university refused to take her back. Maathai has charged that she was "forced out" of her job at the college. "The university told me I could either be an activist or an academic," she said, which eventually led to her resignation.

Fighting the Power

Maathai believes that "you cannot fight for the environment without eventually getting into conflict with the politicians." In fact, she came to believe that bad political leaders caused many of the problems facing her region of the world. "Some people believe that Africans live impoverished lives because they are unproductive and lack initiative," she wrote in *The Green Belt Movement*, "but nothing can be further from the truth. Much has to do with misgovernance by their leaders, and Africans have been poorly governed for a long time."

"A long time" describes the term of Kenya's president Daniel arap Moi, who took power after the death of Jomo Kenyatta in 1978 and remained there for the next 24 years. Moi's administration earned a reputation for corruption. For instance, government leaders were suspected of demanding payments, or "kickbacks," from contractors who wished to work for the government. Also, there is evidence that Moi personally amassed a fortune by misappropriating public money. Many Kenyans were opposed to his actions, but they had no effective way to remove him from office. The constitution prevented the establishment of any opposition political parties, so Moi and his KANU party faced no opposition in elections. Those who spoke out against this system were often arrested and tortured. Opposing President Moi could be very dangerous.

Yet that's the job Maathai took on in 1989. That year, Moi's party announced plans to build a 60-story skyscraper in the middle of Nairobi's Uhuru Park. Accompanied by a four-story-tall statue of Moi, the building

Maathai's work with the Green Belt Movement brought her in opposition to Daniel arap Moi, President of Kenya from 1978 to 2002, whose administration was widely believed to be corrupt.

project would cost Kenya $200 million. In addition, the building's concrete and glass would take over a tree-filled park that was intended to be a refuge for the city's residents. "If I didn't react to their interfering with this park, I may as well not plant another tree," Maathai said. "I cannot condone that kind of activity and call myself an environmentalist." She filed a lawsuit in an attempt to stop the project and publicly denounced the government's priorities. "The people are starving. They need food; they need medicine; they need education. They do not need . . . a skyscraper to house the ruling party and a 24-hour TV station."

Moi and his cronies struck back at Maathai. The president called her "a mad woman" who was "a threat to the order and security of the country," and she was publicly denounced in Kenya's Parliament. Many politicians brought up the issue of her divorce, saying that she was inspired by a hatred of men. Maathai wasn't intimidated, and she continued to speak out against the building. "They think they can embarrass and silence me with threats and name-calling," she said. "But I have an elephant's skin." She lost her legal challenge, but the controversy she created about the tower gave the project's financial backers second thoughts. In the end, the president's skyscraper was never built.

Suffering for Her Actions

Maathai learned that name-calling wasn't the only weapon that could be used against her. The Green Belt Movement was suddenly evicted from the government-owned building where it had its offices. As a result, the group was forced to operate out of Maathai's home for a time. The group's tree-planting work was also interfered with. Still, she was committed to being an outspoken activist. "I may get into serious trouble," she admitted. "They may physically abuse me. . . . But every time you provide leadership — every time you speak out, you expect you may suffer for what you believe in."

Her prediction of physical abuse soon came true. In March 1992, Maathai participated in a hunger strike seeking freedom for political prisoners in Kenya. Riot police attacked the peaceful gathering, and she was clubbed unconscious. She was arrested on numerous occasions but was aided by supporters outside Kenya who pressured the authorities to set her free. In 1993, she tried to stop ethnic violence in Kenya's Rift Valley. Disagreements there between different cultural groups had resulted in more than 1,000 deaths. Maathai charged that Moi's government was inciting the violence so that the president's group (the Kalenjin) could drive out their rivals. She founded the Tribal Clashes Resettlement Volunteer Service to assist those displaced by violence.

"I may get into serious trouble," Maathai admitted. "They may physically abuse me. . . . But every time you provide leadership — every time you speak out, you expect you may suffer for what you believe in."

Though Maathai and other protestors faced many difficulties and dangers, they began to have an effect on the Kenyan political system. President Moi felt the pressure of growing resistance within the country as well as complaints by international governments and organizations. In 1991, the ban on opposition political parties was lifted, allowing greater political freedom. A year later, the first multiparty elections in decades took place, though Moi was once again elected president and his KANU party remained in power. Maathai's supporters urged her to run for office, but she refused for several years. Then, in 1997, she not only ran for a seat in Parliament but also for president. Her campaign as candidate for the Liberal Party of Kenya (LPK) didn't fare well, however. She entered the race late, just a month before the election. Then, on the day before the voting, a rumor circulated that she had withdrawn from the election, though Maathai later claimed this was untrue. According to some accounts, her party deserted her at the last moment. Whatever the cause, she received little support and wasn't elected to either office. Instead President Moi was returned to yet another term.

Defending the Forest

The following year, Maathai returned to a more familiar role — defending one of Kenya's nature areas. The Karura National Forest, near Nairobi, had been established to protect one of the last patches of virgin forest in Kenya. But in 1998 President Moi's government sold one-third of it to developers who wanted to build a luxury housing development. Maathai and other protestors objected to the sale, but that didn't stop developers from beginning to fell trees. The situation became more tense after equipment belonging to the developers was set on fire. Then, in December 1998 and January 1999, violence erupted in a series of confrontations between protestors and private security guards who had been hired by the developers. While Maathai and her colleagues tried to carry out a demonstration, 200 men armed with clubs and whips attacked them. Maathai suffered a blow to the head and dropped to her knees, blood pouring from a scalp wound. Her friends pulled her out of the melee and drove her to a police station. She filed a complaint saying that she had been assaulted, then signed the form in her own blood. From her hospital room she vowed that "as soon as I recover, I shall return to Karura Forest, even if they bury me there."

The controversy over Karura soon grew larger. Prominent religious leaders in Kenya sided with the environmentalists, as did students from the University of Nairobi. In late January 1999, the student protests turned into riots in the streets of the capital. These protests created more negative publicity about the housing development at Karura, and the project was finally abandoned. "We stopped them," Maathai said, but she soon had to take up similar battles in other parts of Kenya. In the early 2000s, the government attempted to give away more public lands, with Maathai and her colleagues fighting them every step of the way.

Winning the Vote

As the 2002 elections approached, many Kenyans wondered if their country was finally about to see an important political change. Thanks to a law passed in 1992, President Moi was prevented from seeking another term in office. He was still very powerful, however, and hoped to see his hand-picked successor become president. Kenya's opposition parties united

After private developers began felling trees in Karura National Forest, a peaceful demonstration turned violent when hired security guards attacked demonstrators. ABOVE: Maathai and others argue with security guards at Karura Forest. BELOW: Maathai was hospitalized after she was injured in the demonstration at Karura Forest.

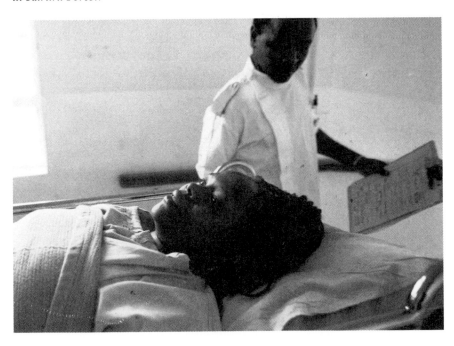

against Moi, forming the National Rainbow Coalition (NARC) with Mwai Kibaki as their presidential candidate. Maathai joined the NARC coalition and once again ran for a seat in Parliament. On election day, NARC swept to victory. Kibaki became Kenya's president, and Maathai became one of the country's lawmakers. Upon taking office, Kibaki gave Maathai an additional responsibility by appointing her Assistant Minister for the Environment in charge of natural resources and wildlife.

"I'm very excited," Maathai said of her new role in government. "For me it is the next step and a very, very important step. I sit in Parliament sometimes and remind myself, 'you're really making laws here.' If a law is made then you actually have an opportunity to influence future generations." At the same time, she came to understand that being a part of government can be as difficult as opposing it. "It's a very slow process," she said. "I try to be persuasive, but [things are] not moving as fast as I would have liked." As usual, she emphasized measures related to the country's trees in her parliamentary work. For instance, she sought funding to purchase seedlings and promoted the establishment of a national tree-planting day.

While her governmental duties keep her busy, Maathai has continued to express her opinions on a range of important topics. Her attitude toward HIV-AIDS has created controversy. *The Standard,* a Kenyan newspaper, quoted her as saying "AIDS is not a curse from God to Africans or the black people. It is a tool to control them designed by some evil-minded scientists." The quote seemed to suggest that Maathai believed AIDS had been purposely invented to harm blacks. She later distanced herself from this view. In an essay entitled "The Challenge of AIDS in Africa" published on her web site, Maathai wrote that "I neither say nor believe that the virus was developed by white people or white powers in order to destroy the African people. Such views are wicked and destructive."

Winning the Nobel Peace Prize

Over the years, Maathai has accepted many awards from international agencies. She's become somewhat accustomed to receiving the news of such prizes, but in October 2004, she got an exciting phone call: The Norwegian ambassador to Kenya notified her that she had just won the Nobel Peace Prize. The Nobel Prizes are some of the most prestigious honors in the world and are given out annually by the Nobel Foundation, which is based in Norway and Sweden. The awards cover several different fields, with the Peace Prize going to the person or group whose actions have promoted world peace. In announcing the award, the Nobel Committee stated that "Maathai stands at the front of the fight to promote ecologically viable

Maathai with her Nobel Peace Prize and certificate.

social, economic, and cultural development in Kenya and in Africa." She was the first African woman and the first environmentalist to win the prize.

"I am absolutely overwhelmed," Maathai said after getting the news. "This is the biggest surprise in my entire life." In addition to the worldwide fame that comes with the award, she received $1.36 million U.S. "That's a lot of money," she said. "I've not had so much money in my life. It's so much I don't know what I'll be able to do with it. But I do know it will go to improve the work we do."

—— " ——

"Some people have asked what the relationship is between peace and environment, and to them I say that many wars are fought over resources, which are becoming increasingly scarce across the earth. If we did a better job of managing our resources sustainably, conflicts over them would be reduced. So, protecting the global environment is directly related to securing peace.... When we plant trees, we plant the seeds of peace and seeds of hope."

—— " ——

Maathai was something of a surprise choice for the Nobel Peace Prize, and some commentators wondered why the prize went to someone best known for environmental work. When she publicly accepted the award, she addressed this subject: "Some people have asked what the relationship is between peace and environment, and to them I say that many wars are fought over resources, which are becoming increasingly scarce across the earth. If we did a better job of managing our resources sustainably, conflicts over them would be reduced. So, protecting the global environment is directly related to securing peace.... When we plant trees, we plant the seeds of peace and seeds of hope."

MARRIAGE AND FAMILY

Maathai married Mwangi Maathai in the late 1960s, and they were divorced in the early 1980s. The couple had three children, Waweru, Wanjira, and Muta, who were primarily raised by their mother. During the years when Maathai's activism earned her powerful enemies, she sent her children to the United States. She felt they would be safer there and could pursue their educations in American schools, just as she had done. In fact, her son Waweru attended the same college in Atchison, Kansas, that his mother attended (it's now known as Benedictine College). Maathai divides her time between Nairobi, her primary home since the mid-1960s, and the Tetu constituency that she represents in Parliament. That area is located near Mt. Kenya, the country's highest mountain, and includes Nyeri, the town where Maathai was born.

SELECTED WRITINGS

The Green Belt Movement: Sharing the Approach and the Experience, 1985; reprinted 2003

HONORS AND AWARDS

Woman of the Year Award: 1983
Right Livelihood Award: 1984
Award for the Protection of the Global Environment (Better World Society): 1986
Windstar Award for the Environment: 1988
Woman of the World Award: 1989
Offeramus Medal: 1990
Africa Prize for Leadership (The Hunger Project): 1991
Goldman Environmental Prize: 1991
Edinburgh Medal: 1993
Jane Addams Women's Leadership Award: 1993
Golden Ark Award: 1994
Member, International Women's Hall of Fame: 1995
Hero of the Planet Award (*Time* magazine): 1998
Juliette Hollister Award: 2001
Montgomery Fellow (Dartmouth College): 2001
McCluskey Visiting Fellow in Conservation (Global Institute for Sustainable Forestry, Yale University): 2002
Outstanding Vision and Commitment Award (Bridges to Community): 2002
WANGO Environment Award: 2003
Arbor Day Award: 2004
Conservation Scientist Award (Center for Environmental Research and Conservation): 2004
Elder of the Burning Spear citation (Republic of Kenya): 2004
J. Sterling Morton Award: 2004
Petra Kelly Prize for the Environment: 2004
Sophie Prize: 2004
Nobel Peace Prize: 2004
100 Heroes and Icons (*Time* magazine): 2005

FURTHER READING

Books

Biography Today World Leaders Series, Vol. 1: *Environmental Leaders,* 1997
Contemporary Authors, Vol. 155, 1997
Contemporary Black Biography, Vol. 43, 2004
Maathai, Wangari. *The Green Belt Movement: Sharing the Approach and the Experience,* 1985; reprinted 2003
Notable Scientists: From 1900 to the Present, 2001
Who's Who in the World, 2005

Periodicals

Chicago Tribune, May 22, 2005, p.C4
Current Biography Yearbook, 1993
Ebony, Mar. 2005, p.22
Financial Times (London), Nov. 5, 1994, p.26; Mar. 12, 2005, p.3
In Context: A Quarterly of Humane Sustainable Culture, Spring 1991, p.55
Independent Sunday (London), Feb. 7, 1999, p.18
Los Angeles Times, Oct. 9, 2004, p.A1; Oct. 17, 2004, p.M6
New Internationalist, July 2004, p.33
New Scientist, July 22, 2000, p.42
New York Times, Dec. 6, 1989, p.A4; Oct. 9, 2004, pp.A1 and A7; Dec. 10, 2004, p.41
O Magazine, June 2005, p.71
People, Oct. 9, 2004, p.71
Time, Apr. 18, 2005, p.98
U.S. News & World Report, Jan. 10, 2005, p.56
Washington Post, June 2, 1992, p.D1; Dec. 26, 2004, p.D1
World Watch, May-June 2004, p.26

Online Databases

Biography Resource Center Online, 2005, articles from *African Biography,* 1999; *Contemporary Authors Online,* 2004; *Contemporary Black Biography,* 2004; and *Notable Scientists: From 1900 to the Present,* 2001

ADDRESS

Wangari Maathai
The Green Belt Movement
P.O. Box 67545
Nairobi, Kenya

WORLD WIDE WEB SITES

http://www.wangarimaathai.or.ke
http://www.greenbeltmovement.org
http://nobelprize.org/peace/laureates/2004/index.html
http://www.goldmanprize.org/recipients/recipients.html

Karen Mitchell-Raptakis 1956-

American Greeting Card Entrepreneur
Creator of the "It's a Sista Thing!"™ Line of
Greeting Cards

BIRTH

Karen Mitchell-Raptakis was born Karen Mitchell on August
14, 1956, in Brooklyn, a borough of New York City. Her father,
Desburnie Mitchell, was a postman and part-time TV repair-
man. Her mother, Frances Mitchell, was a customer service rep
at Macy's department store and later worked for the city of
New York in the Marriage License bureau. Karen has one sis-

ter, Patricia, who is two years younger. In 1969, when Mitchell-Raptakis was 13, the family moved from the projects to a house in Bedford-Stuyvesant, Brooklyn.

YOUTH

Mitchell-Raptakis was raised in the housing projects of Brownsville, Brooklyn. As a child, she enjoyed spending time on creative activities indoors, like reading, writing, and art projects. She loved to draw women's clothing and fashion and to paint the paint-by-number kits that her father occasionally brought her. "Although I enjoyed playing outside with my friends, I actually preferred to stay in my room so I could write, read, or draw," she recalls. "I always carried a book with me. My parents loved reading and passed that love on to my sister and I. But Mama and Daddy didn't understand why their oldest daughter liked to write so much. They wanted me to go outside more. 'I'd rather write,' I'd tell them."

———— " ————

"Although I enjoyed playing outside with my friends, I actually preferred to stay in my room so I could write, read, or draw," Mitchell-Raptakis recalls. "I always carried a book with me. My parents loved reading and passed that love on to my sister and I. But Mama and Daddy didn't understand why their oldest daughter liked to write so much. They wanted me to go outside more. 'I'd rather write,' I'd tell them."

———— " ————

Mitchell-Raptakis remembers making her first greeting card for her mother when she was in kindergarten. She always loved greeting cards. For many years she created elaborate handmade cards featuring original poems, drawings, and collages. They were very popular among her friends and relatives, who always looked forward to receiving them.

Mitchell-Raptakis grew up during the turbulent 1960s. Black people in the South were denied the right to vote and prevented from attending the same schools as white people. Apartheid, the separation of the races, was the law in South Africa. War was raging in Vietnam. And young Karen was being bussed to an all-white school. Legally, schools had been required to integrate during the 1950s. But in fact many schools around the country were still segregated by race. To change that, school districts tried bussing students from one school district to the next. Karen and her sister were bussed to integrated schools in white neighborhoods because her parents believed their children would get a better education there. "The difference I felt from my peers forced me into a sensitive, creative shell," she explains. "I was extremely shy around my classmates and teachers. I rarely raised my hand in school, even when I knew the answer. Writing sustained me as much as breathing. I found my voice while writing."

> *"The difference I felt from my peers forced me into a sensitive, creative shell,"* Mitchell-Raptakis explains. *"I was extremely shy around my classmates and teachers. I rarely raised my hand in school, even when I knew the answer. Writing sustained me as much as breathing. I found my voice while writing."*

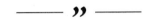

EDUCATION

Mitchell-Raptakis attended Samuel J. Tilden High School in Brooklyn, New York, graduating in 1974. "Writing helped me define my teenage years, when I continued to be the quiet, skinny girl with the glasses, too shy to raise her hand," she recalls. Her favorite classes in high school were art and creative writing. But she viewed these activities as enjoyable pastimes, not steps to a career. When her creative writing teacher wrote on one of her stories "I look forward to reading your books someday," that did not seem possible to Mitchell-Raptakis. She came from a hardworking and practical family, and that meant having a practical job.

From 1977 to 1981 Mitchell-Raptakis attended evening classes at the Fashion Institute of Technology in New York City and majored in advertising design. She learned how to design the old-fashioned way—without a computer—by using T-squares, rulers, x-acto knives, and rubber cement. She learned about the components of good design, typography, color theory, the history of art, and photography. She loved visiting art stores and enjoyed working with her professors, who encouraged students to try something different to stimulate their creativity. So Mitchell-Raptakis bought some pens and a book and taught herself calligraphy. In the mid-1980s she took courses at Parsons School of Design in New York City to perfect her calligraphy skills.

FIRST JOBS

Seeking independence, Mitchell-Raptakis decided to get a job right after high school. Her first permanent job was at Merrill Lynch, a brokerage firm, where she worked from 1975 to 1980 in a variety of administrative positions. From 1980 to 1984 Mitchell-Raptakis worked at another Wall Street firm as the supervisor in the Retirement Planning Department and became a licensed stockbroker. But working in the financial district did not stimulate her creatively. Something was missing. She started making collage-type greeting cards for her family by cutting and pasting ribbons, doilies, dried flowers, and other items on card stock. She also began to sell her hand-made cards and hand-painted T-shirts, hats, and denim jackets at neighborhood craft shows in Brooklyn. In 1982 she started The LDC Design Co. (Let's Design Cards) to do freelance calligraphy work, graphic design, and handmade cards.

By 1984 Mitchell-Raptakis was eager to work in a more creative environment, so she left Wall Street to work in the business office of a small advertising agency/public relations firm on Madison Avenue. After a short stay at another small ad agency, Mitchell-Raptakis was laid off because of a downturn in business. She eventually found a new position at Rockshots, a small photographic greeting card company, where she was hired as a receptionist. The owners were two men who started the business in their kitchen and expanded to a loft with warehouse space and several employees. It didn't matter that she was the receptionist—Karen was thankful for getting on-the-job training in the industry of her dreams. "Every job I've had has always been a training ground for me to learn something and reach new personal goals," she explains.

Mitchell-Raptakis gained valuable experience at Rockshots. She took orders over the phone, sat in on staff meetings to discuss new card ideas, interacted with photographers, models, and artists, and took orders at the National Stationery Show, an annual event where large and small manufacturers showcase their products. The National Stationery Show was vibrant and innovative and full of new ideas—heaven for a person who loved stationery and paper as much as Karen did.

In 1986, Mitchell-Raptakis went to work in publishing as the assistant to the vice-president of production. In 1998, she became the first digital archivist at the company, and she continued to work there as the digital archivist manager until 2003. As such, she ensured that digital copies of her company's books were stored in an electronic archive; she also ensured that all subsequent corrections to the printed books were maintained in the archived versions as well.

CAREER HIGHLIGHTS

Mitchell-Raptakis is the founder of The LDC Design Co., later renamed Karen & Company Greeting Cards. Her business is best known for producing a line of greeting cards called "It's a Sista Thing!"™ Aimed at African Americans, the award-winning cards celebrate the black experience and feature messages that resonate in the black community.

Do you remember...
8 track tapes?
The Bump?
Hot Pants?
Platform shoes?
Afro puffs?

Developing the Idea

Mitchell-Raptakis first got the idea for her company in the early 1990s when she went shopping for a greeting card for her best friend, who was going through a crisis. She wanted a card that would offer encouragement to her friend as well as reflect the African-American heritage they shared. She wanted the card's images and words to look and sound natural, like real black women. There were no cards on the market that fit those specifications, and Mitchell-Raptakis started to think seriously about designing a line of greeting cards for African-American women. "I had a girlfriend who was going through a crisis and I wanted to send her a card, but there was nothing that said what I wanted to say to her," she recalls. "The selection of cards either had syrupy-sweet, unnatural-sounding messages, or the images on them were not representative of who my friend and I were as black women."

After looking closely at the greeting card industry, Mitchell-Raptakis felt that she had identified a niche — a narrow segment of the market that is overlooked by larger companies. The greeting card market is huge — Americans sent about 7 billion greeting cards in one recent year, spending about $7.5 billion, according to the Greeting Card Association. Mitchell-Raptakis decided to try to capture part of that market.

Following Her Heart

Mitchell-Raptakis soon decided to produce a line of greeting cards aimed at African-American women. "I wanted to manufacture my own cards for several reasons," she explains. "First, I was passionate about them! These were the cards that I would have wanted to receive. Second, I was always conscious of where I came from. I'm the granddaughter of sharecroppers and thought about the limited opportunities my ancestors had. I wanted to do this because they couldn't. Third, I wanted to reinvent myself and be challenged in my work. I needed to expand my horizons. Lastly, I wanted to break down the traditional definition of what an entrepreneur looked like and be a positive role model for the kids in my old neighborhood."

At first, Mitchell-Raptakis wanted to use quotations on the cards from famous African-American women, including Maya Angelou, Bessie and Sadie Delaney, Toni Morrison, and Oprah Winfrey. (For more information, see entries on Angelou in *Biography Today*, April 1993; the Delaney sisters in *Biography Today*, Sep. 1999; Morrison in *Biography Today*, Jan. 1994; and Winfrey in *Biography Today*, April 1992, and *Biography Today Business Leaders*, Vol. 1.) She wrote to the Delaney sisters' agent and asked for permission to use their words, but was turned down. She soon learned that any famous person would want royalties for the use of their thoughts. Mitchell-Raptakis didn't have the money to pay for royalties, so she scrapped her original plan. Instead, she decided to write her own messages on each card. She used forthright and natural phrases that were common and familiar in African-American culture. "These cards reflect the black experience and feature phrases that have been around in our community for generations," she stated. "The text is short and to the point, in the same way sisters usually speak with one another."

———— " ————

"These cards reflect the black experience and feature phrases that have been around in our community for generations,"Mitchell-Raptakis stated. "The text is short and to the point, in the same way sisters usually speak with one another."

———— " ————

Then Mitchell-Raptakis teamed up with Fred Harper, a Brooklyn artist whose work had appeared in both New York and national publications, including *Sports Illustrated* and *Essence*. After consulting with Mitchell-Raptakis about her vision for the greeting card series, Harper created artwork featuring bold colors and striking depictions of African Americans. "I wanted a diversity of black women to be depicted in my cards—reflecting the diversity within our culture," she says. "Our hair texture and styles, varied skin tones, creative sense of fashion, and unique vernacular are represented in these cards. . . . I wanted us to see ourselves in all the facets." She took photographs of her friends and gave them to Harper, who incor-

A few words of wisdom:
1. A hard head gets a soft backside
2. God doesn't like ugly and He doesn't care for beauty
3. Every shut eye ain't sleep, every good bye ain't gone

Interior: No matter how old you get, don't forget what Mama taught you.
Happy Birthday!

porated some of those images: a wedding scene of her good friends appears on a wedding congratulations card, and Mitchell-Raptakis's own image appears on a birthday card featuring a young girl with words of wisdom.

The next stage of the project was to find out if the cards would appeal to black consumers. As she developed the cards, Mitchell-Raptakis showed them to women she met in the hair salon, the grocery checkout line, on the subway, and various other places, in order to get objective opinions. She contacted African-American card and gift shops in Brooklyn and asked if they would be interested in purchasing the cards for their shops. Each card buyer gave her an order, which encouraged her even more. But there were so many obstacles. She didn't have the money to produce the cards, a commercial printer to manufacture the cards, or knowledge about starting a new business. Reluctantly, she put the project on hold for several years.

> "I wanted a diversity of black women to be depicted in my cards—reflecting the diversity within our culture," Mitchell-Raptakis noted. "Our hair texture and styles, varied skin tones, creative sense of fashion, and unique vernacular are represented in these cards. . . . I wanted us to see ourselves in all the facets."

Creating the Dream

Then in January 1999 she watched an Oprah Winfrey show with Iyanla Vanzant, who talked about the struggles of her life. She then recited a poem by Patrick Overton that made Mitchell-Raptakis sit up in her chair. "When you walk to the edge of all the light you have and take that first step into the darkness of the unknown, you must believe one of two things will happen: There will be something solid for you to stand upon or you will be taught how to fly." The poem motivated her to take the next step and fortified her belief that God was instrumental in her plan. She felt so strongly about greeting cards for African-American women that she decided to put her faith and her plans into action.

Her family and friends supported her greeting card idea with spiritual, emotional, and physical support, while her mother provided much needed financial support. "It was so important to have such a wonderful support network," Mitchell-Raptakis reveals. "These were the people who believed in me when all I had was a dream. They believed in me when I have been low on faith."

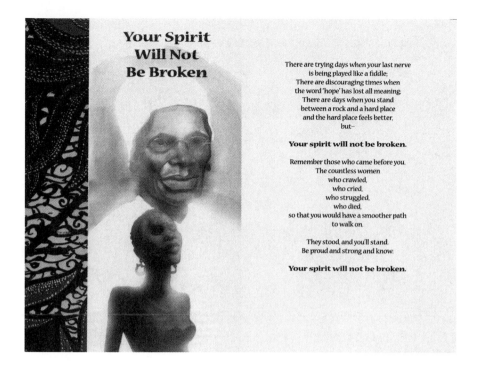

Your Spirit Will Not Be Broken

There are trying days when your last nerve
is being played like a fiddle;
There are discouraging times when
the word 'hope' has lost all meaning;
There are days when you stand
between a rock and a hard place
and the hard place feels better,
but--

Your spirit will not be broken.

Remember those who came before you.
The countless women
who crawled,
who cried,
who struggled,
who died,
so that you would have a smoother path
to walk on.

They stood, and you'll stand.
Be proud and strong and know:

Your spirit will not be broken.

In addition to such support, Mitchell-Raptakis needed the help of a team of experienced advisors. She found a greeting card consultant who taught her the basics about starting a greeting card business—including pricing, distribution, product design, major trade shows, and getting paid. She found a lawyer who specialized in intellectual property and applied for a trademark for the name "It's a Sista Thing!"™ She found an accountant and set up a corporation for The LDC Design Co., Inc. She found a printer who had experience in manufacturing greeting cards and the ability to store and ship her cards.

"It's a Sista Thing!"™

In 1999 Mitchell-Raptakis formally introduced her line of greeting cards—called "It's a Sista Thing!"™—at the National Stationery Show. The series of 24 cards spoke directly to African-American women, offering messages of encouragement, sympathy, and joy, along with birthday, wedding, and holiday greetings. Some examples from the line include:

- "Jumping the broom," a wedding card depicting a couple in traditional African dress preparing to step over a broom lying on the ground (part of the marriage ritual in some African cultures).

- "To the man I love," a Father's Day card illustrated with an image of a black man in dreadlocks with a baby sleeping on his chest.

- "A Christmas letter to Jesus," a holiday card picturing a boy writing at a table in front of a Christmas tree.

- "A few words of wisdom," a birthday card featuring the greeting, "No matter how old you get, don't forget what Mama taught you!"

"The first day I participated in the National Stationery Show was one of the most exciting days of my life," Mitchell-Raptakis observes. "I had attended the National Stationery Show as a visitor since 1983 and always felt that I didn't belong there. But my first day as a participant in the show gave me an extreme boost of confidence. This was my show. I was so happy to be there. The cards even created a 'buzz' among the other African-American card manufacturers and some of them came around to visit my booth and see my cards. The vice president of one large card manufacturer stopped by the booth, nodded, and said he liked the idea. I was ecstatic."

"It's a Sista Thing!"™ cards soon began to catch on in New York and New Jersey. Mitchell-Raptakis managed sales and distribution of the line herself, taking full responsibility for getting the cards into stores. She eventually succeeded in placing her products in more than 80 retail outlets, although the majority of her customers were small specialty bookstores and stationery shops. She also made her cards available on the Internet.

Winning the Louie Award

Mitchell-Raptakis and her company received a big boost in 2001. She entered one of her cards in a contest sponsored by the Greeting Card Association. The top prize was the prestigious Louie Award. Named after German printer Louis Prang, who is credited with introducing color lithography to the United States card industry, the award is considered the greeting card industry's equivalent to the film industry's Oscar.

For the contest, Mitchell-Raptakis entered an inspirational card that featured an image of abolitionist Sojourner Truth on the cover and an original poem entitled "Your Spirit Will Not Be Broken" in the interior. The card celebrates the perseverance of past generations of African Americans who struggled against adversity to create a better future for their children.

More than 1,100 cards from 160 companies were entered in competition for the prize. Judges evaluated each card individually. "Your Spirit Will Not Be Broken" was selected as the winner of the prestigious Louie Award in three categories: friendship, encouragement, and general. Judges cited its

"

"My first day as a partici-
pant in the show gave me an
extreme boost of confidence.
This was my show. I was so
happy to be there. The cards
even created a 'buzz' among
the other African-American
card manufacturers and some
of them came around to visit
my booth and see my cards.
The vice president of one
large card manufacturer
stopped by the booth, nodded,
and said he liked the idea.
I was ecstatic."

"

Mitchell-Raptakis introduced her
greeting card line at the 1999 National
Stationery Show.

originality, impact, artistry, harmony, "sendability," and value. Mitchell-Raptakis attributed the success of the card to her creative process. "I send cards that I would like to get to encourage me," she reveals, "and 'Your Spirit Will Not Be Broken' is the card that I needed, so I had to create it."

Attending the Louie Award ceremony, Mitchell-Raptakis was honored to be part of a group of such talented people in an industry she loved so much. When her category was called and her card was announced as the winner, she was overwhelmed. It had been a long journey of faith and determination.

Growing Pains

Mitchell-Raptakis eventually hopes to expand the "It's a Sista Thing!"™ line beyond greeting cards into calendars, stationery, and other items. She feels just as strongly about the need for her products as she did in the beginning. "If you don't have that one girlfriend who you can tell things to or who you know can lift you up, you're in a bad state," she explains. "I do think of my friends when I create these cards: What will make somebody laugh? What will they want to hear in the way of encouragement? What kind of card can I send them just to say that I love them?"

Even though her cards have gained an enthusiastic following, Mitchell-Raptakis admits that she has experienced periods of doubt and discouragement. Since she spent so much money developing, printing, and marketing the cards, it took a long time for her business to make a profit. In fact, Mitchell-Raptakis continued working at her "day job" in book publishing through 2003. "I was going through some strategy sessions with other business owners, and everything with their businesses was great," she recalled. "They were making money, and here I was, still with my day job and not making money."

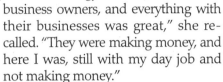

"I do think of my friends when I create these cards: What will make somebody laugh? What will they want to hear in the way of encouragement? What kind of card can I send them just to say that I love them?"

Mitchell-Raptakis is not sure what the future holds for her and her company. She faces difficult decisions about whether to expand her business beyond the level of a "one-woman shop." She has tried to prepare herself to do so by taking business courses in such subjects as marketing, licensing, branding, and financial strategy. But she admits that competing against greeting card giants like Hallmark and American Greetings is quite a challenge.

Despite the struggles, Mitchell-Raptakis says that being an entrepreneur has been very rewarding. "I have learned so much," she noted. "Creating these cards has been a labor of love and a journey of faith. It is my hope that 'It's a Sista Thing!'™ cards will connect African Americans to one another in a meaningful and positive way."

MARRIAGE AND FAMILY

Mitchell-Raptakis was married in 1981, but that marriage ended in divorce in 1993. She married Dimitrios Peter Raptakis, an accountant, on May 27, 2000. They live in East Stroudsbourg, Pennsylvania.

HOBBIES AND OTHER INTERESTS

Mitchell-Raptakis is a Christian and an active member in her church. She believes it is part of her mission to encourage others. In her free time, she enjoys a range of creative activities. She designs handmade cards, silk floral baskets, handmade books, and framed photo collages. She is writing a book of spiritual encouragement for women who have experienced domestic violence. She plans to write a children's book about her favorite cat, Buddy, who passed away. She also loves dancing and listening to music. Some of her favorite recording artists are Donnie McClurkin, Cece Winans, Brooklyn Tabernacle, Michael W. Smith, Babbie Mason, Avalon, Stevie Wonder, and others. She also enjoys going to movies with her husband.

HONORS AND AWARDS

Louis Award: 2001, in the friendship/encouragement/general category, for the Sojourner Truth Card

FURTHER READING

Periodicals

Essence, Mar. 2000, p.64
New York Amsterdam News, July 11, 2001, p.15
New York Daily News, Mar. 22, 2000, Suburban, p.6
USA Today, Mar. 19, 2003, p.B7

Online Articles

http://www.wibo.org
(*WIBO Word*, "Connect with Alumni Spotlight: Karen Mitchell-Raptakis of Karen & Co.," Spring 2003)

Other

Additional information for this biographical profile was gathered from material supplied by Karen Mitchell-Raptakis.

ADDRESS

Karen Mitchell-Raptakis
Karen and Company Greeting Cards
P.O. Box 972
East Stroudsburg, PA 18301

WORLD WIDE WEB SITE

http://www.sistathingcards.com

Queen Noor 1951-

American-Born Queen of Jordan
Author of the International Best-Seller *Leap of Faith:
Memoirs of an Unexpected Life*

BIRTH

Queen Noor al Hussein was born Lisa Najeeb Halaby on
August 23, 1951, in Washington, D.C. Her father, Najeeb Elias
Halaby, was a prominent Arab-American airline executive and
attorney who served as director of the Federal Aviation Administration under President John F. Kennedy. Her mother,
Doris (Carlquist) Halaby, was a homemaker. She has a younger brother, Christian, and a younger sister, Alexa.

In 1978 Lisa Halaby adopted the name Noor al Hussein, which means "Light of Hussein" in Arabic, when she married Hussein ibn Talal, king of the Middle Eastern nation of Jordan. She also became a Jordanian citizen at this time, relinquishing her American citizenship. In alphabetical listings, her name is commonly found under Noor al Hussein, Queen of Jordan.

YOUTH

The Halaby family moved around a lot during Lisa's youth to accommodate her father's frequent job changes. When Lisa was two years old, they moved from Washington, D.C., to New York City. By the time she was ready for kindergarten, they had relocated again, to southern California. "We moved often during my childhood, and the constant changes reinforced my natural reserve," she remembered in her book *Leap of Faith.* "Time and again, I would find myself on the outside looking in —watching, studying, learning—having to familiarize myself with unfamiliar people and communities." At one point, her mother became so concerned about Lisa's shyness around other children that she consulted a child psychologist.

The Halabys spent five years in California. Lisa particularly enjoyed living in Santa Monica, where the family home offered a spectacular view of the Pacific Ocean. She liked exploring the outdoors on her own. She also spent a great deal of time combing through the books in her father's extensive library, reading about exotic places around the world. "I would flip through copies of *National Geographic* and gaze longingly at the globe that helped me chart my parents' international trips," she recalled.

> *"We moved often during my childhood, and the constant changes reinforced my natural reserve,"Queen Noor remembered in her book* **Leap of Faith.** *"Time and again, I would find myself on the outside looking in—watching, studying, learning—having to familiarize myself with unfamiliar people and communities."*

In 1961 the Halabys returned to Washington, D.C., so that Lisa's father could become director of the Federal Aviation Administration (FAA) under President Kennedy. Ten-year-old Lisa felt inspired by Kennedy, whom she met at his inauguration. She was especially attracted to the young president's emphasis on service to less privileged communities and countries.

Najeeb Halaby, father to the future Queen Noor, was appointed by President John F. Kennedy to be director of the Federal Aviation Administration. Halaby is shown here being sworn in as President Kennedy looks on.

For example, Kennedy established an international service organization called the Peace Corps in order to encourage Americans to spend time in developing nations helping to fight poverty, hunger, illiteracy, and other problems. Lisa was fascinated by the program and always wanted to become a Peace Corps volunteer. "I didn't dream of being a fairy-tale princess," she noted.

Sadly, President Kennedy was assassinated in 1963. Najeeb Halaby continued to head the FAA under the new president, Lyndon B. Johnson. Halaby resigned in 1965 to take a job in the private sector with Pan Am World Airways. The family then moved back to New York City.

EDUCATION

Lisa Halaby attended exclusive private schools for most of her education. During her father's tenure as director of the FAA, she attended the prestigious National Cathedral School for Girls in Washington, D.C. She struggled to fit in during her awkward teen years. "[I was] tall for my age, scrawny and awkward, and dependent on Coke-bottle-thick glasses," she recalled. When her father first went to work for Pan Am and the family moved to New York City, Lisa attended the Chapin School. She did not like the sheltered environment at the school, which felt "like a strait jacket" to the idealistic teenager. "The world was held at arm's length at Chapin, with no student involvement in the debate over Vietnam or the civil rights movement or, indeed, anything that smacked of dissent," she noted.

Halaby spent her last two years of high school at Concord Academy in Massachusetts, where she excelled in sports and worked on the school newspaper and yearbook. During the summers, she toured Europe with student groups. Looking back, she praised Concord Academy for challenging her to become a better student and person. "Academic life was extremely stimulating, and expectations were high, but more important to me, the school placed a high premium on individualism and personal responsibility," she remembered.

"I needed time and space to set my own priorities and to discover if I could survive on my own," Queen Noor explained. "That's one of my fondest memories, because it gave me an enormous amount of self-confidence to learn that I didn't need to depend on anyone—a husband, a father, my family—to support me. It taught me that I could take care of myself."

After graduating from high school in 1969, Halaby considered returning to California to attend Stanford University. But then she was accepted into the first co-ed class to enter Princeton University in New Jersey. She eagerly took advantage of the opportunity to become one of the first women to attend the prestigious Ivy League college. Shortly after her first semester got underway, her father was named president and chief executive officer of Pan Am. To her surprise, the media attention surrounding her father's promotion led some fellow students to harass her about her Arab background.

In 1971 Halaby took a year off from college to live on her own in Aspen, Colorado. She worked as a waitress and spent her spare time skiing and studying photography at the Institute of the Eye. "I needed time and space to set my own priorities and to discover if I could survive on my own," she explained. "That's one of my fondest memories, because it gave me an enormous amount of self-confidence to learn that I didn't need to depend on anyone—a husband, a father, my family—to support me. It taught me that I could take care of myself."

Halaby returned to Princeton the following year with renewed energy and focus. She became even more active in social causes and human rights issues, participating in fasts and other nonviolent protests against the Vietnam War. She also chose a new course of study—architecture and urban planning—that she felt would enable her to serve the needs of society. "I loved it," she remembered. "It was a captivating, multidisciplinary approach to understanding and addressing the most basic needs of individuals and communities." Halaby earned her bachelor's degree from Princeton in 1974.

CAREER HIGHLIGHTS

Experiencing the Middle East as a Young Architect

After graduating from college, Halaby took a job with Llewlyn-Davis, a British architecture firm specializing in urban development. Part of the job's appeal was that it offered opportunities to see the world. Her first assignment took her to Australia, and then she was sent to Iran to help modernize the capital city of Tehran. During her time in Iran, Halaby found herself captivated by the history and culture of the Middle East. She also became aware of what she described as "a fundamental lack of understanding in the West, especially in the United States, of Middle Eastern culture and the Muslim faith."

In 1976 the government of Jordan hired Halaby's father to help restructure its airline system. She went along and helped design a training facility at Arab Air University. From the time of her first visit to the capital city of Amman, she fell in love with Jordan. "On that first trip, I explored Amman on foot," she remembered in her book. "Shepherds crossed the downtown streets with their flocks, herding them from one grassy area to another. They were such an ordinary part of life in Amman that no one honked or lost their patience waiting for the streets to clear; animals and their minders had the right of way. I wandered through the marketplace admiring the beautiful inlaid mother-of-pearl objects—frames, chests, and backgammon boards—as well as the cobalt blue, green, and amber vases known as Hebron glass."

During her time in Jordan, Halaby was pleased to have an opportunity to meet the nation's ruler, King Hussein. They first met in January 1977 at a ceremony honoring Jordan's purchase of its first Boeing 747 jet plane. Halaby took a picture of the king greeting her father at this ceremony. Toward the end of that year, she returned to the United States. "I never imagined that I would be returning to Jordan just three months later," she said, "nor did I have any inkling of how fateful that return would be." (For more information on King Hussein, see *Biography Today*, April 1999.)

Halaby had returned to the U.S. with the intention of studying journalism at Columbia University in New York City. But she unexpectedly received a job offer to serve as director of planning and design projects for Royal Jordanian Airlines. She jumped at the chance to return to Amman and to explore further her Arab heritage. "I can't explain why, but going there was something I knew I had to do," she stated. "I wanted to let it become a part of me, and I wanted to become part of it. It was the Arab blood in me that I identified with and that I wanted to discover."

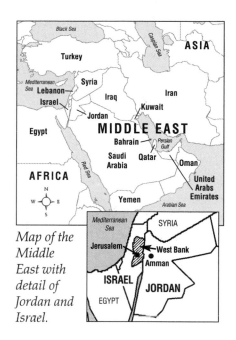

Map of the Middle East with detail of Jordan and Israel.

Jordan and King Hussein

When Halaby returned to Jordan in early 1978, she committed herself to living and working in a small, developing nation that has a proud but often troubled history. Jordan, which is about the same size geographically as the state of Indiana, is located in the heart of the Middle East. It is surrounded by Syria, Iraq, Saudi Arabia, and Israel. Jordan's modern history begins in the early 20th century. Before World War I, much of the Middle East was part of the Ottoman Empire, which had been ruled by Turkish sultans for centuries. During World War I, the Ottoman Turks were allied with the Germans. When they were defeated and the Ottoman Empire crumbled, Great Britain was given the task of governing parts of the Middle East. The area eventually became 11 Arab nations, including Transjordan, founded in 1921. Its first king was Abdullah I, King Hussein's grandfather. In 1946 the country gained its independence from Great Britain and was renamed the Hashemite Kingdom of Jordan.

Two years later, in 1948, the United Nations created the nation of Israel as a homeland for all Jewish people. After World War II and the horrors of the Holocaust, when Nazis systematically murdered some six million Jews, Jewish people felt the need for a land of their own where they would be safe from persecution. The part of the Middle East that became Israel was also home to the Palestinians, an Arab people whose ancestors had lived in the region since ancient times. The creation of Israel angered many Arabs,

311

——— " ———

"I can't explain why, but going [to Jordan] was something I knew I had to do," Queen Noor stated. "I wanted to let it become a part of me, and I wanted to become part of it. It was the Arab blood in me that I identified with and that I wanted to discover."

——— " ———

in part because it displaced the Palestinian people, creating millions of refugees. Jordan and four of its neighbors went to war against Israel shortly after the Jewish nation was formed. The war lasted nine months before Israel defeated the Arab armies.

Even though the Arabs lost the war, Jordan captured part of Israel called the West Bank. This area along the Jordan River was home to 500,000 Palestinians, and it encompassed Jerusalem and Bethlehem—which contain holy sites for Christians, Jews, and Muslims. Once the war ended, thousands more Palestinians fled from Israel and became refugees in Jordan. King Abdullah struggled to maintain control of the country as Palestinians suddenly made up more than half of Jordan's population. Some of the displaced Palestinians formed a group called the Palestine Liberation Organization (PLO) with the purpose of reclaiming lost territory from Israel and establishing an independent Palestinian state. Until his death in 2004, Yasir Arafat was the leader of the PLO. (For more information on Arafat, see *Biography Today*, Sep. 1994, and Updates in the Annual Cumulations for 1994, 1995, 1996, 1997, 1998, 2000, 2001, and 2002.)

From the time of his birth in 1935, Hussein ibn Talal was prepared to become the leader of Jordan someday. After all, he was a 42nd-generation direct descendant of the Prophet Muhammad, founder of the Islamic religion. His family line, known as the Hashemites, had ruled Jordan since its founding. Hussein was educated at exclusive schools in Jordan, Egypt, and England. He also spent a great deal of time accompanying his grandfather and observing his official duties. In 1951 King Abdullah was assassinated by a Palestinian extremist while attending a ceremony in Jerusalem. Hussein, who was standing by his grandfather's side at the time, was hit as well. But the bullet harmlessly bounced off of a medal he was wearing on his chest.

Hussein's father, Talal, was named king of Jordan immediately following Abdullah's death. But Talal suffered from schizophrenia, and the pressures of the position soon made his mental illness worsen to the point that he could no longer rule. Hussein thus took over as king of Jordan in 1952, at the age of 16. He soon became known as a moderate ruler who placed a strong emphasis on education and development. But critics claimed that he was too easily influenced by the United States, which was unpopular in large parts of the Arab world due to its support for Israel. In 1967 Jordan joined Syria and Egypt in another war against Israel. This conflict became known as the Six-Day War because Israel prevailed so quickly. During the war, Israel regained control over the West Bank, which contained half of Jordan's population and much of its industrial capacity. Unhappy with Hussein's loss of the West Bank, Palestinian extremists tried to overthrow the king in a 1970 civil war.

Over the next few years, King Hussein managed to win the civil war and strengthen his rule. In 1974 he made an agreement with the PLO that helped ease tensions with Jordan's Palestinian population. Jordan gave up its claims on the West Bank, which remained under Israeli military control, and recognized the Palestinians as rightful owners of the disputed territory. Following this agreement, Jordan enjoyed a period of increased stability and economic growth. Over the succeeding years, King Hussein emerged as a leading figure in Middle Eastern affairs. He consistently sought ways to make peace with Israel while also securing greater rights for the Palestinians.

Becoming the Queen of Jordan

When Halaby returned to Jordan to become the director of planning and design projects for Royal Jordanian Airlines, the 42-year-old king was mourning the death of his third wife, Queen Alia, who had been killed in a helicopter crash in February 1977. In the spring of 1978, the 26-year-old American accompanied her father to a meeting at the royal palace. King Hussein enjoyed her company and invited her to lunch the next day. Halaby spent that entire day with him and gave him advice on renovating the palace. Before long it became clear that the king's interest in Halaby ex-

——— **"** ———

"I was unsure I would be exactly what he needed, that I wouldn't be a hindrance, being relatively new to Jordan and because it did happen fairly quickly," Queen Noor acknowledged. *"I had lived an independent life, traveled in many different countries. I had a free, open spirit. Would I have the self-discipline necessary to make a good wife for a king?"*

——— **"** ———

313

Queen Noor and King Hussein on their wedding day, June 15, 1978, as they emerge from the wedding ceremony for the cutting of the cake.

tended beyond friendship. She was surprised but also flattered by the attention. "He was a *king,*" she noted. "I was just, you know, a normal person."

King Hussein spent the next several weeks courting Halaby. They spoke on the phone for hours, and she visited the palace often. They both worked hard to keep their relationship a secret. In fact, the king sometimes came to meet her on a motorcycle so they could spend time alone together. After just two months of dating, King Hussein asked Lisa Halaby to marry him. She initially expressed doubts about her ability to become a queen. "I was unsure I would be exactly what he needed, that I wouldn't be a hindrance, being relatively new to Jordan and because it did happen fairly quickly," she acknowledged. "I had lived an independent life, traveled in many different countries. I had a free, open spirit. Would I have the self-discipline necessary to make a good wife for a king?"

Halaby recognized that she would face numerous challenges as King Hussein's wife. He was 16 years older, for example, and had already been married three times (his first two marriages ended in divorce). He had eight children — several of whom were almost Halaby's age, and three of whom were quite young and needed a mother. She also worried that the people of Jordan would have trouble accepting her because she had been born in the United States and did not speak much Arabic.

Yet Halaby ultimately allowed her emotions to overcome her caution. She had fallen in love with the charming king, so she agreed to be his wife. "When you're young and in love," she sighed. "I didn't stand aside, detach myself from the current of feeling, to consider the implications." They were married on June 15, 1978, at Zaharan Palace, the home of King Hussein's mother. The king gave his new bride the name Noor al Hussein because she brought light back into his life. Queen Noor became the first American-born queen of an Arab Muslim country. She also became the first woman in the history of the Hashemite family to attend her own wedding. (According to Jordanian tradition, marriage ceremonies are attended only by men, with a male relative representing the bride.)

Shortly before the wedding took place, Queen Noor converted to Islam. She had nominally been raised as a Christian, but she had never been baptized. Some people criticized her decision, claiming that she adopted the king's religion out of duty rather than true faith, but she said that she felt a real affinity for Islam. "I admired Islam's emphasis on a believer's direct relationship with God, the fundamental equality of rights of all men and women, and the reverence for the Prophet Muhammad as well as all the Prophets and messengers who came before him, since Adam, to Abraham, Moses, Jesus, and many others. Islam calls for fairness, tolerance, and charity," she explained. "I was attracted, too, by its simplicity and call for justice. Islam is a very personal belief system."

> *"I admired Islam's emphasis on a believer's direct relationship with God, the fundamental equality of rights of all men and women, and the reverence for the Prophet Muhammad as well as all the Prophets and messengers who came before him, since Adam, to Abraham, Moses, Jesus, and many others. Islam calls for fairness, tolerance, and charity," Queen Noor explained. "I was attracted, too, by its simplicity and call for justice. Islam is a very personal belief system."*

The wedding attracted a great deal of coverage in the international media. Many reporters seized upon the "fairy-tale" aspect of the union between a

The king and queen.

young American and a Middle Eastern king. But Queen Noor found that her new life did not really resemble a fairy tale. She worked hard to be a good stepmother to the king's eight children. She struggled to adjust to the loss of her privacy, as she suddenly found herself surrounded by bodyguards at all times. Some citizens of Jordan viewed her with suspicion, questioning whether an American made a suitable wife for their king. Arabic television and newspapers followed her every move, ready to pounce on anything they viewed as a shortcoming. Some claimed that she was too ambitious, for example, while others criticized her for spending too much money. "All of a sudden, I was a wife, a queen, a mother," she remembered. "All of a sudden I was inspected and analyzed."

Queen Noor tried to take the attention in stride. She pointed out that she needed time to determine the best ways of dealing with her unique position. "I'm pioneering a role here, as my husband's wife and queen in an ever-changing world, in a developing country that is in some ways backward, in a region that is extremely turbulent," she stated. "I am constantly questioning, as I know he is, the best way to approach certain tasks that we've set for ourselves, whether in social development or international relations or raising a family."

Emerging as a Humanitarian Activist

Once she settled into her new role, Queen Noor emerged as a leading activist in humanitarian causes. She started out working within Jordan to improve the people's health, education, and welfare. For example, the former architect helped convince Jordan to adopt a national professional building code. She also led efforts to preserve Jordan's architectural history through the National Committee for Public Buildings and Architectural Heritage. Queen Noor personally visited Palestinian refugee camps to ensure that they were safe and sanitary, and she also participated in child immunization campaigns throughout the country. In the early years of her reign, she often drove herself to remote villages in a jeep, listening to music by Fleetwood Mac or Bruce Springsteen along the way.

Queen Noor directed some of her efforts toward improving relations between Arab countries and the Western world. "I'm going to continue to the best of my abilities to develop my own understanding and experience, to be a better spokesman for the Arab world, and for Jordan in particular," she stated. "I pray I can be one small block to build greater understanding for everyone in the area."

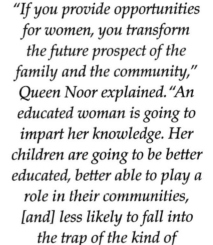

"If you provide opportunities for women, you transform the future prospect of the family and the community," Queen Noor explained. "An educated woman is going to impart her knowledge. Her children are going to be better educated, better able to play a role in their communities, [and] less likely to fall into the trap of the kind of hopelessness and despair that leads to extremism."

Queen Noor also worked tirelessly to promote women's rights. "If you provide opportunities for women, you transform the future prospect of the family and the community," she explained. "An educated woman is going to impart her knowledge. Her children are going to be better educated, better able to play a role in their communities, [and] less likely to fall into the trap of the kind of hopelessness and despair that leads to extremism." She often appeared in public wearing beautiful handmade clothing in order to demonstrate her support for traditional Jordanian women's crafts.

Queen Noor, shown here visiting an orphanage, won the respect of many Jordanians for her commitment to charitable causes.

Over the years, Queen Noor won over the people of Jordan with her commitment to charitable work in the areas of child welfare, environmental protection, and culture and the arts. She started children's reading programs, created parks to promote recreation and tourism, and established the first children's museum in the Arab world. She also initiated the National Handicrafts Development Foundation and the Jerash Festival for Culture and Arts. Queen Noor became actively involved in numerous international organizations over the years, including the World Conservation Union, World Wildlife Fund, International Commission on Missing Persons, Women Waging Peace, Future Harvest, and the International Campaign to Ban Landmines. She earned numerous awards and honorary degrees for her charity work.

Speaking Out on Political Issues

In 1980 Queen Noor returned to the United States for the first time since her marriage. She and her husband met with President Jimmy Carter and his wife, Rosalynn Carter. Later that year Queen Noor gave birth to her first child, a son named Hamzah. She and the king had three more children together over the next few years: another son, Hashim, and two daughters,

Iman and Raiyah. As her own family grew, Queen Noor experienced some difficulty in dealing with the king's older children. In fact, in the mid-1980s they presented their father with a list of 54 grievances about her handling of family issues.

In 1990 the Middle East erupted in yet another military conflict when Iraq invaded Kuwait. Iraqi leader Saddam Hussein (no relation to King Hussein) invaded his tiny neighbor after the two countries failed to settle longstanding disputes over national boundaries, oil reserves, and other issues. Countries around the world condemned the invasion and called for Iraq to withdraw its troops from Kuwait. Many countries sent military forces to the region as part of a U.S.-led coalition against Iraq. This coalition included a number of Arab countries. (For more information on Saddam Hussein, see *Biography Today*, July 1992, and Updates in the Annual Cumulations for 1996, 2001, and 2002.)

King Hussein found himself in a difficult position following Iraq's invasion of Kuwait. He considered Saddam Hussein to be a personal friend, and he appreciated the Iraqi leader's strong defense of Palestinian interests. But he also respected Kuwait's status as an independent nation and expressed concern about Iraq's military aggression toward an Arab neighbor. The king tried desperately to remain neutral in the conflict. He traveled widely throughout the Middle East in an effort to negotiate a peaceful resolution to the crisis. He also met with Saddam Hussein and tried to convince him to withdraw his troops from Kuwait.

King Hussein extolled his wife's virtues in a letter to the people of Jordan. "She brought happiness and cared for me during my illness with the utmost loving affection. She, the Jordanian, who belongs to this country with every fiber of her being, holds her head high in the defense and service of the country's interest. She, like me, also endured many anxieties and shocks, but always placed her faith in God and hid her tears behind smiles."

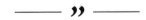

As it became clear that the U.S.-led coalition would go to war to force Iraq to withdraw from Kuwait, King Hussein refused to participate. He knew that Jordan's large Palestinian population approved of Saddam Hussein's actions, and he did not want to risk an uprising that would put his rule at risk. But the king's position proved to be very unpopular with the United States as well as with the Arab members of the coalition. Many of these countries cut off trade with Jordan and refused to help King Hussein deal with the three million refugees who made their way into Jordan from Iraq and Kuwait before and during the 1991 Persian Gulf War.

Throughout this difficult political situation, Queen Noor often spoke out in defense of Jordan's position. She felt that her husband had been treated unfairly, when his only aim was to avoid a costly war. In September 1990 she met with Barbara Bush, the wife of U.S. President George Bush. The queen told the first lady that Jordan had always opposed Iraq's invasion of Kuwait and that King Hussein's position had been misrepresented. "I tried to explain the mounting concern in the Arab world about Iraqi civilian losses and desperate conditions. Mrs. Bush was unmoved. She was a political wife, and she was going to believe what she needed to believe," Queen Noor wrote in her memoirs. "I would continue to speak out after the war started about the humanitarian consequences of the war and the suffering of the people of Iraq, which evidently so angered Mrs. Bush that she sent a message to me through an American official that she considered me a traitor."

In January 1991 the coalition forces launched a major bombing campaign against Iraqi forces. This campaign, which lasted for nearly six weeks, took a devastating toll on both Iraq and Kuwait. The coalition then followed up with a ground assault that quickly succeeded in pushing Iraqi forces out of Kuwait.

Standing by the King

In 1992 doctors discovered a tumor in King Hussein's kidney that contained cancerous cells. Queen Noor traveled with her husband to the prestigious Mayo Clinic in Minnesota, where doctors removed the tumor along with one of the king's kidneys. The cancer scare made King Hussein more energized than ever to seek peace in the Middle East. Over the next few years he repaired Jordan's relationships with its neighbors as well as with the United States, and he gradually emerged as one of the leading statesmen in the Arab world. In 1993 the king played a key role in negotiations that resulted in an agreement between Israel and the PLO that provided for Palestinian self-rule in the West Bank and other Israeli-occupied territories. The following year Jordan entered into a peace agreement with Israel, ending a 46-year state of war between the neighboring countries.

In 1997 King Hussein developed non-Hodgkins lymphoma, a type of cancer that affects the lymphatic system, which circulates antibodies through-

Jordan's King Abdullah II, second from left, Queen Rania, left, and Queen Noor, right, hold special Muslim prayers at King Hussein's grave in the royal cemetery in Amman.

out the body to help it fight infection and disease. The following year Queen Noor accompanied her husband to the Mayo Clinic for intensive treatment, including chemotherapy and a bone marrow transplant. In her book, she describes her initial despair at the prospect of losing her beloved husband. "I felt such fear, such bottomless anxiety at the thought of losing my husband, my best friend, my dearest love and inspiration that it threatened to paralyze me. For 20 years we had been husband and wife, father and mother, life partners through international crises and domestic turmoil in Jordan," she noted. "To lose this man would be a catastrophe on every level imaginable."

Queen Noor spent six months in Minnesota with King Hussein while he underwent treatment. Despite his illness, he still managed to assist President Bill Clinton in arranging further peace negotiations between Israel and the Palestinians. By the end of 1998 it appeared that the king was free of cancer. Queen Noor took her husband back to Jordan in January 1999, where they were greeted by huge, enthusiastic crowds. During the next few weeks, King Hussein met with his younger brother, Crown Prince

Hassan, to discuss the issue of succession. He decided that his eldest son, Abdullah, would replace his brother as successor to the throne. Some Jordanians criticized the king's decision and claimed that Queen Noor was behind the move, because it made it more likely that her own sons would eventually become king. But King Hussein noted that he and his brother had drifted apart in terms of their political philosophy, so he felt that his son would make a better ruler.

> "The spiritual journey that began when I married my husband came to a head during his illness and with his loss," Queen Noor wrote. "Islam was never a greater comfort to me than during that time. I was able to accept God's will and be at peace during and after the king's death in a way that I would never have been able to imagine."

Just a few weeks after his triumphant return to Jordan, King Hussein's cancer returned. He and Queen Noor went back to the Mayo Clinic, where he underwent another bone marrow transplant. The operation was unsuccessful, however, and the queen made the difficult decision to bring her husband home to die. During his final days, Queen Noor and her daughters left the hospital in the middle of a rainstorm to meet with the crowd holding a vigil outside.

King Hussein died on February 7, 1999, at the age of 63. Queen Noor stood by her husband throughout the ordeal of his cancer. When he died, her dignity and composure provided comfort to a grieving nation and earned her the respect of many Jordanian citizens. She noted in her book that her adopted religion helped her cope with her loss. "The spiritual journey that began when I married my husband came to a head during his illness and with his loss," she wrote. "Islam was never a greater comfort to me than during that time. I was able to accept God's will and be at peace during and after the king's death in a way that I would never have been able to imagine."

Shortly before he died, King Hussein extolled his wife's virtues in a letter to the people of Jordan. "She brought happiness and cared for me during my illness with the utmost loving affection. She, the Jordanian, who belongs to this country with every fiber of her being, holds her head high in the defense and service of the country's interest," he stated. "She, like me, also endured many anxieties and shocks, but always placed her faith in God and hid her tears behind smiles."

Moving Forward and Revisiting the Past

Queen Noor's stepson Abdullah became king of Jordan upon her husband's death. For the next few years, Queen Noor stepped out of the public eye. She spent her time doing charity work and supporting her children as they pursued their education abroad.

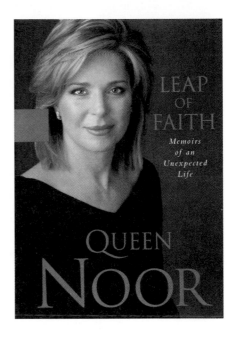

In 2003 Queen Noor returned to the public spotlight with the publication of her book, *Leap of Faith: Memoirs of an Unexpected Life,* which became an international best-seller. The book recounts the story of her courtship and marriage, discusses the challenges she faced in adjusting to a different culture, and documents her husband's efforts to bring peace to the Middle East. It received a great deal of praise for providing an intimate, inside look at some of the important political events of the previous 25 years. But it was also criticized in some quarters for shortchanging the Jewish perspective on recent Middle East history.

Queen Noor explained that she wrote the book in order "to share my perspective on living in two different cultures. Like my husband, I have a conviction that there is much more that binds culture than separates us. I feel a responsibility to highlight our common ground so that both cultures can work together to resolve conflicts peacefully. My husband is the hero of the book; his search for peace is the central theme, and yet it's not meant to be a definitive historical or political account."

"Queen Noor offers a vastly informative and even fascinating memoir," wrote Brad Hooper in *Booklist.* "As the woman who stood behind one of the major players in the Middle East in the second half of the 20th century, Queen Noor brings a unique perspective to the contemporary history of the region." That view was echoed by Julie Salamon in the *New York Times Book Review.* "*Leap of Faith* fulfills its mandate of assuring ordinary readers that real-life fairy tales are suffused with pain as well as magic," said Salamon. "What emerges is a careful yet often revealing account of domestic adjustment and Middle East politics, as well as an affecting wifely portrait of King Hussein." Queen Noor donated all profits from the book to the

King Hussein Foundation, an organization that supports educational programs to promote peace and democracy in the Middle East.

Thanks in part to the success of her book, Queen Noor has emerged as an unofficial spokesperson for Arab political views in the United States. She spoke out in hopes of creating greater understanding between her two cultures, but in some cases her comments generated controversy. In interviews promoting her memoirs, for example, she offered her views on the 2003 U.S.-led invasion of Iraq, which succeeded in removing Saddam Hussein from power. "The United States has won military victories in Afghanistan and Iraq," she noted. "Now the question is, can America win the peace? It takes seconds to destroy something that might have taken centuries to build, and by this I mean not just buildings and monuments, but optimism, trust, and hope. The ability to compromise rests on these things. We've seen a mistaken notion among hardliners in Israel and Palestine — and sometimes in the United States, too — that security comes from guns and building walls. We are hopeful that the United States will apply its historic commitment to justice to this entire region. America can promote peace in the Middle East only if these principles are paramount. This is especially true in relation to the Arab-Israeli conflict, where America's credibility rests not just on its strength, but also on its wisdom and humanitarian ideals."

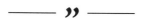

"Leap of Faith *fulfills its mandate of assuring ordinary readers that real-life fairy tales are suffused with pain as well as magic," wrote Julie Salamon in the* New York Times Book Review.

MARRIAGE AND FAMILY

Lisa Halaby married Hussein ibn Talal, king of Jordan, on June 15, 1978. They had four children together: His Royal Highness Prince Hamzah (born in 1980); His Royal Highness Prince Hashim (1981); Her Royal Highness Princess Iman (1983); and Her Royal Highness Princess Raiyah (1986). They also raised eight children from the king's three previous marriages: Princes Abdullah, Feisal, and Ali; and Princesses Alia, Zein, Aisha, Haya, and Abir Muheisen.

Queen Noor and King Hussein lived in Jordan's royal palace, but they also maintained homes in the United States and England. Following her hus-

Queen Noor shown with her husband and their four children in about 1986-87.

band's death in 1999, the queen began spending the majority of her time in Potomac, Maryland, to be near her daughters, who were attending school in the United States. She returned to Jordan for about one week out of every month to oversee her charitable foundations.

Five years after King Hussein's death, the media speculated about a romantic link between Queen Noor and Jim Kimsey, a multi-millionaire cofounder of America Online and prominent Washington-based philanthropist. But she claims that she has no plans to remarry. "Who am I going to marry?" she noted. "I've been married to a charming, attractive king."

HOBBIES AND OTHER INTERESTS

In her spare time, Queen Noor enjoys skiing, water skiing, sailing, horseback riding, reading, gardening, and photography.

SELECTED WRITINGS

Leap of Faith: Memoirs of an Unexpected Life, 2003

HONORS AND AWARDS

Grand Cordon of the Jeweled Al Nahda (Jordan): 1978
Grand Collar of Al Hussein bin Ali (Jordan): 1980
Global 500 Award (United Nations): 1995

FURTHER READING

Books

Collopy, Michael, and Jason Gardner, eds. *Architects of Peace: Visions of Hope in Words and Images,* 2000
Darraj, Susan Muaddi. *Queen Noor,* 2004 (juvenile)
Queen Noor. *Leap of Faith: Memoirs of an Unexpected Life,* 2003

Periodicals

Biography, Sep. 2003, p.44
Current Biography Yearbook, 1991
Good Housekeeping, Apr. 2003, p.125
Ms., Fall 2003, p.39
People, Mar. 1, 1999, p.54; June 9, 2003, p.115
Time, Mar. 29, 1999, p.50
Washington Post, Nov. 6, 1981, p.C1; June 19, 1999, p.C1; Mar. 2, 2004, p.C1
Washingtonian, Oct. 1999, p.50

Online Databases

Biography Resource Center Online, 2004, article from *Contemporary Authors Online,* 2003

ADDRESS

Office of Her Majesty Queen Noor
Bab Al Salam Palace
Amman, Jordan

E-mail: noor@queennoor.jo

WORLD WIDE WEB SITE

http://www.noor.gov.jo

Violet Palmer 1964-

American Professional Basketball Referee
First Woman to Officiate an NBA Game

BIRTH

Violet Palmer was born in 1964 in Compton, a tough section of Los Angeles, California. Her father, James Palmer, was a metalworker in a factory that made airplane parts. Her mother, Gussie Palmer, was a homemaker. Violet was the second of four children in her family. She has two sisters—one older and one younger—as well as a younger brother.

YOUTH

Throughout her youth, Violet enjoyed the stability and support of a close-knit family. Her parents provided for all her needs and always encouraged her to pursue her dreams. She acknowledged that "My friends say, 'Violet, you grew up in Compton, but your family was like *Little House on the Prairie*,'" referring to the book series by Laura Ingalls Wilder that was made into a popular TV show. "It's true. As a child, I never wanted for anything. I think a lot of my confidence and stability comes from my strong family background."

When Violet was about 10 years old, her father put up a basketball hoop in the backyard. She spent hours playing basketball with her brother and the neighborhood boys. "The guys knew that she could play," said her brother, Rod. "She was one of the first to be picked all the time."

EDUCATION

Palmer attended Compton High School, where she became a star athlete. She played softball, ran track, and was the starting point guard for the girls' basketball team. After graduating from high school, she went on to attend California State Polytechnic University at Pomona (Cal Poly-Pomona). She served as captain of the women's basketball team for three years, leading Cal Poly-Pomona to back-to-back NCAA Division II national championships in 1985 and 1986. Palmer earned a bachelor of science (BS) degree, with a major in recreation management and a minor in public administration, in 1987.

CAREER HIGHLIGHTS

Becoming a Referee

At the time Palmer completed her college basketball career, there were no professional basketball leagues for women in the United States. She was not interested in playing in Europe, but she wanted to remain involved in basketball in some capacity. She tried coaching high school basketball, but she only lasted one season. "The kids needed so much attention," she remembered. "I had migraines. I was just so tense and stressed out. I said, 'This ain't for me.'"

Palmer then took a job with the Placentia Recreation Department, near Los Angeles. Part of her job involved refereeing youth basketball leagues. She soon found that she enjoyed working as a basketball official. Her college basketball coach, Darlene May, encouraged her to pursue a career as a referee. May was a top women's basketball referee who became the first woman to officiate a women's basketball game in the Olympics.

Palmer soon began refereeing high school basketball games, and she was selected to officiate the Los Angeles city semifinals in her first year. She quickly moved up to the college level, refereeing women's basketball games in the Big West, West Coast, and PAC-10 conferences. "After just one year of officiating high school, I'm hired to do three college conferences. Unheard of," she stated. "I think my quick rise can be attributed to being an ex-player. I caught on extremely quickly."

Palmer studied basketball rules and regulations and attended special referee training camps during the summers. After impressing observers at summer camps in 1992, she received a schedule that included 40 NCAA

Palmer (#12) battling for the ball in 1985, while playing for Cal Poly-Pomona. The team won the first of the school's five NCAA Division II national championships.

Division I women's basketball games. Unfortunately, her career suffered a setback when she tore ligaments in her knee during a coed softball game. "Guy slides into first, clips me. Blows out my knee," she recalled. "I ended up in a cast from the top of my leg right down to my foot. Out for the year."

At first, Palmer worried that missing a year of refereeing might halt her career progress. "Until my injury, I didn't realize how important officiating was to me," she noted. "How much I really wanted to do it. That year I made a commitment to myself." Luckily, the college conferences recognized her abilities and held her spot until she recovered. "She had an extraordinary amount of talent, terrific personality and communication skills," said PAC-10 officiating supervisor Carter Rankin. "She also had the greatest asset any official can have: anticipatory movement." In 1993 Palmer officiated 50 Division I women's basketball games. The following year she was honored to have the opportunity to referee a Final Four game in the NCAA tournament.

Training for the NBA

By 1995 Palmer was thrilled with the progress she had made in her career as a referee. In the five years since she had officiated her first game, she had rocketed to the highest levels of women's basketball. Since there were no female referees in men's college or professional basketball, however, she thought that perhaps she had advanced as far as possible.

> "I had to become a student again," Palmer said about starting to work in the NBA, where the players were bigger, faster, and stronger than the players she usually officiated. "I was learning where to be, where to look. That's when the training came in. If you learn the mechanics, you become a better referee, instantly."

Then, to her surprise, Palmer received a call from Aaron Wade, who was in charge of developing officials for the National Basketball Association (NBA). Wade told her that the league was hoping to develop some female referees and invited her to attend a training camp. Palmer was one of two women to attend the camp, along with Dee Kantner. She immediately found that she had to make some adjustments, since the NBA players were bigger, faster, and stronger than the players she usually officiated. "I had to become a student again," she recalled. "I was learning where to be, where to look. That's when the training came in. If you learn the mechanics, you become a better referee, instantly."

Palmer was invited back to the NBA's training camp for new referees in 1996. Her performance got the attention of Rod Thorn, the vice president of operations for the NBA, who invited her to participate in another training camp that featured veteran NBA officials. As part of this experience, Palmer was assigned to referee an NBA exhibition game. Up to this point, Palmer had viewed the NBA training as a useful tool that would increase her skills for refereeing women's basketball. It was only after she officiated an exhibition game that she thought she might have a chance to become an NBA referee. "A lightbulb went off in my head," she remembered. "I said to myself, 'You're gonna do this. You're gonna show everybody that thought this was impossible that it is possible.' I wasn't scared—I knew I could do it. I had been an athlete all my life and knew I just needed the training. But I was totally nervous. I couldn't believe it was happening, but that's a normal feeling."

In the meantime, Palmer continued to perform well as a women's college basketball referee. She had a great season in 1996-97, which culminated in her having the opportunity to officiate the NCAA women's basketball national championship game between Old Dominion and Tennessee. That summer Palmer attended the veterans' camp again and officiated five NBA exhibition games. Afterward, Thorn hired her to join the 58-person officiating staff for the NBA. Along with Kantner, who was hired at the same time, Palmer became one of the first female referees in the NBA. "We look for the best possible refs," Thorn explained. "Violet Palmer has an on-court presence. She's a tough, no-nonsense person with excellent referee skills."

Making History

Palmer made history on October 31, 1997, when she took the court to referee an NBA game between the Vancouver Grizzlies and the Dallas Mavericks. She not only became the first female referee in the history of the league, but also the first woman to officiate any major American men's professional sporting event (Kantner took the court for the first time a few days later). "I will never, ever forget the moment I put that jacket on and walked onto that floor," she said. "It was like, 'Wow, you're telling me I'm going to do this every night!' I was more than nervous, I was going to pee in my pants."

That night, Palmer was part of a three-person officiating crew that included veterans Billy Oakes and Mark Wunderlich. All NBA officiating crews consist of three people. The least experienced official is the umpire, the second official is the referee, and the most experienced official is the crew chief. All three officials are allowed to make calls, but the crew chief generally sets the tone for the game and takes responsibility for resolving disputes about rules or the time clock.

The other members of Palmer's first officiating crew recognized the importance of the occasion. In fact, Oakes placed a photo of himself and Palmer on the court in Vancouver in the scrapbook of his career. "I know you cherish that first night," he told her later, "but you would not believe how proud I was to be part of it with you." Thorn made a point of attending Palmer's debut game. Afterward, he praised her performance under pressure. "She did her job, like the other two officials on the court," he stated. "The better she performs, the more anonymous she'll become."

*Palmer in action in her first game as an NBA referee,
in Vancouver, Canada, October 1997.*

Over the first few months of the 1997-98 NBA season, Palmer and Kantner received a great deal of media attention. The introduction of female referees generated some negative reaction around the league—from fans, coaches, and players. For example, the outspoken player Charles Barkley declared that it was a man's game and should only involve men. Other NBA stars questioned whether female referees could keep up with the fast pace of the men's game, or expressed concerns about swearing in front of a woman on the court. But Palmer took it all in stride and tried to do her job. "There are a couple of players saying negative things but that's the way it goes," she noted. "You're always going to have one or two players like that. But most players, I don't think they care who you are. They just want good referees."

A number of other players expressed their support for the addition of female officials to the NBA. "I'm all for it," said Denver Nuggets guard Kenny Smith. "Women have better judgment than men." Chris Mullin of the Indiana Pacers gave Palmer and Kantner a compliment by saying that they were no different than their male counterparts. "They've done a fine job," he stated. "We've had them both for games, but I can't even remember which games. Nothing sticks out."

From the beginning, Palmer was gratified by the reception she received from her fellow referees. "All the referees were supportive. They were unbelievably open and treated me like one of the guys," she noted. "The bottom line is not that I'm a woman but what happens in between that 94

The introduction of female referees generated some negative reaction, but Palmer took it all in stride. "There are a couple of players saying negative things but that's the way it goes. You're always going to have one or two players like that. But most players, I don't think they care who you are. They just want good referees."

feet [the length of the basketball court]. There are three referees on the court and they're the only friends you have down there. So they can't look at me and say 'I don't want to work with her.' You just can't do that. The players don't care. The coaches don't care. They just want the calls to be fair. They won't say a woman screwed up, they'll say the ref screwed up. And we do mess up. We're human."

Gaining Respect

Palmer has continued to progress as a referee since her rookie season. Now an eight-year veteran NBA official, she still finds her job exciting, although she admits that the constant traveling can be tough. Like most other referees in the league, Palmer works from late September through late April each year. She officiates between 11 and 13 games per month, or about 75 games per season. For each game, she must travel to the home team's city and arrive at the arena three hours early to prepare. Palmer and her officiating crew study the teams and players that will be involved in each game. They need to know the disruptive personalities on every team, how long the visiting team has been on the road, both teams' record in recent games, and any personnel changes or controversies. After a game ends, Palmer typically spends another hour or two watching film in the locker room with the other members of the officiating crew to evaluate their performance. She also takes weekly quizzes and video tests to make sure she remains current on the rules.

——— " ———

When asked what factors most contributed to her success as an NBA referee, Palmer responded: "Presence. I think I have that on the court. I know I do. I've never been a follower. I've always been a leader. I feel I have total control out there. I am in charge. I can handle anything."

——— " ———

NBA referees are required to know the rule book inside and out, remain in top physical condition, and undergo a health examination annually. They also must be mentally tough. "This is a tough profession because you're always being scrutinized," Palmer conceded. "If you're a ref, you're going to be booed and yelled at and worse — it has nothing to do with being male or female."

When asked what factors most contributed to her success as an NBA referee, Palmer responded: "Presence. I think I have that on the court. I know I do. I've never been a follower. I've always been a leader. I feel I have total control out there. I am in charge. I can handle anything." In contrast, the NBA's other female referee, Dee Kantner, was fired in 2002. She was the lowest-ranked official among coaches and general managers, largely because she lacked the on-court presence needed to maintain her authority among the best players in the world. Kantner later became the supervisor of officials in the WNBA.

Some observers claim that, as an African-American woman in her 40s, Palmer has a unique advantage in gaining the respect of players. Since many of the NBA's young stars were raised by single mothers, they tend to view her as an authority figure. "She almost looks like your mother," said Golden State Warriors forward Danny Fortson. "She gives you that look

Being an NBA referee requires a certain forcefulness on the court, as in this episode where Palmer ejected Miami Heat player Alonzo Mourning (center) from the court, while Coach Pat Riley (right) looked on.

like, 'Shut your mouth!' I got that look from my mom. I know what that look means." "No question they see her in a different light," said veteran NBA official Nolan Fine. "You can see it in the players' body language." Palmer says that she will accept any source of respect from NBA players. "Everybody has advantages and everybody in this job has to use them," she noted. "I hear guys say, 'We're not messing with that sister right now, she's got that look.' I like that. I'll take it."

Palmer hopes that the next step in her career will be making the 32-person crew that is chosen to referee the NBA playoffs. Since it usually takes between 8 and 10 years of experience before officials are selected to the playoff crew, she appears to be right on track. "I'm not reffing playoff games yet but I'm looking forward to it. I'm just waiting my turn. And it's coming, too. The door will open again and I'm gonna put my foot right in," she stated. "That would be like the pot of gold at the end of the rainbow."

Palmer also hopes that the day will soon come when she is no longer viewed as a *female* referee. "I'm very proud to be a woman referee, don't get me wrong," she said. "But I am not on some woman kick or anything

335

> "*I have a great life.
> I love what I do. I can't
> believe they actually
> pay me to do it. It's like a
> dream come true. I feel
> truly blessed.*"

like that. The recognition I want is to be accepted as a good referee." She hopes to keep working in the NBA for another 15 or 20 years. "I have a great life," she noted. "I love what I do. I can't believe they actually pay me to do it. It's like a dream come true. I feel truly blessed."

HOME AND FAMILY

Palmer, who is single, lives in Carson, California, with her shih tzu dog, Mozhi.

HOBBIES AND OTHER INTERESTS

In her spare time, Palmer enjoys playing golf. She also likes helping young people who aspire to be referees. She spends a good part of each summer teaching at referee camps, and she also makes frequent visits to schools for career days. "I have the opportunity to make a difference," she explained. "I can tell kids the world offers so much — that if they get out there, those doors will open for them. I was working with the city and was happy, but look what happened. I'm at the top of the pedestal for refereeing. You can't get any higher than what I am. I'm blessed and very fortunate."

HONORS AND AWARDS

Top 10 Women Role Models (Ms. Foundation): 1997

FURTHER READING

Books

Notable Black American Women, 2002
Who's Who among African Americans, 2004

Periodicals

Chicago Sun-Times, Apr. 19, 1998, Sports, p.13
Dallas Morning News, Nov. 2, 1997, p.A1
Denver Post, Oct. 21, 1997, p.D12
Ebony, Feb. 1998, p.172
ESPN Magazine, Mar. 4, 2003, p.44

Essence, Aug. 1998, p.60; Nov. 2004, p.42
LA Weekly, Aug. 1, 1997, p.57
Los Angeles Times, Oct. 29, 1997, p.A1; Oct. 30, 1997, p.C6
Newsweek, Mar. 8, 2004, p.38
People, Nov. 17, 1997, p.235
Philadelphia Tribune, June 19, 2001, p.D1
Seattle Times, Apr. 30, 2000, p.D1
Sports Illustrated, Nov. 10, 1997, p.30

Online Articles

http://sportsillustrated.cnn.com
   (*Sports Illustrated*/CNN, "Women of the Court," May 1, 1999)
http://www.referee.com
   (*Referee Magazine,* "Ultra Violet," Jan. 2000)
http://espn.go.com/nba/columns
   (ESPN, "The Truth about Refereeing in the NBA," Feb. 24, 2003)

Online Databases

Biography Resource Center Online, 2005, articles from *Notable Black American Women,* 2002, and *Who's Who among African Americans,* 2004

ADDRESS

Violet Palmer
NBA
645 5th Avenue
Olympic Tower, 10th Floor
New York, NY 10022

WORLD WIDE WEB SITE

http://www.referee.com

Gloria Rodriguez 1948-

American Educator and Activist
Founder and CEO of Avance, Inc., a Nonprofit
Support and Education Program for Low-Income
Hispanic Parents and Children

BIRTH

Gloria Rodriguez was born Gloria Garza on July 9, 1948, in
San Antonio, Texas. Her father, Julian Garza, died when she
was only two years old. Her mother, Lucy (Villegas) Salazar,
raised Gloria and her four sisters—Julia, Susie, Rosa, and
Yolanda—as a single parent, although she later remarried
and had three more children.

YOUTH

Gloria and her sisters grew up in a poor, Hispanic area of San Antonio known as the West Side. After her father was killed in a bar, Gloria's mother, Lucy, moved her five daughters into a housing project where drug-related and gang activity was common. Lucy managed to keep them away from the "negative elements" by laying down strict rules for her daughters' behavior and by keeping a close eye on them. She made sure that there were flowers growing in the family's tiny back yard and that her children had plenty of freshly-made tortillas and other Mexican foods. Gloria's maternal grandfather, whom she called "Papayo," moved in and became like a father to the girls, and an uncle moved in next door. Although her mother had only a third grade education, she "never lost hope," Gloria explains. "She believed with all her heart and soul that her children were going to make it in this world, and that was instilled in us."

Unlike her four sisters, who were "always kind, nice, and did everything my mother said," Gloria was more outspoken and independent. For example, she refused to stay away from the Mirasol public housing project, where some of her friends lived, even though it was known as a place where there were drugs and violence. One of the reasons that she never fell prey to such influences was her grandfather, to whom she gives the credit for her strong sense of discipline and religious faith. It was always clear to Gloria that Papayo had high hopes for her. He called her *mi maestra*, which means "my teacher," because he often saw her lining up her dolls as if they were students in a make-believe classroom.

> *Although her mother had only a third grade education, she "never lost hope," Rodriguez explains. "She believed with all her heart and soul that her children were going to make it in this world, and that was instilled in us."*

EDUCATION

Gloria was a seventh grader at Edgewood Middle School in San Antonio when she began to hang out with the wrong crowd. Her teacher, Daniel Villarreal, immediately stepped in and, in Gloria's words, "basically snapped me out of it." He told her that as an Hispanic-American from a poor family, she would need a good education if she wanted to make a better life for herself.

A childhood photo of Rodriguez with three of her sisters; Gloria is on the right.

By the time she graduated from Kennedy High School in 1967, Gloria was an outstanding student, a member of the Future Teachers of America, a cheerleader, and her school's "sweetheart queen." She had always wanted to be a teacher but knew that her family couldn't afford to send her to college. Then she heard about a program funded by the federal government that would train her in bilingual education if she promised to return to her own community and teach after graduation. But her high school principal refused to write her a recommendation because he didn't think she was "college material." Again one of her teachers stepped in, telling her, "You've got everything it takes to make it [in college], and when you finish, you come back and show him you made it." Still, Gloria didn't think she had much of a chance and applied for a clerical job just in case. To her amazement, she received a letter from Our Lady of the Lake University in San Antonio informing her that she had been selected for the special program in bilingual education.

"I knew college would be difficult," Gloria says. Her English language skills were not the best, and her high school had not really prepared her for the rigors of college life. Once she arrived at Our Lady of the Lake and began her studies, however, "I went daily to the chapel to pray. I vowed that if I did well, I would use my training to help others." It was during her senior year at Our Lady of the Lake that she was chosen as Miss Fiesta, a title Mexican-American girls rarely won. She still remembers the parade and the huge applause she received as she passed through the Mexican-American section of San Antonio.

Gloria completed her bachelor's degree in elementary education in 1970 and immediately went to work as a grade school teacher in her home town. But she returned to Our Lady of the Lake to get a master's degree in education in 1973. Years later she returned to school, earning a PhD (doctorate) in early childhood education in 1991 from the University of Texas at Austin.

> "
>
> *"I knew college would be difficult,"Rodriguez says, because her English language skills were not the best and her high school had not really prepared her for college. Once she arrived at Our Lady of the Lake and began her studies, however, "I went daily to the chapel to pray. I vowed that if I did well, I would use my training to help others."*
>
> "

FIRST JOBS

Gloria had grown up with a very strong work ethic. She and her sisters used to sell their mother's homemade jewelry at restaurants and drive-in movies, and by the time she was nine, she had a job cleaning a neighbor's house. She worked as a sales clerk in a department store when she was in high school, and she claims that learning how to sell "coats in the summer" taught her early on how to overcome seemingly impossible odds.

CAREER HIGHLIGHTS

Rodriguez started out as a bilingual teacher for San Antonio's Northside School District. Her first class consisted of 35 first graders who had already been labeled "slow learners" and "mentally retarded" by the other teachers. At first, Rodriguez assumed that her young students were having problems because they couldn't speak English very well and had never had a bilingual teacher before. But she soon discovered that their Spanish was almost as poor as their English. She was shocked to discover that some of these children had been punished by their teachers for playing with their food, even though sharing food is common in the Hispanic-American culture. And one day she saw a teacher grab a student and shake her simply because she had stayed after school to read to Rodriguez.

Rodriguez was very discouraged. She knew that these children would never catch up with their peers because they weren't receiving any stimulation or encouragement at home. She thought that the best way to make a difference in these kids' lives was to become a principal, so she went back to school. While taking a research class, she surveyed the attitudes of her students' mothers and made a number of disturbing discoveries. The mothers thought that educating their children was entirely the school's responsibility. Because they themselves had dropped out of school, they didn't expect their children to go much beyond the seventh grade. Rodriguez had read the work of several experts in early childhood development and knew that learning began in the home. She concluded that if she wanted to improve her students' chances of succeeding in school, she would have to teach their parents how to educate them at home.

———— " ————

"Parents need to be made aware that they are their children's first and most important teachers," Rodriguez says, *"that taking care of children during the early years of life is so critical and so important."*

———— " ————

Getting Started with Avance

It was in 1973, just after she'd completed her master's degree in education, that Rodriguez first heard about Avance (pronounced ah-VAHN-say, which means "to advance or progress" in Spanish). This program had been started in Dallas the year before by a couple of graduate students from Cornell University. The organization was trying to establish itself in San Antonio and hired Rodriguez as its first director. With three assistants and a corporate grant, Rodriguez started going from door to door in the Mirasol housing project, looking for mothers who were on welfare but who were interested in becoming more independent and improving their parenting skills. The vast majority of the women she met there were de-

Rodriguez reading to an Avance participant.

Rodriguez working with Avance parents.

pressed, isolated, and without hope for themselves or their children. They were under so much financial and emotional stress that they often took their frustrations out on their kids, and child abuse was widespread.

Rodriguez found a handful of interested mothers and set up a nine-month program that offered weekly three-hour sessions for them and their children. During the first hour, the children were cared for in a nearby room while the mothers were given information on child growth and development. They were taught how to stimulate and discipline their child, and how to provide opportunities for them to socialize with other children. They were encouraged to ask questions and to talk about their own experiences. The second hour was devoted to making simple educational toys designed to stimulate language development and learning. Then, during the third hour, people from local health, nutrition, housing, social service, and educational organizations would talk to the mothers about the services they offered. Avance staff members also visited the mothers in their homes once a week and videotaped them as they played with their children using the toys they had made. These videotapes were used as the basis for class discussions and as an opportunity to comment on any problems the mothers might be having as they interacted with their children.

The mothers who completed the Avance program learned the importance of responding to their children's questions and paying attention to them when they spoke. They learned why they should clean behind their children's ears and why letting them fall asleep at night with a bottle in their mouths was bad for them. Over the course of nine months, they made 30 toys that would help their children develop language skills and get ready to enter grade school. They also learned how to handle their own anger in a way that would not make their children suffer. Most importantly of all, they were taught to tell their children that they loved them and were proud of their accomplishments.

The Avance program in Dallas ran out of money and closed down after a few years. Rodriguez was determined to see that the San Antonio program survived and was successful in getting grant money from the city, the United Way organization, private foundations, and government agencies. In the late 1980s she received $5 million from the federal Head Start Bureau to provide services for pregnant mothers that would continue until their children were five years old and ready to start school.

Reaching Out to Fathers and Older Children

As the program for mothers and preschool children thrived, Rodriguez began looking for ways to include fathers, who were often suspicious and resentful of their spouses' involvement in Avance. In 1988 she instituted the "Fatherhood Project," designed to motivate Hispanic-American fathers to get more education and better jobs by attending literacy classes and taking advantage of job-hunting assistance. They were taught how to handle their anger and communicate more effectively with their spouses. Fathers were also recruited to organize scouting activities for older children, and Avance centers throughout the city soon became "home" to a number of Boy Scout troops. Along with the mothers, fathers were encouraged to pursue a GED (General Equivalency Diploma, which certifies that they have met the requirements for high school graduation) and even to apply for college.

—— " ——

"All of us want to see our children become healthy, happy, competent, and successful human beings. We want them to excel in school and grow up to be honest, compassionate, hard-working, and responsible individuals," Rodriguez says. But she also says that "children do not automatically come with these virtues, nor do they come with instructions."

—— " ——

345

Recognizing that Avance mothers often faced challenges with their older children, Rodriguez began offering special classes in parenting grade schoolers and teenagers. The program also provided tutoring and counseling services for older children who were having trouble in school and scholarship aid for those who wanted to attend college.

A Program that Works

In 1991, more than 17 years after Rodriguez had started the Avance program in San Antonio, a reunion of the first graduating class was held. Of the 23 women and 32 children who attended the reunion ceremony, 94 percent of the children had either finished high school, were still in high school, or had earned a GED. In addition, 43 percent of the children went on to college, and 64 percent of the mothers had gone to either college or technical school. "Statistically," Rodriguez says, "that's amazing," especially since many of these children came from single-parent families with mothers who had dropped out of high school. When the Carnegie Corporation of New York conducted a more formal evaluation of the program's effectiveness, it concluded that mothers who had been through Avance's nine-month program provided "a more organized, stimulating, and responsive home environment," had more positive interactions with their children, spent more time teaching them and talking to them, and were less inclined to resort to physical punishment. They encouraged their children to use their language skills, were more likely to take advantage of community resources, and had a more positive self-image as their children's "teacher."

> "Effective parenting does not come naturally," Rodriguez concludes; "it is an art and includes skills that must be learned."

Over the years, the Avance program in San Antonio has been praised by First Ladies Rosalynn Carter, Barbara Bush, and Hillary Clinton — and the latter donated $5,000 from the sales of her book, *It Takes a Village,* to the organization. It has been featured on "ABC World News Tonight" and "Good Morning America," and it has been visited by Prince Charles of England and the Reverend Jesse Jackson. Rodriguez has been asked to participate in the White House Conference on Families and to serve on a number of advisory boards dealing with early childhood education. She routinely travels around the country for speaking engagements and has emerged as a passionate advocate for "at-risk" children. In 2000 Avance was one of eight organizations in the U.S. to receive the Annie E. Casey Award, given for its efforts to "strengthen families and help them overcome the challenges of life in economically disadvantaged communities." And in 2004 Rodriguez accepted an Hispanic Heritage Award at the Kennedy Center in Washington, D.C. — an award that has been given to such well-known individuals as actor Andy Garcia, clothing designer Oscar de la Renta, baseball player Sammy Sosa, and writer Isabel Allende.

Avance now has a budget of $22 million and serves more than 17,000 low-income people in 11 Texas cities and Los Angeles, California. The organization's San Antonio headquarters was recently moved to a renovated building that houses a day care center for 60 to 75 children under the age of 12, as well as classrooms for workshops and training programs.

A Bilingual Guide for Parents

In 1999 Rodriguez published *Raising Nuestros Niños: Bringing Up Latino Children in a Bicultural World*. In what she describes as a "resource guide for all parents," she talks about her own experiences growing up in a poor Hispanic-American family and what she learned from her mother and grandfather. She explains how parents can teach their children about Hispanic culture and religion and encourage them to learn their own language and carry on the traditions of their parents and grandparents. She emphasizes the importance of the support that neighbors and extended family members can provide, and she also stresses the value of maintaining a strong, committed marriage. The book is filled with poems, songs, and common Spanish sayings or *dichos* — such as "The man who knows two languages is worth two people" — so that parents will pass them on to their children. There are even recipes for favorite Mexican dishes like ta-

Rodriguez's book is both a memoir about her own life and a guide for Hispanic parents raising children today.

males, bread pudding, and buñuelos—a New Year's Eve treat in many Hispanic-American homes. Blandina Cardenas, an associate professor at the University of Texas who wrote the foreword to *Raising Nuestros Niños*, called Rodriguez's book a valuable tool for any Hispanic parent, "meant to be treasured and passed down through the generations."

In 2002 Rodriguez and her co-author, Don Browning, published *Reweaving the Social Tapestry: Toward a Public Philosophy and Policy for Families*. The book examines why families fall apart and the devastating effect that this can have on children. *Booklist* called it a "balanced and sober contribution" to the discussion of how family life in America is changing.

> *Rodriguez strongly believes that learning the Spanish language is an important part of early education for Hispanic children. "[They] need to hear their language—to understand, to affirm who they are."*

The First Teachers

"Parents need to be made aware that they are their children's first and most important teachers," Rodriguez says, "that taking care of children during the early years of life is so critical and so important." She adds that "It's not just babysitting. [The parents] are teaching, they're molding, they're influencing children for the rest of their lives." Rodriguez strongly believes that learning the Spanish language is an important part of this early education for Hispanic children. "[They] need to hear their language—to understand, to affirm who they are."

In her introduction to *Raising Nuestros Niños,* Rodriguez points out that "All of us want to see our children become healthy, happy, competent, and successful human beings. We want them to excel in school and grow up to be honest, compassionate, hard-working, and responsible individuals." But she also says that "children do not automatically come with these virtues, nor do they come with instructions." Like other important and demanding jobs, she concludes, "effective parenting does not come naturally; it is an art and includes skills that must be learned."

MARRIAGE AND FAMILY

Gloria married Salvador Rodriguez, an engineer, on June 17, 1972. They have three grown children: Salvador Julian, Steven Rene, and Gloria Vanessa. "I can get so absorbed in my work and community/volunteer activities," Rodriguez admits, "that it is imperative that I schedule time for my family and personal life." She says she is fortunate to have married "a kind, supportive, and understanding husband" who encourages her to challenge herself and at the same time to "smell the roses" once in a while.

MAJOR INFLUENCES

Rodriguez's first and most important influence was her own mother, Lucy Salazar, whom she regards as a "model parent." "She believed in immediate and consistent punishment, she taught us important virtues. More importantly, she had hopes and dreams that her children and grandchildren could become whatever they wanted."

Another important influence on Rodriguez as a child was the grandfather who moved in after her father died. Papayo, as she called him, taught her about discipline and respect. "It made such an impression on me that today," she says, "when I hear teenagers talking rudely to their parents or grandparents, I am appalled because of how horribly those words go against the values that are ingrained in me."

WRITINGS

Raising Nuestros Niños: Bringing Up Latino Children in a Bicultural World, 1999
Reweaving the Social Tapestry: Toward a Public Philosophy and Policy for Families, 2002 (with Don S. Browning)

HONORS AND AWARDS

100 Most Influential National Hispanic Leaders (*Hispanic* magazine): 1988
Texas Women's Hall of Fame (Governor's Commission on Women): 1993
"As They Grow" Award for Social Action (*Parents* magazine): 1994
100 Most Influential Hispanics in the United States (*Hispanic Business* magazine): 1996
25 Most Influential Working Mothers in America (*Working Mother* magazine): 1998
Hispanic Heritage Award (Hispanic Heritage Awards Foundation): 2004

FURTHER READING

Books

Dictionary of Hispanic Biography, 1996
Notable Hispanic Women, 1993

Periodicals

Dallas Morning News, Nov. 14, 1995, p.A23; Apr. 15, 2000, p.A29
National Civic Review, Winter 1993, p.6
San Antonio Express-News, May 3, 1998, S.A. Life section, p.1; Sep. 19, 2004,
    S.A. Life section, p.K1

Online Database

Biography Resource Center Online, 2005, articles from *Dictionary of Hispanic Biography,* 1996, and *Notable Hispanic Women,* 1993

Online Articles

http://www.womenintheeconomy.org
    (The Center for Women in the Economy and the National Center for
    Policy Analysis, "This Month's Woman in the Economy: Dr. Gloria G.
    Rodriguez," Oct. 25, 2002)

ADDRESS

Gloria Rodriguez
Avance
2300 West Commerce
San Antonio, TX 78207

WORLD WIDE WEB SITE

http://www.avance.org

Carlos Santana 1947-
Mexican-Born American Guitarist and Band Leader
Winner of Eight Grammy Awards for His Album
Supernatural

BIRTH

Carlos Santana was born on July 20, 1947, in Autlan de Navarro, a small town in the state of Jalisco in west-central Mexico.
His father, Jose Santana, was a violin player in a traditional
Mexican mariachi band. His mother, Josefina (Barragan) Santana, was a homemaker. Carlos is the fourth-oldest among
the seven children in his family. He has two brothers and four
sisters.

YOUTH

Carlos grew up in a close-knit, religious family. "From my mother, I learned that everything in life is borrowed from the Lord," he recalled. "From my father, I learned that life is service. From both parents, I learned good manners." Like their neighbors in Autlan de Navarro, the Santanas lived in a modest house that did not have electricity or running water. All of the children were expected to help out with the chores and share clothing and other belongings.

Carlos developed a passion for music at an early age. Realizing that music had the power to make people happy, he longed to become a musician himself. "As a kid, I remember watching how people's eyes would light up when my father played his violin," he noted. "I read books about how people in their 30s or 40s are just beginning to find out what their purpose in life is. I found that out when I was five years old." At that time his father started teaching him to play the violin. But Carlos disliked the instrument and grew frustrated at his inability to master it. "My father's a musician, his father was a musician, my great-grandfather was a musician. Dad taught me the violin for almost seven years, and I could never get anything out of it," he remembered. "I just couldn't get a feeling for it. My playing was no good."

> "As a kid, I remember watching how people's eyes would light up when my father played his violin. I read books about how people in their 30s or 40s are just beginning to find out what their purpose in life is. I found that out when I was five years old."

Jose Santana traveled all over Mexico and California with his band, sometimes leaving home for months at a time. During a particularly long absence in the mid-1950s, Josefina Santana grew concerned that her husband might never return. So in 1955, when Carlos was eight years old, his mother packed up the children and moved north to Tijuana, a town along the U.S. border, to look for Jose. Luckily, they were soon able to find him.

Carlos and his family spent the next five years living in Tijuana—a bustling town full of shops, bars, and restaurants, as well as beggars and prostitutes. During this time, Carlos gained his first exposure to American music. He felt an immediate connection with the blues and early rock and roll played by such artists as B.B. King and John Lee Hooker. As a result, he soon rejected the traditional Mexican folk music favored by his father. "Blues was my first love," he explained. "It was the first thing where I said, 'Oh man, this is the stuff.' It just sounded so raw and honest, gut-bucket honest. From then I started rebelling." He stopped playing violin and instead took up the guitar. Playing on the streets of Tijuana in order to collect change from passing tourists, he soon graduated to playing in local bands. By the age of 11, he was appearing regularly in Tijuana nightclubs and earning enough money to help support his family.

In 1960, when Carlos was 13, his family immigrated to the United States. They settled among the large Mexican population in the Mission District of San Francisco, California. At first Carlos felt out of place in San Francisco. Since he did not speak English and had already supported himself by playing guitar in Tijuana nightclubs, he felt that he had little in common with American kids his age. His unhappiness with the new living situation caused him to act out against his parents—arguing, skipping school, and refusing to eat. Finally, in desperation, his mother gave him $20 and sent him back to Tijuana to try to make it on his own.

Carlos lived alone in Tijuana for nearly a year, and it was a difficult time for him. Years later, he revealed that he had suffered sexual abuse during this period. But he also continued his musical education and became an accomplished guitar player. In 1962 his family convinced him to return to the United States. This time he found a reason to stay. At that time, an alternative culture was just starting to develop in San Francisco, and it included a diverse array of musical styles—including jazz, blues, folk, and salsa. "The '60s was the most important decade of the century," he stated. "To me, the [San Francisco] Bay Area was supremely important in creating a whole new frequency for the rest of the world. I was very fortunate to be here at that time."

―― " ――

"Blues was my first love. It was the first thing where I said, 'Oh man, this is the stuff.' It just sounded so raw and honest, gut-bucket honest. From then I started rebelling."

―― " ――

EDUCATION

During his early years in Tijuana, Santana attended a Catholic elementary school. He often complained to his parents that the teachers there were mean, always yelling at or hitting the students. When his family first moved to San Francisco, Santana attended James Lick Junior High School.

"It was a drag," he noted. "They put me back into junior high because I couldn't speak English. I had to adapt to a whole other way of thinking and being around kids, because I thought I was a man of the world after playing in this nightclub in Tijuana and watching ladies strip. To me, I was a grown-up, but when I came here, I had to live the life of an adolescent all over again, and I couldn't relate."

Santana's troubles in school contributed to his desire to move back to Tijuana. Upon his return to the U.S. in 1962, he attended Mission High School in San Francisco. By this time his sole focus was music, and he showed little interest in his studies. "I would only show up in the morning for homeroom. They would take attendance and then I would split," he admitted. "I didn't want to know about algebra or George Washington or whatever. I could hardly wait to get out of school." Nevertheless, Santana somehow managed to graduate in 1965. "They were very gracious to give me my diploma," he acknowledged.

CAREER HIGHLIGHTS

Appearing at Woodstock

Throughout high school, Santana had told anyone who would listen that he planned to become a professional musician and play with great artists. "People would ask, 'What are you going to do when you leave school?'" he recalled. "I'd say, 'I'm going to play with Michael Bloomfield and B.B. King.' They'd say, 'Man, you're tripping.'" After graduation, Santana worked as a dishwasher in a restaurant and played music on the streets of San Francisco for change. As he improved he began joining jam sessions with a variety of musicians and bands. In 1966 he formed his own band with some of these musicians: David Brown on bass; Gregg Rolie on keyboards and vocals; Rod Harper on drums; and Tom Frazer on guitar. Originally known as the Santana Blues Band, the group soon changed its name to Santana. "The reason we chose my name was because it sounded the best," Carlos Santana explained. "Santana was something that could be a galaxy. It could be a planet or it could be the winds. It had a universal resonance to it." The name also proved appropriate for the group, however, because Carlos Santana's soaring guitar solos provided its trademark sound.

Santana started out playing in small clubs in San Francisco. Over the next three years, the band added more Latin rhythms to its sound and rose to regional fame. "We started mixing up jazz and blues, and some African flavor," Carlos Santana recalled. "We had something different than what was being played in San Francisco." In 1968 Santana played a historic series of concerts at San Francisco's Fillmore West Auditorium, a legendary concert

Part of the original poster for Santana's 1968 Live at the Fillmore concerts.

hall. (Thirty years later, the group released a two-CD set called *Live at the Fillmore* featuring songs recorded during these performances.) These shows helped Santana gain a reputation as an exciting and innovative live band. Also in 1968, the group appeared alongside such notable acts as the Grateful Dead and Muddy Waters at the Sky River Rock Festival in Washington State.

By early 1969, Santana had undergone the first in a long string of personnel changes. Original members Frazer and Harper left the band, while drummer Michael Shrieve and percussionists Mike Carabello and Jose Chepito Areas joined it. This incarnation of Santana made a triumphant appearance at the legendary Woodstock Festival in New York during the summer of 1969. Playing in front of an audience of half a million people,

Santana showcased its unusual fusion of Latin rhythms and rock guitar. The highlight of the band's set was the rock anthem "Soul Sacrifice," which was written specifically for Woodstock. This song was featured in a famous 1970 film about the weekend-long concert event.

Although some people criticized Woodstock as a bad cultural influence — citing drug use and lewd behavior among both performers and audience members — Carlos Santana remembered it fondly. "Some people called it a disaster area, but I didn't see nobody in a state of disaster," he stated. "I saw a lot of people coming together, sharing, and having a great time. If that was out of control, then America needs to lose control at least once a week."

Releasing Hit Records

> "When I was in high school, there were certain songs, like 'Louie Louie,' 'Gloria,' or 'Satisfaction,' that made everybody go crazy. The first time I heard 'Oye Como Va,' I knew it was a serious 'party forever' song. And since then, it's like a feeding frenzy every time we play it."

Santana's success at Woodstock brought the band a great deal of attention. Within a few weeks, the group appeared on the "Ed Sullivan Show" and signed a recording contract with Columbia Records. In October 1969 Santana released its debut album, entitled *Santana*. The album featured the hit single "Evil Ways," as well as the songs "Soul Sacrifice" and "Jingo." It was a phenomenal success, spending two years on the pop charts and selling over two million copies.

Santana released its second album, *Abraxas,* in 1970. Widely considered a classic, the band's follow-up effort featured the hit songs "Black Magic Woman" and "Oye Como Va." The latter became a signature song for the band's concert performances. "When I was in high school, there were certain songs, like 'Louie Louie,' 'Gloria,' or 'Satisfaction,' that made everybody go crazy," he noted. "The first time I heard 'Oye Como Va,' I knew it was a serious 'party forever' song. And since then, it's like a feeding frenzy every time we play it." *Abraxas* eventually sold four million copies.

In 1971 Santana released its third album, *Santana III,* which featured the hit song "Everything's Coming Our Way" and sold over one million copies. Around this time, however, the band essentially broke up. Although the members continued to record together on occasion, they no longer performed in concert. Some observers attributed the demise of this early —

Abraxas.

and hugely successful—version of the band to the influence of drugs. Others blamed Carlos Santana's newfound interest in jazz, which the other band members did not share. In any case, the band's first three albums were considered so seminal that they were all re-released in 1998.

Going Solo

Carlos Santana retained the legal rights to the name "Santana," and he continued to use it for bands featuring different collections of musicians over the years. But he also launched a solo career at this time. He recorded a live album with drummer Buddy Miles in 1972, for example, and made guest appearances on albums by such rock and jazz artists as Jefferson Airplane, Alice Coltrane, John McLaughlin, and Herbie Hancock. Although Carlos Santana was best known for his Latin-inspired rock guitar work, he began moving toward a more improvisational jazz fusion sound at this time.

Around 1973, following the drug-related deaths of several prominent musicians, Santana reassessed his lifestyle. His search for spiritual growth led him to become a disciple of the Bhakti Yoga guru Sri Chinmoy. He adopted the name Devadip Carlos Santana during the decade he spent as a follower of Chinmoy. "My time with Sri Chinmoy . . . gave me some discipline and an awareness of Eastern philosophy," Santana explained. "But I look at it like my old tennis shoes from Mission High School. They don't fit me anymore." Santana also met and married Deborah King during this time, and they eventually had three children together.

Santana maintained an active musical career throughout the 1970s and into the 1980s, both solo and with a band. Although none of the albums he released during this time approached the impact of his first three, his live performances continued to attract large crowds. "Mr. Santana's shows can be extraordinary—a fusion of rock, Latin music, and jazz—and they brim with his own improvising," music critic Peter Watrous wrote in the *New York Times.* "It's possible to hear 20-year-old songs sounding totally new; everything the band plays is bursting with intensity." Santana also became involved in a number of charity concerts during the 1980s, and in 1988 he claimed his first Grammy Award—for best rock instrumental performance on the charity compilation album *Blues for Salvador.*

In 1989 Santana moved to Polydor Records because the company offered him an opportunity to start his own record label, Guts and Grace. His label's first release was an album called *Live Forever,* which featured songs from the last recorded concerts of the late musicians Jimi Hendrix, Marvin Gaye, Bob Marley, John Coltrane, and Stevie Ray Vaughn. "We wanted to create the atmosphere that they were all on the same stage doing it, at the same concert, and honor their music and spirit," he explained. By the early 1990s Santana's ongoing spiritual quest led him to become a born-again Christian, although he also incorporated teachings from other belief systems into his life philosophy.

Making a Comeback

During the 1990s Santana's early work continued to receive air play on classic rock radio stations, and his passionate live performances continued to thrill audiences. Music critics viewed him as a guitar virtuoso with a unique sound, and he was widely admired by fellow musicians and studied by young guitarists. In 1998 Santana and his original band were inducted into the Rock and Roll Hall of Fame. The statement announcing their selection read: "After nearly 30 years of musical growth and development, two things have remained constant: the fearless lead guitar of Carlos Santana and the fiery sound which is so identifiable and evocative—a fusion of blues, rock, Afro pan-Latino jungle rhythms, full-throttle vocals, and an always-danceable groove."

Despite such recognition, Santana felt that he had failed to connect with a new generation of fans. He realized that his work from the early 1970s formed the basis of his popularity, and he knew that he had not scored a radio hit since "Winning," from the 1981 album *Zebop!* Not content to settle for "legend" status as he entered his 50s, Santana began considering how to make a comeback. He claimed that an angel appeared to him at this time and told him to reach out to young listeners with positive music.

In 1999 Santana signed a contract with Arista Records and began working on a new album—the 36th of his impressive career. He worked closely with producer Clive Davis, a longtime mentor who had signed him to his first record deal in 1969. Davis encouraged Santana to write some songs himself and collaborate with popular younger artists on others in order to attract new fans. Santana wanted all the songs to offer a hopeful message that would appeal to a large audience. "If you have the right song, you can reach out to junior highs, high schools, and universities, as well as grandparents and little kids," he noted. "The song's the key, and like a house, if it's built correctly, it will not only hold a family but a generation."

> ———— **"** ————
>
> *"Every musician who participated [in making* **Supernatural]** *was on the same wavelength and artistic energy as I was.* **Supernatural** *is a beautiful example of synchronicity. . . . Making it was a truly glorious experience."*
>
> ———— **"** ————

Santana had no trouble finding young artists who were eager to collaborate with him on the new album, which he called *Supernatural*. As it turned out, each of the artists he approached had admired the guitar legend's work for years. Hip-hop star Lauryn Hill, who sang "Do You Like the Way," called Santana "one of the great influences of my life." Wyclef Jean was so excited to participate that he agreed to provide a song, even though he had not yet written one. "I knew I was such a fanatic of the guy that all I had to do was see him and I'd know what to write," he recalled. "We got to the studio and the song ['Maria Maria'] just came to me." The album also

Supernatural.

saw Santana collaborate with Dave Matthews, Eagle-Eye Cherry, Everlast, Rob Thomas of Matchbox 20, and fellow guitar legend Eric Clapton. "Every musician who participated was on the same wavelength and artistic energy as I was," Santana noted. "*Supernatural* is a beautiful example of synchronicity. . . . Making it was a truly glorious experience."

Upon its release in the summer of 1999, *Supernatural* became a tremendous success. It sold an amazing 15 million copies in the United States and more than 25 million worldwide, making it one of the best-selling albums of all time. Its first single "Smooth," featuring Rob Thomas on vocals, spent 12 consecutive weeks in the No. 1 position on the *Billboard* charts to become the longest-running top single of the year. In a review for *Time* magazine, David E. Thigpen said that *Supernatural* drew "an uncommonly diverse coalition of fans: grizzled 1960s hippies; university kids who prefer

Dave Matthews but know a good jam when they hear one; Latin rockers lured by fiery guitar and tropical-tinged rhythms; and, as Santana himself describes them, 'kids who aren't as old as my Metallica T-shirt.'"

Supernatural went on to win eight Grammy Awards in 2000, tying Michael Jackson's 1983 record for the most awards won by an artist in a single year, for his mega-hit *Thriller*. The honors for *Supernatural* included album of the year, rock album of the year, and record of the year for "Smooth." In accepting one of the awards, Santana paid tribute to his humble origins. "This is for all the people who don't have running water or electricity," he stated. "If I could do it, you could do it." *Supernatural* also earned three Latin Grammy Awards and an American Music Award for best album.

Following the release of *Supernatural,* Santana spoke publicly for the first time about the sexual abuse he endured as a teenager living alone in Tijuana. "Part of the reason *Supernatural* is such a fantastic phenomenon is because I chose to face my demons, fear, and pain," he revealed. "I opened the window and stood naked and said this thing happened to me and I'm not ashamed. I opened up that door to say, let's educate our children so this doesn't happen to anyone else."

Santana's success has continued since the release of *Supernatural.* In 2002 he joined forces with a new group of artists — including Musiq, Seal, Michelle Branch, and Placido Domingo — on a similarly collaborative album called *Shaman.* His song with Branch, "The Game of Love," received a Grammy Award for best pop collaboration of the year. Santana repeated this formula for success with his 2005 album, *All That I Am,* featuring Los Lonely Boys, Mary J. Blige, and Big Boi. On his web site, Santana described his most recent album as "an extension and continuation of a vision co-created by Mr. Clive Davis and myself. We equate what we do with the dimen-

> "
>
> *Following the release of* **Supernatural,** *Santana spoke publicly for the first time about the sexual abuse he endured as a teenager living alone in Tijuana. "Part of the reason* **Supernatural** *is such a fantastic phenomenon is because I chose to face my demons, fear, and pain. I opened the window and stood naked and said this thing happened to me and I'm not ashamed. I opened up that door to say, let's educate our children so this doesn't happen to anyone else."*
>
> "

Santana performing at a benefit concert for victims of war.

sions of a three-ring circus . . . where children, teenagers, parents, and grandparents can share unity and harmony in the family of life. We create songs and magic pairing to bring joy and happiness to the listener." Also in 2005, Santana's song "Al Otro Lado Del Rio," which appeared on the soundtrack of the critically acclaimed film *The Motorcycle Diaries,* received an Academy Award for best original song.

Connecting with People through Music

By blending blues and rock music with Latin rhythms and adding his own flaming guitar, Carlos Santana created a passionate sound that helped him earn a devoted following and sell over 80 million albums to date. From the beginning, however, Santana has insisted that music is about self-expression and connecting with others rather than commercial success. He also believes that music has the potential to transform people's lives. "My intention has always been to make people laugh and cry and dance at the same time. When people reach that state, it's not just me playing. A whole other spirit takes over," he noted. "Our music continues to be tremendously appealing to all kinds of people—young, old, black, white, hip, square—and all cultures. I don't deliberately try to make it appealing to lots of different audiences. I just try to get to that next note, to get inside it so the listener can do the same."

Known for his fiery guitar solos, Santana claims that the secret to making great music comes from investing heart and soul into a search for the perfect note. "A lot of times you may hit some really ugly notes, but that's okay in the pursuit of that perfect thing. That's the whole romance of losing and finding yourself when you take a solo. You must lose yourself to find yourself. If you approach everything from an analytical point of view, the mind takes over. By the time you do your solo, it might sound great, but it's not going to penetrate," he explained. "When I hit that note—if I hit it correctly—I'm just as important as Jimi Hendrix, Eric Clapton, or anybody. Because when I hit that note, I hit the umbilical cord of anybody who is listening."

> **❝**
>
> *"My intention has always been to make people laugh and cry and dance at the same time. When people reach that state, it's not just me playing. A whole other spirit takes over. Our music continues to be tremendously appealing to all kinds of people—young, old, black, white, hip, square— and all cultures. I don't deliberately try to make it appealing to lots of different audiences. I just try to get to that next note, to get inside it so the listener can do the same."*
>
> **❞**

MARRIAGE AND FAMILY

Santana married Deborah Sara King, the founder of a health food shop in San Francisco and daughter of blues guitarist Saunders King, in April 1973. They have three children: Salvador, Stella, and Angelica. Santana and his family live in a mansion in San Rafael, California, overlooking San Francisco Bay. "I'm just grateful that I can balance my music life and my family life," he stated. "My family is prime time, and everything else is secondary—including music."

HOBBIES AND OTHER INTERESTS

Throughout his career, Santana has contributed to charitable causes and participated in benefit concerts. "Playing music is easy, like drinking water. But changing the conditions of life is a little more challenging, and infinitely more rewarding," he stated. "The '60s taught me that if you aren't part of the solution, you're part of the problem. It's an old cliche, but I'd rather contribute to the solution." So in 1998 he and his wife formed the Milagro Foundation to support charities that improve the health care and educational opportunities available to underprivileged children around the world. In 2004 the foundation distributed more than $250,000 from the sale of concert tickets and albums to children's charities. "We feel very passionate—my wife and I—that we can make a difference," Santana said.

SELECTED ALBUMS

With Santana Band

Santana, 1969 (reissued 1998)
Abraxas, 1970 (reissued 1998)
Santana III, 1971 (reissued 1998)
Caravanserai, 1972
Welcome, 1973
Greatest Hits, 1974
Borboletta, 1974
Amigos, 1976
Festival, 1976
Moonflower, 1977
Marathon, 1979
Zebop!, 1981
Viva Santana!, 1988
Milagro, 1992
Dance of the Rainbow Serpent, 1995

Live at the Fillmore 1968, 1997
Best of Santana, 1998; Vol. 2, 2000
Supernatural, 1999
Shaman, 2002
All That I Am, 2005

Solo

Live Carlos Santana, 1972 (with Buddy Miles)
Love Devotion Surrender, 1973 (with John McLaughlin)
Illuminations, 1974 (with Alice Coltrane)
Havana Moon, 1983
Blues for Salvador, 1987
Spirits Dancing in the Flesh, 1990

HONORS AND AWARDS

Grammy Awards: 1988, best rock instrumental performance for *Blues for Salvador;* 2000 (eight awards), album of the year and rock album of the year for *Supernatural;* record of the year and best pop collaboration with vocals for "Smooth"; best rock performance by a duo or group for "Put Your Lights On"; best pop performance by a duo or group for "Maria Maria"; best rock instrumental performance for "The Calling"; and best pop instrumental performance for "El Farol"; 2002, best pop collaboration for "The Game of Love"
Chicano Lifetime Achievement Award: 1997
Golden Eagle Legend in Music Award (*Nosotros*): 1997
Rock and Roll Hall of Fame: 1998
Alma Award (National Council of La Raza): 1999
Medallion of Excellence for Community Service (Hispanic Congressional Caucus): 1999
Man of the Year (VH-1): 2000
Latin Music Awards: 2000 (three awards), album of the year for *Supernatural,* record of the year for "Corazon Espinado," and best pop instrumental performance for "El Farol"
American Music Award: 2000, album of the year for *Supernatural*
Blockbuster Entertainment Award for Favorite Rock Artist or Group: 2000
Person of the Year (Latin Academy of Recording Arts and Sciences): 2004
Hispanic of the Year (*Hispanic* magazine): 2004
Academy Award for Best Original Song: 2005, for "Al Otro Lado Del Rio," from the soundtrack to *The Motorcycle Diaries*

FURTHER READING

Books

Contemporary Hispanic Biography, Vol. 1, 2002
Contemporary Musicians, Vol. 43, 2003
Dictionary of Hispanic Biography, 1996
Grove Dictionary of Music and Musicians, 2001
Leng, Simon. *Soul Sacrifice: The Santana Story,* 2000
Remstein, Henna. *Latinos in the Limelight: Carlos Santana,* 2002 (juvenile)
Shapiro, Marc. *Carlos Santana: Back on Top,* 2000
Who's Who in America, 2005

Periodicals

Billboard, Oct. 5, 2002, p.1; Aug. 14, 2004, p.21
Current Biography Yearbook, 1998
Guitar Player, Jan. 1993, p.58; Aug. 1999, p.74; July 2003, p.25
Hispanic, Mar. 31, 1996, p.19; May 31, 2000, p.82; Dec. 2004, p.38
Los Angeles Times, Aug. 9, 1998, Calendar, p.3; Feb. 24, 2000, p.S1
Newsweek, Feb. 14, 2000, p.66
People, Feb. 28, 2000, p.97
Time, Oct. 25, 1999, p.120
Whole Earth, Summer 2000, p.72

Online Databases

Biography Resource Center Online, 2005, articles from *Contemporary Hispanic Biography,* 2004; *Contemporary Musicians,* 2003; *Dictionary of Hispanic Biography,* 1996
WilsonWeb, 2005, articles from *Current Biography,* 1998; *Grove Dictionary of Music and Musicians,* 2001

ADDRESS

Carlos Santana
Creative Artists Agency
9830 Wilshire Blvd.
Beverly Hills, CA 90212

WORLD WIDE WEB SITE

http://www.santana.com

Antonin Scalia 1936-

American Justice on the U.S. Supreme Court
Youngest Supreme Court Justice in U.S. History

BIRTH

Antonin Scalia (pronounced skah-LEE-a) was born on March
11, 1936, in Trenton, New Jersey. He was the only child of S.
Eugene Scalia, a language professor of Sicilian heritage, and
Catherine Panaro Scalia, a first-generation Italian-American
who worked as a schoolteacher. Since early childhood, Antonin
has been called "Nino" by many of his family and friends.

YOUTH

Scalia spent his early years in Trenton. When he was five his father secured a position as a professor of romance languages at Brooklyn College in New York City. The family subsequently moved to Queens, New York, a short commuting distance from the Brooklyn College campus. They lived there, nestled among a wide circle of relatives, through Scalia's teen years.

Both of Scalia's parents were proud members of the Catholic Church, and they raised their son to appreciate the importance of family and the value of religious faith. In addition, they created a home environment that encouraged learning and intellectual stimulation. Smart and curious from an early age, Scalia thrived under these conditions. "He would ask me such questions!" recalled one of his aunts. "He'd ask about the universe, about everything happening around. He floored me many times."

Scalia's youthful energy and intelligence impressed his father as well. "He was good at anything he did," recalled S. Eugene Scalia. "He played the piano when he was very young and I wondered how he managed to do so well and practice so little. He picked up the guitar in nothing at all. The minute I put him on a bicycle he took off, 'whoosh.'"

> "He was good at anything he did," recalled Scalia's father. "He played the piano when he was very young and I wondered how he managed to do so well and practice so little. He picked up the guitar in nothing at all. The minute I put him on a bicycle he took off, 'whoosh.'"

EDUCATION

Scalia attended public school in New York City. For high school his parents enrolled him at Saint Francis Xavier, a Jesuit school in Manhattan. Scalia was a natural leader, both in the classroom and out. First in his class when he graduated in 1953, he also directed the school's marching band and played the title role in a school production of *MacBeth*. "He was brilliant, way above everybody else," recalled one high school classmate.

After earning his high school diploma, Scalia moved on to Georgetown University in Washington, D.C., where he studied history. He dazzled faculty and classmates alike with his affable manner, sharp wit, and intelligence. "[He was] not just bright," recalled former New Jersey Attorney General James Zazzali, who attended Georgetown at the same time. "He was unbelievably brilliant." When he graduated from Georgetown in 1957 with a bachelor's degree in history, Scalia was class vale-dictorian—the graduating senior with the highest grade point average.

Scalia then enrolled at Harvard Law School, where he became editor of the prestigious *Harvard Law Review*. He became known around campus for his deeply conservative political beliefs. Scalia also became known for delivering spirited defenses of his beliefs in friendly debates with faculty and friends. "Conservative" political beliefs have traditionally emphasized low taxes, limited government services, and opposition to social change. After graduating with top honors in 1960 with his law degree, he explored

A rather surpring shot of the future Supreme Court justice as MacBeth in a high school production, in a photo from the Xavier yearbook, about 1952-53.

Europe for several months. It was during these travels that he met and became engaged to Maureen McCarthy, his future wife.

CAREER HIGHLIGHTS

In 1961 Scalia accepted a job in Cleveland, Ohio, with Jones, Day, Cockley, and Reavis, the city's most prestigious law firm. He worked as an attorney in Cleveland until 1967, when he accepted a teaching position in the University of Virginia law program. In 1971 Scalia took his first formal step into the world of public service, accepting the position of general counsel to the White House Office of Telecommunications Policy in the administration of President Richard M. Nixon. In this position Scalia helped media industry leaders reach major agreements on cable television regulations and development.

In 1972 Scalia was appointed chairman of the Administrative Conference of the United States, a federal study group that examines legal and management issues affecting the executive branch of government. Over the ensuing months, a national scandal known as Watergate engulfed the Nixon administration. This scandal concerned revelations that members of Nixon's administration and re-election organization had planned a burglary at the headquarters of the Democratic National Committee in the Watergate office complex in Washington, D.C. These events occurred during the presidential campaign in 1972, when President Nixon was running for reelection. The burglary had been committed by staffers connected to the president's campaign, and it had occurred at the office of the Democratic Party. Even worse, high-ranking staffers had then tried to create a massive cover up to hide these illegal acts. Investigation of this burglary—by the press and by other government agencies—gradually centered on audiotapes and documents held by President Nixon himself.

By 1974 Watergate investigators and Nixon were locked in a bitter struggle for possession of these potentially incriminating tapes and documents. At the height of this battle, Scalia was named assistant attorney general in the Office of Legal Counsel at the U.S. Department of Justice. As such, he was part of the executive branch, like the president. In this position, his responsibilities included providing legal advice to the president on various issues affecting the Oval Office.

Shortly after joining the Department of Justice, Scalia told Nixon that the president—not the federal government—was the rightful owner of the Watergate tapes and documents. Scalia believed that the executive branch of the U.S. government should have the right to keep such information to itself. Nixon embraced this opinion and continued to withhold the tapes. Eventually, however, the U.S. Supreme Court (the judicial branch) rejected Nixon's position and demanded that he turn the tapes and documents over to investigators. Aware that the tapes contained proof that he had engaged in criminal activity and lied to the American people, Nixon resigned from office a few days later. He was the first president ever to resign from office.

A Growing Reputation in Conservative Circles

In January 1977 Scalia left the Justice Department to join the law faculty at the University of Chicago. Around this same time he was named a resident scholar at the American Enterprise Institute (AEI), a nationally known conservative "think tank" based in Washington, D.C. His affiliation with AEI reflected Scalia's growing reputation as one of the most brilliant and promising champions of conservativism in America.

Scalia enjoyed the next several years in Chicago. His family had grown so large by this time that he and his wife converted a former fraternity house into a home to raise their nine children. In the meantime, Scalia balanced his teaching duties with work as coeditor of two scholarly journals that promoted conservative economic and social policies.

There are a variety of philosophies that determine how legal experts interpret and create laws. Some judges follow the philosophy of "judicial activism," which gives judges a lot of freedom in deciding legal issues and interpreting the Constitution. But Scalia took a different approach, developing a reputation during this time as a disciple of the philosophy of "judicial restraint." This philosophy insists that judges should interpret legal questions according to very narrow readings of the Constitution, the Bill of Rights, and other laws. The philosophy of judicial restraint also holds that judges should never make legal decisions for the purpose of changing social and economic policies. In the view of Scalia and other believers in judicial restraint, policymaking in the social and economic arenas should be left entirely to Congressional lawmakers, as stated in the Constitution. Scalia championed this philosophy both in the classroom and in print. As he wrote several years later in his book *A Matter of Interpretation*, "Congress can enact foolish statutes as well as wise ones, and it is not for the courts to decide which is which and rewrite the former."

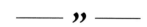

> "[Scalia believes that] laws mean what they actually say, not what legislators intended them to say but did not write into the law's text."
> —Amy Gutmann, preface to Antonin Scalia's book
> **A Matter of Interpretation**

A Rising Star in the Judicial Branch

In 1982 Scalia was appointed to the U.S. Court of Appeals for the Washington, D.C., circuit. This court is widely regarded as second in importance only to the U.S. Supreme Court. Because it's based in Washington, this court hears many cases in which the U.S. Congress, the executive branch, and various federal agencies are deeply involved.

Scalia's seat on the U.S. Court of Appeals gave him numerous opportunities to stake out his positions on various legal and social issues. As the months passed, it became clear that his conservative perspective on issues brought before the court was a pretty close match to that of the administration of President Ronald Reagan. For example, both Scalia and Reagan felt that the U.S. Constitution did not give Americans the right to abortion. They also shared a strong dislike for race-based affirmative action programs and championed private property rights.

By the mid-1980s, the Reagan administration's appreciation for Scalia and his conservative rulings was well-known. In fact, many observers predicted

*In June 1986, President Ronald Reagan announced the retirement of
Chief Justice Warren Burger (far right) and the nominations of
Associate Justice William Rehnquist (second from right) to be chief justice
and Scalia (far left) to be an associate justice.*

that if President Reagan had an opportunity to fill a vacancy on the U.S.
Supreme Court, Scalia would be one of the most likely candidates. As it
turned out, this speculation proved to be right on target.

Joining the U.S. Supreme Court

In 1986 legendary Chief Justice Warren E. Burger retired from the U.S. Supreme Court. He was replaced as head of the court by longtime associate
justice William Rehnquist. On June 24, 1986, meanwhile, the Reagan administration nominated Scalia to fill the vacancy.

Scalia was tremendously excited about the prospect of becoming a member of the highest court in the United States. But he knew that his nomination would first have to be confirmed by the U.S. Senate, in accordance
with the rules of the Constitution. In September 1986 Scalia appeared before the Senate Judiciary Committee, which had the responsibility of making a recommendation for or against his confirmation to the larger Senate.

Prior to Scalia's appearance, many observers wondered if his conservative
reputation would trigger attacks from liberal or moderate members of the
committee. But Scalia's undeniable accomplishments and his thoughtful,

good-humored personality won over the entire committee. His nomination was passed along to the Senate, and on September 17 he was confirmed by a 98-0 vote. Scalia thus became the first Italian-American ever to take a seat on the U.S. Supreme Court. At 50 years of age, he also became the youngest Supreme Court justice in U.S. history.

A seat on the nine-member Supreme Court is both a tremendous honor and a great responsibility. The court decides whether the laws made by all levels of government — federal, state, and local — follow the Constitution. The court accomplishes this by interpreting the provisions of the Constitution and applying its rules to specific legal cases. Because the Constitution lays out general rules, the court tries to determine their meaning and figure out how to apply them to modern situations. After the Justices select a case for review — and they accept fewer than about 100 of the 6,000 cases presented to them each year — they first will hear arguments by the two opposing sides. They begin discussing the case and take a preliminary vote to see which side has a majority of votes. Then one justice from the majority is assigned to write up the court's opinion. Drafting an opinion is complex and time-consuming, and the whole process can take over a year. The court's final opinion has tremendous importance, setting out a precedent that all lower courts and all levels of government throughout the United States are required to follow. The reasoning given in the opinion is also important, because it helps people understand the basis for the decision and how the ruling might apply to other cases in the future.

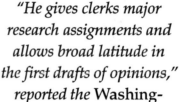

"He gives clerks major research assignments and allows broad latitude in the first drafts of opinions," reported the **Washingtonian.** *"The conservative Scalia frequently hires at least one liberal-to-moderate clerk to play devil's advocate."*

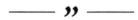

Making His Mark

Scalia made an immediate splash upon joining the court. Legal analysts soon were praising his scholarship, his writing abilities (displayed in opinions on various cases brought before the court), and his engaging personality. One writer even stated that among the other judges, who can seem like silent gray pigeons on a railing, Scalia stood out like a colorful talking parrot.

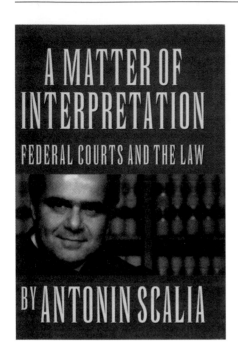

Before long, promising young lawyers were fighting for the chance to serve as one of Scalia's clerks — the lawyers who work with the justices, doing research on upcoming cases and writing legal opinions. This keen competition for these seats derived from his reputation for constantly challenging his clerks to hone their legal skills and their minds. "He gives clerks major research assignments and allows broad latitude in the first drafts of opinions," reported the *Washingtonian.* "The conservative Scalia frequently hires at least one liberal-to-moderate clerk to play devil's advocate."

Scalia also made his guiding legal philosophy clearly known, both to his colleagues on the court and to the world at large. His philosophy, called textualism or originalism, is founded on the belief that the *original* meaning of the Constitution and other laws should continue to govern all legal judgments. Or, as Amy Gutmann summarized in the preface to Antonin Scalia's book *A Matter of Interpretation,* Scalia believes that "laws mean what they actually say, not what legislators intended them to say but did not write into the law's text."

Not surprisingly, this philosophy led Scalia to criticize judges who allow their modern-day "intellectual, moral, and personal perceptions" to override the "text and tradition" of the Constitution and other established laws. In his view, judges should always give greatest weight to the Constitution's original meaning, even if it seems unfair or wrong to modern Americans. Correcting these flaws is, according to Scalia, the responsibility of lawmakers in the executive and legislative branch of American government, not judges in the judiciary branch.

By the early 1990s, Scalia was viewed by many conservative political leaders, writers, and ordinary Americans as their "favorite" justice. After all, his opinions typically reflected their beliefs on such issues as church-state separation, abortion, affirmative action, privacy rights, and property rights. But he did not always side with conservatives. For example, his strong defense of the First Amendment, which ensures free speech for Americans, frustrated some conservative groups. Scalia cited the First Amendment when he voted with the majority in striking down a Texas law that prohibited the burning of the American flag.

In 1997 Scalia published an essay about his political beliefs called *A Matter of Interpretation: Federal Courts and the Law*. This essay, which was published side-by-side with commentaries from several legal scholars, was widely praised as an eloquent defense of the principle of "textualism." "[Scalia] projects a sanguine humor through a robust prose enlivened by sly sallies against what he sees as the gaps in the logic of the opposing camp. He is anything but the angry justice of popular myth," commented the *Wall Street Journal*. The *ABA Journal* offered similar praise, exclaiming that "as a writer of essays he is formidably persuasive, by turns seductive, fierce, funny, charming—and always brilliant."

—— **"** ——

"To be able to write an opinion for oneself, without the need to accommodate, to any degree whatever, the more-or-less-differing views of one's colleagues; to address precisely the points of law that one considers important and no others; to express precisely the degree of quibble or foreboding or disbelief or indignation that one believes the majority's position should engender— that is indeed an unparalleled pleasure."

—— **"** ——

Scalia and His Colleagues

By the late 1990s, however, personal issues seemed to be playing a role on the court. Rumblings that Scalia was disliked by some of his colleagues threatened to overshadow his judicial philosophy and his widely admired skills as a writer and interrogator of attorneys presenting arguments before the court. His reputation as a friendly and engaging person at home and at play remained intact. But many court observers believed that Scalia had developed a bad habit of publicly ridiculing the legal opinions of other justices with whom he disagreed. "No other current justice shows as much contempt for colleagues," declared the *Dallas Morning News* in 1996. "When Mr. Scalia was named to the court 10 years ago, commentators predicted that his intellect and charm would help forge a conservative consensus. Instead, his embittered rhetoric and sarcastic humor drove away the others, except for Justice Clarence Thomas. Demonstrating no interest in consensus building, he revels in dissent. . . .

He places self-importance above the court's prestige as a governing institution—an institution that should be above petty, personal bickering."

Even conservative legal analysts voiced concern about Scalia's public attacks on some of the other justices. They typically agreed with his views, but worried that his blunt criticisms undermined his ability to convince a majority of justices to support rulings he favors. Scalia remained unapologetic about his outspoken ways, however. He also strongly defended his preference for writing his own legal opinions, rather than signing off on those penned by other justices: "To be able to write an opinion for oneself, without the need to accommodate, to any degree whatever, the more-or-less-differing views of one's colleagues; to address precisely the points of law that one considers important and no others; to express precisely the degree of quibble or foreboding or disbelief or indignation that one believes the majority's position should engender—that is indeed an unparalleled pleasure."

Growing Controversy

In the first years of the 21st century, Scalia's reputation as a brilliant conservative mind continued to flourish. But critics sharpened their attacks on him, accusing him of excessive pride and hypocrisy in some of his votes. For example, Scalia was part of the 5-4 court majority that called a halt to the disputed recount of voting in Florida during the 2000 presidential election. This ruling effectively gave the presidency to conservative Republican George W. Bush over Democratic candidate Al Gore. Critics charged that Scalia's vote in the court case *Bush v. Gore* was inconsistent with his previous conservative legal opinions on equal protection issues. "His opponents claim Scalia acted as a ruthless, self-serving politician who put his own boy in power when it looked like the other side might win," summarized *Commonweal.* Scalia and his supporters, though, contended that his vote was based on sound legal principles, not political considerations.

In subsequent months, Scalia's strongly worded opinions on a variety of issues attracted further controversy. He argued, for example, that all-male military schools should not have to open their doors to women, and he insisted that governmental institutions had the legal right to discriminate against gay people if they wished. These opinions were warmly praised by some Americans and harshly condemned by others.

In 2003 Scalia's sense of propriety and impartiality was repeatedly called into question by court watchers. One time, he gave a keynote dinner speech to a group waging a legal battle against gay rights—at the same time that

The Supreme Court in 2003. Front row, left to right: Antonin Scalia, John Paul Steven, Chief Justice William H. Rehnquist, Sandra Day O'Connor, and Anthony M. Kennedy. Back row, left to right: Ruth Bader Ginsburg, David Souter, Clarence Thomas, and Stephen Breyer.

he and other members of the Supreme Court were weighing an important gay rights case. Many considered this a conflict of interest.

On another occasion, Scalia went on a duck hunting vacation with Vice President Dick Cheney. The timing of this trip raised eyebrows even among some Scalia supporters, for it took place shortly before the Supreme Court was supposed to make an important ruling on a fierce legal battle between Cheney and various environmental and governmental watchdog groups. Afterward, Scalia strongly defended himself, stating that socializing should not be automatic grounds for disqualifying a judge from a pending case. But critics such as the *Nation* claimed that Scalia's decision not to remove himself from the case "tells thousands of federal and state judges that it can be OK to vacation with friends who have cases before them and to accept the generosity of those friends while their cases are pending."

In April 2004 Scalia's actions outside Supreme Court chambers once again came under scrutiny. While giving a speech at a Mississippi high school, the justice apparently directed U.S. marshals charged with protecting him to confiscate and erase recordings of his speech made by a teen reporter at the school. "I don't think any public official—and I don't care whether you are a Supreme Court justice or the president of the United States—has a right to speak in public and then say, 'You can't record what I have said,'" said Burt Neuborne, a law professor at New York University. "This doesn't live up to the ideals of the First Amendment. He should know he can't use a U.S. marshal as a private police force to enforce his will."

―――――― " ――――――

"Although Scalia's views resonate with a large segment of the public, his influence within the court appears to be minimal. Without question, he is smart, quick, witty, and devoted to the law. He is considered the court's most gifted writer, and he often dominates the oral arguments. Yet he rarely writes an important opinion for the court. . . . He is known for his sharply worded dissents—but little else."

— Los Angeles Times

―――――― " ――――――

A Pillar of Modern Conservatism

Despite Scalia's recent struggles in the public spotlight, he remains highly regarded by both legal scholars and America's conservative political community. There has even been speculation that if a Republican is in the Oval Office when Chief Justice Rehnquist decides to retire, Scalia might be nominated to be the new head of the court. Most analysts agree, however, that Scalia would have to endure a bruising confirmation hearing to get the seat, given his long record of opposition to abortion rights, affirmative action, gay rights, church-state separation, and other measures supported by liberal and/or moderate Americans.

Today, Scalia's stature within the Supreme Court seems somewhat unclear. In 2003, for example, the *Los Angeles Times* declared that "although Scalia's views resonate with a large segment of the public, his influence within the court appears to be minimal. Without question, he is smart, quick, witty, and devoted to the law. He is considered the court's most gifted writer, and he often dominates the oral arguments. Yet he rarely writes an important opinion for the court. . . . He is known for his sharply worded dissents—but little else."

But other analysts see Scalia as a dominant personality, armed with an intellect and reservoir of energy that outshines every other member of the court. And they believe that he will go down as one of the most important Supreme Court justices in U.S. history. "At the most basic level, Justice Scalia is simply a rascal—a brilliant, hilarious rascal who keeps the rest of

A 1986 photo of Justice Scalia with his wife, Maureen, and their nine children.

the court on its feet, but a rascal, nonetheless," stated the *American Spectator*. "So we all need to just sit back and enjoy it. . . . No, collegiality is not Justice Scalia's strong suit, and that fact alone may deny his fans the pleasure of one day seeing a Scalia court. But, honestly, isn't it his Supreme Court already?"

MARRIAGE AND FAMILY

Scalia married Maureen McCarthy on September 10, 1960. Together they raised a family of five boys—Eugene, John, Paul, Matthew, and Christopher—and four girls—Ann, Catherine, Mary Clare, and Margaret Jane. The Scalias make their home in Virginia, near Washington, D.C.

HOBBIES AND OTHER INTERESTS

Scalia enjoys a wide variety of sports, including tennis and squash. He is also an outdoorsman who likes to hunt all sorts of game animals, from deer to pheasant. Other interests include poker and the piano. Finally, Scalia and his wife have traveled widely, journeying to various corners of Europe and Asia.

SELECTED WRITINGS

A Matter of Interpretation: Federal Courts and the Law, 1997

FURTHER READING

Books

Brisbin, Richard A. *Justice Antonin Scalia and the Conservative Revival,* 1997
Hall, Timothy L. *Supreme Court Justices: A Biographical Dictionary,* 2001
Jost, Kenneth, ed. *The Supreme Court, A to Z,* 1998
Lewis, Thomas T., and Richard L. Wilson, eds. *Encyclopedia of the U.S. Supreme Court,* 2001
Maltz, Earl M. *Rehnquist Justice: Understanding the Court Dynamic,* 2003
O'Brien, David M., ed. *Judges on Judging: Views from the Bench,* 1997
Witt, Elder, ed. *Congressional Quarterly's Guide to the U.S. Supreme Court,* 1990
Witt, Elder, ed. *The Supreme Court A to Z: A Ready Reference Encyclopedia,* 1993

Periodicals

ABA Journal, Jan. 1997, Book section, p.86
American Journalism Review, June/July 2004, p.70
American Spectator, Aug./Sep. 2003, p.20
Amicus Journal, Summer 1999, p.34
Commonweal, Mar. 28, 2003, p.11
Current Biography Yearbook, 1986
Dallas Morning News, July 21, 1996, p.J5
GQ, May 2001, p.190
Los Angeles Times, July 9, 1990, p.A1; June 29, 2003, p.A1; Mar. 8, 2004, p.A1; Apr. 9, 2004, p.A18; Apr. 25, 2004, p.A26
Nation, Oct. 9, 2000, p.32; Apr. 19, 2004, p.21
National Review, Dec. 9, 1996, p.34
New Republic, Jan. 18, 1993, p.20; Apr. 5, 2004, p.14
New York Times, June 19, 1986, p.D27; Mar. 15, 1995, p.A22; May 2, 2004, p.A1
Newsweek, Nov. 6, 2000, p.92; July 14, 2003, p.68
Time, June 30, 1986, p.24; July 8, 1996, p.48
USA Today, July 1, 1996, p.A3
Wall Street Journal, Mar. 19, 2004, p.B1
Washington Post, Oct. 17, 2003, p.A27
Washingtonian, Oct. 1998, p.16

Online Articles

http://www.success.org
(American Success Institute, "Couragously Defend Our Liberty," by Antonin Scalia, undated)

http://www.time.com
  (*Time.com*, "Antonin Scalia, Civil Libertarian," June 14, 2001)

Online Databases

Biography Resource Center Online, 2004, articles from *Contemporary Authors Online*, 2002, and *Encyclopedia of World Biography*, 2004

ADDRESS

Justice Antonin Scalia
U.S. Supreme Court
Supreme Court Building
1 First Street NE
Washington, DC 20543-0002

WORLD WIDE WEB SITES

http://www.supremecourtus.gov
http://www.uscourts.gov
http://www.supremecourthistory.org
http://www.oyez.org

Curt Schilling 1966-

American Professional Baseball Pitcher with the
Boston Red Sox
Overcame Injury to Help His Team Win the 2004
World Series

BIRTH

Curtis Montague Schilling was born in Anchorage, Alaska, on
November 14, 1966. He was one of three children born to Mary
Jo Schilling and Cliff Schilling, a career soldier in the U.S. Army.

YOUTH

Curt inherited an early love of baseball from his father, who placed a ball and glove in his infant son's crib. A native of Pennsylvania, Cliff Schilling was a huge fan of the city of Pittsburgh's professional sports teams, especially the Pirates (baseball) and the Steelers (football). Curt shared this passion from as far back as he can remember. "A lot of the best memories in my life revolve around my father and the Pirates or my father and the Steelers," he recalled. "Because I held my father in such high regard that anybody he talked that way about had to be superhuman to me."

Curt enjoyed playing baseball from an early age. In fact, an early family video shows him swinging a plastic bat when he was just two years old. Almost from the beginning, Curt could throw a baseball much harder than other kids his age. On many youth teams, the player with the strongest arm ends up playing third base, because the third baseman must make long throws across the diamond to first base. Curt started out at third base when he began playing organized baseball, but he always longed to become a pitcher like his favorite players, Nolan Ryan and J. R. Richard. "I always liked power pitchers when I was young, anybody with power," he remembered.

Curt started out at third base when he began playing organized baseball, but he always longed to become a pitcher like his favorite players, Nolan Ryan and J. R. Richard." I always liked power pitchers when I was young, anybody with power," he remembered.

EDUCATION

Shadow Mountain High School

Growing up in a military family meant that Curt moved often and attended school in many different places as a child. After spending two years in Anchorage, the Schillings lived in Missouri, Kentucky, and Illinois before settling in Phoenix, Arizona. Curt loved living in sunny Phoenix, where he could play baseball every day. He attended Shadow Mountain High School, home to one of the best baseball programs in the state of Arizona. He played on the junior varsity team for his first three years of high school, still stuck at third base and close to giving up his dream of becoming a pitcher.

After his junior year, Schilling attended a major-league tryout camp put on by the Cincinnati Reds. The Reds' scouts narrowed the field of prospects by making all the players run a timed 40-yard dash. Schilling was not very fast, so he knew that he could not pass the speed trial. But the scouts did not require the pitching prospects to perform the speed trial, so he decided to try out as a pitcher. His very first pitch hit the catcher's mitt with such a loud "pop" that it turned heads all around the practice area, and every subsequent pitch made the same sound. When his tryout ended, the scouts informed him that his pitches had exceeded 90 miles per hour on their radar guns—a tremendous speed for a high-school player. The team was ready to discuss a formal tryout until they learned that Schilling had not yet graduated from high school.

During his senior year, Schilling pitched for the Shadow Mountain varsity team. Although he would have been the best pitcher on most high school teams, he was one of four equally talented pitchers for Shadow Mountain. This situation limited his opportunities to showcase his talents, but he decided that his own playing time was less important than his team's overall success. "I learned a valuable lesson," Schilling recalled. "I learned that no matter what you think is fair in life, sometimes it's not what somebody else sees. Whether it was fair or not that I didn't play varsity baseball until my senior year was beside the point."

Yavapai Junior College

After graduating from high school in 1985, Schilling decided to attend Yavapai Junior College, which boasted one of the best junior college teams in the country. Many former players had gone on to play at four-year colleges or had been drafted by the pros. But before he took the mound at Yavapai for the first time, Schilling learned that he had been selected by the Boston Red Sox in the January 1986 draft (at that time there were two baseball drafts each year, in January and in June; the January draft is no longer held). The Sox chose Schilling in the second round, shortly before his first season at Yavapai.

Although he was thrilled to be drafted, Schilling knew he had a lot to learn and decided to remain with his junior college team. It proved to be a good decision. Over the course of that season, Yavapai Coach David Dangler taught Schilling to throw his pitches at different speeds and angles, to use the same windup motion on each pitch, and to slow down and stay in control. These lessons helped Schilling post a 10-2 record in the regular season and lead his team to the top position in the national junior college (juco) rankings. Yavapai qualified for the Juco World Series, where the team finished third. "It was one of the greatest, most fun years of my life," he related. At the conclusion of his successful freshman season, Schilling decided to make the leap to professional baseball. Since Boston retained his rights for a year, he signed a contract with the Red Sox on May 30, 1986. He left college without earning a degree.

CAREER HIGHLIGHTS

Moving Up through the Minor Leagues

After being drafted by the Red Sox, Schilling was assigned to play in the minor leagues. Many baseball players start their careers in the minor leagues, also called the farm system. The teams in the minor leagues are affiliated with those in the major leagues. There are a variety of minor leagues, which are ranked according to the level of competition. The top or best league is Class AAA (called Triple A), next is Class AA, then Class A, then below that are the rookie leagues. Players hope to move up through the system to a Class AAA team and then to the major leagues.

Schilling was assigned to play first for Elmira in the Single-A New York—Pennsylvania League in 1986 and then earned a promotion to a higher Single-A team in Greensboro, North Carolina, in 1987. Off the field, however, he faced a more difficult adjustment. He had never lived on his own before, beyond the reach of his father's strict rules, and he suddenly found himself earning more money than he had ever seen. "My first month as a pro I made $6,000," Schilling recalled. "I took that check to the bank and got 300 $20 bills, threw them on the bed in my hotel room, and just lay there, watching TV." With a lack of supervision and an infusion of cash, he soon developed a reputation as a party-loving free spirit. He described his life in the minor leagues as being "like living in a frat house with no classes and getting paid for it. In all these little towns, where the ballpark is the center of things, you're a bigwig. That's a lot of power for a 19- or 20-year-old, and I played it for all it was worth."

Following the 1987 season, Schilling's father was diagnosed with cancer and given only a few months to live. Curt was devastated by the news, since his father had always been his biggest supporter. In January 1988,

> "My first month as a pro I made $6,000. I took that check to the bank and got 300 $20 bills, threw them on the bed in my hotel room, and just lay there, watching TV."

Cliff Schilling came to visit his son. The night before he was scheduled to return home, the two men talked into the wee hours of the morning. "We stayed up late that night just talking about baseball, life, everything," Curt recalled. "He said things that a father usually thinks, but doesn't say. I remember him saying how he knew I was going to make it to the big leagues."

The next morning, Cliff suddenly experienced severe chest pain, collapsed, and died in his son's arms. Curt later learned that he had experienced a burst aortic aneurysm (a weak spot in an artery to the heart). "Now I didn't have that calming voice to tell me everything was all right when I thought it wasn't," he said. Since his father's death, Schilling has come up with a unique way to honor his memory. At every game he starts, he leaves a ticket for his father at the gate as a symbolic gesture. Schilling says that he gets a feeling of inner peace by knowing that there is an empty seat in the stands reserved for his father.

> Schilling described his life in the minor leagues as being "like living in a frat house with no classes and getting paid for it. In all these little towns, where the ballpark is the center of things, you're a bigwig. That's a lot of power for a 19- or 20-year-old, and I played it for all it was worth."

As the 1988 season began, Schilling was promoted to the Red Sox's Double-A team in New Britain, Connecticut. He continued to pitch well, but his off-the-field behavior deteriorated even further. Concerned about his level of commitment, Red Sox management decided to trade him to the Baltimore Orioles' Double-A team in Charlotte. Unlike Boston, which had viewed him as a longshot to make the big leagues, Baltimore considered him one of its top prospects. Schilling received more attention and assistance than he ever had before, and it paid off. On September 1, when major-league teams were allowed to expand their rosters for the playoffs, the Orioles called him up to the big-league squad.

Major League Baseball — The Baltimore Orioles

When Schilling received that long-awaited call from the Orioles, he thought he was ready to play major league baseball. But he was still too interested in partying. "I was such a screw-up when I got to the big leagues," he admitted years later. "I was a total idiot. I ran the nightlife, I drank, I just acted crazy. I did all the stupid things you'd expect from a 21-year-old kid with money."

Schilling made his first major league start on September 7 against his original team, the Boston Red Sox. He pitched well, allowing three runs in seven innings to help the Orioles win by a score of 4-3. But he faltered in his other starts, finishing his first stint in the big leagues with no wins and an ERA above 10.00. He spent the next few years alternating between time in the big leagues and time in the minors, playing for the Orioles and their Triple-A team in Rochester, New York. At one point, after a series of poor performances, Manager Frank Robinson took the young pitcher aside and criticized his bad attitude, shoddy work ethic, and inattention to conditioning.

Schilling waits for the sign while pitching for the Houston Astros, 1991.

"He wasn't a bad kid," Robinson noted. "He just wanted to be noticed." The manager's talk had an influence on Schilling, and his behavior improved for the rest of the season.

In 1991 the Orioles traded Schilling to the Houston Astros. The Astros tried unsuccessfully to make the hard-throwing right-hander into a closer, a pitcher who comes in at the end of games, usually to protect a narrow lead. But Schilling had trouble with his control, walked a lot of hitters, and was demoted to the Astros' Triple-A team in Tucson, Arizona. Soon Houston lost patience with the young pitcher and traded him to the Philadelphia Phillies at the start of the 1992 season.

Reaching a Turning Point

Before he joined his new team, however, Schilling experienced a major turning point in his career. While working out at the Houston Astrodome during the off-season, he ran into Roger Clemens, a star pitcher for the Boston Red Sox who made his home in Texas. Schilling had met Clemens briefly when both players were with Boston, and he admired the Red Sox ace a great deal. Clemens was only four years older, but he had already won three Cy Young Awards as the American League's best pitcher. Schilling dreamed of following in Clemens's footsteps, so he was thrilled when a clubhouse attendant told him that Clemens wanted to talk to him.

But Schilling's excitement quickly turned to embarrassment. Instead of sitting and trading pitching tips with the superstar, Schilling was forced to listen quietly while an angry Clemens berated him for over an hour. Widely known as the hardest-working pitcher in baseball, Clemens had watched in disbelief as Schilling loafed his way through his off-season workout program. He criticized the struggling young player for wasting his enormous talent and disrespecting the game of baseball. Schilling felt humiliated, but he knew that everything Clemens said was true. He vowed to change that very day. Since that time, Schilling has credited "The Talk" with turning his career around. "I can't repeat a lot of what [Clemens] said," he noted. "He just railed at me. He said I was wasting my career and I was cheating the game. . . . It was one of the three or four most pivotal moments of my career. It was one of those conversations your father has with you when you're going down the wrong path and it saves your life."

> "I can't repeat a lot of what [Clemens] said. He just railed at me. He said I was wasting my career and I was cheating the game. . . . It was one of the three or four most pivotal moments of my career. It was one of those conversations your father has with you when you're going down the wrong path and it saves your life."

The Philadelphia Phillies

When Schilling reported to the Phillies a few months later, he was a changed man. He came to training camp in the best shape of his career, and his improved strength and stamina paid off. Working his way into the starting lineup, he posted a career-high 14 victories (against 11 losses), with 10 complete games and an ERA of just 2.35.

In 1993 Schilling became one of the best pitchers in the National League. He finished the season with a 16-7 record and 186 strikeouts in 235.1 innings. The Phillies won the division and advanced to the National League Championship Series (NLCS), where they faced the heavily favored Atlanta Braves. Schilling had an outstanding series. As the starter in Game 1, he set a record by striking out the first five Braves he faced. He ended up

Schilling pitching for the Philadelphia Phillies, 1992.

striking out 10 and giving up only two runs in eight innings, to help the Phillies win the game by a score of 4-3 in 10 innings. Schilling achieved a similar result in Game 5 and was named NLCS Most Valuable Player for his role in helping the Phillies win the pennant.

Advancing to the World Series for the first time since 1983, the Phillies faced the Toronto Blue Jays. The two teams played an exciting World Series that featured a memorable finish. Toronto won three of the first four games in the best-of-seven series and seemed to be on its way to an easy title. Schilling took the loss in Game 1, which Toronto won 8-5. By the time he took the mound again in Game 5, he was asked to keep the Phillies alive in the series. He started out strong, regularly throwing fastballs clocked in the mid-90s on the radar gun. By the seventh inning he began to tire, and the speed of his pitches dropped into the mid-80s. But the Phillies had used so many pitchers the night before—in a heartbreaking 15-14 extra-inning loss—that there was no one available to relieve him. "I looked out in the bullpen and there was nobody there," he recalled. "I knew it was my game, and in many ways, that gave me the adrenaline to keep going." Schilling held on to finish a brilliant complete-game shutout and keep his team alive. His gutsy performance made him a folk hero in Philadelphia.

Unfortunately, the Phillies' reprieve lasted only one game. They lost the series on a home run in the bottom of the ninth inning in Game 6.

During the next two seasons, injuries limited his performance. In fact, Schilling only won a total of nine games in 1994 and 1995. Following the 1995 season he had surgery to repair tendon and rotator cuff damage in his shoulder. During this time, he rededicated himself to being the best pitcher he could be. He built a weight room in his house, improved his workout regimen, and began keeping a video record of every hitter he faced in order to aid his mental preparation. "When [the injuries] happened, it made me stop and think about how I want to be remembered when I'm done," he explained. "I'd like to be thought of as one of the best pitchers of my era."

Schilling's dedication paid off when he returned to the starting rotation in May 1996. Although his record was only 9-10, he struck out 182 batters in just 183.1 innings and led the league with eight complete games. By the end of the season, he was widely viewed as one of the toughest pitchers in baseball. Since his contract with Philadelphia was set to expire, a number of teams attempted to sign him as a free agent. Schilling was happy with the Phillies, however, and passed up higher salaries offered by other teams to remain in Philadelphia. "I make more money than I'll ever need," he admitted after signing a new contract.

Schilling had an outstanding year in 1997. He posted a record of 17-11 with a 2.97 ERA, made the All-Star team for the first time in his career, and broke J. R. Richard's record for most strikeouts by a right-handed pitcher in one season by fanning 319 batters. Schilling's strong performances continued in 1998 and 1999. He won 15 games and made the All-Star team in each of these seasons. His record in 1999 was even more impressive because he missed the last two months of the season after again undergoing arm surgery.

The Arizona Diamondbacks

In 2000, the Phillies decided to trade several veteran players for talented young prospects. Schilling was the Phillies' most valuable asset, and several teams expressed an interest in acquiring him. He was sent to the Arizona Diamondbacks, a talented team that was poised to make a run at the World Series. Combined with perennial All-Star Randy Johnson, Schilling gave Arizona one of the toughest starting pitching rotations in all of baseball. While Schilling had always enjoyed playing for the Phillies, he was excited at the prospect of making a playoff run with the Diamondbacks.

At first the trade appeared to be a mistake. Bothered by arm trouble, Schilling was unable to pitch his best in 2000. The Diamondbacks fell just short of making the postseason, and Schilling took much of the blame. "Ultimately I ended up being one of the reasons we didn't make the play-offs," he acknowledged. "I couldn't get it done." In 2001, however, he turned in a spectacular season. He posted a career-best 22-6 record and a 2.98 ERA, finishing second to Johnson in voting for the Cy Young Award. The two star pitchers combined for 665 strikeouts—the most strikeouts by teammates in a single season in baseball history. Johnson led the league with 372, while Schilling finished second with 293.

To people who knew baseball, it was obvious that each pitcher fed off the other's success. "Randy and Curt raised the bar for each other all year," said Arizona outfielder Luis Gonzalez. "You could see that when one of them pitched a good game, it was as if he said to the other one, 'Here you go, big guy. Now let's see what you can do.'" Led by Schilling and Johnson, the Diamondbacks cruised into the playoffs. After defeating the St. Louis Cardinals and the Atlanta Braves in the first two rounds, Arizona clinched a spot in the World Series, where they faced the legendary New York Yankees—the most successful team in baseball history. But Schilling refused to be intimidated by the Yankees' storied past.

"Randy and Curt raised the bar for each other all year," said Arizona outfielder Luis Gonzalez. "You could see that when one of them pitched a good game, it was as if he said to the other one, 'Here you go, big guy. Now let's see what you can do.'"

The 2001 World Series

The Diamondbacks-Yankees World Series turned out to be one of the most memorable in baseball history, with the outcome decided in the bottom of the ninth inning of Game 7. The Diamondbacks took an early lead in the series by winning the first two games at home. Schilling led the way in Game 1, striking out eight Yankees in seven innings to earn the win in Arizona's 9-1 rout. "I know all about the history of the Yankees," he told reporters after the game, "but I wasn't pitching against Babe Ruth and Mickey Mantle today." Game 2 saw Johnson earn a victory by throwing a three-hit, 11-strikeout masterpiece to beat New York 4-0. But the Yankees came back strong to win the next three games in New York. With their opponents leading the series 3-2, the Diamondbacks faced two must-win

Schilling (in jacket) in the midst of a jubilant celebration after the Diamondbacks defeated the Yankees 3-2 to win Game 7 of the 2001 World Series.

games at home to claim the world championship. In Game 6, Johnson held the Yankees to just two runs, while Arizona scored early and often to trounce the Yankees by a score of 15-2.

Schilling took the mound for Arizona in the deciding Game 7, while the Yankees countered with the ace of their staff, 300-game-winner Roger

Clemens, whose reprimand nearly a decade earlier had helped Schilling turn his career around. In a gutsy performance, Schilling struck out nine batters to take a razor-thin 1-0 lead into the seventh inning. The Yankees finally got to him in that inning, tying the game on a single by Tino Martinez. In the eighth inning, Schilling got the first batter out but then watched in disgust as Alfonso Soriano hit a solo home run to put the Yankees ahead 2-1. Recognizing that Schilling had grown tired, Arizona Manager Bob Brenley decided to replace him with a relief pitcher. Amazingly, Brenley called upon starter Randy Johnson, who had just earned his second win of the series the day before. But Brenley's instincts proved correct, and Johnson retired the Yankees in the eighth and ninth innings without allowing any more runs.

To win the game and the title, the Diamondbacks had to score two runs against the best relief pitcher in baseball, Mariano Rivera, who had yet to allow a run in the series. The Arizona batters came through in dramatic fashion, sending the winning run home with two outs in the bottom of the ninth. Schilling was thrilled with his team's exciting World Series victory. "Nothing could be more meaningful than to beat the Yankees in the World Series," he said afterward. "This was great for baseball. We beat the best team in baseball to win a World Series. You just cannot imagine the feeling looking around our clubhouse and knowing the hard work that went into this." In recognition of his outstanding performance in the World Series, Schilling was named co-Most Valuable Player along with Johnson.

In the two years following Arizona's World Series win, Schilling continued to be one of the anchors of the Diamondbacks' pitching staff. In 2002 he went 23-7 with 313 strikeouts and once again finished second to Johnson in Cy Young Award voting. Although the two pitching aces led Arizona back to the playoffs, the team was swept in the first round by the St. Louis Cardinals. In 2003, Schilling missed more than two months of the season due to injuries and only compiled an 8-9 record. The Diamondbacks missed the playoffs that year and entered a rebuilding phase.

The Boston Red Sox

At the end of the 2003 season, the Diamondbacks started trading older, more expensive players, including Schilling, who was traded to the Boston Red Sox. Schilling welcomed the idea of returning to the team that had drafted him. He knew that Boston fans had waited 87 years for a World Series title, and he hoped to contribute to the team's success. "I love that people are counting on me to be a huge part of winning a World Series," he said. "That's why I'm here. I love the expectations. I have always felt the bigger the game, the better I get. I live on adrenaline. I want to be part of a team that does something that has not been done in almost a century."

Despite the enormous pressure he faced, Schilling delivered exactly what was expected of him in 2004. He led the American League with 21 wins and helped Boston clinch a wildcard playoff spot. Led by Schilling's 9-3 victory in Game 1, the Red Sox swept the defending World Series champion Anaheim Angels in the first round of the playoffs. Boston then faced the powerful New York Yankees in the American League Championship Series (ALCS).

"I love that people are counting on me to be a huge part of winning a World Series," Schilling said after he joined the Boston Red Sox. "That's why I'm here. I love the expectations. I have always felt the bigger the game, the better I get. I live on adrenaline. I want to be part of a team that does something that has not been done in almost a century."

Defeating the Yankees

Schilling started Game 1 of the ALCS, but he was forced to leave the mound after three innings due to an ankle injury. The Yankees then cruised to a 10-7 win. Schilling's ankle had begun acting up during the Anaheim series, but he initially thought that it was a simple sprain. As it turned out, however, the injury was much more serious—he had suffered severe damage to a tendon that would require surgery to repair. The only question was whether Schilling could find a way to continue pitching through the playoffs on the injured ankle.

The Red Sox played poorly in Games 2 and 3 and fell behind the Yankees 3-0 in the best-of-seven series. In the century-long modern era of professional baseball, no team had ever come back from this sort of deficit to win a playoff series. At this point, it appeared that yet another season would end in bitter disappointment for Boston fans. To the amazement of many observers, however, the Red Sox rallied to win an exciting Game 4 by a score of 6-4 in the 12th inning. Boston claimed victory again the following day to close the gap to 3-2.

Suddenly, Schilling's ankle injury occupied the center of the baseball universe. Fans across the country wondered if he would be able to pitch in Game 6. No one outside of the Boston clubhouse knew how badly he was

*Schilling pitching against the New York Yankees in Game 6 of the
2004 American League Championship Series.*

hurt. To the delight of Red Sox fans, the team announced shortly before
game time that Schilling would indeed start Game 6.

In one of the most courageous performances in sports history, Schilling
pitched seven innings and allowed only four hits. Unable to use his normal
throwing motion, he resorted to a variety of off-speed pitches and well-
placed fastballs to keep the Yankee hitters at bay. He remained on the
mound even after the stitches holding the dislocated tendon in his ankle
tore out, turning his sock into a bloody mess. "When I saw blood dripping

395

Still on crutches after surgery, Schilling shows off the 2004 World Series trophy.

through the sock, and he's giving us seven innings in Yankee Stadium, that was storybook," Boston first baseman Kevin Millar said. By the time Schilling left the game, the Red Sox held a 4-2 lead that they maintained until the end. "It's at the top of the list among all the games I've pitched," he said afterward. The Red Sox went on to dominate Game 7, scoring six times in the first two innings on their way to a 10-3 victory.

The Boston Red Sox Win the World Series

Compared to the dramatic ALCS, the 2004 World Series seemed anticlimactic. Boston swept the St. Louis Cardinals in four straight games to win the team's first world title in 87 years. Schilling once again provided an emotional lift by pitching through pain to lead his team to victory. When he took the mound in Game 2, his dislocated tendon was again held together with stitches. As before, he bled through his sock (which is now on display in the Baseball Hall of Fame) but still managed to pitch six innings and shut down the opposing team. The Red Sox went on to win the game 6-2 and take a 2-0 lead in the series. Boston maintained its focus and won the next two games to claim the World Series title. "I'm so proud of being a part of the greatest Red Sox team in history," Schilling said afterward. He also felt relieved that his teammates had completed the sweep. "I was not going to pitch Game 6," he admitted. "I could not do it. I had lost too much strength in the ankle and was unable to get any push-off, even just walking around."

During the off-season, Schilling finally underwent surgery to repair his ankle. Although he started three games at the beginning of the 2005 season, his ineffective performances made it apparent that he had tried to come back too soon. He was forced to go on the disabled list, but returned to the starting rotation in July to help the Red Sox defend their world championship. At the start of the 2005 season, Schilling's career record stood at 185-125, with 2,765 strikeouts and an ERA of 3.35.

MARRIAGE AND FAMILY

Schilling met his wife, Shonda Brewer, while he was living in Baltimore and playing for the Orioles. She worked as an associate producer at a local television station. They married in 1992 and eventually had four children: Gehrig, Gabriella, Grant, and Garrison.

HOBBIES AND OTHER INTERESTS

Off the field, Schilling has many interests, including computer gaming and military history. He combined these interests to form a company, Multi-Man Publishing, that creates military strategy board games. Schilling also collects military artifacts, especially from World War II, and baseball memorabilia, including a uniform and other items once owned by one of his heroes, Lou Gehrig.

Schilling is also active in charity work, with a particular interest in helping people with ALS (amyotrophic lateral sclerosis). Better known as Lou Gehrig's disease, because the legendary Yankee slugger died from it, ALS is a degenerative illness that affects the muscles. In 1992 Schilling founded Curt's Pitch for ALS, through which he donates $1,000 for every victory and $100 for every strikeout to support ALS charities. He also encourages corporate sponsors and baseball fans to donate money. Curt's Pitch has raised millions for ALS research. Schilling has also worked with the Shade Foundation to raise funds to support research into melanoma, a form of skin cancer; his wife, Shonda, was diagnosed with the disease in 2001. "The memories you create on a ball field are pretty insignificant things compared to the changes you can make in the life of a person," he said of his commitment to charity work.

HONORS AND AWARDS

Most Valuable Player, National League Championship Series: 1993
Lou Gehrig Award: 1995
Major League All-Star Team: 1997, 1998, 1999, 2001, 2002, 2004
Branch Rickey Award: 2001
World Series Championship: 2001 (with Arizona Diamondbacks), 2004 (with Boston Red Sox)
World Series Co-Most Valuable Player: 2001 (with Randy Johnson)
Jim "Catfish" Hunter Humanitarian Award: 2001
Hutch Award: 2001
Roberto Clemente Award: 2001
National League Pitcher of the Year (*Sporting News*): 2001, 2002
Sportsman of the Year Award (*Sporting News*): 2001

Co-Sportsman of the Year (*Sports Illustrated*): 2001 (with Randy Johnson), 2004 (with Boston Red Sox)
Philanthropist of the Year (*Worth Magazine*): 2002

FURTHER READING

Books

Hagen, Paul. *Curt Schilling: Phillie Phire!*, 1999
Stout, Glenn. *On the Mound with . . . Curt Schilling*, 2004
Who's Who in America, 2005

Periodicals

People, June 1, 1998, p.73; Nov. 5, 2001, p.73
Sporting News, Dec. 17, 2001, p.8
Sports Illustrated, Feb. 2, 1998, p.78; Mar. 30, 1998, p.99; Nov. 12, 2001, p.36; Dec. 17, 2001, p.112; Nov. 1, 2004, p.48; Nov. 15, 2004, p.58
Time, Nov. 8, 2004, p.38
USA Today, June 22, 2001, p.C1; Oct. 26, 2001, p.C6; Aug. 28, 2002, p.C1; Mar. 15, 2004, p.C3; Oct. 20, 2004, p.C4; Feb. 24, 2005, p.C8; Mar. 9, 2005, p.C8

Online Databases

Biography Resource Center Online, 2005

ADDRESS

Curt Schilling
Boston Red Sox
4 Yawkey Way
Fenway Park
Boston, MA 02215

WORLD WIDE WEB SITES

http://boston.redsox.mlb.com
http://www.shadefoundation.org

Maria Sharapova 1987-

Russian Professional Tennis Player
Winner of the 2004 Wimbledon Women's Singles Title

BIRTH

Maria Sharapova (pronounced shah-rah-POH-vuh) was born
on April 19, 1987, in Nyagan, an industrial town in the Siberian
region of the former Soviet Union (now Russia). She is the
only child of Yuri Sharapova, who worked in the Siberian oil
fields, and his wife, Yelena Sharapova.

YOUTH

Maria's parents are originally from the part of the former Soviet Union that is now Belarus. About a year before she was born, the worst nuclear disaster in history took place at the Chernobyl nuclear power plant, just 50 miles from their home. One of the main reactors exploded at Chernobyl, killing 31 people and exposing countless others to dangerous levels of radiation. The explosion released 100 times more radiation than the atom bombs dropped on Japan to end World War II. This radiation contaminated the air, water, and soil in the surrounding area, leading to the immediate evacuation of over 100,000 people and the eventual resettlement of 200,000 more. To this day, people of the region continue to suffer high rates of cancer and other health problems due to radiation exposure.

Shortly before Maria was born, her parents left Belarus in order to escape the continuing fallout from the Chernobyl accident. They moved to a one-bedroom apartment in Nyagan, in western Siberia. When Maria was two years old, her family moved once again. This time they settled in Sochi, a resort town on the Black Sea, where Yuri Sharapova enjoyed playing tennis. Russia was experiencing a tennis boom around this time. Many Russians took up the sport after watching tennis in the 1988 Olympic Games (the sport's first appearance in the Games since 1924). The increased interest in tennis encouraged many towns to build tennis courts, which gave a generation of Russian youngsters greater opportunities to play.

> *When Martina Navratilova first saw Sharapova play, she was immediately impressed by the girl's potential. "It was not just in the way she played tennis," Navratilova recalled. "It was there in the way she moved, the way she walked, and the way she would kick a ball or pick it up and throw it. You cannot teach that fluidity or that ease of movement."*

As it turned out, Yuri Sharapova's tennis partner was the father of top-ranked Russian player Yevgeny Kafelnikov. He encouraged Yuri to introduce Maria to the game and even presented her with her first tennis racquet. From the beginning of her tennis career, Maria had a major advantage over other young players: she was ambidextrous, meaning that she could make shots equally well with either hand. In fact, her left hand was so strong that she almost became a left-handed player. To this day, her strong left hand makes her backhand a powerful weapon.

Moving to the United States

When Maria was five years old, she attended a children's tennis clinic in Moscow, where she attracted the attention of Czechoslovakian tennis legend Martina Navratilova. The winner of 18 Grand Slam singles titles during her long professional career, Navratilova was immediately impressed by the girl's potential. "It was not just in the way she played tennis," Navratilova recalled. "It was there in the way she moved, the way she walked, and the way she would kick a ball or pick it up and throw it. You cannot teach that fluidity or that ease of movement."

Navratilova suggested that Yuri Sharapova take his daughter to the United States so that she could train under top tennis coaches. In 1994 Maria's father took this advice, moving with his seven-year-old daughter to Bradenton, Florida. When they arrived, neither one spoke a word of English, and they had very little money. Due to visa problems, Maria's mother was not able to join them for two years.

Still, Yuri managed to arrange a tryout for Maria at the famous Bollettieri Tennis Academy, which has trained such top pros as Andre Agassi and Venus and Serena Williams. She impressed the coaches there, and they accepted her as a student. Yuri worked at odd jobs to pay the tuition, and Maria's grandparents sent money from Russia to help out. By the age of nine, Maria had earned a full scholarship to the academy, as well as a contract with the International Management Group (IMG) sports agency. "I had never seen a young woman with so much desire, so much maturity and focus," recalled IMG agent Gavin Forbes.

EDUCATION

Although Sharapova has never attended a traditional school, she has always been a good student. When she lived in Russia, her mother taught her at home. Once she moved to Florida, she completed the early years of her schooling at the Bollettieri Tennis Academy, where she lived in a dormitory with much-older girls and attended classes between tennis practice sessions. After turning professional in 2002, she began taking high-school equivalency courses through an Internet school. She had not yet completed her diploma by 2005.

401

CAREER HIGHLIGHTS

Turning Professional

Sharapova worked hard during her years at the Bollettieri Academy, determined to someday join the Women's Tennis Association (WTA) professional tour. At the age of 11, she began working with Robert Lansdorp, a highly regarded tennis coach who had previously trained such star players as Pete Sampras, Tracy Austin, and Lindsay Davenport. The head of the tennis academy, Nick Bollettieri, predicted that Sharapova's toughness would take her a long way. "She is extremely strict, disciplined, and a perfectionist," the coach explained. "She plays tennis like she's preparing for an attack, a battle. That's Maria Sharapova. There is no monkey business. Every shot has a purpose. She runs for every single, solitary ball."

> "She is extremely strict, disciplined, and a perfectionist," explained Nick Bollettieri, head of the tennis academy. "She plays tennis like she's preparing for an attack, a battle. That's Maria Sharapova. There is no monkey business. Every shot has a purpose. She runs for every single, solitary ball."

Sharapova achieved her goal of becoming a professional tennis player in 2002, at the age of 14. She made her debut on the professional circuit as an unranked player, but she performed well enough in her first few junior tournaments to receive a wildcard invitation to a WTA senior event at Indian Wells. After defeating a player ranked number 302 in the world in the first round of that event, Sharapova joined the WTA rankings at number 532. The rookie went on to win three singles titles that year at tournaments in Gunma, Japan; Vancouver, Canada; and Peachtree City, Georgia. Sharapova quickly advanced through the world rankings, ending her first season at number 186.

Over the course of her breakthrough 2003 season, Sharapova improved her WTA ranking by 154 spots, ending the year at number 32 in the world. Her strong showing in qualifying tournaments enabled her to play in her first Grand Slam events that year. There are many tournaments on the professional circuit of the Women's Tennis Association (WTA), but there are four prestigious tournaments that make up the Grand Slam of tennis: the French Open (also called Roland Garros), the Australian Open, Wim-

*Sharapova in her first match on the WTA Tour, at Indian Wells,
California, against Monica Seles. She was just 14.*

bledon (in England), and the U.S. Open. So it was a great honor for
Sharapova, ranked number 88 in the world by June 2003, to receive a wild-
card invitation from the tournament committee to play at Wimbledon. She
responded with the best performance of her young career, beating players
ranked 21 and 11 to advance to the fourth round of the prestigious tournament. Sharapova's appearance in the quarterfinals was the best-ever
showing by a wild-card player in Wimbledon history.

Due to age restrictions for eligibility, Sharapova could only enter a limited
number of events in 2003. Nevertheless, she managed to claim her first
WTA Tour title in September at the Japan Open. In fact, she won both the
singles and doubles championships (playing with first-time partner Tama-
rine Tanasugarn of Thailand) in that event. In the singles competition,
Sharapova overcame a 5-2 deficit in the determining third set to become
the youngest player to win a WTA Tour event that year. Sharapova claimed
a second WTA Tour title in November at the Bell Challenge in Quebec,
Canada.

In women's tennis, a player wins a match by defeating her opponent in 2 out of 3 sets, while men must win 3 of 5 sets. The first player to win 6 games usually wins the set, but if their margin of victory is less than 2 games, the set is decided by a tie-breaker. Shorthand notation is often used to show the score of a tennis match. For example, 6-2, 4-6, 7-6 means that the player in question won the first set by a score of 6 games to 2, lost the next set 4 games to 6, and came back to win the match in a third-set tie-breaker.

Winning at Wimbledon

Sharapova started off the 2004 season with a bang by advancing to the third round of the Australian Open. In the second Grand Slam event of the year, the French Open, she made it to the quarterfinals. Although few experts expected the young Russian to win a Grand Slam title so early in her career, her performances in these important tournaments attracted attention in the tennis world. Some analysts predicted that Sharapova would make an especially strong showing at Wimbledon. They noted that her skills—such as quickness, a flat volley, and a preference for slice rather than topspin serves—were well-suited to the slow and often frustrating grass surface. Sharapova raised expectations considerably by winning a grass-court tournament in Birmingham, England, just two weeks before Wimbledon.

Sharapova entered the 2004 Wimbledon tournament as the 13th seed. She quickly proved herself, dispatching each of her opponents in the first four rounds without ever losing a set. In the semifinals, Sharapova defeated 1999 Wimbledon champion Lindsay Davenport 2-6, 7-6, 6-1 to claim her first career victory over a player ranked in the top five. The young Russian thus advanced to her first Grand Slam final, where she faced three-time Wimbledon champion Serena Williams. One of the most dominant players on the WTA Tour, the 22-year-old Williams had won the prestigious tournament the two previous years.

The women's final took place on July 3. Sharapova won the coin toss before the start of the match and confidently elected to serve. Her strong serve turned out to be an important factor in the match: she averaged 97 miles per hour, which was 11 miles per hour faster than her opponent's average, and chalked up 14 aces (unreturnable serves). Bolstered by her serve, Sharapova won five straight games on her way to taking the first set by a score of 6-1. Williams rallied to take a 4-2 lead in the second set, but Sharapova recovered and won four straight games to end the match in two sets. She completed her 6-1, 6-4 upset victory in only 73 minutes.

After the match ended, Williams told reporters that she had strained a muscle in her abdomen during the first game. She claimed that the injury had forced her to play in intense pain and had limited her to 20 percent of her

ABOVE: Sharapova facing Serena Williams in the finals at Wimbledon, 2004.

LEFT: Sharapova celebrating with her father after defeating Williams to win at Wimbledon.

BELOW: Sharapova and Williams share a celebratory moment after the match.

usual ability for the remainder of the match. But Sharapova did not let her opponent's comments detract from her accomplishment. After serving for championship point, she ran to the grandstands and hugged her father, Yuri. She tried to reach her mother—who, for superstitious reasons, never attends her matches—on a cellular phone, but was unable to get through. "It's amazing," Sharapova said upon accepting her Wimbledon trophy. "I never, never in my life expected this to happen so fast. It's always been my dream to come here and win, but it was never in my mind that I would do it this year."

Sharapova's Wimbledon championship earned her several spots in the record books. She became the third-youngest winner in the tournament's 127-year history, the lowest-seeded winner in the "Open Era" (since the four Grand Slam events gained additional status), and the first Russian player ever to win at Wimbledon. She also became the fourth-youngest player ever to win any of the Grand Slam events, and only the second Russian woman ever to win a Grand Slam title.

———— " ————

Sharapova was determined not to let her rising celebrity status sway her focus from the game. "The first thing I tell my sponsors is how many days I have in the year to do what they want me to do," she stated.

———— " ————

Becoming a Media Darling

After her stunning victory at Wimbledon, Sharapova suddenly found herself in high demand by both sports and entertainment media. In fact, she received over 300 photo and interview requests over the next few weeks. Some reporters referred to the media onslaught as "Maria Mania." "A lot of people want a piece of me," she acknowledged. "It's been crazy. I've got photographers running around me and driving behind our car all the time." Sharapova made a number of high-profile television appearances, giving interviews on CBS's "Early Show," NBC's "Today Show," "Live with Regis and Kelly," and "The Tonight Show with Jay Leno." She also played table tennis (Ping-Pong) on MTV's "TRL."

In the print media, Sharapova was the subject of feature stories in *Italian Vogue* and *Hello!* magazines, and she became the first tennis player in over two years to appear on the cover of *Sports Illustrated*. As a reflection of her overnight stardom, her name became the third-most-popular search term on Yahoo! (after Jennifer Lopez and Britney Spears) in the weeks following Wimbledon.

Sharapova's photogenic appeal won her many endorsement contracts, including one with Canon for its digital cameras.

Sharapova also started receiving countless offers of endorsement contracts and modeling work. Some observers claimed that Sharapova's photogenic appeal would give women's tennis a much-needed boost. "Women's tennis has been looking for a new hero, a fresh face, and she embodies everything marketers and mainstream corporations are looking for," said sports agent Keith Kreiter. "She is beautiful, young, very well-spoken, and her story is quite remarkable." Although insiders noted that Sharapova could earn as much as $10 million per year in endorsements if her success continued, she was determined not to let her rising celebrity status sway her focus from the game. "The first thing I tell my sponsors is how many days I have in the year to do what they want me to do," she stated.

Getting Back to Business

After winning the 2004 Wimbledon championship, Sharapova had high hopes for the last Grand Slam event of the year—the U.S. Open in Flushing Meadows, New York. But she struggled on the hard, fast surface. After barely beating a lower-ranked opponent in the first round, she was knocked out by Mary Pierce in the third round.

The WTA Tour Championships in November featured a rematch between the two Wimbledon finalists. Sharapova once again prevailed over Serena Williams, 4-6, 6-2, 6-4. Sharapova became the second-youngest player ever to win the tournament and claimed $1 million in prize money. By the end of the 2004 season she had reached number 4 in the WTA world rankings. Her success led to her being named the WTA Tour's most improved player and player of the year.

At the first Grand Slam event of the 2005 season, the Australian Open, Sharapova defeated Svetlana Kuznetsova in the quarterfinals, 4-6, 6-2, 6-2. Advancing to the semifinals for the second time in her last three Grand Slam appearances, she faced Serena Williams once again. This time, however, Williams prevailed. Still, Sharapova's performance earned her enough points to take over the number 3 spot in the world rankings. By April she had improved her WTA ranking to number 2.

Sharapova turned in another strong performance at the 2005 French Open. She reached the quarterfinals of the tournament for the second year in a row before losing to tenth-seeded Justine Henin-Hardenne, 6-4, 6-2. In June 2005 Sharapova made a highly anticipated return to Wimbledon to defend her title. The champion roared through the early rounds of the tournament without losing a set. In fact, an opponent broke her serve (won a game in which Sharapova was serving) only one time in 44 service games. Sharapova thus reached the semifinals, where she faced Venus Williams — the older sister of Serena Williams, her finals opponent from the previous year. Venus Williams broke Sharapova's serve four times and also seemed to break the young Russian's spirit in handing her a hard-fought 6-7, 1-6 defeat.

Staying Tough

As an attractive, lean, six-foot blonde, Sharapova is often compared to fellow Russian player Anna Kournikova. Unlike Kournikova, who never won a major tournament and depended on her good looks as the source of her popularity, Sharapova downplays her looks and wants to be known for her tennis. "I never considered myself a pinup," she explained. "I never will."

Sharapova has also been compared to another former tennis player, Monica Seles, who shared her tendency to grunt loudly when hitting the ball. When several players complained about her noisy habit, Sharapova worked to scale back her outbursts, but she maintains her aggressive, confident style of play. "Whether she's down or whether it gets close or the pressure's on, she keeps hitting harder, keeps going for her shots," said ESPN analyst Mary Joe Fernandez. "The concentration is there all the time. That's what's separating her from the rest of them."

Finally, Sharapova has been compared to American tennis great Jimmy Connors for her mental toughness and determination. This trait has helped her earn the nicknames "Russian Steel" and "The Iron Maiden." Her long-time coach, Robert Lansdorp, argues that Sharapova's determination will help her overcome the pressure of being on top. "She's a sharp girl who knows how to control what she wants," he stated. "Maria is going to do what Maria wants to do. She will succeed the way Maria wants to succeed. She's a lot more mature than people think she is."

Some experts claim that Sharapova is well-positioned to become the next dynasty in women's tennis. "I think she's the most refreshing player to come along in years," said commentator Bud Collins. "No excuses. No shyness. And she just loves what she's doing." Sharapova credits her competitive nature and self-confidence for her success. "I love playing tennis, but I also love competing," she noted. "If you're going to be scared when you walk on the court, you already have a losing mentality. I believe in myself all the time."

> *Sharapova credits her competitive nature and self-confidence for her success. "I love playing tennis, but I also love competing. If you're going to be scared when you walk on the court, you already have a losing mentality. I believe in myself all the time."*

HOME AND FAMILY

Sharapova is single and lives in Florida with her parents. Although she has resided in the United States for many years, she retains her Russian citizenship. Sharapova is very close to her parents, and she describes her mother as her best friend. "The move to the U.S. was an amazing sacrifice," she acknowledged. "Definitely I owe my parents a lot. They always wanted me to be happy, to go in the right direction in life. But there is no pressure from them. Who has an opportunity in life like I do right now at the age I am? Not too many people. At moments like these, I can return my family with favors."

HOBBIES AND OTHER INTERESTS

In her spare time, Sharapova enjoys fashion and designs her own tennis clothes. She also enjoys yoga, singing, dancing, watching movies, and collecting stamps.

HONORS AND AWARDS

Wimbledon, Women's Singles: 2004
WTA Tournament, Women's Singles: 2004
WTA Most Improved Player: 2005
WTA Player of the Year: 2005

FURTHER READING

Books

Who's Who in America, 2005

Periodicals

Detroit Free Press, July 1, 2005, p.D1
ESPN Magazine, June 20, 2005 (cover story)
Miami Herald, June 28, 2004
New York Times, July 4, 2004, p.1; July 5, 2004, p.3
People, Sep. 1, 2003, p.98
Sports Illustrated, July 12, 2004, p.46; July 26, 2004, p.58
Sports Illustrated for Kids, Sep. 2004, p.13
Tennis, May 2004, p.40
Time International, Sep. 1, 2003, p.52
USA Today, Jan. 13, 2004, p.C1; Aug. 30, 2004, p.C1; Nov. 16, 2004, p.C10;
    Jan. 25, 2005, p.C11

Online Databases

Biography Resource Center Online, 2005

ADDRESS

Maria Sharapova
WTA Tour
One Progress Plaza
Suite 1500
St. Petersburg, FL 33701

WORLD WIDE WEB SITE

http://www.wtatour.com/players

Ashlee Simpson 1984-
American Singer and Actress
Creator of the Hit Album *Autobiography* and Star of
MTV's "The Ashlee Simpson Show"

BIRTH

Ashlee Nicole Simpson was born on October 3, 1984, in Waco,
Texas. Her father, Joe Simpson, was a Baptist minister who
specialized in counseling troubled youth. Her mother, Tina
Simpson, was an aerobics instructor. Ashlee has one sister, the
singer and reality-television star Jessica Simpson, who is four
years older.

YOUTH

Throughout her childhood, Ashlee often found herself in the shadow of her beautiful, talented, and well-behaved older sister. In order to gain attention, Ashlee sometimes acted up. As a little girl, for example, she walked barefoot into her father's church, made her way to the altar, and proceeded to pull up her dress in front of the entire congregation. In general, though, Ashlee considered her actions more "edgy" than bad. "I'm not the evil sister," she explained. "I'm the sister who's a little more out there." Ashlee is also quick to note that sibling rivalry did not ruin her childhood. "People always seem to think that I struggled because I was the younger sister," she noted. "Sure, I wanted attention occasionally, but we were such a close family, and Jessica and I were the best of friends."

> "People always seem to think that I struggled because I was the younger sister. Sure, I wanted attention occasionally, but we were such a close family, and Jessica and I were the best of friends."

Both Ashlee and Jessica loved to sing in their youth. But while Jessica often sang in public — she joined the church choir at age five and quickly became a soloist — Ashlee usually restricted her performances to the privacy of her bedroom. "I would sing behind closed doors growing up," she remembered. "Jessica was so good and it made me shy about my own voice."

The two girls also favored different types of music. "Jessica and I are night and day," Ashlee acknowledged. "She grew up listening to Celine Dion and Mariah Carey. I grew up listening to Alanis Morissette and Green Day." The first album Ashlee ever bought — at age 11 and without her mother's permission — was Morissette's alternative-rock *Jagged Little Pill*. She also has fond memories of attending the women's alternative music festival Lilith Fair when she was young. As she watched artists like Joan Osborne and Jewel perform, she knew that she wanted to grow up to be like them.

When Ashlee was young, though, she mostly wanted to become a dancer. She first began taking classical ballet lessons at age three, and at age 11 she became the youngest dancer ever accepted to the prestigious School of American Ballet in New York City. This was a tremendous opportunity, but it required her to move away from her family in Texas and live in a dormitory in New York for two years. She showed enough promise as a dancer that she was invited to study at the prestigious Kirov Ballet in Russia, but her father would not let her go so far away.

Supporting Her Sister

In the meantime, Ashlee's sister Jessica was vaulting to stardom. At the age of 12, Jessica was one of over 30,000 girls nationwide to audition for a spot on the musical-entertainment TV series "The New Mickey Mouse Club." Jessica's five-octave vocal range carried her to the finals, but she froze after hearing Christina Aguilera perform and was not selected to appear on the show. A few years later, however, Jessica was discovered by Tommy Mottola, chairman and CEO of Sony Music Entertainment, who signed her to a record deal.

While Ashlee was continuing her ballet training, her father decided to move the family to Los Angeles, California, in hopes of promoting Jessica's singing career. Ashlee did not mind leaving the School of American Ballet, and she instead turned her attention toward becoming an actress. Within two weeks of moving to Los Angeles, Ashlee had secured an agent and started auditioning for television commercials. Her first commercial was for the Kohl's department store.

In 1999, when Ashlee was 14, the entire Simpson family accompanied Jessica on her first concert tour. Jessica started out as the opening act for the band 98 Degrees, which featured her future husband, Nick Lachey. Grateful to her sister for accepting the move to California, Jessica asked Ashlee to be one of her backup dancers. Ashlee performed with her sister for the next three years.

After opening for several other prominent musical acts, Jessica finally got an opportunity to headline her own concert tour in 2002. The "Dream-chaser" tour was a spectacular success, cementing Jessica's status as one of the rising stars of pop music. By this time, though, Ashlee had begun exploring ways to step out of her sister's shadow. "There were times that it was hard being on tour," she admitted. "My sister was the celebrity pop star, and I just felt like I wanted to do my own thing a lot of the time. I was so sick of everyone telling me you have to look like this, dance like this." These feelings convinced Ashlee that it was time for her to stake out her own identity.

EDUCATION

Ashlee attended Prairie Creek Elementary School while she lived in Texas, then spent two years at the School of American Ballet in New York City. After the age of 14, she obtained much of her education on the road, doing homework between her sister's shows. She nevertheless excelled in her studies and earned her high school diploma by the time she was 16.

Ashlee Simpson as Cecilia, David Gallagher as Simon Camden, and Happy the dog in a scene from "7th Heaven."

CAREER HIGHLIGHTS

Turning Her Focus to Singing

Although she loved the limelight of show business, Simpson was initially hesitant to follow her older sister into the music business. Instead, she focused on building an acting career. Some of her early roles included a guest appearance on the Emmy Award-winning television program "Malcolm in the Middle" in 2000, and a small role in the movie *The Hot Chick* in 2001. Simpson's big break came in 2002, when she received a recurring role on the televised family drama "7th Heaven." The show centered around a minister, Eric Camden, and his large family. Simpson played Cecilia Smith, a girlfriend of one of the Camden sons, Simon (played by David Gallagher). Originally signed to appear in just seven episodes, Simpson was featured on the series for two years, thanks to her popularity with the teen audience.

In an interesting twist of circumstances, Jessica then followed Ashlee into the television business. Jessica had married Nick Lachey in October 2002, when the "reality television" craze was just beginning. Joe Simpson encouraged his daughter to capitalize on the trend. He believed that musical artists could only increase their popularity by letting fans into their personal lives. "I believe reality TV has made America go, 'I want to know you before I buy your record,'" he explained. In the spring of 2003, the reality program "Newlyweds: Nick and Jessica" began airing on MTV. True to her father's predictions, the show became very popular and helped Jessica's musical career reach new heights.

That same year, Ashlee finally got up the nerve to pursue her own music career. "I think that if you love something so much you have to do it," she explained. "I love music so much, there was no choice." Her first recording was the song "Just Let Me Cry," which appeared on the soundtrack to the Disney movie *Freaky Friday*. Following the success of this record, Simpson decided to leave television and dedicate herself to music, which would allow her to better express her own views and emotions. But it took a lot of courage. "When you act, you're in a role," she noted. "If they [the viewers] don't like the character you play, it doesn't mean they don't like you. When you make an album of your own music, you're putting everything on the line."

Making Her First Album

Simpson signed a recording contract with Geffen Records in 2003 and began working on her first album. She drew upon her years of personal journal-keeping and her background as an actress to write all of the songs for the album herself. "My acting experience really helped me get into the characters of the songs and be in the moment with them," she explained. "I was able to go back to the events I'm singing about and bring them to life." One of the first songs she wrote, called "Shadow," was about growing up as the younger sister of a celebrity. The lyrics describe how Ashlee was able to escape from Jessica's shadow and follow her own dreams: "It used to be so hard being me / Living in the shadow / Of someone else's dream / But now that I am wide awake / My chains are finally free / Don't feel sorry for me."

It was clear from the beginning that Ashlee's album would bear little resemblance to the work of her sister. For one thing, Ashlee's voice and singing style were very different from Jessica's. In fact, Ashlee's voice was more similar to the raspy and raw delivery of popular singers from the 1980s, like Pat Benatar and Joan Jett. And unlike Jessica's straightforward pop sound, Ashlee's album covered several musical genres, including rock and punk. "I just wanted to go in and make a record and not worry about what genre it would be," she noted. "I went in to have a good time and I did. It's a rock record, with a cool edge to it. It's the first time people are getting to hear what I sound like." Ashlee collaborated with a number of

*Simpson working on her album in a scene from her MTV reality series
"The Ashlee Simpson Show."*

other artists on the album, including Sugar Ray, Good Charlotte, and John
Feldman from Goldfinger. Finally, to differentiate herself as much as possible from her blonde sister, Ashlee dyed her hair brunette when she
launched her musical career, although she later dyed it blond.

In one respect, however, Ashlee did follow in Jessica's footsteps: she
launched a reality TV show to help generate interest in her album. "The
Ashlee Simpson Show" began airing on MTV in June 2003. It proved very
popular, and within a few episodes it moved into the top five programs for
12- to 34-year-olds on cable television. The program followed Simpson
through the personal trials and triumphs involved in making and launching
her record album. "The show was a success because Ashlee came across as
a real person and not as a glamorous star," said Brian Graden, president of
entertainment for MTV Networks Music Group. "The music she made was
truly expressive of the kinds of things she was going through at that time,
and that kind of connection with viewers made it much more powerful."
"At the end of the day, you see the successes and what it took to get there,"
Simpson added. "It's important to get yourself out there so that people
know you as a person and not just the music."

A month before the launch of her debut album, Simpson released the single "Pieces of Me." Thanks in part to the success of "The Ashlee Simpson Show," the song received a great deal of radio airplay and raised expectations for the album. *Autobiography* was finally released on July 20, 2004. Despite receiving mixed reviews, the album sold a phenomenal 400,000 copies in its first week. It hit No. 1 on the pop charts on July 28 and stayed there for three weeks. It eventually went triple platinum, meaning that it sold over 3 million copies. *Autobiography* was one of the top 10 albums of 2004 in terms of sales, and it was also ranked among *Blender* magazine's "50 Greatest CDs of 2004." The album's success helped Simpson win Teen Choice Awards for Fresh Face of the Year and Song of the Summer.

Damaging Her Reputation

Following the tremendous success of *Autobiography*, Simpson's musical career seemed to be flying high. The album's popularity led to an invitation for Simpson and her band—Ray Brady and Braxton Olita on guitar, Zach Kennedy on bass, and Chris Fox on drums—to perform on the late-night comedy television program "Saturday Night Live." Unfortunately, this live TV appearance turned into a public relations nightmare for Simpson.

Simpson and her band were featured as musical guests on "Saturday Night Live" on October 23, 2004, performing twice. For their first appearance of the night, they performed "Pieces of Me." For their second appearance, the band started to play the introduction to the song "Autobiography." Then a pre-recorded backing track started to play Simpson's voice singing "Pieces of Me," which they had performed earlier. When the musical mismatch occurred, Simpson initially looked around as if confused. Then she danced a little jig on the stage, as if to make a joke out of the incident. Finally, though, she ran off the stage in embarrassment.

Simpson later claimed that she had suffered a bout of acid reflux, a condition in which stomach acid makes its way backward through the digestive

> *"The show was a success because Ashlee came across as a real person and not as a glamorous star," said Brian Graden, president of entertainment for MTV Networks Music Group. "The music she made was truly expressive of the kinds of things she was going through at that time, and that kind of connection with viewers made it much more powerful."*

tract toward the throat. She said that the acid reflux had irritated her vocal chords and compromised her ability to sing. Rather than canceling the "Saturday Night Live" appearance, she decided to pretend to sing (or "lip synch") while her voice played on a backing track. While many singers choose to lip synch at times, the practice is generally frowned upon. After all, when fans pay for concert tickets, they expect to hear their favorite artists performing live. In addition, the use of backing tracks tends to make fans wonder if the voice they hear on an album really belongs to the artist, or if it was created in a music studio through special effects.

Simpson's decision to lip synch on "Saturday Night Live" — a program that built its reputation on live comedy sketches and musical performances — proved especially controversial. The incident received extensive coverage in the media and made her the target of both jokes and criticism.

But Simpson tried to take the negative attention in stride. "I don't regret that happening," she said of the incident. "I'm really glad that it did because it made me stronger. And when you have everybody trying to ask you questions about it and kind of tear you down about it, it helped me grow as an artist because I was finally like, 'I don't care. I'm young. I'm 20. And I'm learning. I'm a new artist. I'm just doing my thing.'" Simpson's father argued that her mistake paled in comparison with those made by other singing sensations. "She didn't expose a boob, she wasn't doing drugs, she isn't anorexic, and she didn't get married in Vegas," Joe Simpson declared.

Bouncing Back

Two days after her ill-fated "Saturday Night Live" appearance, Simpson rebounded to sing live at the Radio Music Awards. In December 2004 she was honored as the best new female artist at the Billboard Music Awards. She suffered another minor setback in January 2005, when she was invited to perform at halftime of the Orange Bowl college football game. Her rendition of "La La" did not go over well with the fans in the stadium, who booed loudly during her performance. Supporters pointed out, however, that Orange Bowl attendees don't fit the typical profile of most Ashlee Simpson fans.

Simpson also continued to dabble in acting. She appeared in an episode of "American Dreams" on NBC, for example, and also began shooting her first feature film. Originally titled *Wannabe,* the film was renamed *Undiscovered* following a legal battle over rights to the first name. Not coincidentally, "Undiscovered" is also the name of a song on Simpson's album. The independent film follows a group of aspiring actors and musicians trying to get their big breaks in Los Angeles. "The movie's all about music," Simpson explained. "I play an actress who's a tomboy type of girl, and music saves her from all the things that she deals with in her life."

— " —

"I don't regret that happening," Simpson said about the SNL lip-synching incident. "I'm really glad that it did because it made me stronger. And when you have everybody trying to ask you questions about it and kind of tear you down about it, it helped me grow as an artist because I was finally like, 'I don't care. I'm young. I'm 20. And I'm learning. I'm a new artist. I'm just doing my thing.'"

— " —

Ashlee with her family at the premiere of her sister's movie The Dukes of Hazzard. *From left: Joe Simpson, Jessica Simpson, her husband Nick Lachey, Tina Simpson, and Ashlee.*

In the spring of 2005, both "The Ashlee Simpson Show" and "Newlyweds: Nick and Jessica" ceased production. But Ashlee has remained busy. She participated in the "Event to Prevent"—a concert held at Gotham Hall in New York to raise awareness of teen pregnancy—and appeared on the covers of *Allure, Teen People,* and *Cosmopolitan.* She remains very popular with her fans, the majority of whom are teenaged girls. Simpson's fans appreciate her warm, "everygirl" appeal, as well as her ability to act tough and "playfully naughty" at times. For her part, Simpson values her fans and tries to open herself up to them. "I think the most rewarding thing is playing shows now while fans are singing my songs at the top of their lungs with me," she said. "It's the coolest feeling. I always get chills. That's when everything is worth it. It's very cool."

HOME AND FAMILY

Simpson lives with her three best friends—Jen, Stephanie, and Lauren—in a house in Los Angeles that she bought from her parents.

Although some magazines have speculated about a difficult relationship between the Simpson sisters, Ashlee insists that she and Jessica are actually quite close. "I'm not jealous of her nor am I in competition with her," she said. "I'm proud of her, and I think that she's proud of me because she knows I've finally done what I wanted to do. And it took me a while to get there. My music is nothing like hers, so there's no competition there."

Both Ashlee and Jessica are managed by their father, Joe Simpson. Not unexpectedly, Joe has sometimes been accused of selfishly capitalizing on his daughters' talent. But he defends the active role he has played in promoting their careers. "I really try to wear three hats," he explained. "I try to wear my dad's hat—'Is this going to hurt my child?' Then I put on a manager's hat and say 'Is this going to hurt my child's career?' and then I put on a television producer's hat and say, 'Is this good television?' We're always walking that line."

HOBBIES AND OTHER INTERESTS

In her spare time, Simpson enjoys going dancing or bowling with her roommates. She also likes to do crafts, like painting and knitting. Like her mother and sister, she loves to shop and has expressed an interest in one day starting her own clothing line.

SELECTED CREDITS

Recordings

Autobiography, 2004

TV Appearances

"Malcolm in the Middle," 2001
"7th Heaven," 2002-2003
"The Ashlee Simpson Show," 2003-2005
"American Dreams," 2004

Film Appearances

The Hot Chick, 2002
Undiscovered, 2005

HONORS AND AWARDS

Teen Choice Awards: 2004, for Fresh Face of the Year and Song of the
    Summer
Billboard Music Award: 2004, for Best New Female Artist
Breakout Star of the Year (*Entertainment Weekly*): 2004
Fun Fearless Female of the Year (*Cosmopolitan*): 2004

FURTHER READING

Books

Norwich, Grace. *Ashlee Simpson: Out of the Shadow and Into the Spotlight,*
    2005 (juvenile)

Periodicals

Cosmopolitan, Feb. 2005, p.54
GQ, Jan. 2005, p.77
Pittsburgh Post-Gazette, Mar. 25, 2005, p.WE23
Seventeen, Nov. 2004, p.86
Teen People, Mar. 1, 2005, p.100
TV Week, Oct. 25, 2004, p.24
Vanity Fair, Jan. 2005, p.109

ADDRESS

Ashlee Simpson
Geffen Records
2220 Colorado Avenue
Santa Monica, CA 90404

WORLD WIDE WEB SITES

http://www.ashleesimpsonmusic.com
http://www.mtv.com/bands/az/simpson_ashlee/bio.jhtml

Donald Trump 1946-

American Real Estate Developer and Business Leader
Star of the Hit TV Reality Series "The Apprentice"

BIRTH

Donald John Trump was born on June 14, 1946, in New York
City. His father, Frederick C. Trump, was a real estate developer. His mother, Mary (MacLeod) Trump, was a homemaker.
Donald was the fourth of five children in his family. He has
two older sisters, Maryanne and Elizabeth, and one younger
brother, Robert. His older brother, Fred, died in 1981.

YOUTH

A Hardworking and Successful Family

Donald Trump inherited his business sense from his father, a self-made man who earned a fortune in the construction business. The son of German immigrants, Fred Trump started his own construction company while he was still in high school. Since he was just 15 years old at the time and his father had recently died, his mother served as his partner. She signed all the checks and contracts for the business, which they called E. Trump & Son.

> ———— " ————
>
> *"My father was the power and the breadwinner, and my mother was the perfect housewife," Trump recalled. "My mom was a wonderful woman who was, in many ways, the opposite of my father — very relationship oriented, very warm and open and generous to people. So I got different qualities from both. It was a great combination."*
>
> ———— " ————

The family business boomed during World War II, when Fred Trump received lucrative contracts to build barracks and apartments for the U.S. Navy. After the war ended, many of the military servicemen needed homes for their families. Fred Trump recognized this need and began building middle-income housing in New York City. He earned a reputation for building homes that were modest but well constructed. Over the years, Fred Trump also began buying apartment buildings that faced financial trouble, then fixing them up and making them profitable.

Fred Trump married Mary MacLeod in 1936, and their son Donald was born ten years later. He grew up in a very traditional family, and he respected the roles that both parents played in maintaining it. "My father was the power and the breadwinner, and my mother was the perfect housewife," he recalled. "My mom was a wonderful woman who was, in many ways, the opposite of my father — very relationship oriented, very warm and open and generous to people. So I got different qualities from both. It was a great combination."

By the time Donald was born, his father's construction business — now known as the Trump Organization — was so prosperous that the family was able to enjoy a wealthy, luxuriant lifestyle. In fact, Donald was raised in a 23-room home in Jamaica Estates, in the Queens section of New York

City. Despite their riches, though, Fred and Mary Trump set strict rules for their children and established high expectations for them. "We lived in a large house, but we never thought of ourselves as rich kids," Donald explained. "We were brought up to know the value of a dollar and to appreciate the importance of hard work."

Fred Trump set an example for his children by being frugal and trying to save money wherever he could. He was even known to go through his construction sites at the end of the day to pick up used nails, which he would give to the contractors to use again the next day. Until he retired in the early 1990s, Fred Trump worked out of the same modest office he had built in 1948. Although he could have easily afforded a fancier office, Donald said that "it simply never occurred to him to move."

A Confident and Aggressive Boy

From the time he was a child, Donald Trump was very confident and aggressive. When he was in the second grade, for example, he punched his music teacher because he felt that the teacher did not know anything about music. "I'm not proud of that," Trump related, "but it's clear evidence that even early on I had a tendency to stand up and make my opinions known in a very forceful way."

Trump also demonstrated from an early age that he could be creative and crafty in achieving his goals. Donald recalled one time when he and his brother Robert were playing with building blocks. Donald wanted to build a really tall building, but he had already used up all his blocks. He asked his younger brother if he could borrow some of his blocks. Robert said he could, as long as he returned the blocks when he was finished. As it turned out, however, Donald liked his tall building so much that he glued the blocks together, and Robert never got his blocks back.

Although Trump was not universally popular, he was always a leader in his neighborhood. "Much the way it is today, people either liked me a lot, or they didn't like me at all," he remembered in his book *Trump: The Art of the Deal.* "In my own crowd I was very well liked, and I tended to be the kid that others followed."

EDUCATION

By the time he reached his teen years, Trump had become a bit of a troublemaker. "As an adolescent, I was mostly interested in creating mischief," he admitted. His parents decided that he needed more discipline in his life. When he was 13 years old, they sent him upstate to the New York Military

Academy. Trump excelled there, both academically and socially. He was elected captain of a student regiment and named captain of the baseball team. "He was a real leader," his baseball coach recalled. "He was even a good enough first baseman that the [Chicago] White Sox sent a scout to look at him." Trump graduated from the New York Military Academy in 1964.

Upon earning his high school diploma, Trump considered attending film school at the University of Southern California. Although he was attracted to the glamorous life of celebrities, he ultimately decided to follow in his father's footsteps and make a career as a real estate developer. He started his college studies at Fordham University in the Bronx section of New York City so that he could remain close to home. After two years, he transferred to the Wharton School of Finance at the University of Pennsylvania. Wharton was one of the top business schools in the country, and Trump knew that a degree from a prestigious school would help him to succeed. He graduated from Wharton in 1968 — at the top of his class— with a bachelor's degree in economics.

> ——— *"* ———
>
> *When he went to work for his father's company, Trump said, "I learned about toughness in a very tough business. I learned about competence and efficiency: get in, get it done, get it done right, and get out."*
>
> ——— *"* ———

CAREER HIGHLIGHTS

Joining the Family Business

After Trump graduated from Wharton, he went to work for his father's company. He had accompanied his father to construction sites throughout his childhood, and over the years he had learned a great deal about the business. "I learned about toughness in a very tough business," he noted. "I learned about competence and efficiency: get in, get it done, get it done right, and get out."

Even though he was the boss's son, Trump still started out at the bottom of the Trump Organization. One of his first assignments involved accompanying the rent collectors who were sent to collect money from the tenants in his father's apartment buildings. He found this job unpleasant and occasionally dangerous, as some of the tenants became violent when approached for the rent money.

Trump with his parents, Mary MacLeod Trump and Fred Trump.

Trump quickly moved up the ladder, however, working for his father in a variety of capacities. He eventually became the president of the Trump Organization. During his five years with the firm, he helped increase its annual revenues from $40 million to $200 million. Despite his success with his father's company, though, Trump always aspired to start his own business. "If I ever wanted to be known as more than Fred Trump's son, I was eventually going to have to go out and make my own mark," he explained.

Staking Out His Own Identity

Part of Trump's strategy for breaking away from his father's legacy involved moving into more upscale real estate and construction projects. After seeing firsthand some of the problems his father faced with his properties, Trump decided that he did not want to have to worry about his tenants finding the means to pay their rent. He felt that one way to avoid such problems was to focus on projects targeted at wealthy people.

Still, when he set out to build his own business Trump applied many of the lessons he had learned from his father. For example, he recognized that

427

Trump poses in the atrium of the Trump Tower in New York City.

the key to success in real estate was finding property that was undervalued (selling for less than it was worth). "I love a bargain," he stated. "I love quality, but I don't believe in paying top price for quality."

Trump made his first major independent deal in 1975, when he purchased the bankrupt Penn Central Railroad's Commodore Hotel and rail yards near the Hudson River. He sold the rail yards to New York City for a large profit. He also convinced the city to give him a $120 million, 46-year tax abatement (reduction) to tear down the Commodore Hotel and build a new Grand Hyatt Hotel. Although some residents objected to the large tax break, Trump's new hotel helped to revitalize a deteriorating part of the city. "Nobody believed I could pull it off," he acknowledged.

Over the next few years Trump continued to negotiate deals in and around the city. He soon became known as one of the most successful — and controversial — developers in New York. In 1982 he opened the 58-story Trump Tower on Fifth Avenue. The luxurious high-rise building features only the finest amenities, including marble flooring, an 80-foot waterfall, and upscale retail stores. Trump Tower attracted many celebrity residents, including Trump himself. He moved into a three-story, lavishly decorated apartment in Trump Tower.

As Trump grew more successful in the world of real estate, he also started to branch out into other endeavors. In 1980 he entered the casino business in Atlantic City, New Jersey. He partnered with Holiday Inn Corporation to open a Harrah's casino at Trump Plaza. Six years later he bought out Holiday Inn and renamed the facility Trump Plaza Hotel and Casino. He also bought a hotel and casino from Hilton Hotels and renamed it Trump's Castle. And in 1990 he opened the largest hotel-casino in the world, the Taj Mahal. Trump also promoted boxing matches that attracted numerous fans to Atlantic City and brought in a great deal of money.

Trump's ambition and energy led him into other interesting business ventures as well. In the early 1980s, for example, he purchased the New Jersey Generals, a team in the newly formed United States Football League. In 1989 Trump purchased the Eastern Airlines shuttle and renamed it the Trump Shuttle.

Living the High Life

In contrast to his frugal father, Trump became known for spending his money freely. He could afford to live a life of extreme luxury, and he did. Among his many personal indulgences were five helicopters, including a black French model that was designed to carry missiles. He also purchased a $29 million yacht from the Sultan of Brunei and named it the *Trump Princess.* The yacht's deck was almost as large as a football field. In addition to his opulent apartment in New York, Trump also owned a 10-acre estate in Palm Beach, Florida, that included a 110-room mansion.

As his wealth increased, so did his confidence and ego. When he was 41, for example, Trump declared, "There is no one my age who has accomplished more. Everyone can't be the best." Although he was often accused of arrogance and exaggeration, his wealth and flamboyant lifestyle helped turn him into a celebrity. For much of the 1980s he was as likely to appear in tabloid magazines as business journals. "I don't think anybody knows how big my business is," he complained to *Fortune* magazine. "People would rather talk about my social life than the fact that I'm building a 90-story building next to the UN [United Nations building, in New York City]. . . . They cover me for all sorts of wrong reasons."

Still, Trump recognized that his celebrity status opened up profitable new avenues for him. For example, he wrote several books about his life and career. Three of his books, *Trump: The Art of the Deal* (1987), *Trump: Surviving at*

the Top (1990), and *Trump: The Art of the Comeback* (1997) appeared on best-seller lists when they were published.

Many companies also tried to use Trump's celebrity status to help market their products. In 1989, for example, toy maker Milton-Bradley introduced a board game with his name on it. Later that year Warner Brothers distributed a television game show called "Trump Card." He also appeared in the TV movie version of *I'll Take Manhattan* as himself.

Facing Bankruptcy

To wealthy New Yorkers, Trump's name became synonymous with luxury and quality products. "I really believe that I build the best product," he stated. "People buy my apartments sight unseen because they know when I put my name on something, it is going to be the best."

> ———— " ————
>
> *"I really believe that I build the best product," Trump stated. "People buy my apartments sight unseen because they know when I put my name on something, it is going to be the best."*
>
> ———— " ————

In 1990, however, Trump's fortunes took a significant downturn. Within a short period of time, several economic factors combined to reduce his income and increase his debts. The New York real estate market entered a slump, for example, while stock markets fell around the world and the junk bond market collapsed. (Junk bonds are investments that have a high degree of risk but also offer the potential for a high return.) "The 1990s sure aren't anything like the 1980s," he acknowledged.

Trump suddenly found himself in serious financial trouble. He had borrowed over $900 million, but he did not have enough money to pay off his creditors. At one point, he saw a man begging for money as he was walking down the street with a friend. "That bum isn't worth a dime, but at least he's at zero," he told his friend. "That puts him $900 million ahead of me." Rumors circulated that his construction company was not paying its contractors. The tabloids claimed that Trump himself was seen nervously pacing around the gambling tables at his Atlantic City casinos to see how the high rollers were doing.

Trump initially tried to deny that anything was wrong with his business, but it soon became obvious that he was in trouble — in fact, he was near bankruptcy. It was estimated that his net worth dropped from $1.7 billion

Trump with hs first wife, Ivana, aboard their luxury yacht, The Trump Princess.

to $500 million. He had to put his airline and the *Trump Princess* up for sale. To make matters worse, he went through a messy divorce from his wife of 13 years, Ivana, around this same time. Stories about his financial situation and his divorce settlement appeared in the news across the country.

Making a Comeback

Trump hired Steve Bollenbach from Holiday Corporation to help him figure out how to avoid bankruptcy. They negotiated with Trump's creditors to work out payment arrangements. Their first success came when they convinced the Bank of Boston to pay the insurance premium on the *Trump Princess*. At the time, Trump was paying $800,000 every three months to insure the yacht. He had borrowed money from the Bank of Boston to buy the vessel, and he was afraid that the bank would take the boat if he did not pay the insurance bill. But Bollenbach talked the bank into covering the bill: "I told them, 'If it sinks [and there is no insurance], you have no collateral [property used to secure a loan].'" Following this initial success, Trump and Bollenbach negotiated a series of other deals that allowed him to keep his casinos and other properties.

Trump avoided bankruptcy and soon pulled out of his financial slump. In fact, within five years he was even more successful than he had been before his financial troubles began. His casinos were doing very well, and he was making huge profits in real estate again. By 1997 Trump was worth an estimated $2 billion. Two years later he was named owner and developer of the year by *New York Construction News*.

Trump's remarkable comeback from near-bankruptcy only increased his celebrity status. A 1999 Gallup poll indicated that 98 percent of Americans recognized his name. Only two other business leaders scored in the 90s in the poll: Microsoft founder Bill Gates and EDS founder H. Ross Perot.

In October 1999 Trump considered taking advantage of his high name recognition to run for public office. He announced that he was forming a committee to determine whether he should seek the Reform Party's nomination for the U.S. presidency in 2000. The Reform Party was established in 1995 by Perot, who believed that voters had become dissatisfied with the two major political parties—the Democratic Party and the Republican Party—and wanted to offer a new alternative.

Trump indicated that he would run for office if he felt he could win. "I think I have a good chance," he stated. "Hey, I've got my name on half the major buildings in New York. I went to the Wharton School of Finance, which is the number one school. I'm intelligent. Some people would say I'm very, very, very intelligent." After investigating the possibility further, however, Trump decided not to run for president.

> *Trump indicated that he would run for the presidency if he felt he could win. "I think I have a good chance," he stated. "Hey, I've got my name on half the major buildings in New York. I went to the Wharton School of Finance, which is the number one school. I'm intelligent. Some people would say I'm very, very, very intelligent."*

Starring on "The Apprentice"

In 2004 Trump became known to a whole new generation of Americans when he starred in the hit NBC reality TV series "The Apprentice." The series was created by Mark Burnett, the force behind the reality series "Survivor." The premise for "The Apprentice" involves a group of young, aspiring business leaders competing for a one-year apprenticeship as the head of one of Trump's companies—a job that came with a $250,000

Trump in the boardroom with "The Apprentice" first-season winner, Bill Rancic.

salary. For the first season, over 200,000 people applied to be contestants on the show.

The 16 contestants on the first season were divided into two teams, men and women. The contestants lived together in a video-monitored space in New York City. In each episode, the teams competed against each other to complete a business-related challenge. The episodes ended with the contestants gathered in the boardroom with Trump and his two trusted advisors, George Ross and Carolyn Kepcher, for a grueling evaluation of their performance. Trump fired one contestant at the end of each episode, and the last person remaining won the coveted apprenticeship. Trump's trademark line, "You're fired"—which he accompanied with a distinctive hand gesture—became synonymous with the show and entered mainstream culture as a popular catch phrase. In fact, whenever he appeared in public, he was greeted with choruses of "You're fired" from fans of the show.

Trump enjoyed the experience of appearing on a reality TV series. "Before I met Mark [Burnett], the reality stuff was of just no interest," he said. "But I think there's a whole beautiful picture to be painted about business, American business, how beautiful it is but also how vicious and tough it is. The beauty is the success, the end result. You meet some wonderful peo-

ple, but you also meet some treacherous, disgusting people that are worse than any snake in the jungle."

"The Apprentice" premicrcd on January 8, 2004, and was an immediate success, attracting more than 18 million viewers each week. Since then, the show has returned with new episodes for two additional seasons. The episodes in fall 2004, which again featured a contest between teams of men and women, was won by male contestant Kelly Perdew. The episodes in winter 2005, the third season, offered a new twist on the formula: 18 apprentices were divided into two teams, with nine book worms with college degrees facing off against nine entrepreneurs with only high school diplomas. "For the third season of 'The Apprentice,' Mark Burnett and I have decided to take the series into a new realm," said Trump. "We wanted to see what would happen if we pitted college grads ("book smarts") against high school grads ("street smarts"). The result makes for fascinating television. Who will you root for?"

MARRIAGE AND FAMILY

Trump has been married three times and divorced twice. His first wife was Ivana Winkelmayr, a fashion model and former Olympic skier who grew up in Czechoslovakia. They met at a party at the Montreal Summer Olympic Games in 1976 and were married the following year. Ivana worked for Trump's business for many years, first as an interior decorator for its properties and later as Chief Executive Officer of Trump's Castle Hotel and Casino. They had three children together — Donald Jr., Ivanka, and Eric — before divorcing in 1991.

Trump's divorce from his first wife received a great deal of media attention. The tabloids speculated that Trump had left Ivana for a young actress, Marla Maples. Trump denied the rumor, claiming that he and Ivana had drifted apart over the years. But Trump married Maples in 1993. Two months before they were married, Maples gave birth to their daughter, Tiffany. Trump and Maples divorced in 1999. In 2004 he became engaged to marry Melania Knauss, a former model from Slovenia. They were married in January 2005 in Palm Beach, Florida. "Melania and I have been together for six years," Trump said in his wedding toast. "They've been the best six years of my life in every way."

Trump enjoys close relationships with his children, whom he once described as "the best thing I've ever done." His three oldest children have followed in his footsteps, attending the Wharton School of Business and working for their father's organization. "The fact is that they get along great," Trump said of his children. "They have an amazing relationship. And I hope it continues on in the business."

Trump, whose parents are now deceased, remains close to his siblings. His oldest sister, Maryanne Trump Barry, is a federal judge in New Jersey. His other sister, Elizabeth Trump Grau, is an executive at a large financial institution in New York. His younger brother, Robert, is the president of their father's property management company. When asked in an interview if there was anything about his life he'd like to change, Trump said, "My older brother, Fred, died at a young age, which was a big loss to me and my family. I wish he were still here."

When asked in an interview if there was anything about his life he'd like to change, Trump said, "My older brother, Fred, died at a young age, which was a big loss to me and my family. I wish he were still here."

Trump claims that his lifestyle has been greatly influenced by his brother Fred, who died of alcohol and tobacco abuse around the time that Trump was starting to build his fortune. "He knew he had the problem, and it's a tough problem to have," Trump noted. "He was 10 years older than me, and he would always tell me not to drink or smoke. And to this day I've never had a cigarette. I've never had a glass of alcohol. I won't even drink a cup of coffee. I just stay away from those things because he had such a tremendous problem. Fred did me a great favor. It's one of the greatest favors anyone's ever done for me."

HOBBIES AND OTHER INTERESTS

Trump works long hours at the office and typically gets only four hours of sleep a night. "I actually like what I do so much that I find it hard to go on vacation," he stated. "I find what other people call relaxation does not feel very relaxing at all." When he does take time off from work, he enjoys playing tennis and golf.

Trump gives some of the profits from his books to various charities, including those dedicated to curing cerebral palsy, multiple sclerosis, and AIDS. He also gave $1 million to the New York Vietnam Veterans Memorial Commission.

SELECTED WRITINGS

Trump: The Art of the Deal, 1987 (with Tony Schwartz)
Trump: Surviving at the Top, 1990 (with Charles Leerhsen)
Trump: The Art of Survival, 1991 (with Charles Leerhsen)
Trump: The Art of the Comeback, 1997 (with Kate Bohner)
The America We Deserve, 2000 (with Dave Shiflett)
Trump: How to Get Rich, 2004 (with Meredith McIver)
Trump: Think Like a Billionaire, 2004 (with Meredith McIver)

FURTHER READING

Books

Business Leader Profiles for Students, Vol. 1, 1999
Blair, Gwenda. *The Trumps: Three Generations that Built an Empire*, 2000
Trump, Donald, with Tony Schwartz. *Trump: The Art of the Deal*, 1987
Trump, Donald, with Kate Bohner. *Trump: The Art of the Comeback*, 1997

Periodicals

Adweek, Oct. 16, 1989, p.54
Business Week, Oct. 9, 2000, p.30
CosmoGirl!, Sep. 2003, p.124
Current Biography Yearbook, 1984
Esquire, Mar. 2000, p.206; Jan. 2004, p.92
Fortune, Jan. 4, 1988, p.92; July 22, 1996, p.86; Apr. 3, 2000, p.188
Good Housekeeping, Oct. 2004, p.130
Life, Jan. 1989, p.45
New York, Nov. 30, 1998, p.36
New York Times, June 26, 1999, p.B7; Jan 25, 2004, p.AR33
New York Times Magazine, Apr. 8, 1984, p.28
New Yorker, May 19, 1997, p.56
Newsweek, Sep. 28, 1987, p.50; Mar. 5, 1990, p.38; June 18, 1990, p.38; Mar. 1, 2004, p.48
People, Jan. 26, 2004, p.63

Teen People, Dec. 2004/Jan. 2005, p.62
Time, Jan. 16, 1989, p.48; Feb. 26, 1990, p.64; Jan. 12, 2004, p.69

Online Articles

http://abcnews.go.com
(*ABC News,* "Trump's Favorite Apprentices," Feb. 6, 2004)
http://www.fortune.com
(*Fortune,* "Reality Check: For Trump, Fame Is Easier Than Fortune," Feb. 9, 2004)

Online Databases

Biography Resource Center Online, 2005, articles from *Business Leader Profiles for Students,* 1999, *Contemporary Authors Online,* 2002, and *Encyclopedia of World Biography,* 1998

ADDRESS

Donald Trump
Trump Tower
725 Fifth Avenue
New York, NY 10020

WORLD WIDE WEB SITES

http://www.trump.com
http://www.nbc.com

Ben Wallace 1974-

American Professional Basketball Player with
the Detroit Pistons
Two-Time NBA Defensive Player of the Year

BIRTH

Ben Wallace was born in the small, rural community of White
Hall, Alabama, on September 10, 1974. He was the youngest
boy in a family of 11 kids (eight boys and three girls) raised by
their mother, Sadie Wallace, who worked on area farms to
support her children. Ben's birth father, Samuel Doss, was not
a presence during his childhood. The man Wallace regards as
his true father was Freddie Payne, a truck driver.

YOUTH

Wallace was raised in a modest house on the outskirts of Benton, Alabama, a small town about 15 miles outside of Selma. He and his siblings grew up without much in the way of material things—the family did not have a car for years, for example, and their house was the last one in the area to be wired for electricity. According to Wallace, though, his mother managed to raise all her children in a loving and secure environment. "I didn't know people went out every other weekend and bought clothes," he recalled. "It was like I was blind to the real struggle. I just remember being happy."

Wallace also has warm memories of his father, Freddie Payne. "My father and I were very close," he said. "He never put any pressure on me—he just told me to work hard, to respect myself and respect others."

As a youngster, Wallace spent most of his free time playing basketball and other sports with his older brothers. It was during these rough-and-tumble games that he began to develop the grit and toughness that would be a hallmark of his NBA career. "As the little brother, I knew they weren't going to pass to me," he said. "If I wanted to see the ball, I'd have to get a steal, a rebound, or save the ball from going out of bounds."

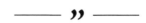

"I wasn't really taking the camp seriously, and [Oakley] wanted to show me how serious basketball really was," explained Wallace. "So he beat on me a little bit, and I beat on him a little bit, but I think he was most surprised that I didn't back down. When he hit me underneath the boards, I just kept coming."

By his teen years, Wallace was known around the neighborhood as a formidable opponent on the basketball court. He was bigger and stronger than all of the kids his own age, and he never tired of playing. "He blocked every shot I ever took," recalled one older neighborhood kid who joined Wallace for after-school basketball games. "He'd get out of school, do his homework, and we'd all go play basketball. We'd play almost every day."

Wallace and his siblings also spent a lot of time working on area farms, picking vegetables and bailing hay. Eager to earn a little extra money for himself, he even established a little makeshift barber shop on the front porch of his home during the warm Alabama summers. Watching the street from his seat on the porch, Wallace would flag down passing neighbors and offer them $3 haircuts.

Wallace was a strong addition to the team at Virginia Union.

rebounds a game. His presence in the middle helped the Panthers sail to a 28-3 record and a Final Four appearance in the season-ending Division II playoff tournament.

Despite his strong performance, though, Wallace was not selected in the 1996 NBA draft. Pro scouts loved his intensity and his knack for snaring rebounds and blocking shots. But most of them felt that his offensive skills were not polished enough for the NBA. They noted that he did not possess a reliable jump shot, and they agreed that his offensive skills in the low post (the area around the free throw lane near the basket) were mediocre at best.

Wallace was extremely disappointed that he was not drafted, but he refused to give up on his dream of a career in the NBA. When the Boston Celtics invited him to training camp to compete for a spot on the team's roster, he quickly accepted. Upon arrival, though, he discovered that the Celtics wanted to convert him to small forward or even shooting guard. Wallace reluctantly agreed to give it a try, though he secretly thought the decision was foolish. "All my life I played center or forward," he explained. "To come to this league, I knew I might have to change something about my game. But I didn't think I'd have to step off the block [the low post] and start shooting threes. That was drastic. I was a little disappointed by that. But I never swayed from my game. I just figured that hopefully they would see me for what type of player I really was. Even when I did play the two [shooting guard] for Boston in a summer league, I still led the team in rebounds and blocks."

> **"**
>
> *"All my life I played center or forward," Wallace explained. "To come to this league, I knew I might have to change something about my game. But I didn't think I'd have to step off the block [the low post] and start shooting threes. That was drastic. I was a little disappointed by that. But I never swayed from my game. I just figured that hopefully they would see me for what type of player I really was."*
>
> **"**

Boston's management finally decided that Wallace was not cut out to play guard or small forward. But instead of giving him a try at power forward or center, the team released him. Wallace then played in Italy for a few weeks before being contacted by the NBA's Washington Wizards, who needed to shore up their bench. He quickly returned to the United States, where he earned a spot on the Wizards' roster.

Bouncing Around the NBA

Wallace played his first three NBA seasons with the Wizards. He spent most of his time on the bench, though, despite the Wizards' mediocre performance. His coaches valued Wallace's defensive tenacity and his hard work on the backboards, but his shooting skills—especially at the free

Wallace bounced around the NBA a bit, playing for the Washington Wizards and the Orlando Magic before landing with the Pistons.

throw line — remained poor. As a result, he never cracked the starting line-up, and he averaged only 3.5 points and 5.2 rebounds per game during his time with Washington.

In 1999 Wallace and three other members of the Wizards were traded to the Orlando Magic for Ike Austin. The trade worked out well for Wallace, who saw a lot more floor time with Orlando. In fact, he started 81 games for the Magic at center, averaging 8 rebounds and 1.6 blocked shots a game.

As the 1999 season progressed, Wallace caught the eye of Joe Dumars, a former NBA All-Star with the Detroit Pistons who had become president and general manager of the team after retiring. Dumars recognized that Wallace, despite his heavily muscled physique and large Afro, was actually a little smaller than many other NBA centers. He also saw that the former VUU star's offensive game needed a lot of work. But Dumars felt that "[Wallace] was a physical presence with Orlando, and I thought he'd be a nice pickup for our team."

Landing with the Detroit Pistons

On August 3, 2000, Dumars engineered a trade with Orlando that brought Wallace and a couple other players to Detroit in exchange for Grant Hill. Projected as the Pistons' starting center for the upcoming 2000-01 season, Wallace signed a 6-year, $30 million contract and began working out with the team.

Some NBA analysts questioned the size of the contract that Detroit gave Wallace, citing his limited offensive game. But once the season began, it became clear that a new force had been unleashed in the league. Wallace immediately emerged as the Pistons' defensive anchor, swatting away shots and grabbing rebounds with reckless abandon. By season's end,

Wallace was ranked second in the league in rebounds per game (13.2) and tenth in blocked shots per game (2.33).

The following season, Wallace and the rapidly improving Pistons made even more noise. During the 2001-02 campaign, Wallace averaged more rebounds (13 per game) and blocked more shots (3.48 per game) than anyone else in the NBA. He thus became only the fourth player (after NBA legends Kareem Abdul-Jabbar, Bill Walton, and Hakeem Olajuwon) to accomplish this feat—and the first sub-seven-footer to do so in league history. Wallace's 278 blocked shots also set a new franchise single-season record, obliterating the old mark of 247 held by Hall-of-Famer Bob Lanier. Most important of all, Wallace's rebounding, defense, and occasional scoring (7.6 points per game) helped lift Detroit to a 50-32 record and the Eastern Conference's Central Division title.

The Pistons were eventually eliminated in the conference playoffs by the Celtics. Despite their brief playoff run, though, the Pistons were clearly a team on the rise. And no one was more responsible for that rise than Wallace. In fact, at season's end he was named the NBA Defensive Player of the Year and honored as a member of the NBA All-Defensive First Team.

As the 2002-03 season approached, coaches, players, and journalists around the NBA were still marveling at Wallace's break-out season. Many of them commented that it was rare to see a player have such a major effect on the outcome of games without scoring. Detroit Head Coach Rick Carlisle admitted that it was unusual. "We've never seen this kind of dominance from a player this size at the defensive end," he said. "He does so many things you can't quantify that impact the game. There are no statistics for changing shots, for setting screens, for helping defense, for stepping out on the point guard and then recovering to block his own man's shots."

Wallace, meanwhile, credited his success to hustle and hard work. "I feel like I'm going to get every rebound," he stated. "If I don't get the ball, I feel

> —— 66 ——
>
> *"We've never seen this kind of dominance from a player this size at the defensive end," said Detroit head coach Rick Carlisle. "He does so many things you can't quantify that impact the game. There are no statistics for changing shots, for setting screens, for helping defense, for stepping out on the point guard and then recovering to block his own man's shots."*
>
>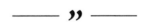

like I'm going to get my hand on it. If I can't get my hand on it, I'm going to be as close as I possibly can get to it. I'm definitely going to attack the boards when the shot goes up."

NBA All-Star

During the 2002-03 campaign, Wallace proved that his success was not a fluke. Urged on by Pistons fans who loved his wild Afro and furious playing style, he played so well that he became the first undrafted player ever to be elected to the NBA All-Star Game.

Wallace was delighted by the honor. "We have so many great scorers that some people have to do other things, and that's what I've tried to do," he said. "To come out and play the way I play, not scoring a lot of points, and people still recognize me as one of the best in the league, is an honor."

Unfortunately, Wallace's joy turned to sorrow when his mother died only a few days before the game. "She was the person I always knew I could turn to, the one person who would ask no questions — it'd just be like, 'It's all right, it's all right,'" he said. "If I felt, at times, that I couldn't stick it out, she'd be like, 'Come home, just come home, you can always come home.'" When Wallace went home to Alabama for the funeral, he expressed doubts about playing in the All-Star game. But his family convinced him to play, pointing out that his mother would have wanted him to participate.

After the mid-season All-Star game, Wallace continued to perform at his usual level of excellence. He finished the season among the league leaders in rebounds, averaging 15.4 a game. He also chipped in with 6.9 points and 3.15 blocks per game. These numbers, combined with his relentless defensive pressure, enabled him to clinch a second straight Defensive Player of the Year award.

Wallace's exploits also enabled Detroit to move deeper into the playoffs. After winning their second straight Central Division title with a 50-32 record, the Pistons rolled over Orlando and Philadelphia to advance to the Eastern Conference championship. They came up short against the New Jersey Nets, however, losing in four straight. Wallace finished the playoffs with averages of 8.9 points, 16.3 rebounds, and 3.06 blocks per game.

Beloved in the Motor City

The Pistons entered the 2003-04 season with a new head coach, Larry Brown, and a cast of veterans who were determined to reach the NBA finals. These veterans included fearless point guard Chauncey Billups and

Rebounding has been a key element of Wallace's game.

sharpshooter Richard "Rip" Hamilton, and they were backed by promising young players like all-purpose forward Tayshaun Prince. But the clear fan favorite in the Motor City remained Wallace. For each home game, dozens of fans cheered their team on wearing big Afro wigs to honor the team's hardworking center. "They love [the Afro]," said Wallace. "In fact, they get disappointed and upset when I wear it in corn rows. They're like, 'Hey Ben, when you gonna let the 'fro out? I thought you were going to wear the 'fro!'" His teammates appreciated Wallace's energy as well. "Ben puts life into the building, and he puts life into us," said Billups.

Dumars, meanwhile, expressed amazement at Wallace's transformation into one of Detroit's most beloved athletes. "I had no idea he would become the 'Fro and the two-time defensive player of the year and a sports icon in Detroit—not in my wildest dreams," he said. "He's probably the most popular athlete in Detroit, and he scores seven points a game. I've never seen a player attract so much love." For his part, Wallace offered a simple explanation for his popularity: "My game is what Detroit is all about, hard work."

Detroit started the 2003-04 season with a bang, roaring into the upper ranks of the NBA standings. At mid-season, the Pistons added another weapon when they traded for forward Rasheed Wallace. "When you look back on the team we started with [in my first year], it's a big change," said Ben Wallace. "We've come a long way. It's a totally different team from

447

when I got here. I'm the last one standing. Over the years, we've been able to make a couple changes here and there every year [that have] made the difference."

Driving to a Championship

The Pistons finished the 2003-04 regular season with a 54-28 record, the second-best record in the conference. For the season, Wallace averaged 12.4 rebounds, 3.04 blocks, and 9.5 points per game. His performance gave him the distinction of becoming the first player in NBA history to register 1,000 rebounds, 100 steals, and 100 blocks in the same season. Wallace also made both the All-Star team and the NBA All-Defensive Team for the second straight year.

> "I had no idea he would become the 'Fro and the two-time defensive player of the year and a sports icon in Detroit—not in my wildest dreams," Dumars said. "He's probably the most popular athlete in Detroit, and he scores seven points a game. I've never seen a player attract so much love."

After knocking off the Milwaukee Bucks in the first round of the playoffs, the Pistons eliminated the New Jersey Nets in a tough seven-game series. In the conference finals they faced the Indiana Pacers, a talented squad led by former Pistons coach Rick Carlisle. The series was a bruising one dominated by defense. In the end, though, the Pistons used the staunch defense of Wallace and Prince and clutch shooting from Hamilton to send the Pacers home in six games.

The victory over Indiana gave the Pistons their first trip to the NBA finals since 1991, when Dumars and his teammates won their second straight championship. Wallace was thrilled at the opportunity to play in the finals. "It's tough to put this into words," he said. "It's a great feeling to be able to compete for something you've always dreamed of."

As the team prepared for the NBA finals, it found that virtually no one believed that they would emerge victorious. The Pistons' opponent was the Los Angeles Lakers, led by superstars Shaquille O'Neal and Kobe Bryant. Many experts, in fact, predicted that the Lakers would easily sweep the Pistons.

When the series started, however, the Pistons sprung one of the biggest surprises in NBA finals history. Using a deadly combination of stifling defense and team-oriented offense, Detroit crushed the heavily favored

*Stifling defense and team-oriented offense — like this rebound Wallace grabbed
from the Lakers — were key to the Pistons 2004 championship.*

———— " ————

"Nobody gave us a chance against these guys [the LA Lakers], but we knew all along that we belonged," said Wallace, who exploded for 18 points, 22 rebounds, and three steals in the clinching Game Five of the NBA finals. "It's a great feeling. There were a bunch of guys on this team who felt they had something to prove. We added a lot of guys over the last couple of years to get to this point. And we took care of business."

———— " ————

Lakers in five games. The Pistons set the tone for the series in Game One, using smothering defense to claim an 87-75 victory on the Lakers' home court. Los Angeles managed to even the series at 1-1 in Game Two, claiming a 99-91 overtime win. But this contest actually increased the Pistons' confidence, for Wallace and his teammates felt that they had been the better team in both games.

The series then moved to Detroit. In Game Three the Pistons rolled to a decisive 88-68 victory, led by Hamilton's 31 points and a defensive effort that held Bryant and O'Neal to a combined 25 points. In Game Four, the teams were tied going into the fourth quarter. But the Pistons ripped the nets for 32 points in the final stanza to claim an 88-80 victory and a 3-1 series lead.

As Game Five approached, the Lakers talked about their determination to turn the series around. But when the game started, Detroit took command. The Pistons led by as many as 28 points on their way to an easy 100-87 victory. "Nobody gave us a chance against these guys, but we knew all along that we belonged," said Wallace, who exploded for 18 points, 22 rebounds, and three steals in the clinching Game Five. "It's a great feeling. There were a bunch of guys on this team who felt they had something to prove. We added a lot of guys over the last couple of years to get to this point. And we took care of business." It was a gratifying win for the team, and the whole city responded with an outpouring of love and affection.

Looking to Repeat

In recognition of their terrific performances in the playoffs, both Wallace and Hamilton were invited to play on the Team USA basketball team in the 2004 Summer Olympics in Athens, Greece. Both men declined, however, citing fatigue from their long run to the NBA title and terrorist-related concerns about the safety of their families.

In August 2004 Wallace underwent successful emergency surgery for acute appendicitis. He was held out of the beginning of training camp so that he could make a full recovery from the surgery.

As the 2004-05 season approached, Wallace expressed great confidence about Detroit's chances of successfully defending their NBA crown. "Winning the championship is something everybody wanted to do," he declared. "With the type of team we have, everyone is geared up to make this run again."

But some of that confidence was squandered early in the season, when a fight broke out at a Pistons game against the Indiana Pacers. A fierce rivalry exists between the teams, since the Pistons had beaten the Pacers in the semi-finals the previous season. Late in the game, with the Pistons losing by 15 points, Ron Artest fouled Wallace, who responded by angrily shoving him back. A few minutes later, Artest was laying down on the scorers' table when a fan in the stands threw a plastic cup on his face. That started a brawl in which Artest and several other Pacers jumped into the stands and fought with fans. A dispiriting range of ugly behavior followed, including players and fans fighting on the court, as well as fans pelting the players with beer, popcorn, and other trash. Someone even threw a metal folding chair at the players' heads.

After the incident, blame was quickly assigned to all parties. The Indiana players were condemned for losing their cool and going into the stands to attack the fans, and the Detroit fans were condemned for their aggressive behavior toward the Indiana players. Heavy penalties were levied against several players on each team, with the most severe being a full-season suspension for Ron Artest. Wallace was suspended for six games for his role in the altercation. After the goodwill and happiness the Pistons and the Detroit fans had enjoyed the previous season, it was a disappointing way to begin the season.

MARRIAGE AND FAMILY

Wallace and his wife Chanda have three children. They live in Virginia during the off-season, but Wallace regularly returns to Alabama to see family and friends. "I like coming back home," he said. "Do it every Fourth of July. Everybody's cooking, and I'm just being Ben, like the little kid I was running around the neighborhood."

HOBBIES AND OTHER INTERESTS

Friends, teammates, and family all say that at heart, Wallace is a "big kid." For example, he enjoys collecting remote-control cars and going motorbik-

——— " ———

"I like coming back home,"
Wallace said about returning
home to Alabama. "Do it
every Fourth of July.
Everybody's cooking, and
I'm just being Ben, like the
little kid I was running
around the neighborhood."

——— " ———

ing with kids around his neighborhood. Wallace also enjoys hunting, fishing, swimming, and other outdoor activities.

HONORS AND AWARDS

Division II All-American: 1996
NBA Defensive Player of the Year:
   2001-02, 2002-03
NBA All-Defensive Team: 2001-02,
   2003-04
All-NBA Second Team: 2002-03,
   2003-04
NBA All-Star: 2003, 2004

FURTHER READING

Books

Detroit Free Press. *Men at Work: The 2004 NBA Champions,* 2004
Detroit News. *Detroit Pistons: Champions at Work,* 2004
Who's Who among African-Americans, 2004

Periodicals

Basketball Digest, Summer 2002, p.42; Mar.-Apr. 2004, p.20; July-Aug. 2004,
   p.40
Birmingham (Ala.) News, July 4, 2004, Sports
Current Biography Yearbook, 2004
Detroit Free Press, Apr. 19, 2004
Detroit News, Apr. 4, 2003, p.H4; Dec. 1, 2003, p.D4; June 16, 2004, p.A1
ESPN Magazine, Mar. 3, 2003, p.40
GQ, Dec. 2003, p.170
Los Angeles Times, June 16, 2004, p.S7
Montgomery (Ala.) Advertiser, July 4, 2004, p.A1
New York Times, May 11, 2002, p.D1; July 4, 2004, p.SP1
Sports Illustrated, Mar. 9, 1998, p.103; Oct. 29, 2001, p.150; Feb. 10, 2003,
   p.42; June 21, 2004, p.48; June 30, 2004 (special issue)
Sports Illustrated for Kids, Nov. 2004, p.24
USA Today, June 4, 2004, p.C21
Washington Post, May 1, 1999, p.D6; Apr. 24, 2002, p.D1; June 16, 2004,
   p.A1; June 16, 2004, p.D1

Online Articles

http://www.hoopshype.com
(*Hoopshype.com*, "Ben Wallace: "Once You Win, Everybody Gets Recognized," Apr. 21, 2002)
http://www.insidehoops.com/wallace-interview-060604.shtml
(*Insidehoops.com*, "Ben Wallace Interview," June 6, 2004)
http://www.nba.com/news/wallace_030423.html
(*NBA.com*, "Wallace Named Defensive Player of the Year," Apr. 23, 2004)

Online Databases

Biography Resource Center Online, 2004, article from *Who's Who among African Americans,* 2004

ADDRESS

Ben Wallace
Detroit Pistons
Palace of Auburn Hills
Four Championship Drive
Auburn Hills, MI 48326

WORLD WIDE WEB SITES

http://www.nba.com/players
http://sports.espn.go.com/nba/index
http://sportsillustrated.cnn.com/basketball/nba/players

Photo and Illustration Credits

Kristen Bell/Photos: UPN/Landov (p. 11); © 2004 CBS Broadcasting Inc. All rights reserved (pp. 15, 17).

Jack Black/Photos: Kevin Winter/Getty Images (p. 21); Melissa Mosely/copyright © Touchstone Pictures. All Rights Reserved (p. 26); Joe Ledrer/copyright © 2001 Columbia Pictures Industries, Inc. (*Silverman*/p. 28); Glenn Watson/copyright © 2001 Twentieth Century Fox (*Hal*/p. 28); Gemma LaMana/TM & copyright © 2001 by Paramount Pictures (*County*/p. 28); TM & copyright © 2003 by Paramount Pictures (p. 31); Brian Hamill/TM & copyright © 2004 Dreamworks LLC and Columbia Pictures Industries, Inc. (p. 32). CD cover: TENACIOUS D Epic/copyright © 2001 Sony Music Entertainment Inc./(P) 2001 Sony Music Entertainment Inc. (p. 26).

Sergey Brin and Larry Page/Photos: Google (pp. 36, 46); copyright © Kim Kulish/CORBIS (p. 40); Peter Morgan/Reuters/Landov (p. 43); Newscom.com (p. 48).

Adam Brody/Photos: R. Sebree/FOX (front cover, p. 51); Jill Greenberg/FOX (p. 55); R. Foreman/ FOX (p. 57); Art Streiber/FOX (p. 58); Stephen Vaughan/SMPSP (p. 60).

Chris Carrabba/Photos: AP/Wide World Photos (p. 63); Kevin Winter/Getty Images (p. 69). DVD covers: SWISS ARMY ROMANCE (p) & copyright © 2003 Vagrant Records (p. 67); THE PLACES YOU HAVE COME TO FEAR THE MOST (p) & copyright © 2001 Vagrant Records (p. 70); A MARK, A MISSION, A BRAND, A SCAR (p) & copyright © 2003 Vagrant Records (p. 72).

Johnny Depp/Photos: Avik Gilboa/WireImage.com (p. 76); copyright © New Line Cinema/copyright © Photofest /Retna (p. 79); Zade Rosenthal/copyright © 1990 Twentieth Century Fox (p. 83); copyright © Bureau L.A. Collection/CORBIS (top, p. 85); Peter Lovino/copyright © 1993 by Paramount Pictures (p. 85); copyright © Touchstone Pictures (p. 85); Clive Coote/copyright © 1993 by Paramount Pictures and Mandalay Pictures LLC (p. 87); copyright © Disney Enterprises, Inc. and Jerry Bruckheimer, Inc. All rights reserved/Elliott Marks, SMPSP (p. 88); Miramax Films (p. 90 top); Peter Mountain (p. 90 bottom). DVD cover: 21 JUMPSTREET copyright © 1987 Stephen J. Cannell Productions, Inc. Package design copyright © 2004 Anchor Bay Entertainment, Inc. (p. 81).

Eve/Photos: Monty Brinton/copyright © 2003 UPN (p. 94); Tracy Bennett/ copyright © 2002 Metro-Goldwyn-Mayer Pictures, Inc. (p. 101); Ron Jaffe/copyright © 2004 Warner Bros. All Rights Reserved (p. 103); Adger Cowans (p. 105). CD covers: LET THERE BE EVE copyright © 1999 Ruff Ryders/Interscope Records (p. 97); SCORPION copyright © 2001 Ruff Ryders/ Interscope Records (p. 99).

Jennie Finch/Photos: Robert Laberge/Getty Images (p. 109); AP/Wide World Photos (p. 112); Chris McGrath/Getty Images (p. 114); Getty Images (p. 117).

James Forman/Photos: AP/Wide World Photos (pp. 119, 133); copyright © Danny Lyon/ Magnum Photos (pp. 123, 127); Francis Miller/Time Life Pictures/Getty Images (pp. 125, 129); MPI/Getty Images (p. 131); Charles Bonnay/Getty Images (p. 135); copyright © Bettmann/CORBIS (p. 137). Cover: THE MAKING OF BLACK REVOLUTIONARIES (University of Washington Press) copyright © 1972, 1985 James Forman (p.121).

Wally Funk/Photos: Matthew Mahon (p. 141); Wally Funk (pp. 144, 147, 149); NASA (p. 151).

Cornelia Funke/Photo: Mark Sullivan/WireImage.com (p. 155, 164). Covers: THE THIEF LORD (The Chicken House-Scholastic Inc.) Original text © copyright 2000 by Cornelia Funke. English translation copyright © 2001 by Oliver Latsch. Original German edition published copyright © 2000 by Cecilie Dressler Verlag, Hamburg, Germany. Cover illustration copyright © 2002 by Christian Birmingham (p. 158); INKHEART (The Chicken House-Scholastic Inc.) Original text copyright © 2003 by Dressler Verlag. English translation copyright © 2003 by The Chicken House. Cover illustration copyright © 2003 by Carol Lawson (p. 161); DRAGON RIDER (The Chicken House-Scholastic Inc.) Original text copyright © 2000 Dressler Verlag. Original English translation copyright © 2001 by Oliver Georg Latsch. This translation by Anthea Bell copyright © 2004 by The Chicken House. Cover illustration copyright © 2004 by Don Seegmiller (p. 162).

Bethany Hamilton/Photos: Vince Bucci/Getty Images (p. 168); courtesy Noah Hamilton and the Hamilton family (pp. 171, 177). Cover: SOUL SURFER (Pocket Books/Simon & Schuster) copyright © 2004 by Bethany Hamilton. Copyright © 2004 MTV Networks/Pocket Books (p. 174).

Anne Hathaway/Photos: AP/Wide World Photos (p. 181); Getty Images (p. 185); Buena Vista Pictures/Getty Images (p. 187); David Appleby (p. 189); Ron Batzdorff, SMPSP (p. 191). DVD cover: THE PRINCESS DIARIES copyright © Disney Enterprises, Inc. Front cover: copyright © Armando Gallo/Retna (p. 186).

Priest Holmes/Photos: Allen Kee/WireImage.com (p. 195); Jamie Squire/Getty Images (p. 199); Rick Stewart/Getty Images (p. 201); AP/Wide World Photos (p. 203); Garrett Ellwood/WireImage.com (p. 205); Cathy Kapulka/UPI/ Landov (p. 207).

T.D. Jakes/Photos: courtesy The Potter's House (pp. 211, 222); AP/Wide World Photos (pp. 216, 219). Cover: WOMAN, THOU ART LOOSED! (Berkley Books) copyright © 2004 by T.D. Jakes (p. 214). CD cover: THE STORM IS OVER (P) & © copyright 2001 EMI Gospel (p. 224).

Pope John Paul II/Photos: AP/Wide World Photos (front cover, p. 228, 235); Religion News Service/Landov (p. 230); Massimo Capodanno/EPA/Landov (p. 232); Jim Hollander/Reuters/Landov (p. 236); Charlotta Smeds/Bloomberg News/Landov (p. 239).

Toby Keith/Photos: AP/Wide World Photos (p. 243); Reuters (p. 248); Reuters/Joe Skipper/ Landov (p. 253). CD covers: TOBY KEITH (P) & © copyright 1993 Mercury Records (p. 246); UNLEASHED (P) & © copyright 2002 SKG Music Nashville LLC (p. 250); SHOCK'N Y'ALL (P) & © copyright 2003 SKG Music Nashville LLC (p. 255).

Alison Krauss/Photos: Mike Blake/Reuters/Landov (p. 258); Kevin Winter/ Getty Images (p. 268); Mike Blake/Reuters (p. 272). CD covers: TOO LATE TO CRY (p) & copyright © 1987 Rounder Records Corp. (p. 262); EVERY TIME YOU SAY GOODBYE (p) & copyright © 1992 Rounder Records Corp. (p. 264); NOW THAT I'VE FOUND YOU copyright © 1994 BMG Music. Cover photography copyright © 1994 High Five Productions, Inc. (p. 266); LONELY RUNS BOTH WAYS (p) & copyright © 2004 Rounder Records Corp (p. 270).

Wangari Maathai/Photos: Ulrich Perrey/DPA/Landov (p. 275); William F. Campbell/ Time Life Pictures/Getty Images (p. 281); Alexander Joe/AFP/ Getty Images (p. 284); EPA/ Landov (top, p. 287); George Mulala/Reuters (bottom, p. 287); AP/Wide World

Photos (p. 289). Cover: THE GREEN BELT MOVEMENT (Lantern Books/Booklight Inc.) copyright © Wangari Maathai 2003. Front cover: Martin Rowe (p. 279).

Karen Michell-Raptakis/Photos: Karen Mitchell-Raptakis (pp. 293, 303). Card covers: copyright © 2000 by the LDC Design Company, Inc (pp. 297, 299, 301).

Queen Noor/Photos: Mehdi Fedouach/AFP/Getty Images (p. 306); AP/Wide World Photos (p. 308, 321); copyright © Bettmann/CORBIS (p. 314); AFP/Getty Images (p. 316); copyright © Nader/CORBIS Sygma (p. 318); copyright © Norman Parkinson Limited/Fiona Cowan/CORBIS (p. 325). Cover: LEAP OF FAITH (Miramax Books) copyright © 2003 by Her Majesty Queen Noor (p. 323). Map: © 2001 Map Resources. Cover photo: Gustavo Cuevas/EPA/Landov (311).

Violet Palmer/Photos: Lisa Blumenfeld/Getty Images (p. 327); courtesy of Cal Poly Pomona (p. 329); Jeff Vinnick/Reuters/Landov (p. 332); Carlo Allegri/AFP/Getty Images (p. 335).

Gloria Rodriguez/Photos: AVANCE (pp. 338, 340, 343, 344). Cover: RAISING NUE-STROS NINOS: BRINGING UP LATINO CHILDREN IN A BICULTURAL WORLD (Fireside/Simon& Schuster) copyright © 1999 by Gloria G. Rodriguez, Ph.D. (p. 347).

Carlos Santana/Photos: Kwaku Alston (p. 351); AP/Wide World Photos (p. 355); Frank Micelotta/Getty Images (p. 362). CD covers: ABRAXAS Legacy/Sony (p. 357); SU-PERNATURAL (p) & copyright © 1999 Arista Records, Inc. (p. 360).

Antonin Scalia/Photos: AP/Wide World Photos (pp. 367, 369, 377, 379); copyright © Bettmann/CORBIS (p. 372). Cover: A MATTER OF INTERPRETATION copyright © 1997 by Princeton University Press (p. 374).

Curt Schilling/Photos: Jed Jacobsohn/Getty Images (p. 380); Rick Stewart/ Getty Images (p. 387); Andrew D. Bernstein/Getty Images (p. 389); Mike Segar/Reuters/Landov (p. 392); Jim Rogash/WireImage.com (p. 395, 396).

Maria Sharapova/Photos: Jung Yeon-Je/AFP/Getty Images (front cover, p. 399); AP/Wide World Photos (p. 403, 405 middle); Phil Cole/Getty Images (p. 405 top); Kevin Lamarque/ Reuters/Landov (p. 405 bottom); Newscom.com (p. 407).

Ashlee Simpson/Photos:,Mark Lidell (p. 411); copyright © The WB/Paul McCallum (p. 414); Mike Yarish/MTV (p. 416); Fred Prouser/Reuters/Landov (p. 420). CD cover: AUTOBIOGRAPHY copyright © 2003 Universal Music Group (p. 418).

Donald Trump/Photos: NBC Photo (p. 423); copyright © Les Stone/ ZUMA/CORBIS (p. 427); Ted Thai/Time Life Pictures/ Getty Images (p. 428); AP/Wide World Photos (p. 431); NBC Photo/Chris Haston (p. 433); Newscom.com (p. 434). Cover: TRUMP: THE ART OF THE DEAL (Warner Books/Time Warner Book Group) copyright © 1987 by Donald J. Trump (p. 429).

Ben Wallace/Photos: Allen Einstein/NBAE/Getty Images (p. 438, 449); Joe Patronite/ Getty Images (p. 440); Virginia Union University (p. 442); Andy Lyons/Getty Images (p. 444); Nathaniel S. Butler/NBAE/Getty Images (p. 447).

Cumulative General Index

This cumulative index includes names, occupations, nationalities, and ethnic and minority origins that pertain to all individuals profiled in *Biography Today* since the debut of the series in 1992.

For cumulative places of birth and birthday indexes, please see biographytoday.com.

For cumulative places of birth and birthday indexes, please see biographytoday.com.

For cumulative places of birth and birthday indexes, please see biographytoday.com.

For cumulative places of birth and birthday indexes, please see biographytoday.com.

For cumulative places of birth and birthday indexes, please see biographytoday.com.

For cumulative places of birth and birthday indexes, please see biographytoday.com.

For cumulative places of birth and birthday indexes, please see biographytoday.com.

For cumulative places of birth and birthday indexes, please see biographytoday.com.

For cumulative places of birth and birthday indexes, please see biographytoday.com.

For cumulative places of birth and birthday indexes, please see biographytoday.com.

For cumulative places of birth and birthday indexes, please see biographytoday.com.

For cumulative places of birth and birthday indexes, please see biographytoday.com.

For cumulative places of birth and birthday indexes, please see biographytoday.com.

    For cumulative places of birth and birthday indexes, please see biographytoday.com.

For cumulative places of birth and birthday indexes, please see biographytoday.com.

For cumulative places of birth and birthday indexes, please see biographytoday.com.

Biography Today

General Series

B iography Today **General Series** includes a unique combination of current biographical profiles that teachers and librarians — and the readers themselves — tell us are most appealing. The **General Series** is available as a 3-issue subscription; hardcover annual cumulation; or subscription plus cumulation.

Within the **General Series**, your readers will find a variety of sketches about:

- Authors
- Musicians
- Political leaders
- Sports figures
- Movie actresses & actors
- Cartoonists
- Scientists
- Astronauts
- TV personalities
- and the movers & shakers in many other fields!

"*Biography Today* will be useful in elementary and middle school libraries and in public library children's collections where there is a need for biographies of current personalities. High schools serving reluctant readers may also want to consider a subscription."
— *Booklist*, American Library Association

"Highly recommended for the young adult audience. Readers will delight in the accessible, energetic, tell-all style; teachers, librarians, and parents will welcome the clever format [and] intelligent and informative text. It should prove especially useful in motivating 'reluctant' readers or literate nonreaders."
— *MultiCultural Review*

"Written in a friendly, almost chatty tone, the profiles offer quick, objective information. While coverage of current figures makes *Biography Today* a useful reference tool, an appealing format and wide scope make it a fun resource to browse." — *School Library Journal*

"The best source for current information at a level kids can understand."
— Kelly Bryant, School Librarian, Carlton, OR

"Easy for kids to read. We love it! Don't want to be without it."
— Lynn McWhirter, School Librarian, Rockford, IL

ONE-YEAR SUBSCRIPTION
- 3 softcover issues, 6" x 9"
- Published in January, April, and September
- 1-year subscription, list price $62. **School and library price $60**
- 150 pages per issue
- 10 profiles per issue
- Contact sources for additional information
- Cumulative Names Index

HARDBOUND ANNUAL CUMULATION
- Sturdy 6" x 9" hardbound volume
- Published in December
- List price $69. **School and library price $62 per volume**
- 450 pages per volume
- 30 profiles — includes all profiles found in softcover issues for that calendar year
- Cumulative General Index

SUBSCRIPTION AND CUMULATION COMBINATION
- $99 for 3 softcover issues plus the hardbound volume

For Cumulative General, Places of Birth, and Birthday Indexes, please see www.biographytoday.com.

503

Biography Today
Subject Series

For ages 9 and above

Expands and complements the General Series and targets specific subject areas ...

Our readers asked for it! They wanted more biographies, and the *Biography Today* **Subject Series** is our response to that demand. Now your readers can choose their special areas of interest and go on to read about their favorites in those fields. The following specific volumes are included in the *Biography Today* **Subject Series**:

- **Authors**
- **Business Leaders**
- **Performing Artists**
- **Scientists & Inventors**
- **Sports**

FEATURES AND FORMAT

- Sturdy 6" x 9" hardbound volumes
- Individual volumes, list price $44 each. **School and library price $39 each**
- 200 pages per volume
- 10 profiles per volume — targets individuals within a specific subject area
- Contact sources for additional information
- Cumulative General Index

For Cumulative General, Places of Birth, and Birthday Indexes, please see www.biographytoday.com.

NOTE: There is *no duplication of entries* between the **General Series** of *Biography Today* and the **Subject Series**.

AUTHORS

"A useful tool for children's assignment needs." — *School Library Journal*

"The prose is workmanlike: report writers will find enough detail to begin sound investigations, and browsers are likely to find someone of interest." — *School Library Journal*

SCIENTISTS & INVENTORS

"The articles are readable, attractively laid out, and touch on important points that will suit assignment needs. Browsers will note the clear writing and interesting details." — *School Library Journal*

"The book is excellent for demonstrating that scientists are real people with widely diverse backgrounds and personal interests. The biographies are fascinating to read." — *The Science Teacher*

SPORTS

"This series should become a standard resource in libraries that serve intermediate students." — *School Library Journal*

Order Annual Sets
of *Biography Today*
and Save Up to 20% Off
the Regular Price!

Now, you can save time and money by purchasing *Biography Today* in Annual Sets! Save up to 20% off the regular price and get every single biography we publish in a year. Billed upon publication of the first volume, subsequent volumes are shipped throughout the year upon publication. Keep your *Biography Today* library current and complete with Annual Sets!

Place a standing order for annual sets and receive an additional 10% off!

Regular price $239
2006 or 2005 Annual Set $192
You Save $47

Biography Today 2006 Annual Set

7 volumes. 0-7808-0940-8. Annual set, $192. Includes:

2006 subscription (3 softcover issues);
2006 Hardbound Annual; Authors, Vol. 18;
Scientists & Inventors, Vol. 11; Sports, Vol. 14

Biography Today 2005 Annual Set

7 volumes. 0-7808-0782-0. Annual set, $192. Includes:

2005 subscription (3 softcover issues);
2005 Hardbound Annual; Authors, Vol. 17;
Scientists & Inventors, Vol. 10; Sports, Vol. 13

Regular price $335
2004 or 2003 Annual Set $268
You Save $67

Biography Today 2004 Annual Set

8 volumes. 0-7808-0731-6. Annual set, $268. Includes:

2004 Hardbound Annual; Authors, Vols. 15 and 16;
Business Leaders, Vol. 1; Performing Artists, Vol. 3;
Scientists & Inventors, Vol. 9; Sports, Vols. 11 and 12

Biography Today 2003 Annual Set

8 volumes. 0-7808-0730-8. Annual set, $268. Includes:

2003 Hardbound Annual; Authors, Vols. 13 and 14;
Performing Artists, Vols. 1 and 2;
Scientists & Inventors, Vol. 8; Sports, Vols. 9 and 10

Regular price $297
2002 Annual Set $237
You Save $60

Biography Today 2002 Annual Set

7 volumes. 0-7808-0729-4. Annual set, $237. Includes:

2002 Hardbound Annual; Authors, Vols. 11 and 12;
Scientists & Inventors, Vols. 6 and 7; Sports, Vols. 7 and 8